Ex Libris
St. Mary of the Springs
College
Columbus, Ohio

THREE WORLDS OF DEVELOPMENT

Books by Irving Louis Horowitz

THREE WORLDS OF DEVELOPMENT
REVOLUTION IN BRAZIL
THE WAR GAME
RADICALISM AND THE REVOLT AGAINST REASON
PHILOSOPHY, SCIENCE AND THE SOCIOLOGY OF KNOWLEDGE
THE IDEA OF WAR AND PEACE

Edited

THE NEW SOCIOLOGY
THE ANARCHISTS
POWER, POLITICS AND PEOPLE
OUTLINES OF SOCIOLOGY
HISTORIA Y ELEMENTOS DE LA SOCIOLOGIA DEL CONOCIMIENTO
SOCIOLOGY AND PRAGMATISM

THREE WORLDS
OF DEVELOPMENT

The Theory and Practice of International Stratification

IRVING LOUIS HOROWITZ

New York   OXFORD UNIVERSITY PRESS   1966

309
H816

To Herbert Blumer

Preface

This work is addressed to those who have felt the impact of a system of false alternatives with respect to the "East-West conflict"; and who are willing to forsake the security of both oversimplified ideologies and over-complicated models. The essential approach is a willingness on the part of the reader to avoid assumptions about the world being "naturally" divided into two irreconcilable antagonists. For this volume is designed as a qualitative study of three worlds of development.

It describes and explains the interaction and interpenetration of the three main sources of economic, political, and social power in the world today: the First World of the United States and its Western Allies, the Second World of the Soviet Union and its Eastern Bloc Allies, and the Third World of non-aligned, but variously committed nations of Latin America, Asia, and Africa. The book focuses on "overdeveloped" societies no less than "underdeveloped" societies; problems of stagnation no less than problems of growth; and national forms of colonialism no less than classical international styles of colonialism.

To undertake an exploration of the developmental process is to be immediately confronted by perennial questions. Whether human relations in socio-economic form and content can actually progress, or whether history is a mere record of changes in such relations, clearly hinges upon how such terms as progress and change are defined. If by development we mean large-scale behavioral revolutions which will change human conduct, then there is, and will always be, much cause for pessimism. If, however, we are more modest, and we assume development in human relations to be an ongoing process of human interaction and the relationships between such interaction to advance registered in the technological means they employ at any given historical point, then it is much more possible to be optimistic. If these processes, whether occurring in revolutionary lurches or by gradual evolution, are without particular appeal to the advocates of *human progress*, we must leave them with their dissatisfaction intact, and take our chances on a more problematic world of *human process*. One can sometimes approach perennial questions implicitly, rather than head-on in a heroic rush which is likely to produce great errors. If, by using heuristic measures for determining the needs and facts of development, one can deduce more significance, that is all to the good. But for our purpose, the issue of development is pressing, and we must make the best of our imperfect scientific condition for the sake of immediate clarification.

Three Worlds of Development offers a language for dealing with international stratification, and a style of handling social facts. For this reason, the book has as its sub-title *The Theory and Practice of International Stratification*. Economists of all persuasions have repeatedly insisted that problems of development are basically social and political, no less than economic and psychological. It is therefore hardly surprising that many younger sociologists and political scientists have entered the world arena to meet the issues directly and freshly. Clichés about "industrial man" or "mass man" will hardly do justice to the task of analyzing backward social relations in a universe of advanced technological achievements; elitism in an age of mass man; modern revolution in stagnant sectors of the economy, or, perhaps the ultimate anomaly, primitive jungle warfare in an age of thermonuclear weaponry.

The principles of stratification have frequently been applied at the national level and at lesser community levels. But in the main, they have resisted analysis at the international level, since industrialization or urbanization are less sophisticated indicators than levels of income or productivity. Yet it is evident that any study of the developmental process is bound to touch upon the main issues of stratification: superordinate and subordinate positions, the tendencies toward and away from egalitarianism, political and psychological as well as economic forms of stratification and differentiation.

I have increasingly been taken with the notion that certain key concepts in social psychology may be very serviceable for social stratification. A line of work extending from Georg Simmel to Anatol Rapoport on differences between dyadic and triadic relations needs to be linked to the more customary figures in the social science cosmos. Studies on the relative instability and the need for coalition characteristic of three-part relationships; on differences between consensus and conflict models for understanding interpersonal relations; on the effect of these models on theories of democracy and authoritarianism; finally on the picture of personality types and the types of reinforcements necessary to induce certain kinds of responses—all of these seemed clearly relevant to any serious examination of "three worlds" no less than "three persons." This reinforces for me the belief that we are living in the twilight of a sociological era in which the object of research can be neatly packaged into conventional lines.

Almost unfailingly, development is written about from the particularized standpoint of "the science of" politics, economics, sociology, anthropology, or psychology. The standpoint is derived from an author's professional commitments rather than from the developmental process as such. Clearly, a mastery of the entire literature on development from each of the disciplines would have been impossible. For studies of a global variety, the standpoint of any single social science is dubious as an intellectual tool and dreary as a bureaucratic reality. The standpoint of social science as a whole, of the collectivity of information, methods, and theories about the human condition is another matter. An integrated approach allows the researcher and the experimenter to concentrate on problems of development in general, no less than its parts. The option to this open-ended approach is a further emphasis on disciplinary boundaries. This would yield formal elegance at the expense of the whole spectrum: economic development apart from political development, political development apart from social development, etc. To underscore who is "entitled" to study which part of the developmental tree still leaves unexamined the genesis, essential features, and types of environment of the development process as such.

The desperate attempt to define "urban sociology" and "rural sociology" in an age of economic affluence, rapid mobility and motility, and a communications network that shows no respect for neat sociological divisions is one symptom of this general impulse toward a reorientation of the social scientific imagination. The same situation obtains in other areas. It is becoming increasingly apparent that political sociology, social stratification, economic development, political socialization, complex cultures, among others, might be useful conventions for indexing and cataloguing purposes, but that such designations are nonetheless nowhere to be found in the real social world. What we do observe are men agreeing, men quarreling, men killing, men loving. And such "atomic" observations are the common property of all who care to look. Thus, social science can lend its distinctive focus and method that extend all the way from personality problems on one side to political problems on the other to help clarify the facts, truths, and meanings behind the dilemmas of the modern world.

Most literature on development is nation-centered. But the nation as an exclusive index of development presents grave difficulties. There is an absence of data on comparative rates of growth, or on unique historical aspects of area clusters which make for contrasting concepts of what is considered development. One purpose of this volume is to etch the elements of favorable or invidious contrast as we move from nation to nation, or even continent to continent. Developmental studies need increasingly not only analyses in depth but also in scope. By focusing on multi-national (no less than sub-national) characteristics of development, further studies along historical as well as analytical lines can perhaps be stimulated. The work already accomplished at the big research centers, and also by independent researchers, would indicate that the time is ripe for a general re-evaluation of the genesis of the problem of development.

This is a study in sociological meanings—a causal and an interpretative study. With few exceptions I have avoided the use of charts and diagrams. Even if it is true, as Galileo said, that nature writes its secrets in numbers, men still require an unraveling of these numbers in the form of words. At some points this qualitative emphasis made my chores more complex, but it also compelled me to think through the mass of data already compiled, without a mechanical reliance upon the mystique of data. In any event the raw data add up to one thing: there is a huge gap between rich and poor nations, and this gap is constantly widening rather than diminishing. The data contain fewer surprises in this area than might be imagined, considering the size of the topic.

The question of wealth and poverty, of superordination and subordination, of elites and masses, of the things which divide men so as to create advantages for some and disadvantages for others, are matters of public *interests* first, and of personal *values* a distant second. If there is a universal interest in survival, there is no such restraining consensus in how or in what style men are to survive. Coercion is not simply the opposite of persuasion, but a response to the limits of persuasion. War is not simply the antinomy of peace, but a response to situations which are unyielding to pacific strategies in the struggles of men for a better life.

This book is neither an appeal to the wealthy nations to spread their goods, nor is it an apocryphal statement of the dire consequences awaiting an absence of such sharing. I have enough confidence in the blind pursuits of self-interest to discount most evaluative claims of superiority. On the other hand, the book is written with a confidence that self-interest can be so defined as to make room for broader social interests. The men of the Enlightenment anticipated by some fifty years the French Revolution of social and economic development. And if their appeals to the benevolence of the monarchs and princes of the time fell on deaf ears, their parallel appeals to a revolution in economy and morality that would entail the maximum use of reason and passion became the common currency of the Revolution.

The same situation seems to be repeating itself today. For the last hundred years appeals to the wealthy nations have not produced the kinds of social changes that could bring poor nations and poor continents of the world into the modern epoch. But it is no less clear that these nations and continents, sometimes with more passion than reason, have taken it upon themselves to settle the question of the redistribution of the world's wealth, and the rearrangement of the centers of power. They certainly have not waited for the benevolence of the wealthy to catch up with the demands of the age.

It may well be that my book will have a greater appeal to those who live and work in poor countries than to those who thrive off the limited affluence found in the wealthy countries. Nonetheless, in the belief that social science represents reason in society, and in the further belief that reason can, at critical ages, replace narrow self-interest in the determination of what is true and useful, I feel justified in submitting my work to all those who share my convictions in the worth of social science as an applied science. And for those who do not share such convictions, perhaps the book will at least serve to sharpen the dialogue between reason

and unreason—which by this time all who think must know is synonymous with the struggle between development and destruction.

I wish to thank first critics and colleagues of mine at Washington
University: Richard D. Alexander, Roger Maconick, Martin Needleman,
Juan Saxe-Fernandez, N. Aguiar Walker, Albert F. Wessen, and Patri-
cia Woo. Their enthusiasm and encouragement were invaluable. Other
friends and colleagues who read the manuscript at one stage or another,
in whole or in part, are Herbert Blumer (University of California), Alex
Fryer (Syracuse University), Paul Honigsheim (late of Michigan State
University), Rollin Posey (New College, Florida), and Roger B. Walker
(Latin American Center for Research in the Social Sciences). Needless
to say, none of the above mentioned persons is in any way responsible for
mistakes or miscalculations that may remain. Throughout the active
period of preparing the manuscript for publication, I was fortunate to
have Adeline Sneider as my secretary and typist. Her proficiency made
additional technical aid superfluous.

Irving Louis Horowitz

Washington University
St. Louis, Missouri
September 1965

Contents

THREE WORLDS OF DEVELOPMENT

I

AN INTRODUCTION TO THE THIRD WORLD

"Everything now tells that we are close upon one of the great revolutions of the human race. If we wish to learn what to expect from it and to procure a certain guide to lead us in the midst of its vicissitudes, what could be more suitable than to have some picture of the revolutions that have gone before it and prepared its way? The present state of enlightenment assures that this revolution will have a favorable result, but is not this only on condition that we know how to employ our knowledge and resources to their fullest extent? And in order that the happiness that it promises may be less dearly bought, that it may be diffused more rapidly over a greater area, that it may be more complete in its effects, do we not need to study the history of the human spirit to discover what obstacles we still have to fear and what means are open to us of surmounting them?"

(Antoine-Nicolas de Condorcet in
Sketch for a Historical Picture of the Progress of the Human Mind)

"It is not difficult to see that our epoch is a birth-time, and a period of transition. The spirit of the age has broken with the world as it has hitherto existed, and with the old ways of thinking, and is in the mind to them all to sink into the depths of the past and to set about its own transformation. It is indeed never at rest, but carried along the stream of progress ever onward...The spirit of the time, growing slowly and quietly ripe for the new form it is to assume, loosens one fragment after another of the structure of its previous world. That it is tottering to its fall is indicated only by symptoms here and there. Frivolity and again ennui, which are spreading in the established order of things, the undefined foreboding of something unknown — all these are hints foretelling that there is something else approaching. This gradual crumbling to pieces, which did not alter the general look and aspect of the whole, is interrupted by the sunrise, which, in a flash and at a single stroke, brings to view the form and structure of the new world."

(Georg Wilhelm Friedrich Hegel in **Phenomenology of Mind**)

Chapter 1

What Is The Third World?

I

In one of the most perceptive and imaginative sentences in *Das Kapital,* Marx wrote: "The country that is more developed industrially only shows to the less developed, the image of its own future."[1] It is amazing to note that what the mid-nineteenth century must have considered a wildly romantic thought is a commonplace today. Current events have become more complex than Marx could possibly have anticipated; more centered on facts than on images. The rise of a Third World, of a social universe in limbo and outside the power dyad of East and West, has generated new queries.

Assuming that the developed countries show to the underdeveloped the image of their own futures, the question arises, do these "expectant" nations accept this image? Are they prepared to accept modernism without qualifications? Does this include the exaggerated consequences of automated industrialism, of alienation and privatization? Will the antagonisms between the rich nations and the poor nations overwhelm potential commonalities of economy and culture? Do the less developed nations apply their energies to careful mending or to revolutionary smashing? Above all, does the developmental process change the terms of description and analysis, or provide them with a renewed urgency?

It is no exaggeration to say that the answers to these questions have been slow in coming. To some extent this is a consequence of the unevenness and lateness of development in some areas; cultural, ethnic, and racial apartness of other areas; and the ways in which resistance to

[1] Karl Marx, *Das Kapital.* Chicago: Charles Kerr Publishers, 1905, Vol. I, p. 13.

3

social change has inhibited these areas from emulating the economic systems of advanced nations. The emergence of a Third World; the transformation of world relations from a dyadic to a triadic balance; the emergence on a mass scale of new nations; new economic systems; new cultural products; new political forms—all bound up with national traditions—not infrequently synonymous with national myths—have created a profusion of new issues for our times. Furthermore, the "image" of a developed nation has been fragmented into "images" of developed nations. There is no question of rejecting development, except among those people overwhelmed with nostalgia; the only question is what direction such development is going to take. In the consciousness of a Third World lives the example of a Second World no less than of a First World—of the socialist Soviet Union no less than the capitalist United States. The *existence* of a development process is a social fact. The *recognition* of a need for development is a social value. What binds the Third World together is not just its being a geographic locale outside the main power centers, but a psychological unity built around a social value. The ideological accoutrements of these processes are responses and effects—which in turn stimulate a desire for accelerated industrialization and rapid modernization. But above all, the ideology of the Third World is a response to the pervasive problem of how to gain worldly pre-eminence. It is always a matter of "catching up" and perhaps ultimately "surpassing" those held to be most advanced. This in itself betrays the fact and shame of backwardness.

Put another way, the developed nations are "causes," not just because they are in the forefront of modernization and material wealth, but because they create the *conditions* for rebellion and revolution. The developed nations thus provide a chain of *effects*.[2] We might introduce the three *effects* as follows: (1) Developing nations define themselves as engaged in a mortal race with the most advanced sectors of the economic world. This is the *demonstration effect*. (2) Developing nations define themselves as economically and socially experimental and lean toward a "mix" rather than a "pure" system. The Third World believes in neither socialism nor capitalism, but also believes in them both. This is the *fusion effect*. (3) Developing nations are those which

[2] See on this Gino Germani, *Politics and Society in Latin America*, edited by Irving L. Horowitz. Englewood Cliffs, N.J.: Prentice-Hall, 1966 (pending).

have the desire and the means to catch up to advanced forms of social and economic organization, and to do so in less time than it took the presently constituted advanced nations to reach their present levels. This is the *compression effect*.

It should be pointed out that the phrase "The Third World" is generally attributed to the Algerian writer, Frantz Fanon. His book on Algeria is probably the first to use it as a colloquial expression for the newly emergent nations.[3] While the French phrase *le Tiers Monde* is quite well known at this point, the English language equivalent is only now entering the vernacular.[4] Nonetheless, it is not useful simply as a definition but also offers a shorthand description of the boundaries of the present work.

At the outset we must undertake to sketch the features of the First and Second Worlds so that differentiation from the Third World is substantially free of clichés or stagnant notions. The "three worlds" are contrasts in social structural evolution, contrasts too in their appearance in historical time.

II

What is meant by the First World is basically that cluster of nations which were "naturally" transformed from feudalism into some form where private ownership of the instruments and means of production predominated. If these nations did not evolve out of feudalism, they at least grew out of the soil of Western Europe and started as capitalist states. Certain properties of this First World are clear: historically they had their initial take-off in the banking houses of sixteenth-century Italy, in the middle-sized industry of seventeenth-century France; and

[3] See Frantz Fanon, *Les Damnés de la terre*. Paris: Maspero Cahiers Libres, 1961. An English language edition has appeared under the title *Wretched of the Earth*. New York: Grove Press, 1965. Also see his *Studies in a Dying Colonialism*. New York: Monthly Review Press, 1966 (pending).
[4] The phrase has now been employed as a title in at least two recent books on the developing areas: Thomas P. Thornton (ed.), *The Third World in Soviet Perspective*. Princeton, N.J.: Princeton University Press, 1964; and Mario Rossi, *Third World: The Unaligned Countries and the World Revolution*. New York: Funk & Wagnalls, 1963. The phrase has also been used in a technical monograph issued by the Food and Agriculture Organization, *Third World Food Survey*. New York: Columbia U.-International Documentary, 1964.

in the industrial mechanization of eighteenth-century England and nineteenth-century United States and Germany. Economically, they share an emphasis on industrialization and technology used for private enrichment and public welfare in uneven dosages.

The First World nations have in common an internal generative power. Changes which took place in Western European nations and the United States have usually come about as a result not of invasion or of foreign conquest, but through the internal breakdown of the older landed classes, a general disintegration of agricultural societies, or through the initiative and creation of new life styles. The basic characteristic of the First World is that economic development was a consequence of the internal machinery of each nation and not the result of international planned agreement. As a matter of fact, there was not even agreement between the nations on a nation-state system until very late in the development of capitalism—the late nineteenth century.

The First World has two geographical parts: Europe and North America. The break with traditionalism in the United States occurs differently as compared with Western Europe. For it gained its national independence only through a struggle with England; and only then could it adopt a central parliamentary system. But it is important to note that in both sectors of the First World the formation of the parliamentary state system followed the bourgeois dominance over the forms of economic production. While they were often supportive of each other, political styles and structures in the First World emerged from the class conflicts of an economic system based on laisser faire.

The rise of industrial capital was preceded by a profound expansion in commercial capital. In this, the United States only repeated the "phasing in" process of capitalism previously undergone in Europe.[5] The factory unit became the keystone of the industrial system and its by-products: hardened national boundaries, protectionist tariff arrangements, heavy migration from countryside to city. And when trade relations became socially expensive, technology stepped in to prevent the premature disintegration of private capital investment. Invention promised savings on labor costs and raw materials, to the point that the factory itself, rather than any individual labor units, became the princi-

[5] See Maurice Dobb, *Studies in the Development of Capitalism*. London: Routledge & Kegan Paul, 1946, esp. pp. 123-76.

pal investment unit. It will be seen that this economic interpretation, however suited it may be for the study of classical capitalism, can hardly be applied to the Third World—since the relationship of politics to economics is reversed.

The system of competitive capitalism which developed in Western Europe was forced to go beyond its own domestic markets. The First World became colonialist as well as capitalist. It established overseas bases from which to draw raw materials or develop potential markets for the purchase of finished products; in so doing it created out of its own dilemmas the master dilemma of colonialism.

Even the most rabid believer in European preeminence would be hard put to deny that the United States of America is the best example extant of the First World—of the highly mobile, commodity oriented, and ideologically egalitarian social system. It witnessed the development of capitalism not only unfettered by feudal structures, but assisted by political legislation. There occurred a crystallization of the state and the economy at roughly the same time and by roughly the same socioeconomic groups; asynchronous and unstable elements were held in check during its development. And whatever interpretation of the origins of the United States is preferred, economist or revisionist, one ineluctable fact emerges—the United States is the most perfect representative of parliamentary democracy and capitalist economics.[6]

The United States also benefited by the continuation, throughout the nineteenth century, of rifts and schisms within Europe. The European powers, especially Spain, Germany, France, and England, were in such keen competition with each other that they were unable to forge any detente against the first new nation. England attempted to capture by economic means what could not be accomplished through military means. During the war of 1812 it blockaded American ports: in the Civil War it played off Northern commercial against Southern agricultural interests; each attempt in turn failed.

[6] The argument between Charles A. Beard, *An Economic Interpretation of the Constitution of the United States*. New York: Macmillan Co., 1913; and his critics, especially Forrest McDonald in *We the People: The Economic Origins of the Constitution*. Chicago: U. of Chicago Press, 1958, effects only a settlement of the type of unique "purity" of America—not the fact of such difference. Indeed, Beard's "economism" and McDonald's "pluralism" can both be embraced by a concept of parliamentary capitalism.

France under both Napoleons attempted to impede the territorial expansion of the United States, but its own internal demands caused it, under Napoleon Bonaparte, to surrender all territorial claims from the Louisiana Purchase, while half a century later, Louis Napoleon removed troops he had put in Mexico. Similarly, the Spanish conquests of America had generated aspirations for independence in all its territories. European colonialism served to stimulate United States expansive economic aspirations in the hemisphere. Whether through Dame Fortune or through Manifest Destiny, the United States was able to consolidate its national economy before it became caught in any extensive European entanglements. Then, at the very point when further possibilities for United States internal geographical expansion were narrowing, the European community was finally riven in combat. World War One committed the United States to European affairs.

The United States should not be dismissed as a model of development for the Third World. The fact that the United States has performed a colonial role is a poor and inadequate explanation of why it does not serve as the perfect model. There are, after all, many cases of the oppressed adopting the methods and philosophies of their exploiters. What is more, the imperialism of the United States was until recently ambivalent and half-hearted. Economically self-sustaining and unlike nineteenth-century England, it was totally independent of imperial holdings. It is only very recently that efforts of the United States to shape the world in its image have given impetus to its imperial thrust in international politics. Still, its anti-colonial sentiments, if not always behavior, set definite limits to its pursuit of influence.

Then why has the United States, despite its enormous power and prestige, failed to capture the imagination of the Third World bloc? It is a failure not of propagandistic devices, but rather of structural inefficiencies. One could say, the failure of success.

First: The United States remains the classic case of national development without a national plan. This is an historical possibility denied to those nations now emerging as economic entities. Indeed, the United States itself, through its various agencies, simply refuses to entertain requests or demands for loans or financial support without some blueprint or plan for over-all growth. Thus, what the United States expects from other nations was not a condition of its own growth. In this, the classic explanation of the mystic hand of the free and mysterious market looms as an apologia for capitalism, while powerful nations like the United States reject the possibility that other nations are entitled to the same sort of laisser-faire apologetics.

Second: Despite the enormous amount of earned income in the United States, distribution of this income continues to be very uneven. Distribution of wealth, in the form of monies and bonds, has remained virtually the same since 1929. The distribution of wages and salaries in the United States also indicates the gap between classes—with the lowest income fifth receiving only 2.5 per cent of the national wage and salary income, while the highest fifth receives an extraordinary 47.0 per cent. Thus, the United States has not solved its class problem, despite the existence of an incredibly high standard of living—the style of life has grown evenly, but economic social division has remained disparate. In the Third World nations, it is precisely the problem of income, wage, and salary equity which looms large, if social development is to be achieved with relative harmony, that is, with a relative absence of class warfare.[7]

Third: Monopolistic and oligopolistic situations obtain in nearly every sector of the American society. This means that competition between private sectors and public sectors continues in the United States with an unabated fury. This can be seen with especial clarity in the "space-race"—where a multiplication of agencies and organizations have arisen, often in competition, for control of everything from property rights on the Moon to domination of the earth satellites. But whatever the net benefits or deficits of this for the United States, it is clear that such competition is precisely what prevents planning for the whole society and inhibits a full drive toward economic equity. The First World has become such an incredible plethora of money and material wealth, that the Third World can no more meet the requirements of this system than it could the traditional, rigorous nineteenth-century capitalist model.

Finally, certain structural weaknesses in the Third World also serve to reduce the role of the United States as a model. The Third World

---

[7] See Bureau of the Census, *Statistical Abstract of the United States—1957.* Washington, D.C.: Government Printing Office, 1957, pp. 315-16. For a good popular exposition of these issues see Gabriel Kolko, *Wealth and Power in America: An Analysis of Social Class and Income Distribution.* New York: Frederick A. Praeger, 1962.

presents a picture of multiplying nations and contrasting politics. Uncritical emulation of the United States social system would mean reversing the current vast trend toward national separatism. Both the United States and the Soviet Union have adopted a cultural pluralism which enables them to absorb rather than crush separatist claims without lessening the quality or the extent of development. The situation in the Third World remains such that ecumenicism of such a variety remains a dream for some, a nightmare for others—but a reality for none.

III

The Second World is historically the Russian orbit, the Soviet Union and its bloc. The center of the Second World presents an ambiguous situation, for the old Russian world was colonized by Poles, Germans, and other Europeans, including the Swedes. Yet Russia also remained a colonial power. While Russian feudalism was accommodating capitalism, the emergence of revolutionary forces in the late nineteenth century inhibited this accommodation. Thus, instead of a movement from feudalism to capitalism, there took place a radical shift from feudalism to socialism. The period of capitalist survival in Russia was extremely short-lived; no more than 25 years. Thus, one can speak neither of the failure nor success, obsolescence nor abortiveness, of capitalism in Russia.

The politics of old Russia was fatally centralized in official functions, residing in the divine royal person of the Czar. Economic and political initiative lay in his hands. For this reason "modernizing" Czars like Catherine or Peter the Great, no less than "backward" Czars, left Russia a legacy of a stagnant agriculture on one hand and an advanced industrial complex on the other. Commercial middle-class elements were considered traitors to Russia's aspirations because of their contacts with foreigners. These business transactions were in turn perceived as direct challenges to royal supremacy; they were thus despised by the traditional and nascent classes alike.

No social class could really carry forward industrialization without the aid of the throne. While Peter the Great's Westernization policy fostered both industrialization and centralization of political authority, it remained for the Bolsheviks to renovate the social structure so as to make possible the completion of industrialization. This combination of an autocratic-Byzantine heritage, and a modern industrialized self-conception arising from a revolutionary movement dedicated to removing this past, makes the Soviet Union a world apart.

In its pre-revolutionary, semi-backward condition Russia resembles the Third World. In its post-revolutionary industrialized status, it resembles the First World. While this descriptive picture helps to explain the Soviet reality, the fact that the Soviet society is also an ideological society further complicates matters. Marxism-Leninism, the ideological context within which all Soviet self-reflection takes place, makes the U.S.S.R. a unique entity, differentiated from China, since the latter's entry in the modern world has compelled numerous doctrinal accommodations. By its past the Soviet Union is an Eastern culture forcibly Westernized under the impact of European powers. Its revolutionary withdrawal from the capitalist sphere of influence gave it a new pride, and also a new destiny—that of being the first socialist state in the world. That it *was* in fact first, further enhances its uniqueness. The advantage of being first separates the Soviet Union from the Third World; while at the same time, being first makes it a model for the Third World. The Soviet Union, unlike Czarist Russia, is no longer a prostrate nation rent by foreign intervention and, even worse, by foreign debts. In its socialist orientation the Soviet Union stands as a model; but in its Russian traditions it stands apart.

The long and ambiguous historical genesis of the relations of Russia with the West, no less than the East, is remarkably well stated by Arnold Toynbee. He noted that an observer who is intimately acquainted with the history of Russia would have recalled that its technological competition with the West, which reached such a dramatic culmination in 1957 (the year of Sputnik), has had a long history. And Russian competition with the West, which we herein call the First World, started not with Lenin in 1917, but with Peter the Great in 1689.[8] Peter's adoption of the Western technology of his day had been so effective that it had enabled him to defeat decisively one of the great powers of the contemporary Western world—Sweden. Russia's historical victory over Charles XII at Poltava in 1709 had been won

[8] Arnold J. Toynbee, "Russia's Place in History," A *Study of History* (*Reconsiderations*). London and New York: Oxford University Press, 1961, Vol. XII, pp. 537-8.

within twenty years of the initiation of Peter the Great's Westernizing program and within twenty-six years of the Polish defeat of the Turks and Mohammedans under the ramparts of Vienna in 1683. Toynbee goes on to point out that Russia, alone of all the geographically non-Western countries, had succeeded in maintaining its political independence. (This is vital because it is a basic characteristic of the Third World that it is dominated by colonial powers.) It was a central fact of Russian development, whatever its former feudal status, that it was never subjugated to a pure colonial status but remained politically independent.

The decisive battle between Russia and Sweden thus signalized Russian achievement near the start of the Industrial Revolution. This interpretation of Russia's role in modern history shows that it served to lead the East, not only in resistance to the modern West's bid for worldwide dominance, but, more important, it offered an alternative form of modernization. In effect, then, there was a long historic struggle between the Russian world (or the Byzantine world) and the Western capitalist world (or Protestant-Catholic world). As political loyalties intensified and as the gap between social classes within nations lost revolutionary dynamism, economic and social competition may be said to have taken a *national* form. The class struggle thus becomes subsumed and swallowed up by the struggle between world empires which symbolically, even romantically, clung to the language and metaphors of social class.

The problem of metaphor and definition now introduced, it remains a fact that Russian society is the first to take seriously the problems of development in their modern, secular sense. Indeed, the Russian economists offered the first major dialogue on the relationship between economic backwardness and political modernization. Russian *fin de siècle* populists, such as Voronstov, Nikolayon, Bulgakov, and Tugan Baranovski, and their more orthodox Marxian critics, such as Plekhanov, Kautsky, and Lenin, raised the essential questions of the twentieth century: Can small nations ever escape from the clutches of big national imperialism? Can the real wants of the masses be best satisfied by an agricultural mode of production or by a coercive system of factory labor? Can economic "stage skipping" actually be brought about in a geo-political climate of hostile nations? Can capitalism promote an international division of labor which is rational and yet not harmful to both advanced and backward economies? Can social development ever really promote the needs of the great public, or must it initially promote the needs of selective social sectors? Can the development of a "self-contained" economy, such as that possessed by the United States, forestall the occurrence of violent anti-imperialist revolution?[9]

While the language of these discussions was strongly dominated by Marxian economics, and by the going rhetoric of Russian revolutionary groupings, the questions posed, no less than the answers finally given, made the late Russian and early Soviet period very special in the annals of economic development. Debates on the strategies of development in old Russia were directly connected to the practice of development in the new Soviet Russia. That there may have been dogmatic interpretations of these earlier discussions was itself not unanticipated. Such is the "inevitability" of the Russian temperament that it could not help but reinforce the infallibility of the Marxian political economy.

The Socialist Revolution of 1917 was guaranteed by the competition between Russia and Germany for European pre-eminence. Perhaps no one in modern times has put the issue of Soviet development better than the once revered and now reviled *Tyrannus Rex*, Joseph Stalin. Speaking to the First Conference of Russian Industrial Managers held in 1931, he puts the issue bluntly:

> It is sometimes asked whether it is not possible to slow down a bit in tempo, to retard the movement. No. This is impossible. It is impossible to reduce the tempo! On the contrary, it is necessary as far as possible to accelerate it. To slacken the tempo means to fall behind. And the backward are always beaten. But we do not want to be beaten. No, we do not want this! The history of old Russia is the history of defeats due to backwardness. She was beaten by the Mongol Khans. She was beaten by the Turkish beys. She was beaten by the Swedish feudal barons. She was beaten by the Polish-Lithuanian squires. She was beaten by

[9] For a brilliant examination of the historical aspects of development theory in Russia, particularly Marxian theory, see Rosa Luxemburg, *The Accumulation of Capital*. London: Routledge & Kegan Paul, 1951, esp. pp. 271-326. Also, for a superior political history of nineteenth-century Russia, one which considers economism and populism as expressions of developmental strategies, see Franco Venturi, *Il Populismo Russo*. Turin: Einaudi Editore, 1952 (two volumes).

the Anglo-French capitalists. She was beaten by the Japanese barons. All beat her for her backwardness—for military backwardness, for cultural backwardness, for governmental backwardness, for industrial backwardness, for agricultural backwardness. She was beaten because to beat her was profitable and could be done with impunity. . . . That is why we must no longer be backward. . . . We are fifty to a hundred years behind the advanced countries. We must cover this distance in *ten* years. Either we do this or they will crush us.[10]

It takes little historical acumen to recollect that ten years later, in 1941, Germany crossed the Russian frontier. And it takes only an added moment to remember that Russia was not crushed. The Soviets were not beaten as their ancestors had been. If the Bolsheviks have long labored under the cult of development, willing to sell short, if not entirely sell out, human liberties in the bargain with industrialization, it might be remembered that the Soviets have a historically minded ideology. History offers dramatic evidence that to be industrially advanced is to be victorious in the military sphere. And Marxist ideology has continually asserted the same doctrine.[11]

Why has the Soviet Union, despite the enormous impetus it has given to developmental theory and ideology, actually had a relatively slender role in directly affecting the institutions of the Third World? It will be noted that there seems to be a reversal—Third World nations seem to reproduce Soviet ideology (although this is in need of great qualification), while at the same time seeking to reproduce American technology. The first and most obvious reason is that American technical achievement is far greater than Soviet technical achievement. The emergence of socialism in one country, in Russia, has bred a rigid giganticism. Customarily, size is mistaken for efficiency, design has been isolated from function. Hence, in the Soviet developmental process, functions may be modern, but form remains baroque. Soviet satellite nations

[10] Joseph Stalin, "We Do Not Want To Be Beaten" (from a speech delivered before the First Conference of Russian Industrial Managers, Moscow, February, 1931) in *Russian Literature Since the Revolution*, edited by Joshua Kunitz. New York: Boni & Gaer, 1948, pp. 455-6.
[11] See, for example, V. I. Sokolovskii, *Soviet Military Strategy*, translated and annotated by H. S. Dinerstein, Leon Gouré, and Thomas W. Wolfe. Englewood Cliffs, N.J.: Prentice-Hall, 1963.

of a more independent persuasion have had to repudiate this strain between social function and cultural norm. And such imbalance stands as a warning to Third World nations.

The Soviets also resolved ethical and political decisions by administrative fiat and bureaucratic enlargement. It is this very institutionalization of a command society that the Third World is subjecting to skeptical scrutiny. Such problems as the dysfunctionality of large-scale organization units, techniques of increasing productivity (which are at the same time not disguised techniques of exploitation), and political tests of bureaucratic enterprise have not been seriously faced by the Soviets, precisely because of their rigid commitment to an ideology. But all of these are now under consideration in subtle ways within the Soviet Union, and even in bolder ways in the Third World nations. The classical nineteenth-century dialogue between capitalism and socialism has yielded to searches for options to both. Economic and political experimentation is nearly as intense within the classic capitalist and socialist blocs as in the Third World itself.

Many of the obstacles which prevent the United States from serving as an effective "model of models" also serve to obstruct, *mutatis mutandis*, the growth of Russia as the model of models.[12] Furthermore, the Soviet Union faces two additional handicaps in its struggle for universal recognition: its own ideological commitments to national self-determination, which, however much violated within its own borders, have been scrupulously observed in its relations to outside nations, and the hostility of the United States, a nation superior in power to itself and one quite ready to support any nationalist movements which adopt an anti-Communist posture. Thus, it may be that "post-imperial" Europe will become the great balance wheel preserving harmonious growth in the Third World. There is increasing evidence that the Third World is turning to Western Europe as a way out from making any ultimate commitment to the American or Soviet model of development.

Finally, the phrase "Third World" itself indicates that a narrow choice between inherited industrial forms is no longer possible. The "natural dyad" which Soviet ideologists have long labored under has in fact been changed into a "natural triad." The Third World is a Third

[12] See John Strachey, *The End of Empire*. New York: Random House, 1960, pp. 292-306.

Force and a Third Position, irrespective of the canons of Marxism-Leninism which say that such a situation is impossible, except as a temporary aberration.

Russian development may be considered a pivot between the First and Third Worlds of development. Russia is both European and Asian. It has looked to the West for its political ideology and turned to the East for its political domain. Russia is both liberator and exploiter, a nation which makes revolution in the name of all humanity, and yet imposes the strictest class and party dictatorship on a nation. Russia is both technologically advanced and artistically backward; jet design aircraft must compete with decadent Edwardian interior decorations. Russia is both a land of advanced workers and of backward peasantry. It represents an imperfect fusion of urban sophistication and industrial secularization. The Soviets substitute giganticism for miniaturization (refined perfecting), size for quality. Such a society cannot provide a "model of models" when it is still in the process of finding its own self-image and its own clear-cut directions.

IV

American political thinking generally focuses on choices between false alternatives. On one side we are deluged with propaganda informing us that peaceful coexistence is impossible between the United States and the Soviet Union. Even if coexistence were possible, it would be better for all concerned to be "dead than red" if coexistence were to lead to a Communist take-over. There are also the absurd "contrasts" between a "God-fearing people" and a "God-less atheistic state," between a two-party system and a one-party system, and between "free enterprise" and "state planning."[13] As a response to these oversimplified versions of social systems, a new super-radicalism is emerging which starts from the abstract notion that the architect of modern evil is the industrial system. Since both the United States and the Soviet Union are archetypes of this industrialization process, they reveal a common condition of dehumaniza-

---

[13] Wladyslaw W. Kulski, *Peaceful Coexistence: An Analysis of Soviet Foreign Policy.* Chicago: Henry Regnery Co., 1959. This is a good illustration of traditional Cold War scholarship based on the premise that the conflict between East and West is basic and structural.

tion of labor, deprivation of historical conscience, and emphasis on the values of material giganticism over any other values.[14] Beneath this *Sturm und Drang* romanticism lies a nostalgic faith in the past. And this longing for paradise lost has led to a drowning out of concrete historicity, of specific differences between capitalism and socialism, democracy and authoritarianism, development and stagnation, poverty and wealth, market anarchy and social planning.

What the nations of the Third World are continually searching for are specific ways in which some sort of "mixture" between the two giant social structures can be brought about without destroying either the vitality or integrity of national development as such. Perhaps the Third World cannot escape the problems of political eclecticism (not even by calling such problems "pluralism"). But it has made a powerful and largely successful effort to define itself over and against both the First and Second Worlds.[15] This it has been able to do only by clearly separating the various reasons for the success offered by the United States and the Soviet Union—particularly those reasons based on technological innovation from those based on rejecting past colonial status.[16]

We might say that the Third World is characterized by the following set of conditions: First, it tends to be independent of both power centers, the United States-NATO complex and the Soviet Warsaw-Pact group. Second, the bulk of the Third World was in a colonial condition until World War Two. Third, it draws its technology from the First World while drawing its ideology from the Second World. Thus, the Third World is non-American, ex-colonial, and thoroughly dedicated to becoming industrialized.

The Third World is a self-defined and self-conscious association of nation-states. Definitions of the Third World position have been made at the Bandung Conference of Colored Peoples in 1955; the Belgrade

---

[14] Herbert Marcuse, *One Dimensional Man*. Boston: Beacon Press, 1964. This is a good example of the new-style romantic critique of industrialism.
[15] See, for example, *United Nations Conference on Trade and Development* (*Final Act*). E/Conf. 46/L.28, 64-15050. 16 June, 1964. Mimeograph.
[16] This fact seems to be better recognized in the Soviet Union than in the United States. The latter still insists on interpreting unfavorable events as proof of the "immaturity" of the Third World, whereas Soviet theorists increasingly speak of "stages of maturation." See Thomas Perry Thornton (ed.), *The Third World in Soviet Perspective*. Princeton, N.J.: Princeton University Press, 1964.

conference of Non-Aligned Powers in 1961; the Congress of African States in Addis Ababa in 1963; and the Second Conference of Non-Aligned Nations held in 1964 at Cairo. The leading nations involved in formulating the politics and ideologies of the Third World at this point are India, Ceylon, United Arab Republic, Yugoslavia, Indonesia, and Ghana. This informal web of association extends to every continent, with a nucleus of membership in Africa, Asia, and Latin America. Marginal membership must be accorded such nations as Canada (a new arrival on the scene of Third World politics), China (which prefers to consider itself "aligned" but "independent"), and Algeria (which although only recently independent is already a powerful voice in the formulation of policies for the Third World).

The very rise and maturation of the Third World points up the instability and schismatic propensities of this coalition of nations. These "underdeveloped" nations have traditionally been the playground for wider international rifts. The Third World sometimes mirrors the ideological disputes between the Soviet Union and China on strategic matters concerning "peace offensives" or "revolutionary actions." At the same time, difficulties in offering an exact definition of the Third World become apparent. In terms of economic and organizational problems, for example, China ranks as a prime member of the Third World. Yet, in terms of its own explicit rejection of the concept of non-alignment, and its own concern for carrying nationalist revolutions to socialist revolutions, China must be considered as outside the Third World on political and ideological grounds.

At this juncture, it is less important to determine where China "fits" than to consider the nations that define themselves as a part of the Third World. From this point of view, all nations not organically linked with the North Atlantic Treaty Organization or the Warsaw Pact are increasingly defining themselves as part of the Third World. The very polarization of the world into a military stalemate has made possible the redefinition of aims and functions of the smaller powers within the NATO and Warsaw Pact Alliances. In the Soviet bloc, strong signs of independence are evident in Poland and Rumania. In the Western bloc the fissures are slower to appear because the control apparatus was weaker to begin with. Nonetheless, they can be found in the new attitudes of France and in the policies of Austria and Finland. Not only are former colonies caught in the crossfire of this organizational dissonance, but even some of the non-imperialist centers of Europe.

Within the bowels of capitalist Europe, Sweden anticipated the rise of a mixed economy. The Third Way of Sweden bears more than a superficial resemblance to the Third World of India. The *Force de frappe* of Gaullist France, however different in ambitions and traditions from the independent deterrent approach of a Maoist China, has a sympathetic relation with the corresponding search for political and military independence in the "inscrutable East." The Third World, is, however amorphous and unwieldy, an expanding entity.

Before going into the special features of the Third World, we ought to immediately point out that there is a Fourth World of undevelopment. That is to say, a world of tribal societies which for one or another reason are unconscious of alternatives to their own ways of life. The undeveloped society has no consciousness of being undeveloped. The Third World nations have a concept of emergence and characterize themselves as being developed socially and culturally, and of being *under*-developed economically and technically. This gulf between *un*development and *under*development is thus central in relation to the definition of the Third World. We are dealing with mature peoples and backward economies.

Any definition of the Third World must account for the powerful psychological force of invidious comparison. To the degree to which a knowledge of differences in earnings and opportunities exists, to that degree there will be a competition in ideologies and orientations. The earning power of each citizen of the United States, measured by the gross national product per capita, is ten times or more that of our "good neighbors" to the south in Brazil, Chile, Colombia, Mexico, Bolivia, and other nations in the hemisphere—outside of Argentina, Venezuela, Cuba, and Uruguay—and at least four times higher than these "exceptional" high income nations. This is in itself a brute fact making for "thirdness."[17]

---

[17] See Gabriel A. Almond and James S. Coleman (eds.), *The Politics of the Developing Areas*. Princeton: Princeton University Press, 1960, pp. 455-63. See also George I. Blanksten, "The Aspiration for Economic Development," *The Annals of the American Academy of Political and Social Science*, 334, March 1961, pp. 10-19.

This conscious awareness of difference is at its core an appreciation of invidious distinctions, what has euphemistically come to be called asynchronous forms of development. Ironically enough, this sense of difference is provoked by the competition of the First and Second Worlds. Through the inundation of propaganda in the form of films, books, periodicals, the peoples of the emergent nations are wooed for their political affections, and in this process they are made acutely aware of the riches of consumer affluence in the United States and the industrial-military complex built up over the past fifty years in the Soviet Union. The impulse for development is thus partly stimulated by these extrinsic features. It may be reinforced by women's magazines no less than political organs, by Hollywood films no less than by Soviet documentaries. However coated this passion for emulation is with slogans about folk identity and national culture, the economic and sociological demands for better living conditions and better credit terms are dictated by standards derived from the cosmopolitan centers. The consciousness of impoverishment gives an aura of frenzied immediacy to the process of social change. To catch up with "fully developed" societies becomes a definition of national purpose. To introduce doubt as to the value of this contest becomes a form of intolerable subversion. This is one primary reason why pluralistic and parliamentary politics have become increasingly scant in Third World nations. Controversy has itself come to be viewed as a luxury which only advanced nations can afford.

What are the character and scope of these asynchronous aspects in the developmental contest?

The developed regions grow rapidly because they are industrialized and sell finished commodities. The underdeveloped regions grow slowly because they are agriculturalized and sell primary products. The developed regions often determine conditions of production and also the price of primary goods.

The developed regions, in order to maintain their own privileged position, induce protective high-level tariffs, price-support programs, customs duties, etc., all of which create a sluggishness for the goods produced in the Third World. The underdeveloped world, for its part, cannot specify its own tariff arrangements without violating the terms of trade and financial loans.

The developed regions exhibit a relative evenness in their demographic patterns, production norms, and planning systems, which make scientific prediction of economic behavior possible. The underdeveloped nations exhibit extreme unevenness in these sociological factors of the economy and hence are disadvantaged in bargaining and negotiating.

These various abrasive features in the world system of invidious comparison are no longer in dispute. What remains open to question is what to do about them. Do these features represent "conflicts" or "contradictions '—items which can be removed without too much difficulty and without too much loss for either the developed or underdeveloped nations by mending, or only by revolution, by smashing? The selection between such alternatives rests on an article of faith, or rather, on contrasting strategies for stimulating social change. For some, contrasts between underdeveloped and fully developed nations can be removed through a concerted effort; that is to say, both "sides" can show long-range net gains by development. Former colonial powers make excellent contacts. The post-colonial status of England is often brought to bear in support of this argument. On the other side, there are those who insist that development and underdevelopment are defined in terms of each other; that underdeveloped nations can "emerge" only by the removal of imperialist economic relations and not simply colonial military occupations. They argue that former colonies make excellent economic partners instead of expensive status hobbies.

V

At one level, the designation Third World is a strategy for economic development rather than a type of economic or social structure. The "mix" in the Third World is ostensibly between *degrees of* (rather than *choices between*) capitalism and socialism at the economic level, and libertarianism and totalitarianism politically. It is not a new synthesis of political economy. One of the typical self-delusions of Third World nations is that they perceive themselves as developing new economic forms, when as a matter of fact this has not been the case thus far. There is little evidence that there will be any real new economic alternatives to either capitalist or socialist development in the immediate future. In the political sphere, however, the Third World seems to have added a new style if not a new structure.

The Third World is a mixture of different adaptations of capitalism and socialism but not an option to either of them at the economic level. The Third World is transitional. It is in a state of movement from traditional to modern society. It is the forms of transition which therefore have to concern us.

The fact that the First and Second Worlds are always in competition within a relative balance of power makes possible the exercise of Third World strategies in determining the role of foreign capital and aid, and not being determined by such capital.[18] To be a member of the Third World, in short, is not to make a choice in favor of one political bloc or another. As a matter of fact, it is to be very conscious and deliberate about not making this decision for the present.

As might be expected, within the Third World there is a wide range of choices of economic methods. Thus it contains some very strange mixtures.

India and Brazil have more than 75 per cent of their productive industries in the capitalist sector, while Algeria and Egypt are more than 75 per cent nationalized. Yet all four nations belong to the emergent bloc. In other words, to be considered part of the Third World it is not necessary to limit the character of the national economic system. The political posture in relation to the main power blocs is central to defining conditions of "membership" in the Third World.

In addition to economic factors, there are politically compelling reasons why the Third World is likely to be expanded further. Nations such as Canada and Mexico in the Western hemisphere are developing sharply independent policies in connection with the United States. Similarly, Yugoslavia, Poland, and Rumania, which between 1945 and 1960 were designated, perhaps not improperly, as satellites of the Soviet Union, are now largely performing a role inside a Third World orbit and ideology. Nations which in the recent past were satellitic and even parasitic are now increasingly linking ideological arms inside an "integral" protective cover of Third World slogans. Paradoxically, at the very moment when the Third World is experiencing great difficulties in defining the scope and character of its economic mix, its political influence is becoming more sharply delineated. The political contraction of Ameri-

[18] See Albert O. Hirschman, *The Strategy of Economic Development*. New Haven: Yale University Press, 1958, pp. 202-8.

can and Soviet spheres of influence has proceeded so evenly that, although an equilibrium of a "delicate balance of terror" is maintained, a great deal is happening in the no man's land between the First and the Second Worlds. This is the widest possible definition of the Third World, but in the absence of clear political-economic guidelines it may turn out to be the only definition which is operationally meaningful.

Many Third World nations have achieved their sovereignty in the present century—and especially after World War Two. The Latin American states are exceptions in that they had at least their formal sovereignty for a longer period of time. They represent old states, and not simply new states evolved out of old nations. This formal sovereignty is primarily political and not economic. Thus the initial phase of entering the Third World bloc is the establishment of national state sovereignty. The swollen membership of the United Nations reflects this process. It has more than doubled its member states inside of fifteen years. This tendency does not foreshadow the breakup of the nation-state for the sake of international government, but rather the development of the nation-state as a prelude to, and the organizing force in, the economic development process.

An essential factor about the international status of Third World nations is that they hold no dependencies. The First World drew political prestige and economic wealth from its colonial holdings. The Second World did likewise with its satellites. But the Third World cannot develop in terms of colonial holdings, since as ex-colonial nations they have neither such possessions nor do they have the possibility of developing colonial ambitions. The development of the Third World nation-state is not tied to foreign colonial expansionism, although it can stimulate what is called "internal colonialism." Third World nations do not compete for membership in the major power blocs. They generally form restricted regional organizations, such as the organization of Arab states, the organization of Pan-African unions, or the Latin American union. The policy of non-alignment militates against entry into such organizations as NATO or SEATO or the Warsaw Pact. Therefore treaty membership for Third World nations is considered undesirable and is avoided wherever possible.

In primary exchange economies, where raw materials are exported and finished commodities are imported, the gap between the Third

World and the First and Second Worlds is widening, not narrowing. Therefore competition between the Third World and First and Second Worlds becomes increasingly keen. Preferential rates and prices between highly developed nations are established; and preferential prices for finished commodities over raw materials are set. As a consequence there is a curbing or unevenness of economic growth.[19]

Very few Third World nations have fully mobilized their industrial potential. As a general rule, when there is such a mobilization, it is of a sectoral nature, usually benefiting elite groups within the Third World nation-state, and it differs widely according to class interest. Thus the gap between classes keeps the level of development low and uneven. Judged by real income per person, 90 per cent of the Third World peoples are between the 400 and 500 U.S. dollar level and another 5 per cent are between the 500 dollar to 750 dollar level and another 4 per cent between the 750 dollar and 1000 dollar level. Not more than 1 per cent earns over $1000. This lag grows greater as the gap between falling prices for agricultural and mineral products confronts the rising costs of finished commodity production. This fact alone casts grave doubt on the theory that a "middle sector" will be the savior of the Third World, or at least, save it from social revolution.

Often "uneven development" is considered erroneously as the antithesis of even development—or as it is more conventionally called, "balanced growth." But this theory of equilibrium as the ideal condition for development, while perhaps of some value for Western European models, is inappropriate for Third World nations—where there is nearly a complete *inelasticity* of demand due to low income levels. What is really at stake is not balanced growth versus uneven development—but the more modest and serious task of less uneven growth than what presently obtains. For example, in a nation such as Venezuela, petroleum accounts for approximately 90 per cent of the exports but employs only 2 per cent of the labor force. The bulk of Venezuelans continue to work in the unproductive agricultural sphere. The settlement is never going to be in terms of parity—90 per cent of the labor force in petroleum production—but an expansion of the domestic economy can serve to offset the degree and extent of imbalance.

Unevenness of development is not a metaphysical curse. It reveals

---

[19] See Raúl Prebisch, *Nueva Política Comercial para el Desarrollo*. Mexico-Buenos Aires: Fondo de Cultura Económica, 1964.

concrete components: money income and outlays above what is warranted by the capacity to produce for the purpose of satisfying consumer demands; imitation of patterns of industrial waste; high tariff restrictions for the purpose of taxing the foreign trade sector in place of a system of graded taxation; disinvestment in the domestic economy for the purpose of paying off purchases in foreign markets; low amounts received for raw materials and high costs for finished goods, etc. And while every economy in some profound sense is "uneven," the difference between developed and underdeveloped societies is the extent of imbalance.[20]

Any sound theory of social change must indicate what development excludes; that is, how it distinguishes itself from such cognate concepts as industrialization, externally induced transformation, growth of population and of the economy.

First, development differs from industrialization in that the latter implies a series of technological, mechanical, and engineering innovations in forms of social production. Social development for its part implies transformation in human relations, in the economic and political status in which men relate to each other, irrespective of the level of industrialization. Industrialization does produce stress and strain in human relationships which in turn has a large-scale effect on the over-all process of social development. But to identify industrialization with development is to run the grave risk of offering prescriptions for economic growth independent of social inequities.

Second, development differs from change in that the latter implies a continual adaptation through small steps and stages to an existent social condition. Development implies a genuine break with tradition —perceptible disruptions of the "static" equilibrium. Social development requires a new set of conceptual tools to explain "reality" whereas social change may leave intact old conceptual tools adapted to modified situations. Indeed, precisely what is modifiable is subject to change; while that which no longer contains the possibility of elasticity and plasticity is subject to development.

Third, development differs from externally induced transformation in that the latter implies a prime mover which is external to the developmental process. Thus, Caesarism, Stalinism, or simple old-fashioned im-

[20] On this topic, see Ragnar Nurske, "Some International Aspects of the Problem of Economic Development," *American Economic Association Papers and Proceedings*, Vol. 42 (May, 1952), pp. 571-83.

perialism may perform important functions with respect to the economic transformation of subject nations, but this is done for the prime, if not the exclusive, benefit of the mother country. Thus the building of a network of roads, communications systems, or the like is designed to expedite the shipment of raw materials to the home country. Similarly, the relationship of the urban complex to the rural regions may undergo similar transformations for the benefit of the city needs, of the needs of "internal colonialism," or of dominant minorities. Here too one cannot speak of development, despite the obvious stimulus such colonial contributions do make to long-run social development.[21]

Fourth, development differs from growth in population or national wealth since, like the simple process of quantitative change, these do not call forth any new process, but are simply processes of adaptation. Furthermore, it should be noted that growth in "natural events" of a society may actually sap development—thus the rapid rise in population may in fact serve to lower the total financial reserves of a nation. In short, some types of growth may be dysfunctional with respect to the needs of a developing society.

Development thus implies a new technology which makes available consumer goods. New methods of production radically alter the position of labor with respect to management. New markets radically alter the position of empire nations to colonized nations. New sources of raw materials and energy supplies radically alter the balance of world commerce and trade, and new forms of social organization radically alter the position of old strata since they now must reckon with a new "technocratic" stratum in addition to their traditional rivals. It is precisely this revolutionary side of the developmental process that has come to characterize the Third World—and precisely this side which is most conveniently forgotten by developmental theorists in the West.[22]

[21] On this matter of internal colonialism, see the following two brilliant studies: Pablo González Casanova, "Internal Colonialism and National Development," *Studies in Comparative International Development*, Vol. I, No. 4 (1965), pp. 27-37; and Rodolfo Stavenhagen, "Classes, Colonialism and Acculturation," *Studies in Comparative International Development*, Vol. I, No. 6 (1965), pp. 53-77.

[22] For a serious theoretical appreciation of the developmental process, at the economic level at least, see Joseph A. Schumpeter, *The Theory of Economic Development*. Cambridge, Mass.: Harvard University Press, 1934. He was the first social scientist to develop a typology of development which distinguished development from change and from externally induced transformations. For criticisms of the developmental economists, see Chapter 12.

In the main, the Third World is a low industrial, goods-producing area no less than a high commodity-cost area.[23] This affects the quality as well as the amount of foreign aid that they receive from the First and the Second Worlds. Disregarding the question of whether this aid is harmful or beneficent, with or without strings, the fact is that the Third World *receives* economic assistance, some kinds of funds, while the First and Second Worlds represent funding agencies for it. Thus national independence does not in itself guarantee an end to foreign domination. This distinction between nations receiving aid and nations rendering aid is central to a definition of the Third World.

The Third World supplies world markets with primary commodities, primary agricultural supplies, nonferrous base metals, etc. The First and Second Worlds basically export not primary commodities but manufactured goods. The Soviet Union has been more sensitive to the international imbalance between raw materials and finished products than has the United States. With the exception of wartime conditions, export of primary commodities is never as financially lucrative as export of manufactured goods. While it is true that without these primary commodities there can be no manufacture of goods, still the source of primary supplies is wider than imagined. Therefore, the First World has tended to maintain the imbalance between the fully advanced and the underdeveloped nations. Contrary to the rhetoric of foreign aid, the extent of First and Second World assistance to Third World development is not so much a question of direct fiscal support but rather of prices paid for raw materials, costs of importing goods, and control of international trade and money markets.

The question of setting market prices is generally allocated to the First and Second Worlds. That is, the Soviet Union can set the price on wool; the United States, along with its Western European cotton manufacturers, can set the price on cotton. This ability to set the price is a characteristic of monopolies in general, and this ability to monopolize prices is a characteristic of the First World. Monopolization is therefore a form for preventing price and wage fluctuation in the metropolitan areas. At the same time, by controlling the flow of vital parts, it is a way

[23] The neglect of this correlation between low industrialization and high commodity costs in the Prebisch thesis has been called attention to by Ramón Ramírez Gómez. "El Informe Prebisch y la Realidad Latinoamericana," *Cuadernos Americanos*, Vol. CXXXI, No. 6 (Nov.-Dec., 1963), pp. 7-72.

for preventing mass expropriation in the backward areas. Underdeveloped regions in the Third World suffer heavy price fluctuations and accentuated inflationary spirals, because they cannot control world markets, set or regulate prices, or expropriate property or resources when this is nationally desirable or feasible.

VI

In the Third World the *formal* systems are nearly always and everywhere republican in character, while their *real* systems are nearly always authoritarian. They are neither monarchies nor total dictatorships. They are under the "rule of law"—that is, they have constitutions—but this lawfulness is deposited in the hands of the dynamic leader of the single party. They have an unchecked higher political directorate, a party charisma. There is neither a developed parliamentary system nor the kind of relatively stable multi-party groupings found in Western Europe and the United States. Where such parliamentary systems have been allowed to expand, they have been a conservative force which has served to fragment the political power of progressive social groups. Parliamentary rule is often present in older sectors of the Third World which already have achieved formal independence, as in Latin America. Here, for instance, the agricultural proletariat has been systematically excluded from effective participation, either directly through disenfranchisement, or indirectly through electoral frauds of various sorts. In such circumstances the legislative branch becomes the legal front for property ownership. In Africa, nations have avoided this situation by abandoning the multi-party system.[24] Thus, in Ghana, Algeria, Tunisia, Kenya, Egypt, and Guinea, there has been the gradual erosion of parliamentary norms in the name of mass participation. The Parliament has become an upper class forum, while the President has become the hope of the masses. This struggle is simply another way of describing the differences between formal and real political systems in emerging nations.

Given the great importance of this element, the revolutionary system is often identified in the minds of the mass with a particular party. Hence, Congress Party, however amorphous its organization may be, re-

[24] See Gwendolen M. Carter (ed.), *African One-Party States*. Ithaca, New York: Cornell University Press, 1962.

tains a virtual monopoly of the political apparatus in India. The same is true of the P.R.I. in Mexico. Thus, even in nations which are traditionally identified with Western values of democracy and libertarianism, parliamentary norms are more formal than real. To achieve even a minimum rate of growth, to enter the "take-off" period, the Third World nations have had to recognize the need for central planning. And such high level planning is in itself a political act, necessarily under the aegis of the state system. The politics of this system, while often "benevolent" in character, cannot be said to be particularly concerned with the observance of parliamentary norms.

A parliament is a forum of conflicting and contrasting interests and opinions. As such, its ability to serve the "whole people" is subject to ridicule and, ultimately, to disrepute. In the cases of the Congo and Pakistan parliamentary rifts prevented the normal functioning of society. And only with the passing of such nominally democratic forums was social order maintained.

Parliamentary development can be afforded as a splendid luxury when time and history allow. This was the case for the United States in the nineteenth century. Whether there is a margin for parliamentary developments in the Third World depends on the role that parliaments perform in these nations. The case histories presently available are hardly encouraging. In Latin America they have tended to preserve the *status quo* and to retard the development of central planning.[25] It is hard to imagine the new African states following such a model. Therefore, there is within the Third World a development of radical political orientations without many basic constitutional safeguards. This is one basic reason why Western social democratic ideology has found it extremely difficult to champion the Third World cause.[26]

The authoritarian nature of the Third World has resulted from the rapid growth and consolidation of the one-party state. Yet, this rarely spills over into totalitarianism, into the control of the total social sys-

[25] See on this Irving Louis Horowitz, *Revolution in Brazil: Politics and Society in a Developing Nation.* New York: E. P. Dutton & Co., 1964, pp. 279-304; and for a more panoramic introduction, R. A. Gómez, *Government and Politics in Latin America* (revised edition). New York: Random House, 1963.
[26] For a sound introduction to this subject see Richard Harris, *Independence and After: Revolution in Underdeveloped Countries.* London: Oxford University Press, 1962.

tem. Technological advance and bureaucratic efficiency have not advanced to the point where this is possible. A verbal commitment to democratic values is retained. The democratic society remains a goal to be attained, while authoritarian solutions are considered temporary necessities. However, its governmental machinery is feared for its total control and the effect on the social system. Yet, almost every Third World nation has a written constitution and a formal legislative body. Oftentimes, these documents are tailored after those extant in the advanced countries. But generally these documents serve to legitimize bodies which act as rubber stamps. Actual political structures bear a much closer resemblance to the Second World of the Soviet orbit than to the First World.

The Third World is subject to a unique set of political circumstances. Nearly every industrial, highly developed society has emerged in the wake of political, economic, or religious conflicts reaching a point of open armed hostilities, and resolved by the play of internal forces with a minimum of external intervention or interference. This is illustrated by the English Revolution of 1640-88, the American Revolution of 1775-81, the French Revolution of 1789, the Russian Revolutions of 1905 and 1917, and even the Chinese Revolution of 1948-49. At present, however, the costs of development under circumstances of international conflict have become prohibitive. Development must now, more than ever, be a response to both international and national pressures. The fact is also that every one of these past revolutionary events resulted in part from the pressures exerted by a newly created working mass for participation in the political process. As much as anything else, these revolutions democratized politics by bringing about the participation of a vast, previously excluded public. These humanistically inspired revolutions were designed to transform the human species from masses into classes.

The Third World nations, as presently constituted, have attempted to develop military alternatives to the First and Second Worlds—not just political options to military power, but genuine large-scale military force.[27] The most powerful Third World nations are nations that had popular revolutions, which means revolutions which have either crushed

[27] See on this Morris Janowitz, *The Military in the Political Development of New Nations*. Chicago: University of Chicago Press, 1964.

or eliminated the old elites rather than just reshuffling power among them. It is no accident that nations such as Ghana, Algeria, Cuba, India, and Yugoslavia are leaders of the Third World; they represent the nations which have had this fully developed "revolution from below." For this reason Mexico can probably be considered a more fully developed member of the Third World than Venezuela, because in the 1910-20 Mexican Revolution the old military caste was crushed. The old military caste was tied up with the feudal aristocracy and the landed nobility. The new military was at the outset a popular peasant militia.

In the Third World, where revolutions have been successful, the traditional military has either been crushed or fully absorbed into revolutionary actions. There has not always been an armed struggle between military groupings. Nevertheless, the national liberation front has been the major stimulus to successful popular reform and revolutionary movements in the Third World nations. The development of these nations in large measure is connected to the outcomes of these internal military conflicts.[28]

Third World nations also cannot really operate with foreign military bases on their soil. Dependent colonial states have in general granted extraterritorial rights to imperialist or colonialist powers. When a nation has a foreign military base, it is almost axiomatic that it is not fully accepted into the Third World. Therefore, one would have to say that East Germany is not a member of the Third World any more than South Vietnam, for both these nations, irrespective of their radically different levels of development, are clear illustrations of regimes buttressed by the presence of foreign military bases, a presence which makes development, as I have defined it, exceedingly difficult.

Ethnic and/or religious differences are exceedingly important in the Third World. With the exception of Latin America, religions of Asia and Africa are neither Roman Catholic, Protestant, Jewish, or Greek Orthodox. They are, basically, Moslem, Shinto, Taoist, Confucian, Buddhist, Hindu, primitive. Even Latin American Catholicism has always been special, often infused, as in Haiti and Brazil, with non-Christian sources of religious practice and ritual. Religious culture remains an element apart, as a cohesive factor for maintaining tradition in the

[28] See J. K. Zawodny (ed.), "Unconventional Warfare," *The Annals of the American Academy of Political and Social Science*, Vol. 341, 1962.

Third World. The religious expression of the value of leisure over work, the sharp distinction between the sacred and the profane, and the separation between castes reinforces the fatalism often linked to ideas opposing development.

The Third World is an area where there are few competing religious institutions, since nationalism and patriotic fervor supercede linguistic and religious preferences. Whether Christian, Moslem, Hindu, or Hebrew, a national Church often accompanies the national State. Where different religions co-exist, there is usually strong conflict. The India-Pakistan partition was made inevitable by religious differences; and the Buddhist-Catholic rift in Vietnam is long-standing and severe. Many of the non-Christian religious organizations do not have established church hierarchies separate from the state bureaucracy. This is particularly true in the Middle East, and was true of pre-war Japan and China. Also, since leadership in the Third World is more tied to ethnic values than to religious values as such, the "secularization" process appears more accentuated than it is in fact. The parochial nature of religions in the Third World tends to force the individual to choose between religious belief and non-belief, rather than between competing religions. Socialist-atheist ideologies, rather than Western-Christian religions, compete with the established religions in Asia and Africa. And in a slightly modified sense, the same is true of Latin America—where Socialism is more tolerated than Methodism.

A large majority of the people in the Third World, prior to their independence, have very little, if any, primary or secondary school training. It is almost axiomatic that once the Third World nation passes through its first ordeal of development, the main push is toward cultivation of its people; at least the technical and primary training that a population needs in order to enter any socially developed world.[29] There is a modifying factor to be considered. Prior to the achievement of national independence, there is a heavy premium on ideological leadership. The new ruling class tends to be recruited from the political elite. In the second stage, once sovereignty and a level of primary education are

[29] See on this Frederick Harbison and Charles A. Myers, *Education, Manpower, and Economic Growth: Strategies of Human Resource Development.* New York: McGraw-Hill, 1964, esp. pp. 49-130; also Adam Curle, *Educational Strategy for Developing Societies.* London: Tavistock Publications, 1963.

also achieved, concern for technical proficiency promotes the demand for higher education for all, a new technical ideology replaces the conventional ideology of revolutionism. This took place in Russia. The first stage was experimentation and freedom followed by an emphasis on heavy industrial growth, which in turn slowly adapted revolutionary Marxism to technical needs—rather than developed a technological ideology as such. This same path seems to be pursued in such far-away places as Rumania and Cuba—where increasingly the political leadership is recruited from technical engineering sources.

This changeover within the Third World, from a militant ideological point of view to a technological point of view, is accompanied by large-scale cultural reorientations. Hence, in all Third World nations, one finds a continuing struggle between humanistic traditions and growing technical predilections between traditional values and scientific innovation. Each newly formed nation is working out the conflict between these "two cultures" that Charles P. Snow has described. As a general rule, the conventional revolutionary ideology lasts longer at the cultural level than at the economic level. Since Marxism, socialism, and the variants thereof represent a general way of life, an effort is made to rationalize technical change within the conventional ideology, rather than risk raising questions about the ideology. Hence, there is considerable disparity and lag between mass sentiments favoring the conventional ideology and technological demands for cultural innovation. This in itself can be an important factor in the emerging nations, as has been made plain in the cultural debates which have taken place in Cuba, almost without letup, since the Castro Revolution of 1959. Nonetheless, if the problem of two cultures is not quite resolved by the evolution of the Third World, thus far it has become a meaningful base for the reexamination of scientific and cultural integration.

"Natural" geographic and demographic factors also directly affect the structure of the Third World. For example, many of the Third World areas have unfavorable climate and/or soil resources. Extreme heat, bacteriological infiltration of the soil, heavy rainy seasons, etc., seriously impede sustained and rapid growth. There is no question that technological advancements such as air-conditioning and artificial irrigation can compensate for these natural deficits, but it would be foolish to deny the grave effects of geographical and ecological impediments in

Third World areas.[30] Indeed, such a natural phenomenon as water supply has played an immense part in the political and economic development of China, determining the character of political control, no less than who shall rule at any given time.[31]

Complicating the tasks of development still further are the demographic imbalances that exist in the Third World. There is today a definite trend toward overpopulation in Asia, Africa, and, more recently, in Latin America. It is a vicious circle, in effect: an agricultural economy can sustain large populations, and large extended families are a requirement for the maintenance of an agricultural economy. The facts and figures on life expectancy rates, infant mortality, and per capita daily intake of calories are too well known to require elaboration. Yet, the demographic factor is complicated by the fact that medical and scientific innovation extends the life span, and in turn places a higher valuation on life. At the same time that mortality is steadily declining, there is no corresponding increase in family planning.[32]

The problems created by the transition from rural to urban life styles leave no aspect of social life untouched. They affect everything from food tastes to cultural preferences. The impact of urban form—the first contact with foreigners and foreign ways—has profoundly shaped the attitudes of social classes in the Third World. People feel as strongly about mass leisure or political participation in Jakarta and Buenos Aires as they do in London or New York.[33] The transitional process is of a special nature. The Third World nations generally have a single metropolitan center, without either middle-sized cities or competing metropolitan centers within their boundaries. Thus they represent highly developed city-states, with a backward countryside surrounding them. This is particularly the case in Latin America. This promotes a great unbalance in mi-

[30] See Wladimir S. Woytinsky and Emma S. Woytinsky, *World Population and Production*. New York: Twentieth Century Fund, 1963.
[31] See Karl Wittfogel, *Oriental Despotism: A Comparative Study of Total Power*. New Haven: Yale University Press, 1956.
[32] See Ralph Thomlinson, *Population Dynamics: Causes and Consequences of World Demographic Change*. New York: Random House, 1965. Such problems are not unlike those faced by the poor in the developed nations. See, for example, Lee Rainwater, *And the Poor Get Children: Sex, Contraception, and Family Planning in the Working Class*. Chicago: Quadrangle Books, 1960.
[33] See Philip M. Hauser, *Population Perspectives*. New Brunswick, N.J.: Rutgers University Press, 1960.

gration patterns. Class and cultural dissonance becomes inevitable because of the gaps between country and city living, and the rapid and often difficult transition forced upon migrants who move to the city.[34] In addition, the large urban centers of the Third World are parasitic rather than promoters of development. They tend to exploit, through the domestic bourgeoisie, the labor and produce of the countryside. And in turn, this parasitism is extended to the international sphere. The cities are not favorably located with respect to further industrialization of the nation, but are evolved in terms of their uses as import-export centers.

It is obvious that the broad outlines of the Third World are easier to define than the precise contours. The selection of variables is a critical factor in this latter task. Thus, if we select "non-alignment" with either the United States or the Soviet Union as the chief criteria, such nations as France and China might well fall within the Third World. However, if we select the character of the social system as central, then France is clearly aligned with the Western bloc, and China no less with the Eastern bloc.

If we try to simplify the definitional problem by asking the "showdown" question—i.e. where would the Chinese Communist regime or a Gaullist France stand in the event of military hostilities between the United States and the Soviet Union—some clarification is possible. From a showdown perspective, it is evident that France is as much a part of the First World as China is of the Second World. The likelihood of a shift at this level in any near future is indeed quite slim. The tensions in the United States and Soviet orbits alike are a consequence of the spread of thermonuclear power, of a general military affluence that has taken place. Thus, France may be considered not so much outside the American power bloc as attempting to set up a countervailing leadership in that bloc. Similarly, ideologically, institutionally, and politically, China remains dedicated to the ideals and principles of Communism, and hence can scarcely afford to allow its criticism of Soviet *policies* to spill over into a general critique of the Communist philosophy.

[34] See Rodolfo Stavenhagen, "Classes, Colonialism and Acculturation," *Studies in Comparative International Development*, Vol. I, No. 6 (1965), pp. 53-77; and for a theoretical exposition of the effects of the urban and industrial processes, see Herbert Blumer, "Early Industrialization and the Laboring Class," *The Sociological Quarterly*, Vol. I, No. 1, January 1960, pp. 5-14.

Nonetheless, the selection of other sets of variables would clearly make China in particular a leader no less than a member of the Third World. China has so many topographic, economic, and sociological features in common with the Third World that it must be said that the Chinese Communist regime seems just as concerned with achieving a directorate in the Third World as it has been in developing a leadership role within the international Communist movement. France for its part is not simply attempting to redefine the relationship between itself and the United States within the First World, but is also attempting to man the bastions of a fourth position—an orientation which sees a "United Europe" as equal in capacity and strength to a "United States." The dilemmas in the Chinese position are graver. China is committed to a socialist economic system built on standardized Marxist-Leninist positions (indeed, China's ideology is more dogmatic than that of any nation in the Soviet orbit), and thus its leadership pretensions are circumscribed by its ideological commitments.

It will be protested that in this discussion of the three worlds of development, far too little emphasis has been given to the "re-emergence of Europe" in the past decade or so. Indeed, there is a new literature speaking of the "fall and rise of Europe,"[35] and various theorists turned enthusiasts now speak of the "New Europe."[36] Perhaps it is a personal bias, grounded in little else than idiosyncrasy, but it seems that Europe, even while engaging in spectacular changes in social relations and scientific inventions, gives the appearance, as one writer put it, of an "antique shop" and a "well-protected aquarium."[37] The continued outward emigration from Europe, its traditional, unimaginative politics (of both Left or Right), the way that the European culture has become a simple footnote to events in either the United States or in the Soviet Union, the relative stagnation of the economies of England, Italy, and France— all these factors weaken the leadership potential of Europe. This is not to deny the role of Europe in East-West relations. But in a volume con-

[35] John Lukács, *Decline and Rise of Europe*. Garden City, New York: Doubleday & Co., Inc., 1965.
[36] Stephen R. Graubard (ed.), "A New Europe?" *Proceedings of the American Academy of Arts and Sciences*, Vol. 93, No. 1 (Winter 1964).
[37] See Gianfranco Corsini, "American Culture and the Italian Left," *The Correspondent*, Number 33 (Winter 1965), pp. 45-52.

cerned with a "natural triad"—with the three worlds of development—Europe does tend to lose a pivotal function.

Nonetheless, one cannot negate the persistent influence of England and France (the "good colonialists") or of Belgium and Portugal (the "bad colonialists") in Africa. There is also the persistent German influence in North Africa and in Latin America. To be sure, Western Europe continues to be the largest buyer of African produce. It is possible that the widening latitude of European commercial activities will have great bearing on the future forms of African development.

France, for its part, has adapted its archaic middle-sized capitalism to the possibilities of bureaucratic technological domination. Even if it were possible for France to continue its independent economic position, this could be done only through the sufferance and forbearance of the United States. United Europe is a dream; the United States is a reality—the French posture has confused dream and reality. It is scarcely likely that this will affect other European nations—which, if they are not satellites with respect to the United States, continue to remain seriously dependent economically. Even if Europe moves away from the United States, which it shows every indication of doing, the likelihood is that Europe will expend its energies forging a new economic synthesis between East and West. When this relatively short-run task is achieved, in some ten to twenty years, only then will Europe be likely to have a deep impact on development in the Third World.

All of this is said not to minimize the theoretical difficulties posed by France or China. There are certainly new features at work which modify any definition of the Third World—but what is really underscored by these schismatic developments within capitalism and socialism is not so much the growth of new and alternative systems of political economy but alternative control agencies within each system. Whether capitalist or socialist economic organization is favored in the allocation of national resources for purposes of full industrial development, the new strategies are circumscribed by the social classes and political means used to exert control over the development process. Doctrines favoring the bourgeoisie and the working class, are being rejected in favor of pragmatic appraisals of who can and will win leadership. Humanitarian, authoritarian preferences are balanced against national needs and sacrifices to be made. As Third World nations are driven by the power struggle between the First and Second Worlds, they have to adopt such postures that enhance their own "freedom of movement." There is no one set of premises which can encompass this whole portion of the world. Perhaps the surest guide to the existence of a Third World view is its own perceived interest as a bloc, despite an exasperating range of variation.

Appendix A

A Digest of Factors Defining the Three Worlds*

Dominated by the United States, including allies in Western Europe and satellites in Latin America and elsewhere.

Economy: Capitalist system; based on private ownership in a free market; development of corporate wealth and strong tendencies toward monopolistic controls of large private power blocs. The typical economy is middle class; based on individual entrepreneurial initiative, with little centralized planning (generally only in social welfare sectors). Emphasis on services and consumer goods production. Open internal market; high international integration created by financial and commodity markets, with slight regulation. Savings policies are individual-voluntary and/or based on democratic tax system. Investment is private, unrestricted, unco-ordinated. Source of funds is variable; based on decisions taken by household, business, bank credit, and international capital market. Currencies are stable. Terms of trade favorable. Growth rates are low, but generally balanced for needs of industrial society. Agricultural sector 5 to 20 per cent of GNP, and 5 per cent of labor force; contraction of this sector is aided by international competition (market forces) and by government subsidy. Industrial level of development is high; growth rate

* Any effort at typification at a universal level is bound to create many problems. It is evident that old nations of the Third World (Latin America) differ profoundly from new nations of the Third World (Asia and Africa) in everything from religion to military orientations. Such variabilities will be taken up in the body of the text, where the social sub-systems are discussed.

39

has plateaued off. Consumption orientation, encouraged as necessary stimulus for growth; restricted by market fluctuations and private savings. Labor unions strong, highly organized, constituting an economic force.

Polity: Parliamentary democracy, which is established by legal authority and based upon economic law of market. Ideologically conservative and centrist. Accepts conflict within rules of game. Emphasis on nation-state is moderate to slight; most prominent in reaction to external threats. Tendency to have few major political parties, with strategic rather than ideological differences between them prevailing. Policy formulation is by these parties and/or associational interest groups. Range of party activity is narrowly political. Party elite membership is small and inactive except at election times. Organization is highly bureaucratized, but centralization is weak. Basic unit is the caucus. Elected representatives forming party leadership tend to come from traditional classes and form oligarchical control, while remaining sensitive to public desires for policy-making. Policy implementing achieved by bureaucrats functioning under political executives. Independent judiciary. Non-participation of religious organizations in governmental or political functions (separation of church and state). Subordination of army to government, though pressure to have voice in international political policies.

Society: Highly urbanized; large growth of medium-sized cities (250,000–1,000,000) in addition to several large cities. Moderate pace of industrial growth, plateaued off at high level of development. Rapid growth of middle class, both professional and entrepreneurial; contraction of lower and working classes. High degree of vertical upward and downward mobility (more upward); increasing specialization of occupations; great status differentiation through occupation and income. Main avenue of mobility is through education, in highly bureaucratized society. Liberal, mass education; education has high income yield and is greatly in demand. Increase in leisure activities, decrease in work activities; considerable separation of occupation from private life. Increased social welfare programs and benefits. High level of mass consumption. Greater geographic mobility. Family unit: small, nuclear; increase in emotional role. Proliferation of highly organized, functionally specific, independent groups. Low birth rate, low death rate; few official demographic policies. Immigration: by quotas; emigration: no restrictions. Religion: Christian. Racial composition: white. Ethnic pre-eminence: Northern European. Cultural affinities: Puritanism and secular enlightenment.

Military: The basic property of the military is its professionalization; that is to say, its general confinement to the execution of decisions made by a non-military civilian body. The armed forces do not have any specific ideological commitment apart from the defense of the nation as this is interpreted and defined by the civilian political elites. The armed forces operate within a well-defined organizational code, with a minimum emphasis, except in wartime and for propagandistic purposes, on personalities. The standing army is generally small to modest in size, with large-scale conscription confined to crisis periods. The centers of actual military power are dispersed throughout the nation; with a bureaucratic core located in the capital city. Engagement in political activities is consciously eschewed, and considered a conflict of interests. Service rivalries exist; but such rivalries are normally confined to which sector of the armed forces gets what and when. There is a noticeable absence of friction between ranks, of "barracks uprisings" against higher military echelon, or open rivalries between military leadership. Requirements for admission and promotion are clearly defined and broadly accepted. *Esprit de corps* is very high, providing a cohesive element in critical junctures.

SECOND WORLD

Dominated by the Soviet Union, including allies and/or satellites in Eastern Europe and parts of Asia.

Economy: Socialist system; based on public (state) ownership in a strictly controlled internal and external market; centralization of all sectors of the economy by political elites; based on total planning. The typical economy is geared to proletarian values. Emphasis is on heavy industrial production. Highly regulated internal and external markets, determined primarily by economic considerations. Trade agreements are largely within Eastern bloc countries; not subject to severe trade fluctuations. Savings policies are non-voluntary; state determined and government controlled. Investment is through the public sector; highly restricted and co-ordinated. Source of funds is stable; based on internal budgeting. Currencies are generally stable. Growth rates are high; imbalances controlled through economic regulation. Agricultural section 15 to 30 per cent of GNP, 40 per cent of labor force; contraction due to prohibition of individual private agriculture. The factors making for land speculation are strictly regulated in order to release resources and increase output at a rate integrated to industrial expansion. Industrial level of development is high, and growth rates have just begun to plateau off. Direct and manifold controls on production and distribution of consumer goods; discouraged as deterrent to industrial development. Labor unions perceived as part of state directorate, worker councils play minor role.

Polity: Democratic centralism; legitimated by rationalized authority, and based upon economically grounded ideology of Communism-socialism, interpreted through ruling elite with very high doctrinal rigidity. Very strong emphasis is put on building common forms of economic socialism in a brotherhood of political nation-states; most prominent in times of independent political dissension of a member nation-state. Prohibition and suppression of opposition. Strong one-party system dictating all interest articulation. Discipline tends to be very strong and centralization is from the top. Basic unit is the cell. Although working class oriented, party elite membership is rather large (up to 10 per cent of population); leadership based on bureaucratic principles of selection, and elites rising solely through Party lines. Party activity is all-encompassing and continual; no separation of policy-making from policy implementing, no separation of powers; legislation from above, achieved through bureaucrats functioning under political executives, judiciary not independent. Army entirely subordinate to civil control. Subordination or repression of religion and church. Enthusiasm and commitment are highly praised and broadly based, emphasizing community as well as national affairs.

Society: Highly urbanized; large growth of medium-sized cities, generally with several large ones; still a sizable peasant sector. High pace of industrial growth, just beginning to plateau off at a high level of development.

Rapid growth of working class, moderate increase of middle professional class (increase in non-bureaucratic white-collar workers). High degree of social mobility, with a greater amount than in First World due to technological change; slowly increased specialization of occupations; lower degree of status differentiation. Main avenue of mobility is through occupational hierarchy, although education is becoming more important with increased specialization, complexity, and bureaucratization of industrial structure. Technical-scientific, mass education are emphasized. The educational sphere is unique in that it alone can claim manpower priorities over economic production. This is based on notion of education as postponed economic improvements. Slight increase in leisure activities, little decrease in work activities; general separation of occupational and private spheres. High social welfare benefits. High level of mass comunication; low level of mass consumption. Slight geographic mobility. Family unit: slightly extended nuclear family (often due to limited housing). Low birth rate, low death rate; variety of policies to integrate population increase with industrial growth rate. Immigration and emigration prohibited. Religion: Christian. Racial composition: white. Ethnic pre-eminence: Slavic—Central and Eastern European. Cultural affinities: Byzantine and secular enlightenment.

Military: The basic property of the military is its professionalization; but while it is generally confined to executing rather than formulating policy, it works closely with the political elite at the decision-making level. The armed forces do not have a specific ideological commitment apart from the general social commitment to the socialist ideology as defined by the civilian political elites. The armed forces operate within a well-defined organizational code, with a minimum emphasis, except in wartime and for propagandistic purposes, on personalities. On the other hand, the political elites often simulate military modes of dress and behavior. The standing army is generally larger than in the First World; but again, large-scale conscription is confined to crisis periods. The centers of actual military power are dispersed throughout the nation, with a bureaucratic core located near capital cities. Engagement in political activities is part of the role of the higher military elites, but eschewed among the rank and file (with the exception of political commissioners, either civilians attached to the military base or non-commissioned officers of political orientation within such bases). Service rivalries are frowned upon, and the organization of the branches of the military are made in terms of functional activities. The political system further discourages such rivalries by insisting on a higher military loyalty to state and party. There is a noticeable absence of friction between ranks, barracks uprisings against higher military echelons, or open rivalries between military leaderships. Requirements for admission and promotion are clearly defined and broadly accepted. *Esprit de corps* is very high, and provides a cohesive element in critical junctures.

THIRD WORLD

Non-aligned and non-satellitic nations with a general tendency toward clustering in Africa, Asia, and Latin America—a spectrum conventionally covering Algeria to Yugoslavia in economy and India to China in polity.

Economy: Mixed economy; with both private and public sectors, but moving toward some form of socialism. Economy reveals conflict between desire for integration based on self-sufficiency, and need for aid in development. There is a dilemma between strong internal regulation (foreign/internal investment ratio) and moderate external regulation (freedom of bloc trading) and ability to implement development schemes. Decline in terms of trade; balance of payments problem. Variety of planning techniques (total, national flow, national budget, project, labor, etc.). The typical economy is based on the peasant sector; basic level of economic production is agricultural; although emphasis is on basic industry. Desire for contraction of primary sector: mechanization of agriculture, overwhelming push factors, and imposed plans (rate of collectivization is presently reducing); agriculture often neglected in favor of emphasis on basic industrial development (the highest premium is placed on heavy industry whatever the costs in terms of man-hours) to create import substitute mechanisms. Successful integration of shift from agricultural to industrial sector is therefore uncertain, and dependent upon national planners' ability to control. Compounded by "demonstration effect," which government often tries to dampen through inflationary policies. Source of funds is variable and generally short term; foreign aid and investment supplement domestic savings (which are mitigated by unstable currency). Savings policies mostly voluntary and due to inability to control. Growth rates are high; attempted control of imbalances through political regulation. Short-run private-sector gains often vitiate effects of long-run public-sector planning. Labor unions are radical and unstable, with little economic role.

Polity: Mass democracy; legitimated through highly articulated and politically grounded ideology of nationalism and socialism, with a strong charismatic leader. Ideology is radical and socialist; but with considerable variation; polycentric rather than monolithic. Basic unit is the party branch. Highly centralized state, under virtual one party rule. Elite desire for total control and suppression of conflict groups, with no disjunction between policy-makers and policy-implementers. This is mitigated by: low level of party discipline; enthusiasm and commitment often attached to party personages rather than to party policies; absence of institutionalized charisma; responsiveness to masses' desires. Source of change in policies due less to minority parties than to multiple interest articulation and application. Often independent and over-participant role of military, executive branch, and/or prematurely overdeveloped bureaucracy (sometimes much too underdeveloped). Although oriented toward the "popular" class or the nation as such, party membership is somewhere between the First and Second Worlds. Leadership often based on educational-technological-military criteria; except under highly revolutionary circumstances, leadership alliances with elites of traditional prestige where latter not resistant to development.

Society: Rapidly urbanizing; problem of developing middle-sized cities, often the major city more powerful than nation as a whole. Industrial growth still attaining take-off stage. Social mobility: still low in traditional areas; occupational mobility slowly increasing in industrial areas. Labor market still unspecialized. Traditional status differentiation diminishing. Main avenue of mobility is through occupational and political hierarchy. Education: emphasis on mass literacy, technical-scientific secondary education, with planning to integrate industrial needs into educational programs. Little leisure activities; increase in work activities; often no clear distinction between occupational and private spheres of life. High social welfare benefits. Development of mass communication; low consumption rates. Individual geographic mobility is low; occasional shifts of large groups in population (due to force, planning, natural disasters, etc.). Family unit: extended family, deteriorating. High birth rate, low death rate; difficulty in introducing birth control policies. Immigration and emigration: generally restricted by occupational skills. Religion: Moslem, Hindu, Buddhist, Christian (not major). Racial composition: yellow, black, brown, red; in short, basically non-white. Ethnic preeminence: Negroes and Indians. Cultural affinities: philosophical rationalism closely linked to religious expressions. No clear separation between the secular and the sacred as in the Western tradition; but rather close fusions between theological doctrines and political credos.

Military: The basic property of the military is its politicalization, i.e. its role as a formulator and executor of political decisions. The "new nations" witness the rise of military politics, either as a prime mark of sovereignty or directly, as the political ruling group. The armed forces have specific ideological commitments—in "pre-revolutionary" Third World countries to conservative Caesaristic models and in "post-revolutionary" Third World countries to radical-charismatic models. The organizational code of the military is ambiguously defined, with an extreme emphasis on personalities, on the military leader as a national redeemer. The standing army is relatively small in numbers, but with a "top-heavy" ratio of elite to rank and file. But the level of financial expenditure is relatively quite high to the size of the standing army—in part this is a consequence of the necessity of purchasing arms from foreign industrial powers, and in part the consequence of maintaining a potential agency of maximum coercion with minimum numbers. The centers of military operations are usually highly concentrated in or near the capital cities or the industrial centers, hence enhancing the possibility of "palace revolutions"; also a symbolic reflection of the military near the centers of political decision-making. Political activity is most noticeable at the elite level, but in periods of discontent, rank and file leadership will oftentimes manifest itself. Service rivalries are exceptionally high, with the navy and air force often representing a posture to the political right of the army. Friction among military elites is very high. Factionalism oftentimes becomes noticeable in pre-*coup d'état* situations. *Esprit de corps* is not particularly strong—except within "in group" or barracks factions.

Chapter 2

Sociological and Ideological Conceptions of Development

Since twentieth-century thinkers began to "expose" the romantic and utopian fancies of inevitable progress, the social sciences have been plagued with the problem of accounting for "progress." Historians like Arnold Toynbee and Oswald Spengler tend to see in every kind of change the force of historical destiny.

Perhaps as a reaction to the concept of an inevitable succession of stages social scientists have turned "anti-historical"—erecting a barrier between social change and social development. This is the counterpart of the fact-value dualism in methodology. Change can be conveniently linked to "matters of fact" and hence studied, while social development entails matters of judgment and "statements of value" and hence cannot be scientifically valid. Given such a methodological injunction, it is no wonder that contemporary efforts in the field of social development do not compare with such "nineteenth century" works as Bury's *The Idea of Progress* or even Lecky's *History of European Morals*. Instead, current textbooks treat social change as an "area" of sociological investigation. This tendency toward compartmentalization violates the essential nature of change, which occurs in *all aspects of social life*.

The reasons for neglecting the question of change as human development are manifold. First, sociology has so sundered history from the social sciences that development is considered an accoutrement rather than a necessary aspect of the study of any society. Second, empirical sociological studies tend to focus on internal structure and consistency, stressing pattern maintenance, models of equilibrium, consensus systems, structural hegemony, etc. This approach leaves little place for conflict situations, forms of radical change, spontaneous and unstructured behavior, and other "unstable" forces producing change and development alike. Third, there is a fear that to discuss human development leaves one open to charges of utopianism. This is an age which takes forward strides self-consciously. Fourth, there is a widespread doubt that the concept of development is scientifically definable since it has for so long exclusively been the rallying cry of political ideologists.

In our age the struggle for social development takes place in the context of a developing social struggle. The question of what constitutes social development has itself become part of the general ideological struggle. Facts and figures on everything from consumer production to rates of capital re-investment now serve as "evidence" for the superiority of capitalism over socialism or socialism over capitalism. In such circumstances the social scientist hesitates to leap into the controversy over what contitutes development. This is the most important single reason why sociology has been so tentative about the question of human development.

Before examining differences between ideological and sociological definitions of human development, we can look briefly to historical concepts of change. Ancient Greeks provide some anchor-points. Correlated to the rather sophisticated Platonic and Protagorean notion of the basic unreality of change, is the concept that changes take place in "appearances" only, while a "substratum" remains essentially one and unchanging. For Plato change in space or time meant decadence, and objects which changed were intrinsically worthless. His identification of the good and the true with a changeless state represented the conservative position, which opposed all forms of development as threats to the established order.

The Aristotelian tradition removed the pejorative connotations from things which change. Thus, while Aristotle also held that there is an essentiaily unchanging substratum or reality (the categories of logic and mathematics), there exists an empirical reality, which is not quite as worthwhile, subject to laws of birth, growth, maturity, and decay. From a social point of view, Aristotle shared Plato's mistrust of things subject to alteration and progression. Empirical change was thought to "actualize" the "potentialities" inherent in all things rather than to create new phenomena.

Among the pre-Socratics, Heraclitos was the first to express a general theory of change. Several cardinal principles are offered in his dialectical picture of the world: (1) change is real, and therefore all reality must be defined in terms of change; (2) there is no aspect of physical, biological, or social life that can resist the general process of change—birth, development, and decay; (3) change is patterned and proceeds in accordance with well-defined general "laws"; (4) these general laws are "dialectical," that is, they proceed in a struggle of contrary and internal forces until a new stage of reality is achieved. Contrary to the Protagorean-Platonic view, Heraclitos placed exclusive emphasis on change and growth as the essential elements of reality.

Democritus took another approach to the problem of change. He considered atomic particles the ultimate stuff of the universe. All complex organisms are built up from these atoms, with the type and level of clusters determining the characteristics of the object. Change takes place through the combination and dissolution of basic atomic entities. The Epicureans advocated "reductionism," or an explanation of change in terms of uncomplicated material entities. Change was authentic and development feasible. But the basis of social change was still considered "physical" in essence; social laws were extensions, albeit complex, of principles of atomism and mechanics.

Although the ancient Greeks developed some highly refined and imaginative general theories of change and development, they evolved no working set of principles to account for social change and social progress. Until the start of the Industrial Revolution, concepts of human development remained highly theoretical. There evolved a variety of notions of what constitutes development: in one conception development signifies innovative possibilities of discovery. Development is also viewed as the unfolding in definite stages of the new in place of the old. There is also the "aesthetic" approach which views development as the working out of a theme or of variations on a theme. Finally, in the humanist tradition, development depended on knowledge and the bringing to light of new information.

The variety of these developmental theories should caution the social scientists from viewing development merely as a matter of "common sense." Such an attitude, which sociologists call "self-definition" or "auto-perception" of change, is dangerously limited—witness the endless multiplications and sub-divisions in the "self-definition of social class."[1] Human development involves factors which are definite and can be studied—such as quantity and quality of education, level of welfare, and the gap between attitude and actions, membership and commitment, costs and benefits—not mere arbitrary and capricious feelings of individuals or groups.

The rise of modern industrial society gave a new and robust dimension to the concept of development. Raw materials were turned into finished artifacts *en masse*; machines replaced human labor as the essential agency of production; organic, e.g. feudal, societies gave way to consensus, e.g. capitalistic, societies. The perception of change quickly followed the fact of change. There was an intense interest in new forms of social production, ownership, and consumption to fit the changing circumstances in the industrial world. Standards of "normal" life-span and infant mortality were no longer accepted; hygienic measures to guarantee maximum growth and life were demanded. Salvation became naturalized, and "man's lot" was no longer necessarily synonymous with "man's fate." The feudal contentment with the *status quo* crumbled before the onslaught of the capitalist world's concern with how things might and ought to be. Capitalist society fostered new standards of achievement no less than new forms of production.

Development becomes a general human concern only at the point of dramatic changes in the material culture. With the Industrial Revolution population burgeoned, inventions proliferated, and colonization began in earnest. The new social forces of production and the economic reorganization of life affected the whole mass of English people as had no prior political or religious event.[2] There was a great shift from rural

[1] See Ruth R. Kornhauser, "The Warner Approach to Social Stratification," *Class, Status and Power: A Reader in Social Stratification*, edited by Reinhard Bendix and Seymour M. Lipset. Glencoe: The Free Press, 1953; and also C. Wright Mills, "The Social Life of a Modern Community," *Power, Politics and People*, edited by Irving L. Horowitz. New York: Oxford University Press, 1963, pp. 39-52.
[2] See Gordon Childe, *Man Makes Himself*. London: Watts & Co., 1941, pp. 12-14.

to urban life, a change of emphasis from agricultural to commercial production, and a general change from relative scarcity to relative abundance.

Clearly, the precondition for the scientific study of social development is the fact of social change, just as a theory of progress can only arise in a changing world. These social changes wrought by industrialism turned traditional men into pragmatic risk-takers. Though the advantages were not the same for all men, opportunities for all were greater than ever before. The Industrial Revolution also highlighted problems and obstacles to change. Thus, Protestantism, Enlightenment, Liberalism, and Socialism can each be viewed as responses, at the ideological and philosophical levels, to the problems made evident by the facts of industrial development.

Weber's classic studies of the inter-relations between the Protestant ethic and the capitalist economy attempted to show how the traditional bourgeois belief in the curative power of work and the Protestant notion of "a calling" were fused into a monumental frontal assault against traditionalism.[3] This fusion of industry and religion was not made solely on grounds of abstract principles (e.g. the need of capitalism for integrity and honor in contract relations and the parallel need of Protestantism to link salvation to a practical work-ethic). It was based on a shared belief that if the individual as an active agent were to count at all, there would have to be a break with feudal "collectivism," which assumed that the things which could be changed were not worth changing, while the things worth changing were unchangeable.

The pietistic puritan and the worldly ascetic each saw development as apocalyptical rather than historical. Nonetheless, development was deemed necessary for grace. Man's redemption became more important than man's fate. The bourgeois consciousness likewise viewed development in apocalyptical terms—i.e. "windfalls," "good fortune," "business shrewdness," or just plain "luck." But even though the Lutheran concept of the calling remained traditional and the capitalist view of suc-

---

[3] Cf. Max Weber, "The Religious Foundations of Worldly Asceticism." *The Protestant Ethic and the Spirit of Capitalism*. New York: Scribner's and Sons, 1930; also "The Protestant Sects and the Spirit of Capitalism," *From Max Weber: Essays in Sociology*. New York: Oxford University Press, 1946, pp. 302-22.

cess remained utilitarian, both strongly hinted at a scientific view of change. In place of supernatural intervention as a means of attaining either Divine Grace or Nature's Wealth came a stress upon hard work, patient effort, and slow and tedious results. Such attitudes paved the way for the establishment of a doctrine of social change in place of the stratified and stultified view of the medieval feudal and religious world.

The concept of human development could not emerge until apocalyptic and capricious notions of change were discarded and development could be seen as a natural process proceeding independently of providential design. The French Enlightenment, characterized by Turgot's *Tableau philosophique successif de l'esprit humain*, Helvetius' *De l'esprit*, and Condorcet's *L'Esquisse d'un tableau historique des progrès de l'esprit humain*, gave the industrial world its first fully articulated theory of social development. This theory incorporated both Protestant and bourgeois modes of social explanation. The *philosophes* expounded a new humanism, extending the concept of development to include every department of human activity and every class of people.

The Enlightenment thus established a new view of social realities. History was no longer to be written in terms of "great men" or "individual genius" but in terms of the flow and the thrust of humankind. By conceiving of development as social, philosophers like Diderot and historians like Michelet fashioned a theory of change which was simultaneously "scientific" and "moral"; from illiteracy to universal education; from the rule of autocracy to a democratically oriented oligarchy and universal suffrage; from a law based on power and prestige to equality of all before the law; from *pax romana* to national sovereignty; from concentration to rational distribution of wealth; from women as slaves to women as partners. In this new humanism history became the story of man's progress, and true morality was said to consist of a radical critique of the present.

Some noted historians[4] have presented us with a sophisticated denigration of Enlightenment achievements, claiming that the philosophers confused religious belief and rational faith and muddled the idea of progress with that of redemption. But we still owe the Enlightenment

---

[4] Cf. Carl Becker, *The Heavenly City of the Eighteenth Century Philosophers.* New Haven: Yale University Press, 1932; and also, Crane Brinton, *The Anatomy of Revolution.* New York: W. W. Norton & Co., 1938.

the first significant formulation of a general theory of social development. The social scientists continue to frame the question of what constitutes development in Enlightenment terms. The Enlightenment not only took seriously the realities of development but predicted that the problem of development would become increasingly urgent. For example, Condorcet anticipated an era in which statistical and scientific methods would be enlisted to support the cause of progress.

While the French Enlightenment produced a theory of *social* development, it did not evolve a causal basis, an historical accounting, by which social science could be liberated from arbitrary forms of utopianism. French formulations viewed development as essentially a matter of *esprit, Zeitgeist,* and moral imperatives. Thus it tended to ignore the concrete, historical locus of development. Historically there has been decline as well as growth, decay as well as achievement. Rather than face the problem of decline, the Enlightenment chose to cast development in anti-historical terms, pitting human will against the dead hand of the past. The French *philosophes* in particular were troubled by discrepancies between the fact of inequality and the idea of equality. Unable to resolve this divergency empirically, they resorted to a moral posture. The progress of mankind was said to culminate in the final fusion of reason and self-interest—in short, in hedonistic utopianism.

The German Enlightenment tradition of Lessing, Herder, and Nicolai managed to fuse the Protestant doctrine of millennialism and the rationalist faith in progress into a historical theory of development. This was made possible by a concerted effort to connect reason and revelation into a general theory. Revelation is a moment in time which takes on meaning only through a painstaking process whereby reason connects one great moment with another. By framing laws governing both the continuities and discontinuities in social life, the German theorists supplied the missing link to the French Enlightenment theory of development. In the highest stage reached in pre-sociological discourse on the problem of development, change is seen as linked to the religion of humanity. The theory of development as progress became one with the religious base of human evolution. With this, "philosophical anthropology" was born. Change was no longer an accidental property of society but its very essence. Feuerbach, by bringing about materialistic theology, gave the summation of this entire tradition and, more important, the first glimmer of the critical spirit upon which nineteenth-century scientific theories of progress came to rest.[5]

The socialists, from Saint-Simon to Marx, connected the concept of development with that of particularized class interests and thus introduced the first full-fledged ideological (in contrast to religious) note to development. Progress in human affairs was no longer a total undertaking of society but a class enterprise. The "great man" was transformed into a "great class" and history became collectivized. The agencies and the bearers of change became the hitherto anonymous proletarian collectivity.

If Marxian and socialist tradition represents the substitution of ideology for religion, it no less represents the replacement of philosophy with science. By viewing development as a social question, a secular question, and insisting on the specific, interest-laden dimensions of the problem, Marxism made it unfeasible to consider development in terms of Hegelian historical categories. Marx himself developed a parallel theme: one side of development is seen as occurring in the "natural society" in which "man's own act becomes an alien power opposed to him, which enslaves him instead of being combatted by him"; development takes place also in "civil society" and actually constitutes the history of class society, the history of the division of human labor. These lines of development are resolved and synthesized in socialism; the communism of "natural society" is joined to the material achievements of "civil society." Marx waxed rhapsodic on this theme; through socialism, man's nature is "restored to himself."[6] Marx, however, clearly saw the problem of development as one which must account for both continuities and discontinuities in social life; and more specifically at the political level, development signified the replacement of state power with social authority.

At the same time Marx sought to enunciate principles of development in terms of the natural history of socio-economic production. The concept of an inexorable progression from slavery to feudalism, capitalism, socialism, and ultimately to communism arose out of Marx's con-

---

[5] Cf. Irving L. Horowitz, "Lessing and Hamann: Two Views on Religion and Enlightenment," *Church History*, Vol. 30, No. 3, September 1961, pp. 334-48.
[6] Cf. Karl Marx, *The German Ideology*, ed. by Roy Pascal. New York: International Publishers, 1939; and also his *Economic Philosophic Manuscripts of 1844*, trans. by M. Milligan. Moscow: FLPH, 1957.

viction that social development is the key to prediction and explanation in the social sciences. Just as the appearance of capital announces a new age in the process of social production, the appearance of labor (and the laborer as a class affiliate) signifies the next higher stage of development —socialism.

Marx's was the first system of social science framed primarily (if not exclusively) in terms of developmental models; particularly important is the fact that by relating development to social interests this system fed the streams of both modern political ideology and modern sociological inquiry. Marx asked the scientific question: What is development? But he did so in the context of ideology, and he tried to promote specific agencies to stimulate development. Under the impetus of Marxism, development became a class task; hence development did not proceed harmoniously or mechanically, since there were always classes which depended for their existence upon the *status quo*. Only after the downfall of bourgeois society and bourgeois consciousness could there be national, and even international, development as a general, social phenomenon. It should be mentioned that, with the discovery that power and status are independent variables that continue to divide men, the vision of a general harmonious development has receded to an ever more distant future.

Until now we have discussed general orientations toward the question of social development. But the metaphysical orientation loses relevance when we make a clear distinction between sacred and profane. When analysis hinges upon specific problems—e.g. who progresses, at what rate, and at what costs—we leave behind such questions as how do we know we have progressed or how should we progress.

It should be understood that we do not view the ideological approach as bad and the sociological as good; indeed, sociology often lags behind ideology in the promotion of useful and beneficial goals. The ideological approach, which rests on the standpoint of particularized interests, has generally asked the right questions.[7] The difficulty is that it asks such questions in a biased way, with specific ends in view, irrespective both of the instrumentalities employed and of any contravening evidence. If sociology followed the reverse approach—i.e. were unbiased,

[7] Cf. Irving L. Horowitz, *Philosophy, Science and the Sociology of Knowledge.* Springfield, Ill.: Charles C. Thomas, 1961.

not influenced by personal or social interest factors, and always operated according to scientific canons of evidence—then our problem would be considerably eased. The fact is, both sociological and ideological discussions of development contain many unscientific and sometimes even anti-scientific formulations. Thus, while in theory it is clearly superior to argue from a sociological rather than an ideological standpoint, these two modes of thought interpenetrate to a significant degree.

Sociology confronts a human complex which is of two minds on the issue of development. Public attitudes are split not only on the worth of development but on its facts. If we distinguish between change and progress, we can see more clearly why this split has occurred. In defining human development it is important to distinguish social development from change in the physical sense of movement in space and in time, and from growth in the biological sense of alteration in the nature of an organism. For the sociologist, simple physical or biological processes do not constitute development, for such changes occur *de rerum natura* and are not subject to alteration by human decision. The orbiting of the Earth about the Sun, the growth of a fetus or of a human being—these are indeed changes, but not development processes. Human development, however, reflects at some level culture and consciousness and factors which are "unnatural" (electricity to defy the night, airplanes to defy gravity, machines to defy the limits of human labor-power, etc.). In human development alternative forms of social structure are not only possible but almost inevitable. But to conclude from these facts, as some sociologists have, that it is impossible to arrive at a scientific statement of human development is simply to abandon the major question posed for social science. The separation of "facts" and "values" is not a mandate restricting the sociologist to the former "realm" alone—but only a methodological caution for avoiding undue subjectivity. When this separation becomes a sanction for avoiding the problems of human development, it is no longer a heuristic tool but a positive hindrance.

The sociologist confronts social forces which are contradictory or at the very least ambivalent. For every utopian dream of a world of technological innovation, social justice, and material abundance, there is the sober warning of those who envision the same future as a robot-age, inhabited by technological idiots and political scoundrels.[8] To further

[8] Cf. Irving L. Horowitz, "Formalización de la Teoría General de la Ideología y la Utopía," *Revista Mexicana de Sociología*, Vol. 24, No. 1, Jan.-April 1962,

complicate matters, the sociologists themselves are divided in their judgments of the content and meaning of human development. One current
commentary indicated that "recent developments in technology suggest
heretofore unimagined possibilities in the way of human well-being."[9]
Though the author pauses to indicate the dangers of such developments,
he concludes "that we are only on the threshold of the possibilities and
problems occasioned by these technological developments." For another
contemporary sociologist the dangers far outweigh the advantages of
technological achievement, which has "degraded man to the level of a
mere reflex mechanism, a mere organ motivated by sex, a mere semi-
mechanical, semiphysiological organism, devoid of any divine spark, of
any absolute value, of anything noble and sacred."[10]

Nor should it be imagined that only sociologists differ in their attitudes toward development. The industrial world itself exhibits similar
confusions and dichotomies. Managerial attitudes toward automation are
often dictated by a blithe optimism: "Guided by electronics, powered
by atomic energy, geared to the smooth, effortless workings of automation, the magic carpet of our free economy heads for distant and un-
dreamed of horizons." In contrast is the conclusion drawn recently by a
labor leader:

> I am not reassured by those who tell us that all will work out well
> in the long run because we have managed to live through radical
> technological changes in the past. Human beings do not live long
> enough for us to be satisfied with assurances about the long-run
> adaptation of society to automation. And while it is true that
> radical technological improvements have been introduced in the
> past, it is well to remember that they were accompanied by vast
> social dislocations, recurring depressions and human suffering.[11]

Even within the social sciences development is variously defined.
The demographer may measure development in terms of gross popula-

pp. 87-100; and also, "Formalization of the Sociology of Knowledge," Behavioral Science, Vol. 9, No. 1, January 1964, pp. 45-55.
[9] J. O. Hertzler, American Social Institutions: A Sociological Analysis. Boston:
Allyn and Bacon, 1961, p. 220.
[10] Pitirim A. Sorokin, "Social and Cultural Dynamics," in The Making of Society: An Outline of Sociology, ed. by Robert Bierstedt. New York: Random
House, 1959, p. 481.
[11] Both statements are contained in Robert P. Weeks (ed.), Machines and the
Man: A Sourcebook on Automation. New York: Appleton-Century-Crofts,
1961, pp. 171-6 and 202-17.

tion growth or declining rates of infant mortality; in geriatrics the problem may be considered primarily in terms of human longevity; the economist may use indices of industrial reinvestment, or consumer goods produced and bought, etc.; the psychiatrist may see the situation in terms of increasing the proportion of "normal" people or decreasing mental illness; and for the criminologist development may mean either the care and treatment of criminals or the abolition of the causes of crime. If there were a harmonic coalescence of all of these developmental elements, then there would be no problems. But this is not the case. The uneven distribution of wealth in the affluent society is often coupled with a high incidence of mental sickness and criminal behavior, especially among the poor. Therefore it is the maldistribution of wealth, rather than the absolute annual earnings, which most significantly affect "deviant" patterns.

The alternative approaches to human development are not necessarily mutually exclusive. Indeed, these various approaches all contribute to an overall definition. There are certain fundamentals common to a scientific notion of development.

Development can be seen as an aspect of human will. It can be viewed as a particular kind of planning aimed at transforming an underdeveloped country into one which will eventually resemble either the First or Second World or some combination of the two. According to this viewpoint, all planning is done by a dedicated development-oriented elite supported by loyal, self-sacrificing masses.

Another approach emphasizes the products of advanced technology, or some concrete evidence that development is taking place. These products can be the types of social structures, levels of technologies, and life styles found in the First or Second Worlds. Mass production, for example, can yield intermediary forms of social structures, technologies, and life styles. Specifically, these intermediary consequences of mass production can produce a dedicated elite, can stimulate a self-sacrificing mass, and can change handicraft activities into large-scale automated factories.

From this perspective, total social planning is not a necessary condition for development. The intermediary products of the development process, as well as the "terminal" products or stages, may or may not be produced by a dedicated elite. This open-ended view of development allows us to consider as a developing nation one which has little central planning by a dedicated elite but a plethora of modern factories and well-clothed, well-fed citizens who are politically, economically, and socially mobilized. This viewpoint makes it possible to distinguish between a "modernizing" country, with few or even no factories, and a "mobilizing" nation. This "product" way of looking at the developmental process forces us to say that Venezuela is a modernizing nation, since it has shown a marked degree of industrial development, particularly in the oil industry. It is possible that Venezuela will ultimately surpass Cuba's economic development. At the present time, however, Cuba is further along the road of development than Venezuela, for Cuba has the political forms and a mobilized dedicated mass suitable for sustained development. Thus far, Venezuela has neither.

Countries may remain underdeveloped for opposite reasons. Guinea, for example, has a dedicated elite which has done an extraordinary job of mobilizing the population politically. While the elite has tried and is still trying desperately to develop the country economically, it is unlikely to succeed. Poorly endowed in resources and population and with little to offer her own people or the world, Guinea is little more than an unfortunate accident of imperialistic map-making. Only if it can unite with richer nations will Guinea become part of a developed state. Venezuela, on the other hand, is rich in both mineral resources and population, but it may never develop if it is not successful in producing a dedicated elite supported by self-sacrificing, loyal masses.

The basic elements in a definition of development must focus on the main features of the Third World but still must not lose sight of the measurements which distinguish one nation or territory from another.

First. A developed society is one made up of the social structures, technologies, and life styles that exist today in the First and Second Worlds. In other words, these two worlds, represented by the United States and the Soviet Union in particular, will be used in this work as models of developed nations. There are obvious "pitfalls" in treating these two countries as models. But unless the development analyst makes the value judgment as to what a developed society is he will not be able to determine which changes are part of the developmental process. In short, the taboo against making value judgments has little place in the study of social and economic development.

Second. The concept "developmental process" refers to those planned and unplanned activities which produce the social structures, technologies, and life styles found in the First and Second Worlds, or else the means for obtaining these advanced forms. The developmental process includes those social and economic changes which tend to make the nations of the Third World more closely resemble the nations of the First or Second Worlds or some combination of the two.

Third. Whatever form development may take, it is universally an asynchronous process. The political, economic, and social sectors of a nation do not advance at the same rate. The economic sector of a Third World country such as Brazil or India may be rapidly approximating the economic sector of the First World, while the masses continue to live in a state of poverty unknown to the lowest classes of the United States.

Fourth. The asynchronous nature of the developmental process makes it extremely difficult to determine whether a nation is developing or stagnating. Such a judgment assumes that the investigator has measures for determining the degree of development in the various sectors which make up the nation as well as some kind of technique for weighting the "development scores" assigned to each sector. The techniques for measuring economic development are fairly adequate; those for measuring political and social development are relatively crude. While we cannot be precise, we can still speak with a fair degree of certainty as to whether a particular sector of a nation is developing. However, no generally accepted method exists for weighting and averaging the "scores" accorded to each sector. Consequently, any judgment as to whether a nation rather than a sector is developing or stagnating, while not entirely arbitrary, ultimately rests on the technique the investigator sees fit to use.

Fifth. The ideological viewpoint of development attempts to determine in advance not simply the goals but the instruments, tactics, and strategies of planning social change. The sociological viewpoint, while readily granting ends-in-view, does not have a determined scheme for the realization of such ends. It contains a pragmatic dimension which enables it to shift its theoretical focus if plans do not work out in practice. Developmental ideologies tend to compel types of change along pre-directed channels.

These are modest steps in the clarification of meaning. But if the issue of development is raised within a perspective which recognizes both a common humanity and diverse culture patterns, then this can serve as a starting point for constructive social action. Under certain conditions there is a relative absence of any perception, much less conception, of social development. An understanding of developmental processes is inhibited by two factors:

(1) An absence of comparative criteria, between nations and a period of time. Under conditions of social or group isolation within a larger community spatial comparisons between social sub-systems become difficult. Similarly, the absence of historicity or self-consciousness blocks a society from judging itself in terms both of past and future goals.

(2) Extended periods of structural equilibrium without external, counterbalancing challenges. Since primitive societies neither retrogress nor progress, they maintain a belief in the fixity of social relations. Thus, while what we term underdeveloped societies change slowly, traditional societies lack not only the fact but the very idea of human development; that is, they do not possess a plan, a direction, or a goal.

This distinction between traditional and underdeveloped societies is pivotal. The traditional society is characterized by little change from generation to generation; a behavioral pattern governed almost exclusively by custom; status determined almost entirely by inheritance (ascriptive); low economic productivity; and a social organization and life style grounded on the principle of hierarchical command. The underdeveloped society has a great deal in common with the developed society; the phrase "underdeveloped" is used as a measure of technical and technological inferiority *vis à vis* the developed society. This society exhibits rapid change; behavior governed by law as well as custom; status based on achievement as well as on inherited patterns; low economic productivity in some sectors of the economy, high productivity in other sectors; and a life style geared to rapid social mobility, despite intensive stratification though not defined by it.

Conceptions of social development depend therefore both upon the facts and upon consciousness of change. These in turn owe their existence to a consciousness of being different, i.e. an awareness that shared values do not necessarily represent shared wealth. The rise of rapid, universal communication and transportation systems is fast transforming traditional societies into "underdeveloped" societies—if not through structural shifts, then certainly through the rise of consciousness and the growth of spatial and temporal comparisons.[12]

We can turn now to the "developed" society in which change is first and foremost a social fact. In considering the theories advanced for or against development, we become involved in the effect of ideology on the theory and practice of development. Ideology is not concerned with the ethical aspects or the morality of development. The ideological posture naturally assumes a general dissatisfaction with the present and the necessity and feasibility of change. Though the ideologist does not consider the ethical question whether development is worthwhile or needed, he must still evaluate the worth of available types of development. Ideological debates over such slogans as "revolutionary socialism" and "evolutionary socialism," or in American society over "government control" versus "laisser-faire," take on a strong ethical flavor. It is patently clear, however, that there is a huge difference between those arguing the worth of change (the moralists) and those arguing the types of change which are worthwhile (the ideologists).

What should not be lost in the fog of competing political loyalties is the similarity between capitalist and Communist industrial ideologies: material abundance, rapid urbanization, educational facilities, military strength—these indices define both American and Soviet notions of development. This is not to say that all differences between capitalist and Communist ideologies have been eliminated or that this would be advantageous. The similarities do, however, far outweigh the dissimilarities. The Russians and the Americans must face a similar set of social questions: Are large-scale changes best accomplished spontaneously or through planning? What mixture of persuasion and coercion most facilitates progress? How can the growth of a particular society be turned into a model for "underdeveloped" areas?

The ideologists tend to obfuscate and distort fundamental similarities between systems for the sake of preserving the separateness of their own, whether it be called "The American Way" or "The Communist Road." Ideologists tend also to assume a world of total voluntarism, as

[12] For a dissection of the problem of change in relation to traditional societies, see Everett E. Hagen, *On the Theory of Social Change: How Economic Growth Begins*. Homewood, Ill.: The Dorsey Press, 1962, esp. pp. 55-8.

if human development were dictated exclusively by choice and consensus, without limitation imposed by national boundaries, traditions, political systems, or economic potential. If the sociologist is not himself to become an ideologist, he must cut through the ideological rhetoric and search out areas of convergence as well as differentiation. At the same time, due recognition must be accorded the role of ideology in defining developmental goals.

We are now in an age dominated by a common industrial ideology which is just as much the property of the Soviet Union as it is of the West. Industrial demands are sufficiently potent eventually to win out over traditional political forms. This may not be obvious in the short run, since Soviet and American societies share not only an emphasis on technological and scientific achievements but they also share a willingness to absorb the human losses which will insure them world leadership. A cardinal feature of any definition of "Western culture" is anchored to the notion that human development results from scientific achievement. The present competition between Russia and the West comes about precisely because there is so much (rather than not enough) common ground. A statement by Sorokin seems particularly relevant:

> Both nations are fairly similar in scientific knowledge and technological progress. In normal conditions, without the misuse and abuse of scientific and technological achievements by the governments and militarists, both countries would have mutually profited from scientific discoveries and inventions of each other. This means that science and technology as values do not give any ground, any reason, any justification for continuation of the belligerent policies "for Salvation of Science and Technology from the Destruction by the Russians (or the American) Barbarians." The scientists of both countries are quite successfully taking good care of scientific and technical progress, especially if they are not hindered by governmental interference in their highly important research.[13]

The definition of economic development in terms of per capita output and rates of capital investment has become standard currency for

[13] Pitirim A. Sorokin, "Mutual Convergence of the United States and the U.S.S.R. to the Mixed Sociocultural Type," *International Journal of Comparative Sociology*, Vol. 1, No. 2, Sept. 1960, pp. 143-76.

both "Marxian" and "Keynesian" economists.[14] The convergence of East and West has proceeded so rapidly and at so many levels since World War Two that there remains an ideological lag. Apologists for capitalism expend their energies discussing the pre-revolutionary *political* ideology of Marxism instead of the functioning Soviet system.

In terms of the concept of development, the ideological struggle is not between East and West but between two styles of Western thought.

> We must not forget that Marxism and communism are also Western ideas, and that modern Russia is also culturally, intellectually, and socially in the Western tradition. Indeed, the Russian Revolution can be seen, in part, as the Westernization of a formerly "Eastern" peasantry . . . In their general drift into the mainstream of Western history, the leaders of the underdeveloped world will have a choice between divergent currents of Western development: the one represented by the free-enterprise, free-dissent nations of the Atlantic, and the other by the planned enterprise, limited or no-dissent nations of the Soviet orbit.[15]

The choice for other nations is not between capitalism and Communism—or perhaps between oligopoly and state capitalism—(the growth of the economic "mix" in both societies makes a choice implausible if not entirely impossible), but rather between the industrial ideology shared by Americans and Soviets and the pre-industrial ideology of the Third World countries. This choice may be singularly unpleasant for those reared in inherited political ideologies. But nostalgia, while comfortable, simply does not face up to the realities of functional and ideological convergence.

The accent on development is ingrained in technological societies exhibiting high degrees of social mobility. For an American trade union leader turned businessman this signifies "self-development for everybody, everywhere."[16] For a Soviet engineer turned manager such self-

---

[14] Compare, for example, the capitalist apologetics of John K. Galbraith, *American Capitalism*. Boston: Houghton-Mifflin Co., 1952, with the socialist apologetics of Paul A. Baran, *The Political Economy of Growth*. New York: Monthly Review Press, 1957.

[15] Robert L. Heilbroner, "The Revolution of Economic Development," *The American Scholar*, Vol. 31, No. 4, Autumn 1962, pp. 541-9.

[16] F. J. Roethlisberger, "Introduction" to Elton Mayo, *The Human Problems of an Industrial Civilization*. New York: Viking Press, 1960, p. xi.

development involves "the radical improving of the management of enterprises and institutions through the extensive automation and mechanization of engineering and administrative jobs."[17] In each case, the price of change is a disruption of older norms and even older patterns of culture, and development is justified in terms of the same goals, e.g. higher productivity, shorter working hours, increased leisure time, more goods to consume at lower prices. What emerges is a two-fold typology of value preferences which sharply demarcate the industrial ideology of spending from the political ideology of savings. The situation in both the United States and the Soviet Union demonstrates that a technological society requires, and usually gets, an ideology built upon expertise. That the "debate" over inherited political ideologies such as liberalism and Marxism is most furious in the traditional nations merely supports the contention that Russia and the United States represent alternative means for reaching the same industrial goals. Nonetheless, it might be kept in mind that even when an ideology is built upon some well-defined principle, that principle does not necessarily dominate behavior. The "experts" do not completely dominate in the United States, and the same is undoubtedly the case in the Soviet Union. The ability to allocate and distribute wealth is still in the hands of the politicians.

It has been particularly painful for the "American way of life" to come to terms with the problem of the costs of development, and to understand that traditional patterns are not necessarily and always inimical to development.[18] For the American, for the proponent of the liberal rhetoric, the idea of progress through science has become, as Robin Williams noted, "a slogan to defend the course of technological innovation and economic rationalization and concentration. If small entrepreneurs, farmers, or urban workers felt economic distress, their condition could be considered a regrettable but necessary and temporary by-product of the triumphant march of progress."[19]

Given the combination of provincial ingenuousness, Puritan piety, and a technological definition of progress, which in large measure defines the present American mood of self-congratulation, a sociological study of

[17] A. I. Berg, "Cybernetics and Society," *The Soviet Review*, Vol. I, No. 1 (1960), pp. 43-4.
[18] Ralph J. Braibanti and Joseph J. Spengler, *Tradition, Values, and Socio-Economic Development*. Durham, N.C.: Duke University Press, 1961.
[19] Robin M. Williams, Jr., *American Society*. New York: Alfred A. Knopf, 1960 (2nd rev. edition), p. 433.

the negative aspects of social change borders on a subversive reading of American history.

W. F. Cottrell's brilliant analysis of the death of a railroad town in the southwestern United States illustrates the costs of development and the potential social consequences of technological changeover. In this town of "Caliente" everything was predicated on the railroad's need for continued growth.

> Men built their homes there, frequently of concrete and brick, at the cost in many cases of their life savings. The water system was laid in cast iron which will last for centuries. Business men erected substantial buildings which could be paid for only by profits gained through many years of business. Four churches evidence the faith of Caliente people in the future of their community. A twenty-seven bed hospital serves the town. They believed in education. Their school buildings represent the investment of savings guaranteed by bonds and future taxes. There is a combined park and play field which, together with a recently modernized theatre, has been serving recreational needs. All these physical structures are material evidence of the expectations, morally and legally sanctioned and financially funded, of the people of Caliente. This is a normal and rational aspect of the culture of all "solid" and "sound" communities.[20]

"Rational" economic forces and laws of technological development worked to undermine this well-defined urban structure. When the railroad converted from steam to diesel power, Caliente, totally dependent on its water and repair facilities, was shorn of its reason to exist. The victory of technology, of the very industrial ideology of progress which the citizenry of Caliente espoused—since they were by all standards good Americans—paradoxically substantially destroyed their carefully nurtured social structure.

Development, in other words, is often preceded by social disorganization. There is a dialectic to socialization, namely privatization. The end of the parochial rural and semi-urban standards leads to Jean Gottmann's *Megalopolis*. But it also feeds a collective *anomie*, a drive for

[20] W. F. Cottrell, "Death by Dieselization: A Case Study in the Reaction to Technological Change," *American Sociological Review*, Vol. 16, 1951, pp. 358-65.

escapism and frenetic leisure-time activities, and a nihilist attitude about the future, as described in Leo Srole's *Metropolis*. The overdeveloped society is tentative about the future and cynical about the present— characteristics to which the Third World societies would do well to pay closer attention.

The enormous increase in the types and rates of technological growth has created other immense problems. Even if we accept the business ideology that technological change does not create large-scale unemployment, the problem of mass mis-employment remains. As one writer recently stated:

> The underlying assumption is that one job equals another, that income is the sole criterion and it makes no difference what you do or become in order to get it. Technological unemployment may be a myth, but what about technological mis-employment? From 1880 to 1940, the percentage of Americans who were self-employed declined sharply. The percentage employed in clerical work, or in more or less parasitical service activities, rose sharply. The percentage employed in actually making useful articles declined; and even among the productive workers, millions were downgraded from skilled craftsmen to mass-production hands, with little skill or responsibility. It may be that these changes were not, in the long run, harmful. It may be—as Henry Ford insisted—that a worker gains from the transformation into a kind of zombie, if that transformation leads to so great an increase in production that the worker can acquire a car, a refrigerator, and other objects he could not otherwise possess. But it is absolute nonsense to pretend that there is no problem, that a job is a job.[21]

The problem for the sociologist, one which the ideologist dare not recognize, is to discover the forms of creativity possible in a highly impersonal and mechanized society. The real failure of industrial ideology is that it provides a false alternative to traditionalist-conservative ideologies. For while the latter seem solely preoccupied with the costs, the former is exclusively concerned with the benefits of industrial change.

[21] Geoffrey Ashe, "Technological Mis-Employment," in *Machines and the Man*, ed. by Robert P. Weeks. New York: Appleton-Century-Crofts, 1961, pp. 200-202.

The sociologist must deal with the problem of the price of change and who has to pay this price. The decision to orient a society toward rapid industrial and technical development is basically a value decision, most often made by an elite group for the mass of people.

Sociology should caution us against any "iron laws" of industrialization. Such "laws" are pernicious as well as unscientific. A decision in favor of industrial expansion may entail large-scale and long-range hardships, and short-run costs may well outweigh long-term results. An agricultural-export economy, which satisfies consumer demands by buying rather than making automobiles, television sets, washing machines, etc., does not necessarily have to be reoriented toward industrialism. Often industrialization is demanded in the name of nationalism, the common assumption being that affluence and greatness are synonymous with industrialism. Doing without the products of General Electric or General Motors because they come from an imperialist nation may be materially damaging to a nation which could trade wheat for radios and beef for cars. The problem exists not only in capitalist economies; the dogmatic application of the industrial ideology, of the assumption that home-grown goods are always cheaper to make than imported goods are to obtain, has boomeranged in Yugoslavia, Hungary, Poland, China, and Cuba.

This is not to be construed as a nostalgic critique of industrial society. To recognize the weaknesses in industrial ideology is not to condemn industrial values. A modern and efficient agricultural system must basically have industrial values. It does point up the need to distinguish between absolute underdevelopment, when the basic tools whereby a citizenry can survive are lacking, and relative underdevelopment, when rates of social change are slower than in developed societies. Surely, there is a vast difference between a form of underdevelopment which witnesses mass starvation (as in parts of India) and a form of underdevelopment in which industrial capacity is low while everyone is essentially well-fed and well-clothed (as in Argentina and even peacetime Vietnam). Precisely because the word underdevelopment is charged with emotive meanings, it is doubly necessary to distinguish the actual, empirical contents of "underdevelopment" in any given society.

It should be noted that the nineteenth-century liberals' prophesies of progress through science were, indeed, realized. The extent of modern creativity would surprise and delight even an Edward Bellamy. Why then should there be such widespread disillusionment and dismay in the developed societies? Clearly, it is because the very giganticism of our achievements has made it possible for the individual to be overwhelmed and for whole populations to be annihilated. In short, technical and industrial development is not total development and does not settle the major problems of politics, economics, war and peace, etc., but only raises such issues to a new pinnacle of desperation. For human development we still require some kind of "science of values," some analytical tools for expressing the new situation in meaningful terms.

Development will take place. For an overwhelming majority of people the costs of development are well worth the price. Most "backward" tribal associations—such as the Sironis in Bolivia, the Guayaki in Paraguay, the Macu of Brazil—join with their brothers in La Paz, Asuncion, and São Paulo to demand entrance into the gateways of tomorrow. But development will have its price. The task of the sociologist is not only to indicate the dangers of social dislocation but to anticipate and work out solutions for potential problems. This requires some courage. Traditional relations between parents and obedient children and between male and female may likewise have to be altered. The idea of the state as a dispenser of welfare may indeed supplant the older notion that a government governs best which governs least. The sociologist must become a physician of society.

The sociologist considers the problem of development in terms of various methods, rates, directions, and consequences, while the ideologist thinks of development as a matter of national pride, and is mainly concerned that his society reach development before others. Mills made a very pointed statement in this connection.

> When we think about the "underdeveloped society" we must also think about the "overdeveloped society." There are two reasons for this: first, if we do not do so, we tend to think of everything as moving towards *the developed*. It is the old notion of nineteenth century evolutionism. And this is no longer a very fruitful idea. Second, to think of the polar types leads us to think about a third type—an ideal which we should always keep in mind: the properly developing society. We need all three types, not just the two.[22]

[22] C. Wright Mills, "The Problem of Industrial Development," in *Power, Politics and People: The Collected Papers of C. Wright Mills,* edited by Irving L. Horowitz. New York and London: Oxford University Press, 1963.

Mills indicates that the underdeveloped society is characterized by a limited standard of living, whereas in the overdeveloped society the life style is dominated by the living standards. The fetish of production becomes a fetish for consumption. And without adding a theological note, social science should maximize human possibilities by helping to design, no less than understand, the proximate future. It is this maximization that Mills considers to be the substance of "proper" development.

We know considerably more about the differences between development and underdevelopment than we do about differences between development and overdevelopment, or what may just as readily be called mis-development. The latter is a more recent phenomenon. Also, it is easier to describe the sociology of scarcity than of affluence, since there are so many illustrations of the former and so few of the latter. Nonetheless, the need for a clear view of overdevelopment is urgent; for otherwise we shall be providing instruments to developing nations which can reproduce the worst rather than the best features of modern civilizations.

As a general rule, overdevelopment can be defined as that social condition in which material wealth is maldistributed and the human skills available are not used to a maximum extent. This occurs when there are social impediments—for instance, when there exist radical imbalances between social classes; or when there are organizational impediments—for instance, when available energy and power sources are not properly utilized. An overdeveloped society is furthermore one in which failures at both the social and technical levels lead to breakdowns in production and in distribution and create a perennial crisis in the political institutions and educational establishments. Like underdevelopment, overdevelopment is relative to a given type of social-economic organization, one that has the technical capacity to satisfy basic human needs but is lacking the social instrumentalities to utilize such a capacity.

Thus, while the United States can by no stretch of the imagination simply be relegated to the realm of overdevelopment—by the above-named criteria at least—it does reveal certain properties of overdevelopment, which, if not curbed, could lead to exaggerated mis-development. For example, there has been a vast slowing down in the development of inexpensive electrical power for rural regions. There has been no follow-up to the TVA (Tennessee Valley Authority) and MVA (Missouri Valley Authority). Regional planning continues to be viewed as something the nation does only in times of economic crisis. Similarly, despite an upward trend in the 'sixties, United States industries continue to operate below maximum capacity—often by as much as 50 per cent—except during wartime periods. Agricultural underproduction is encouraged to keep market prices inflated, federal subsidies given for not planting certain key crops, and tax write-offs for failing business enterprises.[23] Nor can we leave out of this inventory the military build-up. Military expenditures have most often been measured exclusively in terms of the benefits to labor and management, without a corresponding regard for the ultimate social costs involved. Galbraith has put the risk of overdevelopment clearly.

> As matters now stand, we have almost no institutions that are by central design and purpose directed to participation in modern scientific and technological progress and its large-scale application. We have no organization capable, for example, of taking on the large-scale development of atomic power generators or radically new departures in passenger-carrying aircraft in advance of knowledge that these will be commercially feasible. Much has been accomplished by research and development, not immediately subject to a commercial criteria, under the inspiration of military need. This has done more to save us from the partial technological stagnation that is inherent in a consumers' goods economy than we imagine. But it is also a narrow and perilous prop, and it has the further effect of associating great and exciting scientific advances with an atmosphere of fear and even terror.[24]

What this should teach the newly emerging nations is that the problem of development is not exclusively one of technological or natural resources or exclusively one of sociological or human resources, but rather the interrelation and interpenetration of the two. Indeed, the

[23] See L. N. Naggle, "Scylla and Charybdis of Engineering Education," *Proceedings of the 1961 Syracuse University International Conference on Electrical Engineering Education.* Syracuse, N.Y.: 1961, pp. 52-3.
[24] John K. Galbraith, *The Affluent Society.* Boston: Houghton-Mifflin Co., 1958, pp. 354-5.

more "mature" a society becomes, the more it needs instruments for orderly social change, but the less does it provide for such agencies. Similarly, the greater the technological achievement, the more the social system is pressured to accommodate such achievements. Any prolonged and exaggerated imbalances between the social and technical sectors lead to stagnation. And the pressures for development are such that stagnation is intolerable over a long period. This is what revolutions are all about.

II

THE OLD WORLDS IN PERSPECTIVE

"Parliamentarism and Communism are political systems, but they are also something more than that. Just as Western technology involves Western science, so Western political systems imply Western moral ideas — conflicting ideals reflected in conflicting systems. Ideologies and ideals cannot be understood or appraised without taking some account of their history. The spiritual history of the West has therefore to be taken into consideration in any twentieth-century estimate of the prospects of the World as a whole."

(Arnold J. Toynbee in **A Study of History,** vol. XII)

"We men of the Western Culture are, with our historical sense, an exception and not a rule. World-history is **our** world picture and not all of mankind's. Indian and Classical man formed no image of a world in progress, and perhaps when in due course the civilization of the West is extinguished, there will never again be a Culture and a human type in which 'world-history' is so potent a form of the waking consciousness."

(Oswald Spengler in **The Decline of the West**)

Chapter 3

The First World of United States Development

There are two ways of assessing life in the United States with a minimum margin of error: one way is to rely exclusively upon the decennial
Census Report; the other is to rely upon any of a dozen omnibus anthologies about the American nation, especially its politics and culture.
But when one attempts to fuse the economic statistics given in the reports with the generalizations found in the various anthologies, there
does not seem to be much of a match. The difficulty is that the economic reports are optimistic, indicating a rate of growth based on increased spending, greater production, higher profits, and more people
working shorter hours. But other reports are pessimistic, indicating such
factors as divorce as a social problem, the displacement of specific interest groups by masses, the political apathy of the "Main Street" population, and the high incidence of mental illness and crime; then the
contradiction between economic and non-economic types of information
is revealed. To achieve some direction then, we must first reconstruct
some picture of what the United States was like and then compare it
with a picture of what the United States is now; and, finally, identify
those specific characteristics which make the United States the First
World of social development.

We should begin by examining the historical judgments of Europeans about the United States. This is little more than an application
of the norm of reciprocity. For we shall apply throughout the standards
of the United States in judging the rest of the world. Then we shall try
to see how these historical judgments have been rendered inept by the

passage of time. It is strikingly characteristic that American apologetics place an emphasis on its historical continuity which is all out of proportion to historical evidence. A peculiar type of conservatism refuses to face the implications of radical departure from tradition. Thus one writer has even observed the seeds of current Latin American revolution in the Lincoln-Douglas Debates of the eighteen-fifties,[1] while another writer can observe the traces of George Washington's legacy in the current political behavior of the political elite.[2]

To presume breaks rather than continuities helps us to speak with some objectivity about the United States as a First World in a historically new international setting. Such a frame of reference should enable us to avoid the extreme relativism of considering the United States as "a nation among nations"[3] or the extreme absolutism of the United States as one nation with a manifest destiny over all other nations.[4]

I

There has been a remarkable consensus about the United States in Europe. One critic may be more friendly than another. Another may be more or less elitist or feminist in orientation than others; but in the main, what European observers have chosen to praise or condemn about life in the United States follows strikingly similar patterns. Generally, the United States is recognized as embodying a synthesis of European traditions. This synthesis is precisely what European commentators most respected and were most troubled by. Here was a society which indeed absorbed many pluralistic strains, yet demanded very exacting loyalties.

(1) The most common of the recurring themes was America as "a wave of the future." The United States was viewed as that nation which

[1] Harry V. Jaffa, *Equality and Liberty: Theory and Practice in American Politics.* New York: Oxford University Press, 1965.

[2] Seymour Martin Lipset, *The First New Nation.* New York: Basic Books, 1964. For a discussion of this, see Irving L. Horowitz and Seymour Martin Lipset, "The Birth and Meaning of America: A Dialogue on *The First New Nation,*" *Panoramas,* No. 17 (August-Sept.), 1965.

[3] See on this Hans Kohn, *American Nationalism: An Interpretive Essay.* New York: Collier Books, 1961.

[4] See especially *The Works of Theodore Roosevelt* (twenty volumes). New York: Charles Scribner, 1926. Volume 19 in particular contains perhaps the most bellicose pronouncements, coupled with an extreme paternalism, representative of turn-of-the-century American policy.

would carve the path for all other yet unborn civilizations. It attracted such curious onlookers and observers because its historical leadership, even by 1835, was recognized. It would show other nations and peoples what their own future would look like. This has been a prevalent theme since de Tocqueville designed his study of the United States with the express purpose of seeking there "the image of democracy itself, with its inclinations, its character, its prejudices, and its passions, in order to learn what we have to fear or to hope from its progress."[5] De Tocqueville, and other educated commentators, were so convinced that the United States embodied the future of the democratic spirit that in his masterpiece he oftentimes drops the term "America," even when describing a peculiarly American characteristic, and simply uses the word "democracy." He employs the United States throughout as a surrogate for democratic "social conditions."[6] Beyond that, he drew the irrational conclusion that democracy was the wave of the future just as mass society was the inevitable replacement for an elitist society. While de Tocqueville may have said this with a certain caution and aristocratic nostalgia, others who followed him abandoned caution and merely assumed that America plus Democracy equaled Progress; that this was a magic formula for development.

This notion of the United States as the vanguard of industrial nations has been so common that a tone of admiration persists even when the faults of American development are discussed. André Siegfried points out, for instance, that "the assimilation of things of the spirit is the real lesson offered by the study of the humanities but America appears to consider this old-fashioned. In an examination for the recruitment of administrative staff, 80 per cent of the questions were on scientific and technological matters, while the 20 per cent reserved for general culture were not allotted to literature or philosophy but to sociology—a very significant replacement. There is a whole new conception of life there, and it is one toward which our century is moving with the United States in the vanguard."[7] These same sentiments are still fre-

[5] Alexis de Tocqueville, Democracy in America, edited with an introduction by Henry Steele Commager. New York and London: Oxford University Press, 1947, p. 16.
[6] Alexis de Tocqueville, ibid., p. 41.
[7] André Siegfried, America at Midcentury. New York: Harcourt Brace, 1955, p. 355.

quently expressed by humanists such as Howard Mumford Jones.[8] But what is most impressive is, whether the spirit is critical or celebratory, it is taken for granted that the United States is certainly the wave of the future—insofar as the future entails industrialization, urbanization, and mass dissemination of information.

(2) The United States was seen as the land of equality both in eighteenth- and nineteenth-century literature. All foreign observers noted the egalitarianism and the conscious dedication to minimizing stratification. The United States represented social equality—equality of status, of manners, and of deference. What is more interesting is that, until the twentieth century, there was much emphasis upon political equality. There was also a very strong emphasis on economic equality—not seen so much as an achieved fact but rather as an aspiration. The emphasis on equality did not preclude the desirability of an unequal distribution of ambition.

De Tocqueville attributes all equality to a basic economic equality of conditions, in contrast to the psychological inequality of talents. This dynamic tension is reinforced by the laws of equal inheritance which obtained in the United States in the nineteenth century. He saw in this law of inheritance the elimination of the ultimate barrier to equality. He speaks of juridical safeguards of economic equality as "tending powerfully to the destruction of large fortunes and especially large domains." He notes that in the United States the last trace of hereditary ranks and distinctions is destroyed. This is why "in a foreign country two Americans are at once friends, simply because they are Americans." This, in contrast to the English, for whom "the same blood is not enough; they must be brought together by the same rank."[9]

Harriet Martineau provided a most powerful second to this when she indicated that it was an "admitted truth" that for Americans "enormous private wealth is inconsistent with the spirit of republicanism. Wealth is power; large amounts of power ought not to rest in the hands of individuals . . . the popular feeling is so strong against transmitting large estates, and favoring one child, that nobody attempts to do it."[10]

---

[8] Howard Mumford Jones, *One Great Society: Humane Learning in the United States*. New York: Harcourt Brace, 1959.

[9] Alexis de Tocqueville, *op. cit.*, pp. 370-71.

[10] Harriet Martineau, *Society in America*, edited with an introduction by Seymour Martin Lipset. Garden City, New York: Doubleday & Co., 1962, pp. 263-4.

The completeness of this egalitarianism strikes the present-day observer. The irony is not only how far the United States has moved away from an image of egalitarianism, but how it was possible for European observers to see in the nineteenth-century United States such exaggerated egalitarian strains while at the same time the crystallization and the encroachment of class, race, and ethnic distinctions of a rather profound type was occurring.

By the mid-nineteenth century the leveling effects of the frontier were still able, to some extent, to maintain this equilibrium between economic equality and psychological drives for wealth. For if the pursuit of money did not yield real wealth, it at least provided the illusion of equality. But by the twentieth century, serious commentators ceased to raise the image of economic equality in the United States. Yet whether or not social and political equality has been based upon economic equality, the classless society has been a major ideal for Americans. De Tocqueville began his second volume on America with a discussion of the American passion for equality and the American neglect of liberty. He noted that in the United States men endure poverty, servitude, and barbarism, but they will not endure fixed class differences.

The characteristic egalitarianism of the American stems from three types of rejection. First, because of the "continual movement which agitates a democratic community," family ties are severely loosened, and "every man readily loses the trace of the ideas of his forefathers or takes no care about them." Second, there is no respect for the ideas of a master class, since "there are no longer any classes, or those which still exist are composed of such mobile elements that their body can never exercise a real control over its members." Third, egalitarianism is a consequence of a society in which intelligence is "placed on the footing of a general similitude," and men see each other as not being incontestably greater than each other. But because of this extreme independence, egalitarianism becomes the tragic enemy of libertarianism, of the spirit of being linked in a common cause which is led by uncommon men. But for our purpose, de Tocqueville's aristocratic perspective is less relevant than his strictly sociological conception of equality.[11]

The egalitarianism de Tocqueville speaks of is primarily one of manners and mores. What he fails to see is that this sociological egalitarianism, curiously enough, has become a major bulwark against eco-

[11] Alexis de Tocqueville, *op. cit.*, pp. 251-7.

nomic egalitarianism. But in this he was only expressing a common American dream. For, as long as Americans perceive themselves as politically equal, and as long as each American has a theoretical chance of rising out of his economic class as an individual, huge differences in economic status are not only tolerated but become the mark of distinguishing the achiever from the non-achiever, the "successful" man from the failure. This view maintained intact the idea of personal, rather than societal, responsibilities for development.

As James Bryce noted,

> There are no struggles between privileged and unprivileged orders, even that perpetual strife of rich and poor which is the oldest disease of civilized states. One must not pronounce broadly that there are no classes, for in parts of the country social distinctions have begun to grow up. But for political purposes classes scarcely exist. No one of the questions which now agitate the nation is a question between rich and poor. Instead of suspicion, jealousy, and arrogance embittering the relations of classes, good feeling and kindliness reign. Everything that government, as the Americans have hitherto understood the term, can give them, the poor have already political power, equal civil rights, a career open to all citizens alike. . . . Hence the poor have had nothing to fight for, no grounds for disliking the well-to-do, no complaints to make against them.[12]

How interesting this sounds in retrospect, to have someone, eighty years ago, indicate that the poor have no common denominator which would give them class consciousness. Indeed the present "war on poverty" is being largely waged by the relatively well-to-do to pull the poor up as if by an Archimedean lever. It is by no stretch of the imagination illustrative of the poor hoisting themselves up by their own bootstraps. The war on poverty assumes that everyone has an equal desire for advancement, while the structure of poverty is based on motivation or lack thereof. Hence, even at this stage, there is no common consciousness of poverty or common destiny which unites the poor against other classes. Indeed, among Negroes there is an absence of "social myths."

[12] James Bryce, "The American Commonwealth (1888)," in *America in Perspective: The United States Through Foreign Eyes*, edited by Henry Steele Commager. New York: Random House, 1947, p. 224.

Simone de Beauvoir has pointed out that, even in the present epoch, "no class hierarchy has been superimposed on top of any qualities of wealth and the average standard of living is high enough to prevent wealthy people from creating an inferiority complex. The rich American has no grandeur. The poor man has no servility. Human relations in daily life are on a footing of equality. Pride in the title 'American citizen' which is common to all makes for understanding." Here one detects the huge gulf which exists between the United States as a land of social equality and as a land of economic inequality; and how one serves to undermine much concern for the other. As de Beauvoir herself indicates:

> Each individual can disguise the poverty of his lot by believing he shares in the life of a great nation and each sees himself in his neighbor and wishes him to enjoy the dignity of man and the rights to which he is entitled just like himself. Americans have never demanded economic equality so much as economic opportunity. They admit of different standards of life so long as each citizen can by his own efforts climb from one rung of the ladder to another. Of course a few accidental successes maintain the cherished legend of the self-made man fluttering on the horizon, but this hoax is like comparing a lottery ticket with a treasury bond; any ticket may be the winning one, but only a tiny percentage of them actually do win. The equivocal meaning of the word "chance" is exploited, for its precise statistical meaning is very different from the vague meaning it has for the individual dazzled by doubtful promises.[13]

(3) The United States was also seen as a land of plenty and opportunity. The lush abundance of the United States has been held by observers to account for its liberality of spirit and for its egalitarianism as well. From the time of its first discovery, visitors were bewildered by the vastness of the United States and the bounty of its harvest, which formed such a stark contrast to the nations of Europe. William Cobbett looked with wide eyes on the table of the unperturbed American farmer: "You are not much asked, not much pressed, to eat and drink; but, such an abundance is spread before you, and so hearty and so cor-

---

[13] Simone de Beauvoir, *America Day by Day*. New York: Grove Press, 1953, pp. 260-63.

dial is your reception, that you instantly lose all restraint."[14] As the wilderness revealed its great wealth of raw materials and as the United States began to expand industrially, her riches became legendary.

By the time Harriet Martineau came to America, there was a virtual rhapsody of praise for the natural wealth of the new land.

> The United States are not only vast in extent: they are inestimably rich in material wealth. There are fisheries and granite quarries along the northern coasts; and shipping from the whole commercial world within their ports. There are tanneries within reach of their oak woods, and manufactures in the north from the cotton growth of the south. There is unlimited wealth of corn, sugar-cane and beet, hemp, flax, tobacco, and rice. There are regions of pasture land. There are varieties of grape for wine, and mulberries for silk. There is salt. There are mineral springs. There is marble, gold, lead, iron, and coal. There is a chain of mountains, dividing the great fertile western valley from the busy eastern region which lies between the mountains and the Atlantic. These mountains wield the springs by which the great rivers are to be fed for ever, to fertilize the great valley, and be the vehicle of its commerce with the world. Out of the reach of these rivers, in the vast breadth of the north, lie the great lakes, to be likewise the servants of commerce, and to afford in their fisheries the means of life and luxury to thousands. These inland seas temper the climate, summer and winter, and insure health to the heart of the vast continent. Never was a country more gifted by nature.[15]

Here a decent living standard was to be had for the common man. Here lay unlimited raw materials and opportunities making both overseas expansion and revolutionary civil strife unnecessary. This wealth made inconsequential if not inevitable the wastage of natural resources which resulted. When man has to conquer nature rather than adapt himself to it, his attitude tends to be more concerned with exploiting nature. He is eager to harvest its wealth by transforming natural objects into raw materials for the industrial process. But Mrs. Martineau was perceptive enough, and knowledgeable enough in economics, to realize

[14] William Cobbett, "The Material Well-Being of the Americans," in *America in Perspective, op. cit.*, pp. 28-9.
[15] Harriet Martineau, *op. cit.*, pp. 130-31.

that the greatest material wealth of America was its peoples. "However it may gratify the pride of a nation to be descended from one stock, it is ultimately better that it should have been compounded from many nations. The blending of qualities, physical and intellectual, the absorption of national prejudices, the increase of mental resources, will be found in the end highly conducive to the elevation of the national character. America will find herself largely blessed in this way, however much she may now complain of the immigration of strangers."[16]

The notion of American abundance is classic, but its existence was not a challenge in itself. How it would be used to maximum capacity was what intrigued and interested observers from other shores. And here the first announcement of the American ideology was to perform its role. "Opportunities for work and business activity were richly abundant. Idleness and shiftlessness, when associated with poverty, were condemned as moral delinquencies. The resultant mentality developed in this environment was one which glorified the 'hustler' and the 'go-getter' and deprecated devotion to anything which was not immediately practical."[17] In brief, every social fact was translated into moral currency, into what Perry termed the "moral economy." The American past was thus pegged to a divine mission; success was not a social good so much as it was a proof of moral competence. The "moral economy" was strangely linked to the "moral athlete," which made for the "ultimate individual."[18] In such a scheme, society could never be more than instrumental to the drives and directions of the person. And the laisser-faire economy served as a model for the fusion of material plentitude and human opportunity. This is made clear in Mackay's interesting observation on American stratification, his basic point being that, while the love of money may be a universal psychological characteristic, the availability of money is a particularized social characteristic.

> The love of money is regarded by many as a striking trait in the American character. I fear that this is a weakness to which humanity must universally plead guilty. But it is quite true that it

[16] Ibid., p. 131.
[17] Morris Raphael Cohen, *American Thought: A Critical Sketch*. New York: Collier Books, 1962, p. 33.
[18] Ralph Barton Perry, *Puritanism and Democracy*. New York: The Vanguard Press, 1944, esp. pp. 245-96.

is an absorbing passion with the Americans. This cannot be denied, but it may be explained. America is a country in which fortunes have yet to be made. Wealth gives great distinction, and wealth is, more or less, within the grasp of all. Hence the universal scramble. All cannot be made wealthy, but all have a chance of securing a prize. This stimulates to the race, and hence the eagerness of the competition. In this country England, however, the lottery is long since over, and with few exceptions the great prizes are already drawn. To the great bulk of the people, wealth is utterly unattainable. All they can hope for is competency, and numbers fall short even of that. Men soon flag in a hopeless pursuit. Hence it is that, in this country, the scramble is neither so fierce nor universal.[19]

(4) A strange ambiguity about American political structure prevailed throughout the nineteenth century. Practical politics in the United States was most frequently described as corrupt and subject to the whims of the ignorant masses.[20] Political morality often shocked foreign observers. Elected officials were rarely found to be people of higher sensibilities; and even less so, appointed "Tammany Hall" type officials. They were rarely businessmen who were inspiring, and even less frequently were those in the political ranks drawn from men of intellectual substance. Dicey noted that the less "Anglo" and the more "American" the United States became, the less interest educated men took in American politics. In contrast with the colonial period, quality of leadership went down and mass consensus, what Dicey bluntly called "uniformity," went up. In other words, in setting the democratic framework, the nation paid the price in the form of a lower level of public servant.[21] What Dicey was really reflecting upon was the transformation of the American value system under the impact of the double process of urbanization and industrialization.

Lord Bryce found the same condition of public immorality wide-

[19] Alexander Mackay, "Every American Is an Apostle of the Democratic Creed," in *America in Perspective, op. cit.*, p. 119.
[20] This was a profound motivation in even the best analysis of the American political system. See, for instance, M. Ostrogorski, *Democracy and the Organization of Political Parties*, Vol. II: *The United States*, edited and abridged by Seymour Martin Lipset. Garden City, New York: Doubleday & Co., 1964.
[21] Edward Dicey, *Six Months in the Federal States* (two volumes). London: Macmillan Co., 1863.

spread among administrators and legislators. Since they were in fact "average men," and thought of by themselves and by others as "average men," a sense of high purpose rarely went along with their high responsibilities. What most disturbed Bryce was not its effects on the society as a whole, but its reinforcement of the democratic ethos. Political corruption produced a certain apathy among the ruling classes and among fastidious types. Since they perceived themselves as being no more important than the ordinary voter, and since they were disgusted by the superficial vulgarities of public life, they ostensibly retreated into nonpolitical or cultural activity. Bryce's vision of America was mostly confined to the large cities he visited.[22]

Despite the vulgarities of American political life, it became apparent to most commentators that the American had an extraordinary faith in his formal political institutions. Not only was the American loath to challenge the political order; he was hardly prone to challenge even its sordidness. The American saw in the exaggerated displays of vulgar politicians the populism which was thought to be the essence of democracy and the democratic spirit.

Ostrogorski saw the way out of this dilemma of political formalism and political populism through the widest possible use of populist sentiments of the Americans.

> The moral basis of political action was laid in the struggles for emancipation throughout the United States, in the form of "committees of seventy" or of "one hundred," of the "citizens' movements," of the "mugwumps," or the "leagues," or "civic federations" all of which represented free associations of men brought together for a particular cause, and completely setting aside, for the nonce, their views on other political questions. In these movements the new method received its baptism of fire and showed what it could do. By its means it has been possible to combine all the living forces of American society for the struggle against political corruption, and to win victories which enable us not to despair of American democracy and of the government of the people by the people. In the sphere of the great national questions, as well as in municipal life, everywhere the "leagues" have been the instigators of the civic awakening; all the great reforms

[22] James Bryce, *The American Commonwealth* (two volumes). New York: Macmillan Co., 1888.

which have been passed to purify political life, beginning with that of the civil service, are due to their initiative or to their efforts; they have broken the prescription set up in favour of party tyranny and corruption, by opposing to the traditional conventions and the rigid forms that congeal and stifle everything that falls into their grasp, liberty of movement for the citizen in public life and the full light of free consideration.[23]

Whatever the contemporary significance of Ostrogorski's suggestions, he did pinpoint the achievement as well as the dilemma of nineteenth-century American politics. In retrospect it might be said that the conflict between political corruption and mass participation had a stimulating effect on the developmental process, for it kept the political machinery from hardening into an obstacle to development. The necessary price was paid but the work got done. This was true at the national level and at the ward level, and because of this, economic development in America was not fettered by an admittedly cumbersome political process.

(5) One of the most frequent charges against Americans is that they are dominated by monetary values. Charles Dickens claimed the American was infatuated with the real to the exclusion of the ideal. De Tocqueville, for his part, explained American materialism as an inevitable and natural consequence of an egalitarian state of mind. The Polish writer Adam de Gurowski saw the emphasis on material acquisition as something every American could be proud of. All observers, however, sensed one distinctive peculiarity in American materialism, namely, that the passion for money-making did not stem from an innate propensity to avarice, nor from a desire for opulence, but resulted from Americans' love for the game of chance. "With all the numerous and dark drawbacks of this propensity for money-making, it does not generate avarice in the Americans. If generally they are infuriated in the pursuit of money, they spend it as freely as they make it. If they are called men of the dollar, at any rate they are not hunters of cents. Parsimonious economy is not their characteristic, and in general the racing after dollars, the thirst for gain, does not make them contemptible misers or calloused to others." As de Gurowski sees it, this drive is basically autonomous, what in modern terms would be called a search conducted

[23] M. Ostrogorski, *op. cit.*, p. 365.

anomically, that is, independent of any firm frame of reference or set of goals. "Money is made not merely for the sake of becoming independent and rich or enjoying both, but from habit—on account of finding any other congenial occupation impossible. It becomes an intellectual drilling, and a test of skill. It becomes a game, deeply combined, complicated—a struggle with men and events, exciting, captivating, terrible, hand-to-hand, man-to-man, cunning-to-cunning." Interestingly, de Gurowski sees this drive for material acquisitions as taking place in an atmosphere of cultural scarcity. "The socially passionate life in Europe, diversified, and full of various enjoyments, gives to a successful winner, new scopes, attractions, and pleasures, such as society does not proffer, yield, or create in America."[24]

For Hugo Munsterberg this economic materialism ends up as a philosophical idealism. He sees the money-making orientation involved in a transference of values.

> The real attraction which the American feels for money making does not lie in the having but only in the getting, from the perfect equanimity, positively amazing to the European, with which he bears his losses. To be sure, his irrepressible optimism stands him in good stead; he never loses hope, but is confident that what he has lost will soon be made up. But this would be no comfort to him if he did not care much less for the possession than for the getting of it. The American chases after money with all his might, exactly as on the tennis court he tries to hit the ball, and it is the game he likes and not the prize.

One can see that the gaming analogy is almost endemic to the American scene; it is surprising how many nineteenth-century observers used the game metaphor to describe the American way of life. But they also emphasized that idealism prompted the performers. "It is fundamentally false to stigmatize the American as a materialist and to deny his idealism," Munsterberg goes on to conclude. "The economic life means to the American a realization of efforts which are in themselves precious. It is not the means to an end but is its own end."[25]

[24] Adam G. de Gurowski, "The Practical Genius of the American," in *America in Perspective, op. cit.,* pp. 157-70.
[25] Hugo Munsterberg, "A Philosopher Explains the American Passion for Money," in *America in Perspective, op. cit.,* pp. 261-9.

George W. Steevens saw American materialism in much less flattering terms. It was not an illustration of philosophical idealism so much as an adolescent empiricism. The keynote of this materialism is its impulsive need to express all sentiments externally by the crudest and most objective means. "The Americans are the most demonstrative of all the peoples of the earth. Everything must be brought to the surface, embodied in a visible, palpable form. For a fact to make any effect on the American mind it must be put in a shape where it can be seen, heard, handled. If you want to impress your fellows you must do it not through their reasoning powers but through the five senses of their bodies." Steevens also sees this materialism as the foundation for the peculiar type of patriotism the American exhibits:

> The most patriotic of men, his patriotism seems always to center rather on his flag than on his country. He can see the flag but he can't see the country. Why does he cover his person with childish buttons and badges? Because you can see them and you can't see the sentiments in his mind. They do not read Shakespeare but would think it almost a sin to visit England without seeing Shakespeare's house. In business they are the most unwearied and ingenious advertisers in the world. In dress they appear vain, out of just the same reverence for the concrete and indifference to the abstract.[26]

In sum, American materialism is actually equivalent to development as an economic notion, that is to say, concepts of development in terms of cultivation or culture did not impress the American citizen. It was not that the Americans did not believe in art. It was that their view of art was itself functional. The aesthetic was embodied in the object— in the object as a performing instrument. The continued awe in which the American holds Automobile Shows or Boat Shows is certainly not different from the awe with which an Italian holds the Sistine Chapel. The aesthetic is different, but it is there. It was this genius for linking aesthetic judgments to practical judgments that so fascinated men like de Tocqueville, who indeed saw not only the influence of democracy on science and the arts, but also appreciated the degree to which the arts and science influenced the structure of America.[27]

[26] George W. Steevens, "The American is an Electric Anglo-Saxon," in *America in Perspective, op. cit.*, pp. 254-60.
[27] Alexis de Tocqueville, *op. cit.*, pp. 265-78.

(6) This practical materialism thus gave rise to a whole new aesthetic quite different to, and alien in spirit, from the European system. Americans were not known as people of artistic or intellectual excellence, and therefore they have not been judged by their cultural productions, at least not in the nineteenth century. Not only was there a general decline of "cultivated gentlemen" in America from the days of the founding of the Republic, but the educated men themselves seemed to treat the intellect quite differently from the Europeans. Thus it might be said that the American became educated as he became massified—less concerned with cultivation and manners and hence unaffected in his developmental goals by education. Madariaga says in a rather whimsical fashion:

> They are hungry and thirsty for information—facts, stories. But they dislike thought, as all sound, healthy children do. None of your highbrow stuff for fine lads who can enjoy themselves making toys and playing with them. Knowledge, yes. By all means. Some boys must know all about how toys are made and moved to and fro and distributed fairly in the nursery, or there would be no fun. Knowledge is all right. It can be checked and put to some use, both made something of and kept busy, so to say. It can be turned into a toy, so that by means of little machines with colored lamps and buttons and switches the springs of the soul-machine may be shown to the whole nursery.[28]

Madariaga, however, undoubtedly has in mind a much later period in American history. In the formative years there was indeed a deep desire to educate people and not simply to manufacture fact machines. There was not yet the kind of professionalism which now pervades education. The division of labor did not extend to the sphere of learning, where the notion of general education, liberal arts education, and all-round competence prevailed throughout the nineteenth century. The rise of professional training did not take place till the end of the nineteenth century with the consolidation of the American industrial system. The concept of knowledge as a bank account, as something one can dip into according to how much wealth of information is stored, corresponds to a stage in American development where industry overshadows agriculture as the main source of wealth.

[28] Salvador de Madariaga, "Americans Are Boys," in *America in Perspective, op. cit.*, pp. 297-309.

What eased this transition from humanistic learning to professionalism was an emphasis on methods of work rather than on products of work. Lack of abstract knowledge never prevented the American from plunging ahead on an experimental and operational base.[29] As Siegfried put it, "The new world is in no way hostile to the general idea used as a source of inspiration, but, though the American feels in spite of everything that there is an empty space to be filled, his response is not that of the classicist. He is not tempted to consider educating specialists in general ideas, that is to say, another class of experts. In everything he seems to be interested in methods rather than things themselves."[30] The methodological orientation was the bridge which enabled the American to cross over from an agricultural to an industrial base. The leisured educated class of an agrarian society was replaced by specialists and the "usefully" educated, thus encouraging a "particularistic" over a "universalistic" emphasis.

In the nineteenth century, criticism of the United States from within was mainly confined to the grafted aristocracy, that minute portion of the American scene which remained unabsorbed and preferred the culture of France and England and the courtesy of Spain to the roughhewn philistinism of America. The American intellectual, therefore, has a largely conservative tradition in contrast to the European intellectual, who, since the period of eighteenth-century France, has been classically a radical, isolated from other classes and even from members of his own class. By contrast, criticism of the United States by Americans during the nineteenth century tended to be imitative and almost trivial in character. Not until William James's anti-imperialism near the end of the century is there a meaningful liberal criticism of American foreign policy. Thus it is necessary to use the European writers' image of America because of this peculiar divorce of the American intellectual from the industrialization process.

It is remarkable how uniform the interpretation of the United States has been from within. Allusion is nearly always made to Ameri-

---

[29] Irving Louis Horowitz, "Professionalism and Disciplinarianism: Two Styles of Sociological Performance," *Philosophy of Science*, Vol. 31, No. 3, July 1964; also Everett C. Hughes, *Men at Work*. Glencoe, Ill.: The Free Press, 1958; and C. Wright Mills, *Sociology and Pragmatism: The Higher Learning in America*. New York: Paine-Whitman, 1964.

[30] André Siegfried, *op. cit.*, p. 356.

can initiative, optimism, materialism, faith, and devotion to hard work. Even when interpretations of these variables sharply differ, few challenge the facts surrounding the First World *Weltanschauung*. Perhaps the reason why this is so has less to do with the facts than with the projections of what constitutes Americanism. Few nations on earth, overdeveloped, properly developing, or underdeveloped, have such a passion for a teleological goal as the Americans. They pursue "purpose" with the same zeal, though with less assurance, than the religiously devout reach out for Providence and the politically devout reach out for utopia. The spate of literature on the "national purpose" which appeared in the late 'fifties demonstrates clearly the collective anxiety of Americans. As Riesman notes: "There is something oddly regressive in the spectacle of the United States reducing itself to the size of a new nation that needs a manifest destiny."[31] Perhaps in this search for a future role, one aspect of United States leadership of the First World becomes clear: from the pragmatic, pluralistic, and uncertain orientation claimed for the United States by de Tocqueville, the country has evolved into a monolithic unity. It has sought out a singular purpose characteristic of historic bureaucratic world empires.[32]

Those who seek to celebrate the United States as the first new nation, or who see in it only the realization of its original purpose, would do well to recollect the words of Gilbert Keith Chesterton.

> When once we cast aside, as we inevitably have after a moment's thought, the fanciful physical metaphor involved in the word "youth," what serious evidence have we that America is a fresh force and not a stale one? It has a great many people, like China; it has a great deal of money, like defeated Carthage or dying Venice. It is full of bustle and excitability, like Athens after its ruin, and all the Greek cities in their decline. It is fond of new things; but the old are always fond of new things. Young men read chronicles, but old men read newspapers. It admires strength and good looks; it admires a big and barbaric beauty in its women, for instance, but so did Rome when the Goth was at the gates. All these are things quite compatible with fundamental

[31] See David Riesman, "The Concept of National Purpose," *Council for Correspondence Newsletter*, No. 27, June 1963, p. 11.
[32] See S. N. Eisenstadt, *The Political Systems of Empires*. New York: The Free Press of Glencoe, 1963, especially the conclusion, pp. 361-71.

tedium and decay. There are three main shapes or symbols in which a nation can show itself essentially glad and great: by the heroic in government, by the heroic in arms, and by the heroic in art. Beyond government, which is, as it were, the very shape and body of a nation, the most significant thing about any citizen is his artistic attitude toward a holiday and his moral attitude toward a fight—that is, his way of accepting life and his way of accepting death. Subjected to these eternal tests, America does not appear by any means as particularly fresh or untouched. She appears with all the weakness and weariness of modern England or of any other Western power.[33]

II

The American self-perception remains fixed, atrophied, characterized by buoyant optimism about the future, by concern for material well-being, moralizing, a faith in egalitarianism, and an egalitarianism of faith. As Boorstin indicated, it is a society whose members are still convinced that they are misunderstood by everyone, and that this misunderstanding arises out of a basic jealousy of have-not peoples.[34] Interestingly, even those who do their utmost to revise this "image," who are dedicated to the elimination of "ethnocentricism" in American thought, are not infrequently guilty of moralizings which read like some catalogue of false stereotypes. Thus, in one recent effort along the lines of self-purification, "a manual for Americans overseas,"[35] we find out everything but what counts: Why are millions of Americans overseas in the first place?

Perhaps the greatest single study of the United States was made by Alexis de Tocqueville over a century ago. Nevertheless, de Tocqueville is done no honor by a number of recent writers who are remarkably jejune in their uncritical acceptance of his work. These are the writers who present themselves as implacable foes of dogmatism when it comes to Marx's writings.[36] In some measure this is simply a response to an

[33] G. K. Chesterton, "Is America a Young or a Dying Nation?" in *America in Perspective, op. cit.*, pp. 270-74.
[34] Daniel J. Boorstin, *America and the Image of Europe: Reflections on American Thought.* New York: Meridian Books, Inc., 1960.
[35] Conrad M. Arensberg and Arthur H. Niehoff, *Introducing Social Change: A Manual for Americans Overseas.* Chicago: Aldine Publishing Company, 1964.
[36] See for example Seymour Martin Lipset, "Political Sociology," in *Sociology Today: Problems and Prospects,* edited by R. K. Merton, Leonard Broom, and L. S. Cottrell, Jr. New York: Basic Books, Inc., 1959, pp. 81-114.

impulse to celebrate those who praise the United States and criticize those who condemn it. De Tocqueville spoke well of the United States. Even his aristocratic criticisms of American democracy were made with generous respect for the revolutionary achievements of the first new nation and could hardly irritate the devoted believer in manifest destiny.

There is little advantage in basking in the judgments of the nineteenth century, unless we are prepared to say that the empirical conditions which prevailed at the time of the writings of de Tocqueville, Martineau, and Ostrogorski still obtain. But if the situation is radically different, as I maintain it is, then judgments must similarly be cast in terms which reflect the present. Indeed de Tocqueville himself knew this. He wrote of democratic government in America, "The foreign policy of the United States is reduced by its very nature to await the chances of the future history of the nation, and for the present it consists more in abstaining from interference than in exerting its activity."[37] Such abstinence came to an abrupt end with World War One. At this point the United States became the leader of the highly industrialized part of the world.

Hans Kohn appreciated this when he indicated that "the turning point for the United States was the war of 1914." He went on to explain that "it linked the destinies of the two shores of the North Atlantic again as closely as they had been in the eighteenth century." But this time the superordinate and subordinate positions were drastically altered.

> Though the Europeans were not aware of it, and continued their struggle to maintain a European balance of power, bidding for European hegemony as if no fundamental change had happened, the end of the war marked also the political eclipse of Europe. It was a misfortune for both Europe and the United States that neither realized it or wished to acknowledge it. Yet in 1917 only the entrance of the United States into what had been until then a war for the maintenance of the balance of power in Europe saved Europe from the consequences of a German victory on the eastern and western fronts and from German hegemony over the whole continent.[38]

But if the United States "saved" Europe from German hegemony, it

[37] Alexis de Tocqueville, *op. cit.*, p. 138.
[38] Hans Kohn, *op. cit.*, pp. 205-6.

made clear its own stake in the affairs of the world. From that point on, the United States has in fact been the leader, acknowledged or otherwise, of the First World.

The United States becomes leader of the First World (and not just the industrial world) only when there are comparisons to be made with the Second World of Soviet development and with the Third World of Latin America and the Afro-Asian bloc. As long as the United States represented one part of a homogenous Europeanized world, it had no reality as a First World. It had no leadership possibilities; for however much an object of curiosity the United States must have appeared in the previous two centuries, European observers never dreamed that the New World tail would wag the Old World dog.

In other words, this era has a special kind of distinctiveness. It is neither useful nor instructive to think of the United States only in historical terms. It has to be recognized that a radical break has occurred between the past and the present, between the time when the United States was a part of European expansion and a time when the United States is the leader in an expansive phase of what has come to be known as Western civilization.

Despite the wars carried on in the name of democracy, economic inequality has become more pronounced. The gap between rich and poor nations has become greater. At the same time the main center of traditional economic wealth has moved from Europe to the United States. European nations—most specifically England, France, and Germany—have declined as world powers. Europe, not merely the Axis powers, was defeated in World War Two. Militarily, economically, politically, and culturally, the United States has become the power center of the Western bloc. At this point it consolidated its substance and style into a veritable First World—a measure of universal wants as well as universal needs.

In the process of rising to the fore of a First World the United States paid an indirect tribute to the power and the potency of the Second World of Soviet development. The First World maintains a string of international military and political affiliations, a network of associations calculated to prevent the Second World from expanding its powerful international influence; and in a more ultimate sense, intended to keep the Third World from adopting concrete anti-Western "socialist" strategies or principles. The emergence of the First World as a conscious entity has been accompanied by a drastic inflation of nationalism and nationalistic rhetoric. Precisely to the extent that the First World has become mobilized and homogenized into an "Atlantic Community," a "Western democratic" orbit, a "civilized front against barbarism," the United States itself has been transformed from a nation-state into a world civilization.

The United States has become an international purchaser of "good will." Economically, it has sealed off its orbit; and in various ways it deploys its economy as an instrument to gain political and military ends. Even the trade-union movement has become fully incorporated both into the national economy and America's larger nationalistic designs. Those strata not yet absorbed, such as Negro and other ethnic minority groups, have had their protest movements severely circumscribed. Often they only seek participation in the national celebration rather than real equality.

Louis Hartz has described the impact of the United States' sealing itself off from developments in the rest of the world:

> The American failure to understand revolution derives not merely from the formal experience of fragmentation. It derives from the point at which the American detachment from the European development took place, the bourgeois point, which by the complicated mechanism of fragment evolution cut off the socialist "future." Hence it is an inability to understand the appeal of socialism itself which is involved. McCarthyite virtue at home is accompanied by bafflement with respect to the origin of sin abroad. But it is precisely the promise of modernity which socialism offers, in the context of the traditionalist order, which is the root of its appeal . . . Life within the American fragment, which does not know that ethos, as either a burden or a lure, as either something to forget or something unforgettable, cannot seize the meaning of this promise.[39]

Perceptive as this formulation is, one important point is left unanswered: the United States has not simply "fragmented" or become "detached" from the mainstream of development; for it offers to the

[39] Louis Hartz, "United States History in a New Perspective," *The Founding of New Societies.* New York: Harcourt Brace, 1964, pp. 119-20.

Third World a highly successful model for further development. And here is where the contradiction becomes especially apparent. It is not just American failure to understand revolution that is at stake, but its failure to come to terms with social revolution. What is truly novel in twentieth-century experience, is that nearly all of the definitions bear on the technological, and few innovations in economic organization can be claimed. Even those social changes that have taken place are largely a consequence of technological and scientific invention. The constitutional basis of American society serves to undermine social revolution just as assuredly as it serves to promote technological innovation. It is then this internal contradiction which makes the United States a difficult "model" for the rest of the world, and in turn makes it so impermeable to internally induced social revolutions.

The United States role as a model for the future has been subject to competition from other styles of economic and social development and other forms of political organization. On the internal scene it has been severely circumscribed by the closing of the frontier and restriction of immigration. This dramatic change is underscored by a recent report issued by the Rockefeller Foundation:

> The picture of the United States held at least unconsciously in the minds of Americans is that of a large continent, endowed with virtually unlimited resources, enjoying an easy power and favored with a comfortably large and growing population. That picture will change in the decades ahead. In comparison with the vast, amorphous new regional groups now obtaining political expression, the outstanding fact about the United States may come to seem its compactness. Notable among its characteristics will be a high degree of skill, elaborate organization, a refined technology. Its conviction of self-sufficiency will be replaced by awareness of how greatly it is dependent on its relations with other countries for essential materials and for a supporting atmosphere in which it can breathe and be itself.[40]

As long as the United States had open frontiers, unexplored regions, and free land it retained many of the values of an agricultural so-

---

[40] *The Mid-Century Challenge to U.S. Foreign Policy,* Panel 1 Report of the Rockefeller Brothers Fund Special Studies Project. Garden City, New York: Doubleday & Co., Inc., 1959, p. 58.

ciety. The first hundred years of American experience were unique in that they revealed little anxiety over economic development. The doctrine of inevitable progress covered everyone. Even if we explore the character of technological innovation and invention in this early period we often find its orientation directed toward farm machinery and ways of creating crop efficiency. While there can be no doubt that these technological developments stimulated the movement of men toward cities and in themselves generated technological unemployment on the farm, their consequences were almost wholly absorbed by lateral mobility, by movements to fresh lands and new territories. Conservation, for example, was no concern between 1780 and 1870 precisely because of the abundance and fertility of virgin territories.

The real end of the frontier coincided with the growth of mutually incompatible economic systems in the United States. From an economic viewpoint the Civil War involved an acute confrontation of the emerging industrialism represented by Northern interests and the declining agriculturalism represented by Southern interests. Considered in this way, slavery was a hindrance to the North and to the West, for it prevented the rapid mobilization of primary factory labor, while for the South it was a necessity because it alone of all forms of economic relationships was cheaper in cost than technological substitutes. The liquidation of slavery meant that whatever form the economic question took in the post-Civil War period, it would have to be based on the triumph of machine over human labor, of "scientific technology" over "natural law." The humanitarianism of the Civil War, the outcry against slavery, was thus a response to the needs of an industrial society. The Civil War brought about not simply an end to slavery—a debatable point—but hastened the end of the agricultural epoch in American history, to the period when economic solutions could be based on free lands and open frontiers.

Thus, the post-Civil War take-off period in the United States, from 1870 to 1914, witnessed an immense industrial growth in the north and central regions. The industrial belt was fused to an urban belt. *Megalopolis* extended from New York to Chicago westward, and from Boston through Philadelphia along the coastal plain. States such as Pennsylvania, Massachusetts, and Ohio were the great beneficiaries of this sectional development, since their cities represented, as they still do, what has come to be known as the industrial heartline.[41] During the same period, despite chronic agricultural stagnation in the South and New England, the total agricultural sector expanded at least as rapidly as the industrial sector. What has been referred to, in describing the Third World, as the sacrifice of the agricultural sector to the industrial sector actually took place in the United States. The exploitation of agricultural workers in the post-Civil War period corresponded to the needs of a growing industrial empire which was at the same time an urban empire. The agricultural portions of the community were made intolerable, driving excess labor into industry. At the same time concentration was placed on the mechanization of industry, the application of this mechanization to the farm lands further weakened the agricultural sector. What is amazing about American development is that the agricultural sector continued to yield higher productivity in the face of a rising urban labor force recruited into relatively well-paying jobs in an expanding industrial economy. This is in marked contrast to development in the Second World of the Soviet Union and in most portions of the Third World.

The genius of the United States was expended in devising ways and means of making capitalism viable. There was nothing to indicate that this was possible. European capitalism in the nineteenth century had already entered a period of deep stagnation. The peculiarities of American capitalism can be seen from the electrical engineering field. Despite the fact that the basic scientific knowledge had been discovered, with Faraday showing in 1831 how to convert mechanical power into electrical current, mass electricity was not made available to a mass public until the end of the century. The problem was not how to produce electrical energy, but how such energy was to be marketed and sold. Selling energy reached its pinnacle in the natural resource monopolies of the United States. Through the dual process of industrialization and urbanization, such new energy sources could be commercially marketed. And they were. Even at present, the "electrification process" has nowhere reached the degree of achievement it has in the United States. Furthermore, the profits from such electrical activities were partially used to sponsor new

---

41 For a significant work covering these trends, see Jean Gottman, *Megalopolis: The Urbanized Northeastern Seaboard of the United States.* New York: The Twentieth Century Fund, 1961.

research and new styles of research. "Edison's Menlo Park laboratory may have been a crude affair, but it was the prototype of the great governmental and industrial research institutions of today. It is in the electrical industry that we can see most clearly how economic success can, so to speak, *fix* and establish scientific *development*."[42]

Despite this remarkable achievement of converting society from agriculture to industry with minimal friction, and despite this technological compensation for problems of the transition period, the United States has still failed to capture, in ideology at least, the imagination of Third World leadership. Paradoxically there seemed to be more enthusiasm and more interest in the genius of America when it was less developed than when it is more developed.

To some degree at least, the answer must be sought in the economic operations of American society, particularly its inability to operate at maximum capacity, which has given rise to underutilization of resources coupled with overproduction. The dynamics of this contradiction has placed financing in American society on a shaky credit basis in which the ability to repay is constantly being threatened by underutilization, and the capacity of the lender to foreclose equally threatened by the vast problems of overproduction. The gap widens. Even with this new reservoir of credit the industrial complex in the United States operates at between one-half to three-fourths of its capacity. At least ten billion dollars worth of goods and services have been lost in the last decade alone. Thurman Arnold in a recent updating of his study on *The Folklore of Capitalism* has pointed out that:

> For the past ten years we have been able to use only about 75 per cent of what we produce. As a practical matter, it would not be difficult to avail ourselves of that unused production. As an ideological matter it is a present impossibility to carry on the public works and services which our economy could so easily afford. This is because private money and credit are not available for such things as conservation of our water supply, our health, our recreational facilities, and so on, through a long list of public necessities. Things which cannot be bought and sold for dollars on

[42] See J. D. Bernal, "Science, Industry and Society in the Nineteenth Century," *Essays on the Social History of Science*, edited by S. Lilley. Copenhagen: Ejnar Munksgaard, 1953, pp. 138-65.

the marketplace cannot be financed by private credit. Therefore we must do without them even though this means a colossal waste of our real production resources.[43]

Even if we adjust Arnold's version to account for huge philanthropic activities, his criticism is forceful, since the underutilization of planned capacities is itself the cause in holding down the public works required for further development of the economy. The idea of setting in motion a free-floating private sector is for this reason unappetizing to most nations entering the developing stage. The conflict of interests within the United States acts to prohibit its identification with revolutions taking place abroad. These interests prevent the formation of an ideology that does not fit in with some modified version of laisser faire.

Ideologically the United States no longer functions as the wave of the future. But technologically this country has never been more of a model for the rest of the human race. Admiration for the United States has been transferred from its political institutions to its industrial capacity to provide immense quantities and high-quality creature comforts, mass electrification, super-highways, consumer goods, and a host of other technological specialties. At this level the United States serves as a prime model of efficient modernization for the developing regions and for Western Europe and the Soviet bloc as well.

Compared to the Soviet Union the United States is more aware of what is and is not important in the technological order. In the 'twenties and 'thirties the United States emphasized the tallest, the largest, the most gigantic. This was particularly so in the fields of electronics and architecture. Such items as enormous cabinets for minute radios or one-hundred-story buildings, the top halves of which were unoccupied, showed the planners the limits of giganticism. Ironically, in the Soviet Union one still finds this emphasis on the gigantic: the largest rockets, the biggest buildings, the greatest amount of thrust, the most number of orbits. Therefore it is exactly at that point when technology in the United States has become interested in "miniaturizing," the Soviet Union has adopted the braggadocio of greatness through bigness.

[43] Thurman W. Arnold, "The Folklore of Capitalism Revisited," *The Yale Review*, Vol. LII, No. 2, Winter 1963, pp. 188-204.

The egalitarian spirit in the United States has undergone a transformation. The orientation toward achievement still remains; only it is now in uneasy balance with ascribed values. Thus there remains enormous upward striving among Jews but with intense attachment to Jewish identity. Similarly there is an increase in striving among Negroes but with developing attachment to the virtues of Negritude. The Protestant Establishment, for its part, has remained firmly intact. It has consolidated itself around the banking and financial interests of the country. And the existence of Catholic separatism has been well documented in all areas and walks of life.[44] Within the framework of the United States there is taking place a crystallization of three religious power groups focused on different spheres of activity. Broadly, one might say that the Roman Catholics have a higher than average involvement in the political arena; the Jews have a concentrated leadership in the academic and intellectual areas; and the Protestants have become the administrators of the general economy and the big organizations of the nation.[45] The extent to which religion in America hinges on considerations of status remains to be explored, but their increasing intensity is no longer in much doubt. With the individual pressured to "climb," the immensity of the modern environment pressing him down, there is resort to "group mobility," uniting group identification with individual ambition.

One way of putting the model of America in meaningful perspective is to note how radically the United States has become "sociological" in its fundamental values. The actual membership in a church has tended to rise over the years, with upwards of 50 per cent claiming membership or affiliation of one kind or another, and over 90 per cent professing a belief in one religion or another. But the quality of such affiliation has drastically altered. In a recent study of church commitment in the American suburb, the following results were obtained. (1) It was found that one of the chief reasons for joining a church was "familism," promoting family unification and children's religious needs through authoritative agencies. (2) A central factor was belonging, social affiliation

---

[44] See Will Herberg, *Protestant-Catholic-Jew.* New York: Doubleday & Co., 1955; and Milton M. Gordon, *Assimilation in American Life: The Role of Race, Religion, and National Origin.* New York: Oxford University Press, 1964.
[45] See E. Digby Baltzell, *The Protestant Establishment: Aristocracy and Caste in America.* New York: Random House, 1964.

on the basis of the commercial advantages of certain friendships. (3) Peace of mind, religion as a psychoanalytic surrogate, providing mental well-being in a tormented and aggressive society, was also frequently mentioned by the new parishioners. (4) Moral orientation, the belief that to identify with a church is to achieve a degree of value orientation which is absolute and meaningful was important. (5) Success, the church as a means of validating and legitimizing already achieved economic or political gains, was a further motivation. Two other items, often stressed in the classical sociological literature—a need for ritual and a corresponding need for religious and ethical understanding—ranked lowest on the scale of reasons for church affiliation. Thus, contrary to a religious revival, there is a tendency to subvert religion by converting it into a sociological celebration, by employing religion as a role.[46]

The trade union movement has also undergone a transformation of large proportions and serious consequences. It has moved from a search for redress of grievances derived from poverty to a search for economic security within the hierarchy of positions. This is particularly evident in craft unions, which have changed their goals from the total unionization of employed labor to the practice of rigid exclusion of the unorganized portions of labor from the benefits of unionization. The American union system, like the religious system, has itself become a mark of ascribed status. In certain unions, the union card is virtually passed on from generation to generation.

Such differentiation has been enshrined as the doctrine of the functional necessity of stratification: "If the rights and prerequisites of different positions in a society must be unequal, then the society must be stratified, because that is precisely what stratification means. Social inequality is thus an unconsciously evolved device by which societies insure that the most important positions are conscientiously filled by the most qualified persons. Hence every society, no matter how simple or complex, must differentiate persons in terms of both prestige and esteem and must therefore possess a certain amount of institutionalized inequal-

---

[46] See Dennison J. Nash and Peter L. Berger, "Church Commitment in an American Suburb: An Analysis of the Decision to Join," *Archives de Sociologie des Religions* (Centre National de la Recherche Scientifique), Vol. 7, Whole No. 13, Jan.-June 1962, pp. 105-20; and for a more detailed study, see N. J. Demerath III, *Social Class in American Protestantism*. Chicago: Rand McNally & Company, 1965, particularly the theoretical discussion, pp. 177-204.

ity."[47] This kind of position is not a defense of conservative virtues so much as a reflection of a generalized apathy that has spread throughout the American social system in which things are taken for granted as immutable laws. The American ideology has accepted the canons of inequality as being natural to capitalist development, just as in the previous century it relied on capitalist development to prove the necessity of social equality.

The land of plenty and opportunity has become classic and mythic. While lush abundance has increased dramatically, its distribution has remained remarkably uneven. The most noticeable gap, for example, that between Negro and white, has actually increased in relative terms despite the fact that the actual condition of the Negro has improved. According to the latest census figures, Negro personal income in the South varies anywhere from one-third to one-half that of white personal income.[48] Most notable also is that the rates of upward mobility are widening, and this seems to be true generally of the gap between affluence and poverty. If we take three variables—race, ecology, and family income—and combine them, the result is a dramatic picture of atrophied economic equality, coupled with significant social gains.

Despite wide industrialization in the South, Negro job opportunities have hardly improved in the last fifty years. During the twentieth century nearly all increase in Negro purchasing power has been due to the family shift from the rural to the urban centers of the South and of the North. As a result, the Negro urban family has more income than the Negro rural family.

This increased circulation of personal income stimulated the growth of and provides the material base for the Negro bourgeoisie.[49] Shopkeeping, real-estate and insurance activities, and in general those commercial establishments primarily connected with everyday needs of the Negro form the hub of this marginal middle class. The kind of work that the Negro jobseeker in the city receives is linked to low status and low-paying positions. The new industries identified with recent economic

---

[47] Kingsley Davis, *Human Society*. New York: Macmillan Co., 1949, pp. 367-8; also see Kingsley Davis and Wilbert E. Moore, "Some Principles of Stratification," *American Sociological Review*, 10, 1945, pp. 242-9.
[48] U. S. Census, *Families and Unrelated Individuals*. Washington, D.C., 1960.
[49] See E. Franklin Frazier, *Black Bourgeoisie: The Rise of a New Middle Class in the United States*. New York: Collier Books, 1962, pp. 42-55.

growth in the South, such as clothes manufacturing, aircraft manufacturing, and communications industries, have followed the traditional Southern practice of confining Negroes to the same low-wage job categories. At the same time the introduction of various automation processes in the older industries is eliminating the kind of unskilled and semi-skilled jobs that Negroes have traditionally held. In sum, the income gap between the average urban Negro family and the urban white family is wider than the gap between the white and Negro rural families.[50] The substantial growth of a Negro bourgeoisie has not altered the basic classical pattern of underdevelopment, in part because the Negro bourgeoisie remains a small section of the total Negro population, and in part because the geographic distribution of wealth in the North and South has become more rather than less concentrated.

A "great war on poverty" may very well attempt to stave off economic class struggle as an irritant in an already difficult racial conflict. But "a war on poverty" without a concomitant critique of opulence may perform a double role; on one hand it may reassert the existence of class barriers, and on the other hand it may provide a stimulus for high achievement among the present generation of wealthy who have not lost the desire nor economic drive of their forefathers. It may be that the war on poverty will prove to be an exceptionally brilliant way of stimulating an achievement orientation among those who thus far have not been touched by the American dream. As Kolko points out:

> From the point of view of access to economic status symbols, the position of the upper tenth of the nation's income earners should be the dominant concern of students of social inequality in America. For in almost any given year the average dollar income of the upper tenth of the income earners will be twice as high as the average income of the next highest income tenth; and about 25 to 30 times higher than the average income of the lowest income tenth. Recent assertains on the purported tendency towards income equalization have concentrated on the position of the upper fifth of the income earners and the decline of the number of annual tax returns at very high figures—$100,000 and up. This latter assertion is of little relevance, since if it can be shown

[50] J. H. Odell, "The Negro People in the Southern Economy," *Freedomways,* Vol. 3, No. 4, Fall 1963, pp. 526-48; also see S. M. Miller, "Poverty, Race, and Politics," *The New Sociology,* edited by Irving L. Horowitz. New York and London: Oxford University Press, 1964, pp. 290-311.

that the centralization of economic power and status symbols has not moved out of the control of a small economic elite, then the problem of the elite's relation to society remains with us despite minor shifts within the elite itself.[51]

American abundance can hardly be better celebrated than by a war on poverty, a war which would increase the living standards of those poor who already live better than comparable groups in nearly all parts of the world. The possibilities for realizing great wealth with little effort have not only vanished for the poor but are rapidly vanishing for the middle classes. As one writer pointed out: "Even among the highly paid and responsible businessmen and salaried executives only a small fraction were actually able to reach the top. Thus, insofar as the American people were committed to the American ideology of personal success, they were attempting to accomplish something that for most of them was impossible. Judged by the prevalent standards of American society, most Americans were compelled to regard themselves as having failed and to attribute their failure to some shortcoming within themselves."[52]

While social mobility has slowly increased, it has not kept pace with the actual growth of the economy. Thus, there is enormous stress to participate in the American celebration and to gain a measure of plenty while at the same time there has been no dramatic or significant change in social mobility since World War Two. The formal educational apparatus which was intended to further social mobility and economic opportunity has served at the same time to stratify the American society. As one group of findings show, the stratification process is reinforced by the educational system no less than the mobility process.[53]

[51] Gabriel Kolko, "The American Income Revolution," *America as a Mass Society*, edited by Philip Olson. New York: The Free Press of Glencoe, 1963, p. 107. It is interesting to note that the situation in the United Kingdom shows no more of a trend toward leveling than in the United States. See Richard M. Titmuss, *Income Distribution and Social Change*. Toronto: University of Toronto Press, 1962.
[52] Henry Bamford Parkes, *The American Experience: An Interpretation of the History of Civilization of the American People*. New York: Alfred A. Knopf, 1955. See Chapter 11.
[53] See Murray Gendell and Hans I. Zetterberg, *A Sociological Almanac for the United States* (2nd edition). New York: Charles Scribner's Sons, 1964, pp. 21-2; also, Elton F. Jackson and Harry J. Crockett, Jr., "Occupational Mobility in the United States: A Point Estimate and Trend Comparison," *American Sociological Review*, Vol. 29, No. 1, February 1964, pp. 5-15.

In its very structure, American education ties social mobility to personality rather than to knowledge as such. Here we may note Fromm's acute observations on this marketing orientation:

> The gospel of working loses weight and the gospel of selling becomes paramount. In feudal times, social mobility was exceedingly limited and one could not use one's personality to get ahead. In the days of the competitive market, social mobility was relatively great, especially in the United States; if one delivered the goods one could get ahead. Today the opportunities for the lone individual who can make a fortune all by himself are, in comparison with the previous period, greatly diminished. He who wants to get ahead has to fit into the large organizations and his ability to play the expected role is one of his assets.[54]

Popular American political character has significantly changed. At the "mass" level it has revealed an increasing response to questions of section, race, age, and family. In its latest phase people have moved away from questioning national policies. Citizens participate in the political process by working for the civic culture, in such activities as the passage of a local bond issue or a highway construction plan. Politics as a general system of governing or a critique of that general system has dissolved. Apart from radical movement, politics is now concerned with parochial matters. In the process, politics based upon universalistic values has disappeared.[55] There remains the question to what extent the public accepts the narrowing of political choice, the sameness of the different political factions and parties in the United States.[56] The growing strength of conservatism as an organization no less than as an ideology would indicate that ideological politics may increase with the sharpening of the international crisis.

The basis of national and international politics has shifted from a widespread dialogue to a maneuvered consensus. Abstract politics has dissolved into the political sciences. Elective offices are giving way in importance to the appointive offices. Few elected officials in the history

---

[54] Erich Fromm, *Man for Himself*. New York: Holt, Rinehart, & Winston, 1947, pp. 81-2.
[55] Gabriel A. Almond and Sidney Verba, *The Civic Culture*. Boston and Toronto: Little, Brown & Co., 1965.
[56] Daniel Bell, *The End of Ideology: On the Exhaustion of Political Ideas in the Fifties* (Revised edition). New York: Collier Books, 1961, esp. pp. 393-402.

of the United States have had anywhere near the power and the prestige of such appointed officials as the Secretaries of Defense and State; men who in the present case have never run for office yet exercise enormous political controls. In this large-scale shift from competitive politics to policy-making, from elective to appointive styles, and in the corresponding rise of the expert as arbiter in the decision-making processes, nineteenth-century political styles seem outmoded and even quaint.[57]

The debate over whether there is in fact a power elite which runs the United States or whether there are countervailing veto groups has become, in the short span of a decade, an outmoded question. If one examines in some detail the arguments of Riesman, it becomes evident that while there are a series of groups, each of which struggles for and finally attains a power to stop things conceivably harmful to its own interests, the ability to start things is something Riesman fully recognizes as the responsibility of those who are the strongest, namely, those who have power within such veto groups.[58] Likewise, if we examine Mills' position, we find something more sophisticated than a blunt representation of the Franco-Italian concept of power. For what he does is to divide the power apparatus into three sections: a mass which lacks political power and lacks the agencies for attaining such power; a middle stratum which does indeed settle matters of local issue and is in what Mills calls a "semi-organized stalemate" condition; and at the third level, the power elite, which is not issue-bound but rather value-oriented and makes decisions affecting national and international policies independent in large measure of democratic norms.[59] This is not to minimize the existence of differences between Riesman and Mills. Nonetheless, it has become clear that the genius of two-party systems, multi-party systems, or of a democracy of the top based on veto groups does not alter the fact that in larger institutional and international matters the policy of the United States is as unitary as that of any other great power.

[57] See Henry A. Kissinger, "The Policy Maker and the Intellectual," in *International Politics and Foreign Policy*, edited by James N. Rosenau. New York: The Free Press of Glencoe, 1961, pp. 273-8.
[58] David Riesman, Nathan Glazer, and Reuel Denney, *The Lonely Crowd: A Study of the Changing American Character*. Garden City, New York: Doubleday & Co., 1953, pp. 246-59.
[59] C. Wright Mills, *The Power Elite*. New York: Oxford University Press, 1956, pp. 3-29.

The technological innovations which distinguish the United States in the twentieth century have at the same time produced profound effects on American politics, for they have streamlined the agencies of power and in so doing minimized the exercise of popular political control of that power. In place of the responsive politician there arises the irresponsible expert. As Seligman notes:

> Political differences are also becoming blurred: American political debate is increasingly conducted in a planned, even tempered atmosphere, and extremists of any kind are becoming rarer. The political expression of the new society in which more and more families are bunched around the middle income levels and adapting to middle class ways is a congress in which more and more politicians are bunched around the middle of the road, in which both parties are increasingly dominated by "reasonable" liberals.[60]

Nor has this process of political disintegration been confined to political agencies alone; there have been large-scale social and psychological consequences. Basically it has meant the collapse of the pragmatic, innovative political style. If pragmatism meant anything in the past, it required at the very least participation, action, a statement of commitment. But what we now have is political behavior manipulated to such a degree as to create what Lazarsfeld and Merton have referred to as a "narcotizing dysfunction." As they point out, vicariousness sets in, a rarefied removal from actual commitment. The modern American

> comes to mistake *knowing* about problems of the day for *doing* something about them. His social conscience remains spotlessly clean. He is concerned; he is informed; and he has all sorts of ideas as to what should be done. But after he has gotten through his dinner and after he has listened to his favorite radio programs and after he has read his second newspaper of the day it is really time for bed. In this peculiar respect mass communications may be included among the most respectable and efficient of social narcotics.[61]

[60] Daniel Seligman, "The New Masses," in *America as a Mass Society, op. cit.*, pp. 254-6; also see, Richard E. Neustadt, *Presidential Power*. New York: John Wiley, 1960.
[61] Paul F. Lazarsfeld and Robert K. Merton, "Mass Communication, Popular Taste, and Organized Social Action," *Mass Culture: The Popular Arts in America*, edited by Bernard Rosenberg and David Manning White. Glencoe, Ill.: The Free Press, 1957, p. 464.

To what then have the attentions and ambitions of the American mass been drawn, now that its mind has been relieved of political considerations? Here it should be recorded that it is not simply mass culture or mass leisure that defines the new situation, but the character and quality of present-day work styles. For culture and leisure are still defined in terms of the labor process, and not the other way around. It would be erroneous to think that the search for alternatives to work means an end to the definition of the labor process as central.

In a generalized celebration of "American values" political ideologies have lost competitive fervor and have increasingly become economic ideologies. While on the surface a conservative recrudescence challenges this, it was effectively defeated in a recent election. Perhaps the most perfect representation of this economic determination is American unionism, which paradoxically exhibits a violent history of labor class struggles accompanied by an early lack of political direction. The goals which unionism set for itself were distinguished by the almost exclusive concern with economic well-being. Although this is mitigated by political affairs committees in recent history, political concerns center on economic issues. Thus, while there was a very high degree of class consciousness, there was a simultaneously low degree of political consciousness, the reverse of Marxist expectations. This ideological economism served to stimulate socio-economic development rathen than, as in Europe, act as a brake on its development. The ideology of "bread-and-butter" unionism corresponds to the recruitment of large numbers of skilled workers. What are these ideological needs?

(a) That labor is to be rewarded for the amount of work done, with harder work and more productivity deserving better rewards. Thus, at the outset, the working class of the United States is tied to the ideology of a rewards system, which was what the owning classes attempted to inspire in them. (b) The ideology of economism rarely led to the formation of political parties along class lines. When such parties were formed, they were generally farmer parties or farmer-labor coalitions and not industrial working-class parties such as have existed in Europe since the nineteenth century. This made possible a consensus at the political level which emphasized common class interests and class needs in terms of more industrial wealth rather than in terms of new social relationships. (c) The ideology of economism was not confined to the trade union movement. It was in fact characteristic of business and professional groups as well. From their point of view, it seemed natural and organic to lay emphasis on the economy, since they were the prime recipients of its benefits. On the other hand, where class feeling took on a political cast, it was strongly colored by nostalgia, by the desire for the return of a former condition on the part of a newly displaced or threatened class. American society has been unique in the degree to which it separated the "political" from the "economic." Politics in America is run not so much by a "power elite" or by "veto groups" as by businessmen. But quite unlike the predictions of Marxist "economic determinism," the proletariat takes an active part, and in certain instances a leading part, in the maintenance of the American power structure. Politics increasingly becomes, in an American context, a formal science, while the politician is that person in possession of the keys of truth.

Anti-intellectualism in American life has taken on nuances that distinguish it from past forms of the "knowledge through experience" doctrine. Whereas in the last century to be anti-intellectual was to be anti-educational, this no longer holds. What is distinctly modern is the way in which education has been sundered from intellect. That is to say, mass education, even higher education, has been given an enormous impetus by those technological innovations which require more refined skills. But the professional and occupational emphasis of the educational plant leads not so much to the cultivated personality as it does to a higher philistinism.[62] The learning process becomes instrumental to economic goals. Knowledge itself becomes subservient to acquisitions. Money is its measure. Occupational choices, based as they are on high monetary compensation, become the goal of education, and in this way the liberal arts tradition is destroyed with more certainty than by any directly anti-intellectual assault. Instrumentalized education is perfectly in accord with bureaucratized labor. But any critique of the new educational style must still take into consideration its success with respect to the developmental process.

Recently much importance has been attached to where and how one is educated, and thus education has become not only a means of achievement but more recently a means for guaranteeing one's family's status. When education *per se* becomes less important than the education received, the divorce between intellect and practice is particularly no-

[62] For a detailed historical account see Richard Hofstadter, *Anti-Intellectualism in American Life*. New York: Alfred A. Knopf, 1963.

ticeable. And occupations of middling status become elevated when a college degree is required as a prerequisite. Even occupation and education lose their connection in the race for status. When the *raison d'être* for education is money or status, there is a tendency for an educational system to become crisis-ridden; the break-up of education along class lines between academic schools and trade training centers is itself symptomatic of a crisis.

Even with its current emphasis on non-working time, America still remains a productive society; and the definition of its wealth is hardly more Veblenesque now than it was at the turn of the century.[63] The wealth of America, while visible in terms of a search for status, is still measured in terms of economic productivity. The worth of the person is measured not in terms of leisure but in terms of his working capacity and productive skills. Although the rise of a technological order has changed relationships between labor and leisure, production and consumption, machine labor and manual labor, it only alters the mix, it does not alter the facts. The facts are plain enough. The measure of American worth in foreign eyes is its immense material wealth and its high degree of skilled labor, not the way in which non-working time is employed.

To speak of development in the United States in the twentieth century is to speak almost exclusively about technology; for the characteristic stamp of the First World is its technology. Standardization, automation, and a host of technological cultural influences, such as the tendency toward miniaturization and interchangeability of parts, are all innovative devices calculated to make work less severe and life easier. The processes involved in standardization are absolutely essential to development, since they allow for the richest production diversity with minimal confusion or retooling. At the same time, automation is, a long-range process in the United States. Factory assembly-line techniques have incorporated every possible device to liberate labor from the burdens of manual work and of course to liberate management from the burdens of labor even at the administrative level.

Standardization maximizes output and minimizes the labor necessary for it. It makes machine tools available for multiple uses and cheapens costs of repairs and replacements at the same time that the cost of

[63] See Eric Larrabee and Rolf Meyersohn (eds.), *Mass Leisure*. Glencoe, Ill.: The Free Press, 1958.

labor rises. It brings forward new machine goods to such a state of mass production as to make unnecessary and even burdensome repair work as such. Therefore the process of standardization bypasses the problem of obsolescence. Old goods in a modern United States are not so much obsolete as they are simply too expensive in contrast to new commodities. The same is true at the production level, where it is cheaper to buy new machinery than to maintain used machinery.

Automation cuts labor costs by cutting the time necessary to produce commodities, while at the same time it expands the energy output of machines. At least short-range planning is necessary with automation, for the level of productivity must be correlated with the level of consumption needs and the ability to pay for these goods and services.

Together standardization and automation lead to new types of laboring man and managerial man. The distinction between the technician and the professional tends to be minimized, since the processes they are engaged in tend to become like each other. These twin processes of the technological society have made possible the first consumer-oriented society in the world, the first society which consciously dedicates itself to solving the problems of consumption and takes for granted the solution of problems of production.

Technological processes also tend to transform men into instruments, commodities, or things which are themselves measured by the products they create, and thus give an "anti-human" and "pro-machine" quality to society. Human valuation may become converted from a human act into a technological fact. Thus a person may come to be defined in terms of an all-purpose computer, which is easy to produce but difficult to control.

The mechanical age has succeeded in displacing human labor power, but this displaced labor power has not developed into new creative channels. On the contrary, it has become fragmented, alienated, and deeply torn from the social fabric. At the least, displaced labor searches out new mechanized jobs. At worst such labor power falls into aggressive and anti-social forms of mental and social disorder.[64]

[64] Joseph Bensman and Bernard Rosenberg, "The Meaning of Work in Bureaucratic Society," in *Identity and Anxiety: Survival of the Person in Mass Society*, edited by Maurice R. Stein, Arthur J. Vidich and David M. White. New York: The Free Press of Glencoe, 1960, pp. 181-97.

In the light of this, it is little wonder that the American celebration has turned sour before it has begun. It is remarkable that in the light of United States development, criticism of it by others has been so restrained, so imbued with good will. Perhaps this is the ultimate cut. The rest of the world may still consider the United States an adolescent society rather than a developed nation. In this case the adolescent holds the ultimate possibility of life and death; therefore he must be humored as well as cajoled. Seen from this point of view the absence of criticism may not be so much an absence of resentment as a fear that we have not grown mature enough properly to absorb criticism without recourse to armed violence.

Little more than a decade ago, nothing seemed more important than knowing what the future of the United States would bring. There was a sense of urgency which derived from the central position of America in the world scheme of things. The kinds of questions posed by Commager in *The American Mind* seemed especially vital. The Americans "had created an economy of abundance; could they fashion a political mechanism to assure the equitable distribution of that abundance? They had become the richest people on the globe; would they use their wealth to prosper society or to display power? They were democratic in law; would they be democratic in fact? They were equalitarian by conviction; would they be equalitarian in conduct? They had developed technology to its highest point; would they learn to make technology their servant rather than their master?" And then there were yet the newer questions. The Americans "had made the atomic bomb; would they use it for purposes of civilization or of destruction? They had achieved such power as no other nation had ever known; would that passion for peace . . . triumph over the temptation to establish a Pax Americana by force?"[65]

Two observations deserve to be made on such typical (and rhetorical) remarks. One, that the answers remain as obscure as they were then. And this very fact indicates a certain stagnation in the American style, if not in the American soul. But more significant than the fact of stagnation is the implication that the answers to such questions lack the

[65] Henry Steele Commager, *The American Mind: An Interpretation of American Thought and Character Since the 1880's.* New Haven: Yale University Press, 1950, esp. pp. 442-3.

urgency they once possessed. This is because the United States lacks the urgency it once had. In its assumption of the leadership of the First World, it indicated its power; but a power over only a small sector of the universe. There remained the Second World of the Soviets, who noted how rapidly and readily development in the United States had come. And there came into being a Third World either indifferent or indignant about the American Century. It became apparent that the "dialogue" of Americans was more with themselves than with the rest of the world. Thus, it is less important whether these questions receive immediate answers than that the questions be placed in a universal context, which would recognize the ethnocentricism and even the parochialism of the questions themselves. When being an American ceases to be an all-consuming way of life and style of morality, then perhaps the United States can make a genuine contribution to international friendship and understanding.

Chapter 4

Third World Perceptions of the United States

The most meaningful aspect of present Third World perceptions about the United States is how radically they differ from the traditional positive sentiments which representatives of Asia, Africa, and Latin America have held toward it. The positive feelings were based neither on romantic adulation nor covert jealousy, but on hard fact. The United States came into being through an anti-colonial revolution. Because it had only this one revolution, it must continually make this solitary eighteenth-century revolution symbolically and realistically relevant to the present. Perhaps Nehru summed it up best when he pointed out that the birth of the United States was a consequence of the revolt against economic injustices and, secondarily, against the social consequences of these injustices. "The colonists did not begin fighting for the sake of independence. Their grievances were taxation and restrictions in trade." As a consequence of the revolution, independence became a rallying cry and a unifying idea among the colonies. "The United States republic was a new kind of country. It had no past as the countries of Europe and Asia had. It had no relics of feudalism except in the plantation system in the South. It had no hereditary nobility. The bourgeois or middle class had few obstacles to its growth and it grew rapidly."[1]

In addition to its anti-colonial origins, the United States had a traditional policy of non-involvement in the internal affairs of other nations. Of course, like any expanding power, the United States engaged in questionable forms of diplomacy—military, economic, and otherwise—

[1] Jawaharlal Nehru, *On World History*. Bloomington: Indiana University Press, 1962, pp. 69-70.

115

but in the main, until the end of the last century, the United States was not decisively involved in colonial occupations. Even the boldest critic would be hard pressed to demonstrate that its attitudes toward traditional feudalist empires in Japan and China were more than negative. Deep into the present century it supported revolutionary movements in China and later in India. And even the United States occupation of Japan in the post-World War Two period was marked by an anti-colonial effort to liquidate the remnants of a landed nobility and of the parasitical military caste. The United States sponsorship of land reform under the MacArthur period was typical of its "colonial policy" rather than exceptional.[2] Who ever heard of old-fashioned colonialists sponsoring, or even allowing, extensive land redistribution?

Historically, the situation in Latin America has been less decisive. United States policy, clearly under the constraint of the "spheres of influence" doctrines made current in Europe by Prince Metternich and in America by President Monroe, tended to adopt colonial attitudes and economic imperialism much more rapidly and decisively in the Western Hemisphere than elsewhere.[3] If some doubts were raised about the "one nation above all others" and "manifest destiny" policy with respect to Europe and Asia, only the boldest or the blindest were prepared to deny that in the Western Hemisphere such slogans were in fact realities. But even here the character of American intervention was much more circumspect and more concerned with the maintenance of certain formal legal norms than was European colonization in Africa and in Asia. If Grover Cleveland was prepared to defend hemispheric colonialism, others like William Jennings Bryan were prepared to attack such colonialism. Republican forms of government were encouraged; economic self-sufficiency was put forward as a slogan; independent foreign policy was encouraged as long as such policy did not impinge directly on United States financial or political interests.[4] In short, the American

[2] Wolf Ladejinsky, *Farm Democracy in Japan*. Tokyo: Preliminary Report, The General Headquarters, Supreme Commander for the Allied Powers, Natural Resources Section, Report No. 79, 1947.
[3] For an exceptional historical study of "Bolivarism" and "Monroeism," see Antonio Gómez Robledo, *Idea y Experiencia de América*. Mexico-Buenos Aires: Fondo de Cultura Económica, 1958.
[4] For a useful collection of documents and readings see Louis L. Snyder, *The Imperialism Reader*. New York: D. Van Nostrand Co., 1962, esp. pp. 385-413.

style of colonialism was republican in form and financial in substance, whereas the European style was Caesarist in form and military in substance.

Of all the great powers in the capitalistic era, the United States alone could lay claim to an anti-colonial, or at least a non-colonial, diplomatic and political tradition. In contrast, the British, however humane and administratively innovative their imperialist policy, never ceased to operate within the fictional framework of a "white man's burden" and hence they treated the nation they colonized as an outright possession or inferior entity.

While attempts have been made to prove that American colonialism became rigidified at the same time the Civil War gains of the North were consolidated, the actual involvements of the United States in international power relations were far too few at this early stage to warrant much attention. The Europeans did not welcome, and the Americans did not understand, their new power. It is only in consequence of the two world wars that the United States became cosmopolitan. Given the huge benefits the United States business and military establishments derived from two world wars, it is significant that the American nation even at this stage is still reluctant to enter "international power politics." There remains within the nation a profound inability to accommodate itself to conventional standards of colonial behavior or belief.

The terms by which the Third World views and describes the United States derive precisely from the nation's ambiguous legacy. Third World identification with the origins of the American Revolution contrasts markedly with its rejection of the present conduct of American nationalism. The Third World offers a wide angle for viewing the First World. This in turn provides a looking-glass effect, a way of viewing the Third World by seeing what it objects to in the United States. Even now, twenty years after World War Two, attitudes toward the United States are far from crystallized. The United States has rarely practiced outright ownership or prolonged occupation of colonial lands. The absence of such oppressor-oppressed contact makes the United States a special case in the developed world.

The Third World has increasingly come to view both the United States and the Soviet Union as some sort of "generalized other." There is a declining sense of distinction between developed sectors of the enemy. Backgrounds and traditions will coat attitudes—for instance, the ideological similarities between India and the United States or between Yugoslavia and the Soviet Union—but the sense of the developed *versus* the developing increases. Sekou Touré expressed this sentiment very clearly: "It is not Africa which should be asked whether it belongs to one camp or another. It is rather to the two camps, to the European as to the Western, that we must put the question we consider fundamental: yes or no, are you for the liberation of Africa? The answer to this question will determine the attitudes of Africa *vis-à-vis* the existing systems."[5] The developing regions are therefore not so much interested in criticizing or attacking the United States as they are in distinguishing themselves from the developed world in general. The United States has failed to appreciate this fact, and instead has taken every critique made of capitalism or of parliamentarianism to be an assault on the behavior of Americans, a personal and direct assault on the American Way. Since the Soviets have not made this mistake, it *appears* that the Third World is identified in aims with the Second World.

As a matter of record, there are few policy-launched attacks emanating from the Third World against the United States. An exhaustive survey of the literature will turn up a wide spectrum of sentiments about the United States but (outside of China and Cuba) very little in the way of open condemnation. As a general rule, there is an inverse correlation, strangely enough, between the weakness of a participant nation in the Third World and the strength of its condemnations of the United States. Thus one finds the most powerful and forthright criticisms of United States policy emanating from Latin America; and the most cautious and reserved statements emanating from Africa. One explanation for this difference is that in Africa anti-American statements are modified because the rulers themselves speak for the official position of the entire nation, while in Latin America such statements often come from those out of power. In addition, of course, the United States does have a colonial "tradition" in regard to Latin America.

Instead of showing militant anti-Americanism, African leaders such as Robert Sobukwe of South Africa and the late Patrice Lumumba of

---

[5] Sekou Touré, "Africa's Destiny," quoted in Charles F. Andrain, "Democracy and Socialism," in *Ideology and Discontent*, edited by David E. Apter. New York: The Free Press of Glencoe, 1964, p. 194.

the Congo have advocated a United States of Africa.[6] While the merits of the phrase as well as its actual meanings have often been debated, it demonstrates an obvious respect of the achievements of the American federated union and, also, a symbolic recognition of the United States' opposition to *apartheid* and Congolese separatism.[7]

The Third World is not so much hostile to the United States as it is disenchanted with it. The disenchantment has come from high expectations; it is not the kind of resentment reserved for implacable enemies. The Third World was irritated during the years when the United States equated neutralism with betrayal and treated neutrals as surreptitious enemies. A recent symposium on *The Dynamics of Neutralism in the Arab World* makes this point. Friendly Egyptian-Western relations were greatly harmed by American policy during the first two years of the Eisenhower administration. The United States aroused Afro-Asian as well as Arab resentment by demanding their participation in American-sponsored Cold War pacts. The passionate "pactomania" ascribed to Dulles was as irritating to proud and pressure-sensitive new nations as was its corollary, "neutrophobia." The latter dashed the cherished hopes of the Third World for speedy economic development, for the United States, acting on the belief that "he who is not with me is against me" and treating neutrality as immoral, translated this into the maxim "I am against those who are not with me," which meant in practical economic and political terms that there were no military pacts or economic assistance available to neutralist nations.[8]

Non-alignment has become a cornerstone not only of Third World policy but of a great many advanced industrial nations as well. Thus, a leader of the European Economic Community has noted that "the road for real completion of national independence is the road of non-alignment, of non-polarization."[9] For the African nations, non-alignment does not imply a passive neutralism, but rather the active pursuit of inter-

[6] See on this Rolf Italiaander, *The New Leaders of Africa*. Englewood Cliffs, N.J.: Prentice-Hall, Inc., 1961, esp. pp. 121-2, 155, 209-10.
[7] See Pierre L. van den Berghe, *South Africa: A Study in Conflict*. Middletown: Wesleyan University Press, 1965, pp. 257-62.
[8] Fayez A. Sayegh, *The Dynamics of Neutralism in the Arab World*. San Francisco: Chandler Publishing Company, 1964, pp. 194-5.
[9] Vassos Lyssarides, "Socialism, Non-Alignment and Under-Developed Countries," *Voice of Africa*, Vol. 4, No. 2, February 1964, pp. 15-16.

tional peace through the mediation of the claims of the big powers. "Our foreign policy has never been one of neutrality, but rather non-alignment. We have never, for instance, been neutral in African affairs, nor can we be neutral in matters pertaining to world peace."[10]

The United States has been reluctant to see that the alternative to non-alignment is not alignment with the West but a perennial anti-colonial crusade under the auspices of mainland China. To understand the attitude of the Third World one does not start with the peculiarities of individual nations. Nations of the Third World behave as nations generally do, in terms of their self-interest and general area-wide interests. It is inevitable that these will from time to time conflict with the interests of the United States, a fact which should be viewed as a normal part of international relations. In addition, this conflict of interests does not necessarily have to spill over into a conflict of values, which is to say that American values can be held in very high esteem and most often are, without making it necessary for them to support a free-enterprise economy. And, conversely, the conflict of interests does not necessarily raise the specter of long term animosity. This said, let us now turn to the spectrum of sentiments expressed in the Third World about the United States.

Basic to the Third World "profile" of United States shortcomings is its economic policies, and the effects of such policies in weakening the process of development by draining the poor nations of their already limited capital. The main lines of criticism made by Third World leaders about the conduct of the United States can be summarized as follows:

(1) Under various forms and in various degrees, the United States maintains, by the selective manipulation of the international economy, various kinds of military, political, and cultural privileges which encroach upon the sovereignty and independence of Third World countries. (2) Although Third World industries are nominally free, American business firms often control the major branches of production and technology, which means they can influence the political structure and the internal social life of each nation. (3) The United States controls the international trade market and, not the least significant, the money market.

[10] Abubakar Tafawa Belewa, "Nigeria Looks Ahead," *Foreign Affairs*, Vol. XLI, No. 4, October 1962, pp. 19-39.

In this way it manipulates world prices and arbitrarily lowers the values of primary products or the kinds of products manufactured in the Third World. With equal arbitrariness it manipulates the prices of finished manufactured goods, thus creating a constant drainage on the developing nation. (4) The United States is able to raise interest charges at will; and even when it does not do so, its credit position provides it with a constant economic edge, since, given the unequal starting point of the Third World, its member nations can barely repay the interest, let alone the principal on loans issued. (5) The United States controls and monopolizes a considerable portion of the communications and transportation industries and by so doing controls a good deal of what can and cannot be traded and between whom. For example, it uses its maritime shipping as a political weapon against opponents.

These charges against United States *economic policies* do not in any way imply criticism of its *value system*. Nor is there any negative reaction to its social system. The political literature of the Third World shows that there are more pointed criticisms directed against the social system of the Soviet Union than of the United States. What preserves the Soviet Union from even more damaging criticism is precisely its positive economic policy toward and political identification with the Third World.

The United States is repeatedly called the most developed nation in the world. From the technological point of view, it holds up the future to the rest of the world. With the exception of a relatively small but articulate group of European intellectuals, with whom a relatively small and articulate group of Third World intellectuals identify, there is little criticism of United States technological achievements, either at the production or at the consumer level. Similarly, the Soviet Union tends to be viewed as that society which has best resolved the question of economic organization. This is so, if for no other reason than it is a society based on planning. At the same time the Soviet Union has the moral advantage of having introduced a non-competitive economy. But this initial advantage has been largely liquidated by the political repressions of the Stalin era. Interestingly, there is far sharper criticism in certain sections, particularly in Africa, of the Soviet achievement than of the American achievement. This in part is due to the acceptability of criticism of a political system and the relative inaccessibility of a technological system to the same sort of criticism. It also reflects the extent to which the many and varied definitions of African socialism are made with an eye toward distinguishing socialism from Soviet Communism no less than from American capitalism. Men like Tom Mboya say so openly; others like Julius Nyerere only whisper this truth.

There is a constant din of intellectual activity in the Third World concerning folk values, regional conditions, and national cultures. Oftentimes the concepts of Negritude, Moslemism, and regionalism represent a disguised fear of the impact of both the United States and the Soviet Union on the traditionalistic aspects of Third World cultures. For example, in many areas where there has been a successful liberation movement, traditionalism seriously retards the developmental process. In India it is the caste system and Hinduism as an economic philosophy. In Tunisia it is the Moslem culture. In many of these instances there is a tendency to revert to a type of theocratic state, or tribal social order, similar to what existed before the European conquest began. Thus the form of anti-colonialism can be reactionary insofar as it views liberation as a return to a pristine pre-conquest era.[11] But reactionary anti-colonialism does not represent a direct assault upon the United States so much as an attempt to prevent the more militant marginal sectors, such as the radicalized military and the socialist intelligentsia, from taking complete charge of the developmental process. In other words, anti-Americanism can have a backward content, and is not always illustrative of the revolutionary sectors.

The three parts of the Third World react differently to United States involvement in their affairs. For Latin America the main fears tend to be economic encroachment; in Africa, political encroachment; in Asia, direct military encroachment. Each form of United States involvement produces profound negative sentiments throughout the Third World. The character of the criticisms tends to be slightly different, depending on the nation's stage of development, the historical relationship between a particular nation and the United States, and whether the nation is within the United States sphere of influence.

Latin America represents the most economically advanced sector of the Third World. It has the highest per capita earnings, the most de-

[11] See on this section, Gilles Martinet, *Marxism of Our Time: Or the Contradictions of Socialism*. New York: Monthly Review Press, 1964, esp. pp. 84-108.

veloped industrial complex, and the best trade balance. Therefore one expects and does find a reaction toward United States economic impingements. It is only when an area begins the long developmental process that it can afford to become competitive. Africa, which for the most part remains economically a raw material depot and not much else, boasts the highest degree of political stability in the Third World. It has achieved this high degree of cohesion and consensus on a continent-wide basis, as well as within each nation, by appeals to ethnicity and racial unity even more than to economy. It has therefore achieved an independence and a maneuverability with respect to both the United States and the Soviet Union that is absent either in Asia or in Latin America.[12] It would be expected, and is indeed the case, that criticism here is directed against the political impediments and restrictions imposed by the United States. Asia, for its part, represents the greatest land mass with the greatest economic independence from the Western Powers. It is the section of the Third World which has been in a constant state of military struggle since the beginning of World War Two. And it is here that one finds the engagement of the Third World with the United States to have assumed a direct and prolonged military form. In the light of the constant stress in Southeast Asia, what is impressive is not so much the extent of local wars, but the fact that they are still local; a significant tribute to the operations of the non-alignment doctrine. Nonetheless, it is apparent that in the Asian sector of the Third World the United States as a military threat is the central and decisive factor.

From what has been said it is clear that the attitude of the Third World as a whole and in its parts toward the United States is richly textured and widely varied. Nothing could possibly be more dangerous than to flatten out the Third World and imply a uniformly implacable hostility. But in the absence of significant distinctions and refinements on the part of United States foreign policy between various forms of Communism, between various types of economic mixes, between one-party states which encompass and engage opposition within their structure and multi-party states that may really be more autocratic than a one

[12] See on this Alex Quaison-Sackey, *Africa Unbound: Reflections of an African Statesman.* New York: Frederick Praeger, 1963; and Leopold Senghor, *African Socialism.* New York: Frederick Praeger, 1959.

party system, and ultimately between neutrality pertaining to matters of world peace and non-alignment pertaining to economic-power blocs, we may expect a continued increase in anti-Americanism as a surrogate for anti-colonialism.

Perhaps the most important single step which the United States can now pursue is to make a simple recognition of the historic importance of the Third World. Even a complete and thoroughgoing settlement of all outstanding issues between the United States and the Soviet Union would do very little to reduce the problems with which the Third World confronts the developed world. As Sukarno has recently pointed out in no uncertain terms, from the Third World point of view, the Soviet Union "has established a status quo with imperialism in following a policy of peaceful coexistence." Speaking of his own country, Sukarno notes that Indonesia "does not believe in peaceful coexistence between the oppressed and colonial countries."[13] It has become one of the fundamental schemes within the Third World to base a policy either on anti-imperialism, what has come to be known as the "Chinese position," or on peaceful coexistence, which has come to be known as the "Soviet position." The great irony of the situation is that the United States somehow seems to be left out of the reckoning. There is no "American position" in the same sense. This is another way of saying that the United States has not thus far provided strategies and tactics with which the member nations of the Third World can identify.

As a result of World War Two, the United States sought to provide maximum leadership to the emerging nations—as indeed it did in relation to India—but as a result of its obsessive return to European politics, it forfeited its opportunity. The only real question seems to be whether the Soviet Union or China, each representative of variations upon classical socialist tactics, is best suited as a model to be emulated. The Soviet Union is moving rapidly to build an image of itself as an Asian nation. Not only is two-thirds of its land mass in Asia, but its political, economic, and military aid, however tentative and halting when made, has been on the side of revolutionary factions.

Thus, even the forces of "conservatism" in Asia and in Africa are

[13] Associated Press Wire Service, June 16, 1965. The attempted *coup d'état* which took place late in 1965 apparently has not dulled Sukarno's militant formulas, since many similar statements were made after the *coup*.

more likely to be demonstrating support for Soviet foreign policy than for the United States.[14] The United States has avoided the implications of the Sino-Soviet rift, not because, as its official spokesmen declare, it does not want to upset the course of that rift, but because it is unable and unwilling to make a real dent in the socialist bloc by a positive policy of support for the economic phase of revolution in the Third World. The United States has recognized the distinction between nationalism and Communism when such recognition was clearly a disadvantage to the Soviet Union—as in the case of such eastern European nations as Poland and Hungary. But the same distinction has not been made for the emerging nations because the United States would then be placing at a disadvantage its own large foreign investors. This diplomatic appreciation of the difference between the needs of the American nation and the needs of private commerce has not yet registered. Until the United States puts its own interests ahead of the protection of private American business overseas, the Third World will remain suspicious that the First New Nation seeks to establish a claim to being the Only New Nation.

[14] The extraordinary diplomatic tug-of-war within the Afro-Asian bloc about whether to consider the Soviets as part of its conference structure is indicative of the growing split between the Chinese and Russian "factions" within the Third World—but it shows little tendency to adopt a posture of pro-Americanism or free-enterprise philosophy.

Chapter 5

The Second World of Soviet Development

I

The development of the Soviet Union holds a certain fascination for the Third World which no amount of dismay at Communist political patterns can quite deter. First, the Soviet Union represents a civilization which became powerful in the twentieth century. Second, the Soviet Union withstood the challenges of foreign aggressors and emerged from a condition of "encirclement" as a world military power second to none and equal to any. Third, the Soviet Union demonstrated that social and state planning, whatever their political deformities and technical deficiencies, can create full economic mobilization and complete integration of a society. Fourth, the Soviet Union demonstrated that historical "stage skipping" is not only possible but necessary. This last point, since it contradicts some basic ideological tenets of Marxism, is often underplayed by the Soviets themselves. Nonetheless, it is in keeping with the idea that through mastery of the environment men can tame history. Planning and socialization, when joined to urbanization and industrialization, reveal the extent to which the processes of development can be consciously manipulated. This is precisely what the elites of the Third World are searching for. And this is in marked contrast to the pragmatic daring of the development process in the United States.

The Marxist theory of class struggle tends to be forgotten in these circumstances. Marxism becomes a theory of national liberation from foreign exploitation, instead of an ideology or social science technique for the liberation of masses from ruling classes. The Soviets have themselves encouraged this construction. Increasingly, the Soviet elite has at least admitted the fact that social distinctions exist inside Russia. Through the *ad hoc* notion of compatible classes, Soviet officials, by sending business and managerial personnel all over the Third World to elicit support and negotiate trade agreements with their business and professional elites, have created an appeal to the Third World across class "barriers"—although this technical appeal is seriously restricted by the fear that Soviet wealth is compromising Soviet policy. Thus the very "realism" of present Soviet policy may create suspicion as well as admiration.

The most obvious fact about the Soviet Union is at the same time the most impressive. In less than a half century, Russia has gone from a backward peasant economy based on rural life-styles to the second largest industrial complex in the world. The present Soviet output of pig-iron, steel, coal, and oil are roughly 80 per cent of United States production figures.[1] But given the relatively slight concentration of consumer goods, the gap between United States and Soviet productivity is less than the statistics reveal, since this basic production impetus translates itself in heavy machinery, armaments, and other goods which are vital from a perspective of national power. The development of a military machine capable of enormous offensive action, no less than a defensive series of actions, should not be undervalued.[2] As has recently been noted, "as a country considerably less powerful than the USA, the USSR is generally satisfied with less complex apparatus and equipment than the USA and is more inclined to concentrate on relatively few projects, whereas the USA can afford to invest in a great diversity of programmes. All this points to a somewhat less expensive Soviet military and space research and development programme, although the great progress made by the USSR suggests that the difference cannot be enormous."[3]

[1] Cf. Henry J. Bruton, "Contemporary Theorizing on Economic Growth," in *Theories of Economic Growth*, edited by Bert F. Hoselitz. New York: Free Press of Glencoe, 1960, pp. 239-94.

[2] I have eliminated charts and tables from this chapter, since statistical information is available in great abundance about the Soviet Union. Further, a recent paper of mine contains what I believe to be the essential information about present-day Russian industrialization and urbanization. See Irving L. Horowitz, "The Political Sociology of Soviet Development," *Il Político*, Vol. XXIX, No. 1, 1964, pp. 28-47.

[3] David Ingram, *The Communist Economic Challenge*. New York: Frederick Praeger, 1965, p. 163.

Like many nations of the Third World, the Soviet Union has been subject to considerable foreign intervention and invasion. And the size of the military establishment represents an extremely considerable factor in Third World nation evaluations of the Soviet system. At the same time, the Soviet Union has transformed an essentially rural society into a "citified" one. And because of the productive (rather than consumption) pattern, it has done so with a minimum of economic drainage, such as high-priced automotive production, expensive televisions, and status buildings. Nor is this urbanization process a simple consequence of a population boom. The Soviet Union has maintained a large but well balanced population (tragically, this is in part the consequence of twenty million casualties in World War Two). Industrialization, military strength, and urbanization are the magic words for the Third World, and represent the achievement of the Second World.

The Bolshevik Revolution was the first occasion in history when a society consciously dedicated itself toward the realization of an ideal model of social change, namely, the Marxist model. True enough, this model was designated a scientific plan. But for our purposes, whether Marxism represents an ideology or a science, or some combination of both, is irrelevant to the overriding significance of a society dedicated to the realization of a blueprint blanketing all *social* sectors.[4]

In previous revolutions the connection between the pre-revolutionary ideological build-up and the actual course of revolution were, at best, tenuous. In discussing the relationship between the French Enlightenment and the French Revolution, for instance, one must carefully distinguish ideological stimulants to the Revolution itself from the *ad hoc* manufacture of a pre-revolutionary tradition after the fact of revolution. Let us turn, therefore, to Marx's discussion of the nature of past social development. Essentially, he uses the dialectic as a method somewhat akin to a bookkeeper's balance sheet. Every social system Marx describes has positive and negative factors. The ultimate positive factor in each social system is that it gives rise to "its other" or to some other form of social existence potentially more advanced than itself. Even within each

---

[4] Cf. Lewis S. Coser, "Prospects for the New Nation," *Dissent*, Vol. X, No. 1, pp. 43-58. See also Kalman H. Silvert, "Peace, Freedom and Stability in the Western Hemisphere," paper read at Georgetown University Colloquium on Latin America, June 1962 (mimeo).

social system, Marx adapts a "trial-balance" approach to history. Feudalism may have been an evil in terms of the increased misery of the masses and in the formalization of the gap between servant classes and noble classes; however Marx recognizes in feudalism an advance over slavery, an advance in social relations. Such advances are measurable insofar as they match up with advances achieved in the techniques of production. As feudalism evolves, it produces a multiplication of economic classes, the development of a system of rights and obligations which, however uneven, is at least mutually shared and reciprocally understood. Capitalism resolves this fragmented condition by producing two great class contenders for power—capitalists and proletarians. It is a system which introduces mass industrial innovation, which substitutes secular for theological values, which moves the people from rural to urban life-styles, and makes possible for the first time abundance and affluence which hold out the promise of freedom, if not always its actual realization. As with feudalism, capitalism is said to have its negative aspects. This system estranges men from the source of creativity and alienates labor from the values embodied in productivity. Capitalism is a system which indicates how the tower of massive wealth no less than the abyss of poverty can be reached. It is a system which intensifies both strife between social classes and achievement by human beings. Thus, capitalism for Marx is the ultimate dehumanization of man, precisely because the distance between humanity and inhumanity is never so plain as it is under the modern, privately operated industrial factory system. It is Marx's unique contribution that he saw the process of social change emanating from "below" rather than instigated from "above."

It might be thought that with the "leveling tendencies" set in motion by Keynesian economics, the force of Marx's argument would be considerably diminished, particularly for Third World countries in a pre-industrial condition. But this is not what takes place. Instead, while the class struggle between the emergent nations and established imperial powers tends to become sharper, it will be "internationalized," becoming a conflict between "have" and "have not" nations. As a matter of fact, there is substantive support for this. According to a United Nations report, the gap between the rich and poor nations is steadily widening. From 1950 to 1960 the poor nations had the slowest growth rate and the rich ones showed moderate growth. Middle-income nations had the fastest growth—and this is a fact easily overlooked. The per capita annual increase in the gross national product is 1.3 per cent for India and 0.4 per cent for Pakistan. Latin American nations such as Ecuador and Colombia show a parallel low growth rate of between 1.0 per cent and 1.6 per cent. To this must be contrasted the growth rates of Japan with 7.2 per cent and West Germany with 6.1 per cent. More damaging still is the fact that 87.1 per cent of the world's total population has an annual income of $700 or less, with 64.5 per cent of these earning less than $200.[5] It may well be theoretically improper to transfer Marx's concept of class struggle to the international arena. However, what we should note is that the practical consequences of perceiving an uneven distribution of poverty has been an unrelenting search for radical means to eradicate it.

When we turn to Marx's description of socialism, this dialectical bookkeeping procedure breaks down. There is no longer an analysis of the cost of socialism, of negative factors in development once political power is transferred to representatives of the working class, or of the possibilities of socialist exploitation of peasant economies. Analysis turns into rhetoric, and the language of distant ideal refutes that of dialectics. No longer is there stocktaking of real material costs, new social problems, but only the movements of men from the realm of necessity (which is the realm of economic determinism) to the realm of freedom (which is the realm of political indeterminism). In essence, socialism is made synonymous with the good life. In consequence of this, Marx's analysis is no longer balanced in the same way. As equality replaces stratification, science gives way to a longing after paradise. There is a substitution of a moral goal in place of scientific law. Socialism is not subject to the iron laws of economic evolution the way all previous social systems are said to have been. The justification for the breakdown of these iron laws is that freedom itself replaces necessity as social ownership of production replaces private ownership.[6] But while Marxism offered few guidelines on how to plan an industrial empire, this in itself had a liberating effect in a Russian context.

[5] The New York Times, Sunday, April 21, 1963. On this whole problem of the "widening gap," see Raúl Prebisch, Nueva Política Comercial para el Desarrollo. Mexico-Buenos Aires: Fondo de Cultura Económica, 1964, esp. pp. 125-43.
[6] Ralf Dahrendorf, Class and Class Conflict in Industrial Society. Stanford: Stanford University Press, 1959, Chapter 1.

The attraction of the Russian Revolution for the Third World is heightened by the fact that it occurred under economically backward conditions. This attraction is most forceful where development is increasingly difficult due to the existence of a highly developed and competitive industrial capitalist social system in the West. Societies such as England, France, and especially the United States developed under conditions of unimpeded change. There were few interference mechanisms, few factors to upset the historical timetable. The Western nations, in their formative years, did not have to cope with powerful colonial empires, with communication and transportation facilities which make or break revolutions, or with large-scale counter-insurgency and para-military operations.

The development of Russia more nearly approximates the obstacles faced by developing areas in the modern world. Here, too, was a backward nation with an uneducated, illiterate peasantry. Here, too, there was an imbalance between the agricultural and the industrial sectors. And here, too, there was a heavy investment of foreign capital in those areas which, prior to the revolutionary buildup, had already been subject to some degree of industrialization. Hence, it should occasion little wonder that the developing areas of the Third World would be magnetized—perhaps even hypnotized—by the Soviet model.

What we should note is that, contrary to those economic diagnoses concerning the advantage of those who come last in the developmental race,[7] the Soviet Union's model for development is important for precisely the reverse reasons. There are, in fact, powerful economic and sociological disadvantages for those who develop last. For example, the conception of development in the United States and in England comes attached to the revolution of political liberties and the rise of humane industrial relations. In the older European civilizations there is no contradiction or conflict between political liberties and economic growth.

The first full-scale model of development through planning came

---

[7] This refers to the avoidance of reduplicating historical forms of development. For example, in transportation the move from horse and buggy to jet airliners is direct. Ostensibly, the Third World nations do not have to cope with each intermediary stage of problems in transportation. This was anticipated in the Russian Marxist literature by Trotsky's "law of uneven and combined development." See Leon Trotsky, *The History of the Russian Revolution*. New York: Simon and Schuster, 1932, pp. 264-8.

out of a supposedly "non-Western" area. The specific geo-political conditions which backward Russia had to confront proved to be magnetic. This magnetism stems from a belief in the Third World that Russia faced and resolved first, the problem of foreign occupation; second, the problem of internal colonialism; and third, the relationship between rural and urban working sectors. The structural similarities of Russia to the underdeveloped areas of today cannot be dismissed by making loose statements about political freedom and political liberties. Soviet attempts to break feudal relations by means of peasant mobilization and land appropriation provide the impetus for rapid development in the Third World. The Soviet Revolution was unique, not because of its adherence to principles of socialist economics, which were well known and which to some small degree had been put into practice in various parts of Western Europe, but rather because the Russian Revolution combined well-defined ideological goals with a political machinery which could help achieve these goals.[8] If the American Revolution can be described as pragmatic, forging its theory in the crucible of the revolutionary action itself, the Soviet Revolution has to be described in highly rationalistic terms. Both in its origins and its present-day status, the Soviet Revolution is compelled to justify even its changes in terms of an ideal typification, an ideal model brought forth a hundred years ago in Marx's theory.

It must be understood, but rarely is, that Marxism in a Russian context does not so much represent an economic as a political determinism.[9] The ideology derives its power and its strength not from the economics of social equality but from the politics of mass movements. The limits of Marxian theory include a description of the forms of making a successful revolution, the means for mobilizing publics in the capture of state power, and the kind of political structure (euphemistically called dictatorship of the proletariat) which is necessary for the solidification of government power. In its political and social planning aspects, Marxism can be described as a rational action system of society, and not simply a

[8] See S. Swianiewicz, *Forced Labour and Economic Development: An Enquiry into the Experience of Soviet Industrialization.* New York and London: Oxford University Press, 1965, esp. pp. 208-35.
[9] Cf. Stanley W. Moore, *The Critique of Capitalist Democracy.* New York: Paine-Whitman Publishers, 1957.

theory of economic growth. It is a science of the seizure of power, or, rather, a science of political relations. The justification of Marxism is that the chief goal of socialist revolution—human liberation from the class system—is at the very outset separated from the political instruments for achieving this democratic end. But Marxism as Leninist practice provides a series of contradictory propositions for reaching the free society. It uses a theory of dictatorship to arrive at practical freedom, a theory of political coercion to justify an historical withering away of the state, and a theory of mass affluence to be brought about by an organization of select political elites headed by a "vanguard" party.

It was inevitable that the socialist tradition would cleave. Those who called for a socialist revolution prior to settlement of anticipated negative consequences and those who insisted on settling the purposes of a revolution before engaging in any actions, which could have unanticipated negative effects, were inevitably pitted against each other. The ideological controversies *between Communism and socialism*, between the ideologies of the first and second internationals, thus form the essential background of contemporary discussions on development. Actually, there is no such thing as "plain Marxism" because Marxism is ambivalent about socialism as a form of freedom and socialism as a form of control.[10]

II

The economic history of the Soviet Union provides ample verification that Marxism contains the incompatibilities of social democracy and social authoritarianism. The Civil War period temporarily delayed consideration of internal problems of development. Revolutionary euphoria and party slogans carried the government a long way. But underneath the superficial activities of the Communist Party, the Red Army, and the

---

[10] The inability of C. Wright Mills to see that the problem of Marxism inheres in its ambivalence permits him to set up a trichotomous distinction between Social Democracy, Bolshevism, and Plain Marxism. In point of fact, what Mills describes as Plain Marxism is precisely the kind of pragmatic makeshift view of life that was alien to the spirit of both the founders of Marxism and its Russian and German advocates. Cf. C. Wright Mills, *The Marxists*. New York: Dell Publishing Co., 1962.

Council of Soviets, the broad outlines of economic crisis were looming. As one observer reported: " 'War Communism' could be defined as follows: firstly, requisitioning in the countryside; secondly, strict rationing for the town population, who were classified into categories; thirdly, complete 'socialization' of production and labor; fourthly, an extremely complicated and chit-ridden system of distribution for the remaining stocks of manufactured goods; fifthly, a monopoly of power tending toward the single Party and the suppression of all dissent; sixthly, a state of siege, and the Cheka."[11] But once "war Communism" ended, and problems of the succession to Bolshevik leadership came to the forefront, an open schism between social democratic factions and social authoritarian factions emerged.

The Social Democrats could properly argue that the Russian Revolution was rapidly becoming an aberration; that Marx would never have called for a revolution merely for the sake of a change of rulers; that he would never have offered intellectual sanction to a revolution made in the name of humanity that required so much sacrifice and so little possibility of the political realization of popular liberties. On the other hand, the Bolsheviks could argue, just as righteously, that everything about the later Marx was geared to the seizure of power and the mobilization of the population. The long-range liberation of men was held to be subordinate to the necessary tasks of forging a socialist society and a political party which would be responsive to this new society. Thus to jeopardize the *Russian* Revolution on behalf of an abstract principle of *Socialist* Revolution was held to be an irresponsible form of nihilism.

The codification of socialism under Stalin was bought dearly—by bureaucratizing politics. At the ideological level Stalin represents an end to the Russian Marxist dialogue. The first socialist nation entered the developmental race with a coherent and unified ideology and proceeded to settle intellectual issues by policy edicts. But this coherence rapidly degenerated into intellectual rigidity. Thus codification of Soviet ideology under Stalin resulted in serious confusion over the role of the Party in the life of the nation, and serious setbacks in the actual performance of the society. Giganticism in engineering, falsified statistics in industry,

[11] Victor Serge, *Memoirs of a Revolutionary, 1901-1941* (translated and edited by Peter Sedgwick). London and New York: Oxford University Press, 1963, p. 117.

careerism in the bureaucracy—all accentuated the fact that the "new Soviet Man" was much like the "old Russian Peasant."[12]

The Soviet assertion and insistence on the monolithic appearance of socialist politics, particularly as this developed under Stalin, was a response to the absence of genuine theory, an inability to make useful generalizations concerning strategies for social development. The bitterness of early policy strife within the Soviet leadership, as well as the continued, agonizing ideological discussions within Soviet rank-and-file Communist Party members throughout the 'twenties, indicated powerfully that "plain Marxism" was nowhere to be found inside the Soviet hierarchy. As a matter of fact, the choice had to be made between two types of Marxism, one humanistic but without power, the other authoritarian and with great power. Indeed, the leadership oftentimes made decisions which weighed both strains of Marxism in different historical periods. The Soviet Revolution announced the liberation of women from marital bondage, but twenty years after the revolution (by 1936) the Soviet Union became the most difficult country in the world in which to get a divorce, with the possible exception of Ireland. Marriage, which Marx called a form of legal prostitution, became sacrosanct in the Soviet kinship system. In every aspect of cultural activity, the same pattern reveals itself, a task of social development irrespective of social costs; and without considering the positive consequences of developing "social deviance."

The positive results of the bending of all portions of Russian society toward a common goal are not to be minimized. It resulted in Russia's rapid industrialization. It compelled the Russian peasant to abandon his small primitive holdings and set up collective farms. It ruthlessly tore primeval plowshares from the hands of the peasant and forced him to come to terms with the modern tractor. It transformed a society of illiterates into a society with bulging schoolrooms. It compelled adults to enter technological and industrial plants where for the first time reading and writing were essential. It made the factory a learning experience, and brought science to factory management. The "hardness" of government rested on the malleability and plasticity of human nature.

[12] See Herbert Marcuse, *Soviet Marxism: A Critical Analysis.* New York: Columbia University Press, 1958.

The rewards of the Soviet Revolution were astonishing. It succeeded in transforming a rural society, in which peasant masses and other social classes were clearly rent, into an industrial society, in which all sectors were linked through the instrument of planning. Part of this reorientation involved the partial detachment of Russia from Europe. This detachment did not rest exclusively on the confiscation of the business holdings of European capitalists, but was also a spiritual detachment from political agencies and institutions of European democracy. As Isaac Deutscher indicated, this political detachment was not at all inherent in the early program of Bolshevism. The idea of a multi-party system was readily assumed.[13] But there was enough evidence in the history of Marxist ideas and in the conduct of Western socialism to offer precedence for both economic confiscation and political totalitarianism.

The disputes and disagreements among early leadership of the Russian Communist Party convey the impression of men amazed rather than aware of having actually concluded a successful revolution. That they were little conscious of just how unique and rocky an enterprise the Russian Revolution represented is reflected in their obsession with ideology and their lack of concern about empirical necessities.[14] Even after the Revolution and the conclusion of the Civil War period, its leaders spoke in terms of compromise and conciliation. Lenin, speaking on February 2, 1920, before the All Union Executive Committee of the Communist Party of Russia, addressed himself to the Social Democrats. He pointed out that terror was perhaps a necessary part of the victory over the foreign enemies of Russia who were occupying its soil during the period of revolutionary ferment. But he declared that, with the simultaneous achievement of three aims—the victory over the foreign enemy, the successful completion of the capture of state power, and the mobilization of the basic elements in the productive apparatus—terrorism was no longer necessary.[15] As a matter of fact, from Lenin's point of view, terrorism was not compatible with the needs of the country. He encouraged open

[13] Isaac Deutscher, *Stalin: A Political Biography*. New York: Vintage Books-Random House, 1960, pp. 224-5.
[14] This is the distinct impression left by the most knowing observers. See, for instance, E. H. Carr, *The Bolshevik Revolution* (Vol. I of *A History of Soviet Russia*). London: Macmillan & Co., Ltd., 1950, esp. pp. 70-101.
[15] Vladimir Lenin, *The Essentials of Lenin*. London: Lawrence and Wishart Ltd., 1947, Vol. II, pp. 683-6.

debate and criticism with the anarchists, social revolutionaries, and Mensheviks, and even utilized portions of the old Czarist apparatus in the armed forces and the civil service.

What took place is indicative of the self-deception of an ideology, its inability to think outside of its own ideals. Two major events, little reported, occurred in the years 1921-22: the victory of the Communist Party apparatus over the Soviets, or the Council of Workers; and an intensification of tension between rural and urban interests. The victory of the Communist Party over the Workers' Soviets was first announced in the debate over the Red Army which took place at the close of the Civil War period. The concept of a professional and permanent standing army was against all socialist tradition. Hence, at the conclusion of the Civil War period there were demands for a transition to a national militia in the hands of the Soviets. Leon Trotsky advanced a proposal under which the future militia would be centered in the industrial centers so that the leading army cadres could be organized through the close co-operation of the army and trade unions, both under the direct control of the Soviets. This proposal, which amounted in effect to an operational military dictatorship of the Soviets, was approved in principle but never carried out. The Kronstadt sailors' uprising, peasant rebellions, and the unrest among industrial workers all combined to make any thought of developing an army of Soviets too dangerous to contemplate. There was also opposition to a Soviet militia on principle. The professional officers regarded such a system as less efficient than a standing army and impotent in the face of foreign encirclement.[16] Others felt that a national army was necessary in order to lend support to socialist revolutions elsewhere. Russian Communists, it must be remembered, felt revolutions were as imminent as they were desirable.

Once Trotsky's plan for a proletarian Soviet armed guard was abandoned, it was inevitable that the army should be thoroughly under the control of the Communist Party leadership, particularly the Central

[16] The theory of imperialistic encirclement, which rationalized the "party army" at the time of War Communism, still persists in Soviet Communist statements. However, the concept of the Red Army as an instrument of internal repression has ceased. The Red Army has, in fact, been transformed into an instrument of the Party for the guardianship of the nation. See on this V. D. Sokolovskii (ed.), *Soviet Military Strategy*. Englewood Cliffs, N.J.: Prentice-Hall, Inc. (A Rand Corporation Research Study), 1963, pp. 82-3.

Committee of the Communist Party. The possibilities of terrorism became manifest once a "party army" (or a Soviet Army) triumphed.[17] It had its first opportunity to exercise this national power in the conflict between the urban and rural sectors. In the early 'twenties, the situation between the two sectors grew increasingly desperate. The distribution of goods was dependent on private traders. The peasantry clamored for more and cheaper goods, while at the same time they demanded higher prices for their own products. Industry, only slowly rising from the ruins of revolution and civil war, produced few goods at high prices. Indeed, the idea of socialism as *immediate* gratification of wants served to reinforce industrial confusion. Factory laborers clamored for cheap food and inexpensive raw materials, but could not see the need for a corresponding effort on their part.

Given this situation, the solutions proposed by the Communist leadership were desperate. The group around Bukharin was willing to have a degree of capitalism in the peasant sector in order to maintain some kind of social peace, while the group around Zinoviev was anti-peasant and vowed "no compromise" on the issue of socializing the rural sector.

The Bukharin faction reasoned that the organs of state power were in the hands of the socialist sector. Therefore the drain of a private-sector agricultural economy would not be sufficient to upset the basic economy. At the same time, compromise with the peasant groups would give the public sector of the economy a necessary breathing space for consolidating its power. In contrast to this, the Zinoviev faction stressed the incompatibility of a private sector in the agricultural sphere with a public-sector-dominated industrial sphere. The reasoning of the ultra-left faction was that inevitably the rural sector (particularly the wealthy landholders) would increase their wealth at the expense of the factory workers. In long-range terms, they feared that appeasement of the peasants would undermine the Revolution. Moreover, they saw the peasants' demand for a greater return for their produce as an attempt to reintroduce private enterprise, free-market economy which would in effect be a betrayal of the socialist revolution. It would stimulate the economic conditions of class warfare and cause strife among the disenfranchised. These factors,

[17] Leonard Schapiro, *The Communist Party of the Soviet Union.* New York: Random House, 1959-60, pp. 325-7.

the Zinoviev faction felt, far outweighed the short-run gains which the Bukharin plan would bring. The Bukharin faction was essentially non-violent in its strategic position, moving to an opening up of the private sector and a surrender to peasant demands. The Zinoviev group was ready to engage in the slaughter of the rich peasantry as part of a meaningful termination of War Communism. At the same time, this would bring about the collectivization of the poor peasantry and help start the social-ization process.

This controversy also has a significance in relation to contemporary strategies of development. It is the kinds of responses held to be avail-able which are important today. Stalin makes his entrance into Soviet politics as the great compromiser between the two factions. It must be understood that prior to the mid-'twenties there was no such thing as Stalinism. There is no ideology which can properly distinguish Stalin's from that of his colleagues. As a matter of fact, his position as Secretary of the Communist Party was the most ambiguous one within the Councils of the Soviet ruling elite. It was thought to be the least likely position from which ideology could emanate. The early image of Stalin the organizer did not include any comparable image of him as a theorist.

Throughout the period of Lenin's rule, Stalin represented the per-fect bureaucrat, the man who executed the plans of others and went to the "field" only to file efficiency reports. But he scarcely made plans of his own. Since Stalin had an abrupt, brusque character and mostly lacked any charismatic qualities of leadership, it appeared unlikely, all things being equal, that Stalin would ever be in a policy-making position.[18] All things were not equal. And in this controversy between compromise and coercion, between the public sector and the private sector, was born the hybrid phenomenon of Stalinism.

It must be appreciated that Stalinism as a strategy of economic and social development passed beyond Stalin as an individual. The doctrine of forced collectivization, of the bloody repression of the peasantry, of the necessity of terror exceeded Stalin. This raises the efficacy of at-taching an "ism" to Stalin's name, any more than we might be justified in attaching an "ism" after the names of Andrew Carnegie, Cornelius Vanderbilt, Jay Gould, or any of the nineteenth-century railroad mag-

[18] See Bertram D. Wolfe, *Khrushchev and Stalin's Ghost*. New York: Frederick Praeger, 1957, p. 263.

nates who built the American transportation system with conscript labor and with European and Asian immigrants "outside the law." What these men share is a beatific vision of the future and a general disdain for human obstacles in gaining the brave new world.

There developed in Russia a phenomenon over and above what Stalin as a leader or an individual implied or advocated. When the peasants had been crushed in 1930, Stalinism was victorious. But Stalin the leader backed away from the implications of his own adoption of the methods of terror. At this point, we find him advocating caution and avoiding a revolutionary euphoria which made regional Bolshevik cadres "dizzy with success." Throughout his whole career, Stalin showed a political ambivalence, an inability to face up to the theoretical implications of his own policies. He had little faith that the rapid development he was encouraging, contingent as it was on the high risks he was taking, would produce the desired developments, but in the absence of a theory of development, Stalin became a desperate pragmatist—like many before and after him.

III

Development in modern Russia is ironically a matter of an economy haunting politics. Even under the socialist regime planning becomes willy-nilly subject to the "iron laws" of "surplus value." The political commissariat lagged behind economic transformations at every stage of Soviet development. Stalin himself lagged behind the phenomenon of Stalinism. In effect, then, when we speak of Stalinism, we are not speaking of the individual capacity for terror. Terror is not a new phenomenon in the social or economic history of Europe. What we are speaking of is a method for control of the economy through the political apparatus. Insofar as this method was successful, and real development could be accelerated through central-planning agencies, socialism represents a new phenomenon. Bureaucratic socialism, where planning, party, and politics are fused into one gigantic machine presided over by an industrializing autocrat, is similarly unprecedented. Thus, the victory of the Soviet Revolution represented the triumph of bureaucracy no less than of socialism.

We cannot measure development exclusively or even primarily in terms of agriculture. The Russian Revolution only rationalized, but did not eliminate, the uneven nature of the developmental process. But even this asymmetry has made its "economic experiment" fascinating to Third World leaders. The drama of one sector surrendering its sovereignty to another sector has been played out in all post-Soviet revolutions. It is in this context that the essence of Stalinism was realized. There were byproducts of development in the Soviet Union, accidental features Stalin contributed, which can hardly be overlooked. But it is doubtful that such features are organic to the nature of the planning system involved. Terrorism, for instance, formed part of the package. Development for Russia represented a recognition that industrialization is war-like. It was a war against famine, hunger, illiteracy, potential foreign enemies. It is also true that development was seen as a war to prevent war. This image of a military undertaking helped to legitimize the political control of economic development. In a sense then, Soviet Russia has from the outset been on a wartime footing.

The cost of development under Stalinism can hardly be vindicated simply on grounds of economic achievement. In effect, Stalinism is the justification of the forced reorganization of an economic and political structure, despite the social and cultural costs. This very economic vindication is at the same time perhaps its strongest social condemnation. The Soviet regime trained a generation of educated men, a generation of literate men, and a generation of machine-oriented men. By what it excluded (the liberal arts, for instance) this training furnished exactly the kind of selective information geared to prevent any bottlenecks in the process of social development. Nonetheless, this education in technology produced an uneven form of development. It dehumanized Marxism and led to grotesque and arrogant notions of Party members as "engineers of the soul" and the Russian people as the engine. The effect of this bureaucratic corruption by the Party which was greatly facilitated by the liquidation of the old intelligentsia, produced a generation geared to false claims and improper estimates of Soviet industrial output.

The reliance on terror itself proved to be a partial bottleneck. As Fainsod has pointed out, a secret police develops its own laws of conduct. The concept of secrecy breeds an atmosphere of fear even in the leadership which created the instrument of terror. It tends to preserve the fiction of permanent dangers since the bureaucratic apparatus of terror, like any other, seeks to survive and extend its domain, even when it becomes dysfunctional. But Fainsod also notes how well terror "worked" in Russian society.

The full circle of the Great Purge offers a remarkable case study in the use of terror. Arrests ran into the millions. The gruesome and harrowing experiences of the victims blackened the face of Stalinist Russia. The havoc wrought in leading circles appeared irreparable. Yet despite the damage and the hatred engendered, the dynamic momentum of the industrialization program was maintained. The arrests of responsible technicians and officials frequently produced serious setbacks in production, but, as their replacements acquired experience, order was restored and production began to climb again. While many functionaries reacted to the purge by shunning all responsibility, others responded to the fear of arrest by working as they had never worked before. Terror functioned as prod as well as brake.[19]

Terror may have helped bring Russia into the modern technological world while at the same time it cut down industrial efficiency; but the important point is that it did not disturb the momentum of industrialization and urbanization. The very success involved and implied in Stalinist developmental strategy is its greatest source of weakness. Stalinism created new forms of unevenness, new bottlenecks to development, that were unknown in the capitalist sectors. We may list some of these contradictions in Soviet socialism: (1) The rise of a preferred political bureaucracy, unchecked by popular control; (2) the loss of labor incentives prior to the institutionalization of the socialist system; (3) a toleration of regional sub-national groups which offered but slight allegiance to the Soviet Union as such.

If we look at the dislocations of the forced labor system, many of the lesser contradictions can be put in perspective. The institutionalization of police terror, aside from its other functions, provided a cheap source of labor—prisoners, political or otherwise, for the industrial march. Large-scale arrests put a large reservoir of labor at the disposal of the state and its supervisory organs. Penal and conscript systems were fused in the "labor camps," and "labor therapy" was prescribed for "criminal"

[19] Merle Fainsod, *How Russia Is Ruled* (revised edition). Cambridge: Harvard University Press, 1963, pp. 443-61.

offenses. The chief virtue of this conscripted labor force was its "cheapness." Conscript labor was used "entirely without investment of capital." Industrial equipment to a great extent had to be bought abroad at a time when export opportunities were limited by the small amount of *valuta* on hand. Forced labor was largely manual labor and did not require modern industrial equipment. And what is more, an iron bound discipline "can be imposed upon the personnel, both technical and staff workers."[20]

Providing a system of incentives, rewards, and even awards for this conscript labor system may have maintained a relatively high level of output, but it did little to refine or advance individual productivity. Since there was little concern about the physical maintenance of conscript labor, there was a permanent problem of "recruitment." Even when periods of high arrest and confinement solved the "personnel problem," the efficiency of this labor was minimal. There was a general lack of human incentive and an equal lack of modern equipment. But in terms of the whole Soviet system, the use of conscript labor was an undoubted success—given the circumstances in which Russian development took place. Thus, while the average efficiency of conscript labor was perhaps half that of free labor, its value in Russia's "take-off period" can hardly be questioned.[21]

If today in Russia the system of conscript labor has been reduced, if not entirely eliminated, it is not only for humanitarian motivations. With the introduction of more complicated machinery requiring greater technical skills, such labor has become obsolete. Russian conscript labor may be considered a substitute for the immigrant labor flow in nineteenth-century America. In the absence of a flow of free labor, it provided the Soviet Union with a cheap labor source for rapid industrialization. But when the relative advantages of free and skilled labor far outweighed those of conscripted and unskilled labor, the developmental process underwent drastic changes.

The basic dilemma of the post-Stalin period is that few measures exist for dismantling the coercive apparatus—a task made doubly difficult by the Soviet's insistent denial that such an apparatus even existed.

[20] David J. Dallin and Boris I. Nicolaevsky, *Forced Labor in Soviet Russia.* New Haven: Yale University Press, 1947, pp. 89, 91.
[21] Ibid., pp. 105-6.

Strong discipline will be necessary to raise consumer production and create better living standards. The growth of differences between incomes and positions of power, wage rises, and increasing professional and labor specialization, has made "inequality" a more widespread phenomenon. Thus, achievement of social mobility in a Soviet context required an increase in social stratification. And what this shows is that the degree of mobility is not uniquely determined by the presence or absence of broad social distinctions in rank and earnings.

With all of its pitfalls, the field of economic statistics remains the most reliable single indicator to the paradoxes of the post-Stalin period. The Soviet regime promised an improvement of more than 250 per cent in per capita consumption between 1960 and 1980. But this would have necessitated an increase at a compound annual rate of more than 6.4 per cent. Yet, the Soviets achieved this growth rate in only one period of their existence, between 1948 and 1958. And even this high rate of growth may have been partially due to the destruction caused by World War Two, for the real starting urban wage for 1948 was less than half that of 1928. Thirty years later, by 1958, the real urban wage was still not up to the 1928 level. And by the present decade, the Russian rate of growth had slowed to approximately 4.0 per cent.[22] Thus, while the rate of economic growth is roughly equivalent to that of the United States, since the starting points are quite different, the possibilities of the Soviet Union delivering on Khrushchev's promise to achieve a high enough per capita production to equal that of the United States can hardly be redeemed. Indeed, to "catch up" would mean an abandonment of present Soviet social and political norms. It would signify either a definite return to Stalinism and an economy of primary production, or a turn to Libermanism and an economy of consumer production.[23] In either case, this would occasion pressures on the regime from many and diverse social sectors. And as long as present Soviet commitments to the

[22] See Oscar Gass, "Soviet Economic Developments," *Commentary*, Vol. 37, No. 2, February 1964, pp. 54-68; and for more recent data consult the Senate-House Joint Economic Committee, *Current Economic Indicators for the U.S.S.R.*, Washington, D.C.: United States Government Printing Office, 1965.
[23] "Libermanism" refers to the unorthodox approach to the Soviet economy advocated by Yevsel Liberman, Professor of Economics at Kharkov University. The basis of his approach is that any great improvement in the quality and the quantity of national production can best be brought about by making profits the principal indicator of the success or failure of any enterprise.

world socialist bloc and to the developing regions must be moderated in terms of internal pressures for greater consumer satisfaction, there is unlikely to be any radical shift in Soviet economic strategy.

The backwardness of Soviet agriculture is the perfect illustration of the nation's uneven economic development. It reveals in the most acute form the problems Soviet policy planners now face with respect to the acceleration of growth and the corresponding relaxation of tensions inside the Soviet Union. As of 1960, there were 160 farm laborers to 100 factory workers. The projection for 1980 is 50 farm laborers for every 100 factory workers.[24] This compares quite unfavorably to the United States, where in 1960 there were between 8 to 10 farm workers for every 100 factory workers. While there has been a drop of 17.7 per cent between 1913 and 1961 in the proportion of the Russian population living on farms, the absolute numbers of farm workers has continued to increase. This high agricultural overpopulation represents an unabsorbed and untapped labor force. The Soviet Union is seeking to readjust its population, to move it from rural to urban situations. What complicates this task is the further need to reallocate at least six million of its citizens east of the Urals to maintain its industrial growth rate.

Soviet planners hope to reduce the size of the agricultural labor force while increasing the yield per acre through increased efficiency. But certain problems arise. In the first place, an industrial existence is in many ways less enjoyable and more difficult than farming. And, second, the geography of the Soviet Union may make it difficult for agriculture to increase its yield beyond present capacities. For areas of comparable climate, grain yields in the Soviet Union and in the United States are about equal per acre, but not per worker. On both scores, Soviet development will probably not only remain uneven but become even more so. The much vaunted liquidation of the distinction between farm and factory labor or between manual and intellectual labor will probably not only fail to be realized, but will most likely become greater.

This raises the question of what is considered legitimate in the process of development and what must be viewed as illegitimate. The moral question in a sense precedes the social question. Stalinism in one country has become an accepted political formula despite the inevitable

[24] Louis Aragon, *A History of the USSR: From Lenin to Khrushchev.* New York: David McKay Co., Inc., 1964, pp. 650-51.

corruption of the bureaucratic state. But Stalinism as an economic pro-gram is not obsolete in the same sense. Terror was vindicated as a neces-sary feature of accomplishing the tasks of the social revolution. Once these tasks were accomplished, once it was demonstrated that the social-ist revolution was possible, it became a desired goal for other countries. Given this new high value, terror was no longer a main source of con-tention but became only a necessary consequence for social development and social planning in a backward economy.

It is useful to compare modern China and the Soviet Union in this regard. True to the predictions of Stalinism, party strife has been held to a minimum and much less internal violence has existed in China since its revolution than existed in the first years of the Russian Revolution. Consequently, there has been a reduction in the use of overt terrorism. The "law" of development through self-criticism has replaced the aber-ration of destruction.[25] We can then ask why China has been unable to maintain its timetable for development. Why do its collectivization schemes fail to have the same success as Stalin's did, even though there is less dependence on terror?

In Russia during its period of rapid take-off, controversy performed the function of thrashing out social problems in a concrete and meaning-ful way.[26] The very fact that there is little internecine strife in China's Communist Party, and only sterile, debased forms of "auto-criticism," has shown that artificially induced consensus is less meaningful than con-flict as such. But despite such aberrations, the Chinese have demon-strated that it is possible to have rapid industrial expansion with a sus-tained rate of growth at minimal cost in human life.[27] This is a lure to the underdeveloped areas induced by the socialist ideology of develop-ment. However dissimilar Soviet and Chinese forms of politics are, they show a strong similarity in agriculture.[28] Socialist ideology demands ex-

[25] For a positive account of the importance of "self-criticism" in Chinese Com-munist society, see Felix Greene, *Awakened China*. Garden City, New York: Doubleday & Co., 1961.
[26] Isaac Deutscher, "The French Revolution and the Russian Revolution; Some Suggestive Analogies," *World Politics*, April 1952, pp. 369-81.
[27] This combination of minimal costs in life but maximal costs in goods is made by most observers. See Edgar Snow, *The Other Side of the River: Red China Today*. New York: Random House, 1962; and Felix Greene, *op. cit.*
[28] See W. K., "Soviet Agriculture as a Model for Asian Countries," *The China Quarterly*, January-March 1961, pp. 116-30.

propriation which is to be followed by collectivization. This is counter-posed to the capitalist ideology of agricultural development through technological innovation and scientific management.

Soviet development was greatly helped by the pre-revolutionary domestic bureaucracy, one which was thoroughly Russian, and thus could not easily be removed as was the colonial bureaucracy in so many parts of Africa. At the same time, the Russian bureaucracy was sufficiently separated in fact and in function from the rest of the Soviet class system as to be able to give its direct allegiance to the political apparatus. It has been pointed out that the social basis of Stalinism was this bu-reaucracy, which gained disproportionately in the industrialization proc-ess.[29] We can appreciate this factor when we note that the traditionalism of the Chinese bureaucracy drastically reduces China's potential for rapid development after the Sun Yat Sen Revolution of 1910. As one writer recently pointed out: "The weak point lay in the reluctance of the Chinese bureaucracy, imbued with the ethical standards of the man-darin system, either to allow effective management to pass into the hands of those competent to exercise it or to adapt their own ideas to changed circumstances. It was exacerbated by the inability of the Chinese government to maintain order and political unity, a defect which per-sisted until 1949."[30] In Russia, the bourgeoisie bequeathed a "value free" bureaucracy to the Soviets, while in China the examination system, based as it was upon class privilege, was unable to liberate the bureauc-racy from traditionalism.

Socialism as set forth in the Marxist program does not answer the questions of nationalism, racism, and militarism. It is on these grounds, and not in the argument of alternative roads to development, that social-ism faces its most severe challenge from the Western capitalistic democ-racies. While problems of electrification, military build-up, and steel and

[29] See Max Shachtman, "Bureaucratic Collectivism: Two Eras," *The New In-ternational*, Vol. XXIII, No. 3, Summer 1957, pp. 156-60. Also see H. Malcolm Macdonald, "Revisionism and Khrushchev," *The Southwestern Social Science Quarterly*, Vol. 44, No. 4, March 1964, pp. 335-45.
[30] C. D. Cowan, *The Economic Development of Southeast Asia: Studies in Economic History and Political Economy*. New York: Frederick Praeger, 1964, pp. 17-18. For a particularly relevant statement of the current status of Chinese polity and economy, see Franz Schurmann, "China's 'New Economic Policy'—Transition or Beginning," *The China Quarterly*, January-March 1964. (Reprint No. 134, Institute of International Studies, University of California, Berkeley.)

iron-ore production are central to the major large nations of the world, these are not the biggest problems in the underdeveloped or developing regions.

Behavioristic manipulation through the propagandistic obliteration of political memory has displaced outright terrorism. Stakhanovism, the Soviet blend of time, motion, and terror, has given way to psychological manipulation, to a mechanical scheme of punishment-reward incentives. Leading technicians of the new socialist society concentrate on making the productive process work rapidly and precisely. Through punishment and reward, incentive schemes are designed to end criticism. This could be considered a type of brainwashing typical of rapidly developing nations. It is no exaggeration to say that some technicians have learned the wrong things from self-sacrifice in the developmental process. Mechanical validity, or *prima facie* accomplishment, becomes the basic characteristic of practically all automated societies.[31] The power of the automated socialist society to reward its members depends upon their uncritical acceptance of what is offered in the form of those signals which mean "well done" or "how right you are." But this turns the full circle. What is wrong with Soviet life is thus closely connected to what is wrong with industrialization as an ideology.

The power of the machine to condition the populace would be decreased if it were suspected for a moment that the rewards given to workers in particular planning tasks did not correspond to those expected from the general population. This assumption of perfect economic rationality is a key reason why the development of the Soviet system has been so uneven. Actions which might prove to be unrewarding or even fatal in a wider context might be the most rewarding within the planning zone. But any suspicion that the plan might not be perfect would tend to destroy the popular faith in the artificial forms of manipulation held necessary for development.

Clearly, the Soviet development has given enormous stimulus to new forms of controlled development. But it has also bequeathed to the

---

[31] Recent discussions in the United States should make it evident that such uncritical acceptance of behavioristic canons is not confined to any single industrial society. See Robert Boguslaw, *The New Utopians: A Study of System Design and Social Change*. Englewood Cliffs, N.J.: Prentice-Hall, 1965.

Third World new forms of uncontrolled terror. The final question here is not an easy one: To what degree is the terrorism warranted on pragmatic grounds? And for a partial answer, we must necessarily compare and contrast the Soviet Union and the United States.

IV

We begin by noting the obvious difficulty of establishing criteria of comparability between the United States and the Soviet Union. For one thing, there is the sociological fact that the United States is a modernist society, while the Soviet Union is a structural society. To put the matter somewhat differently, the United States places great emphasis on factors of consumption (creature comforts, personal property, quality of goods marketed, etc.), while the Soviets give precedence to factors of production—to surpass the United States in coal and steel production becomes a major undertaking.

The United States and the Soviet Union both think that their differences are far greater than their similarities. This has led them to be more intensely competitive in the struggle for world influence than any actual economic differences warrant. Third World countries similarly see them as antithetical. Yet major powers like France or England may see these similarities as important. But the United States and the Soviet Union can really be only imperfect models, for their own history and experience are in many ways unique.

The difficulty with much political and economic analysis of similarities and dissimilarities between the Soviet Union and the United States is the tendency to maximize ideological factors; to take at face value statements about the extent of differences in means and ends between the two economic goliaths. While there is no doubt that differences of ideology permeate the social structure, and even serve to define the differences between some leadership groups, the serious observer cannot help but feel that ideological differences have been overtaxed and freighted at the expense of structural similarities. If we eschew ideological self-definitions of the international political situation, and move to some statistically and empirically based generalizations, then the variations can for the most part be considered as those which might be expected to exist between two countries of such different geographical and historical backgrounds, rather than those which obtain between ideological adversaries.

Thus the difference between the United States and the Soviet Union can be expressed as a lag, rather than as a structural deficiency in either society. The American Civil War took place between 1861-65, and its outcome guaranteed the victory of industrialism over agriculturalism. The Russian Civil War took place between 1919-22, and its outcome similarly guaranteed the victory of industrialism over agriculturalism. If we take this event in both countries as the trigger for rapid economic development, then the gap between the United States and the Soviet Union can be considered a function of the period in which each Civil War took place, rather than as a consequence of the social system.

Now we can turn to several incongruous aspects of development in the Soviet Union and the United States—differences which at the same time cancel each other out.

The United States developed in a military atmosphere relatively free from foreign pressures toward conquest. The profound isolation of nineteenth-century United States from "European involvements" placed minimal pressure on the industrial machine, for it did not have to divert a portion of factory production for such non-valuable goods as military hardware. The Soviet Union was born in the midst of World War One, and the extent of military adventurism against it in its formative stages has now passed over into mythology. From the "imperialist cordon sanitaire" of 1920 to the "ring of bases" which Stalin saw in 1950, the Soviets have developed with the fact as well as the psychology of being surrounded by hostile military forces. While this undoubtedly rendered the Russian worker more willing to engage in the rituals of self-sacrifice for the fatherland, it also served as an effective drain on Russian economic growth roughly between 1918 and 1948. In recent post-World War Two conditions, military waste has become less significant—since the United States has world-wide military commitments draining its productivity, while the Soviet Union, because of the new technology and the Khrushchev "New Deal," has been able to level off its military investments with respect to its total economic output.

In comparing the relative advantages and disadvantages of the developmental process in the United States and the Soviet Union, special mention should be made of the role of organized labor. The arguments at the ideological level between worker representatives in each nation often reflect the different character of labor and the different notion of success. Labor organization in the United States, despite the high costs of class conflicts, served as a vehicle for rapid development. In the nineteenth century unions served to maintain labor discipline more than to elevate mass labor rights. In the present century, the continuing pressure by unions for higher wages has provided one of the absolutely essential underpinnings for expanding mass demand, and has thus served to accelerate the nation's economic growth. The pressure of labor costs has also become one of the main reasons for increased productivity. Above all, unions, their leaders and members alike, have had a shared value in the fundamental transformation of the worker's status. The goals of the workers themselves are close to those of other parts of American society, thus guaranteeing a formal consensus between Americans on the appropriate developmental goals.[32] Hence, industrial unionism contributed to the general developmental process.

The Soviet Union, for its part, was so bound by Marxist formulas concerning the co-operative nature of social classes under socialism, that it suppressed all displays of labor independence and labor strife as indicative of counter-revolutionary activity. There is no doubt that the forced labor system had advantages in the earliest stages of the Soviet regime, and similarly, it is quite possible that the suppression of independent labor agitation led to a higher rate of production. But if the Soviets hoped to achieve by their methods the full liberation of productive energies in a co-operative situation in replacement of the American system of formal consensus, it failed dismally.[33] The Soviet Union was forced to increase the proportion of externally inflicted terrorism, constant propaganda, and postponement of hopes to arrive at the same point which the United States managed to gain by being more tolerant and, at times, sensitive, to the role of labor independence and its stimulus to

[32] See Sanford Cohen, *Labor in the United States*. Columbus, Ohio: Charles E. Merrill Books, Inc., 1960, pp. 68-94.
[33] See S. Swianiewicz, *Forced Labour and Economic Development*. London and New York: Oxford University Press, 1965, pp. 50-53.

development. This is one reason why the Soviet Union, in its formative period, has advanced at a rate parallel to, rather than in advance of, the United States. And this with higher social costs.[34]

While we are on the subject, it should be said that the coexistence of the United States and the Soviet Union as major industrial powers has served to puncture some favorite myths about developmental ideology. The idea that Protestantism *per se* represents the driving force of development, rather than only one strain or variety of development in the West, is now firmly put to rest. It is not only that the Soviet Union has few if any Protestant worshippers, but more to the point, no religion has dynamized the U.S.S.R. toward development. Indeed, "delayed gratification" can be urged on religious grounds (as in England or the United States), but it can also be urged on nationalist grounds (via the medium of the Communist Party as in the Soviet Union and China). It is also quite clear that whereas the elite in the West was indeed touched by the "Protestant Ethic," this elite did not labor in the vineyards of God. This was left to Irish hod-carriers, Jewish garment workers, Italian bricklayers, and the whole universe of a non-Protestant labor force in the United States.

Another fairy tale exposed by the comparative examination of the U.S.A. and the U.S.S.R. is the idea that development is somehow a consequence of political liberalism—of a belief in progress through free choice and free science. Alternatives allow for development at a faster rate than dictatorship. Political pluralism necessarily minimizes the effectiveness of planning, and it makes the decision-making process so complex and subject to countervailing pressures as to substantially slow down the rate of industrial growth. While on the other hand, totalitarianism minimizes precisely these types of obstacles to development. Stalinism was not simple rule by terror. Rather, terrorism was the consequence of an approach to development in which planning, decision-making, and policy-determination were all centralized and expected to be realized—whatever their human cost. Thus, the choice is really the other way around. Not only is political liberalism less viable with respect to sustained high industrial growth rates than totalitarianism (up to the

---

[34] A significant beginning of such comparative-historical study is contained in Reinhard Bendix, *Work and Authority in Industry: Ideologies of Management in the Course of Industrialization*. New York: John Wiley & Sons, 1956.

"primitive accumulation" point). However, this is far from the naïve notions prevalent—at least until Sputnik—that economic liberalism is the best possible state for high rates of development, and that dictatorship is somehow incompatible with modern industrial life.

Another myth punctured by the coexistence of the United States and the Soviet Union is that high growth rates require, as a metaphysical necessity for their realization, the destruction of the middle classes. It may be true that the liquidation of the Russian bourgeoisie as a social class was necessary to achieve high levels of social production, but it is also clear that in the evolution of the United States the bourgeoisie performed the significant role as the directorate of development. Through significant investment procedures, industrial combinations, foreign holdings, and philanthropic services, the bourgeoisie of the United States proved its exceptional qualities—its capacity for self-sacrifice to gain development. Too often the talk about American exceptionalism has focused on the character of the labor force. In fact, what has made the United States "exceptional," at least with respect to Marxist "laws" about socio-economic transformation, is its bourgeoisie.

It is simpler to assume that the similarities between industrial organization in the United States and the Soviet Union drive them both to similar economic peaks and plateaus, and leads to a convergence of productivity rates, than it is to make the opposite argument. Indeed, both the United States and the Soviet Union are rapidly growing, in like manner, and the gap between them and the rest of the underdeveloped world is widening sharply. Both are self-sustaining economies; both are exporting economies; both are industrial economies. The Third World nations, for their part, tend to reveal less of a capacity for self-sustained growth. They are importing economies (of finished goods), while they export their materials. Furthermore, they are pre-technological, in both scientific and industrial senses, and hence it scarcely pays for these nations to "nationalize" one isolated economic sector, since the finished goods are usually bought far more cheaply abroad than from domestic labor.

What is actually taking place today is the very slow growth of industrial parity between the two giant powers. But since the starting points differ significantly, and since most other independent variables favor the United States in terms of high growth rate, the actual date of coalescence is much later than the Soviet Union has envisioned it. The target date, the rendezvous with economic destiny, is more likely to be around the year 2050 rather than 1980. The industrial gap, with great crudity, may be expressed in terms of about fifty years, and by 1980 it may, all things remaining equal (meaning no major shift in balance of political power or no thermonuclear war), be about thirty years. Again, this suggests the striking structural similarities between the United States and the Soviet Union—similarities which Khrushchev has been more ready to grant exist in the military sphere than in the economic sphere; even though one might expect that from a Marxian point of view, the military capacity of a nation would be considered directly linked to and forged by a nation's economic potential.

The statistical information adds up to a bright picture for both the United States and the Soviet Union. True, there are dark spots in each. The Soviet agricultural system is in a shambles—but the declining importance of this sector and the introduction of scientific technology can overcome this handicap. The United States, for its part, continues to avoid making full use of its industrial potential. But this can also be rectified through "welfare" investment or by raising the threshold of consumer wants and demands by new products and services.

Despite the similarities between the two nations which advanced industrialization has produced, there is little point to First and Second World characterizations if existent structural likenesses are the only focus. Methods, traditions, and types of development, in other words, "procedures," still make of both nations two distinct entities in world political culture. And Third World countries attest to these differences by the sheer fact of being driven back and forth between "the camps" for aid, for "models," for support. Perhaps their similarities and differences are both best illustrated in this fact.

Appendix B

The Transition from Totalitarianism to Authoritarianism

The second Soviet revolution was announced in a joint communiqué issued, in mid-October 1964, by the Central Committee of the Communist Party and by the Presidium of the Supreme Soviet (the Government). It said two important things: First, that Nikita Khrushchev had been released from the duties of First Secretary of the Party and Chairman of the Russian Council of Ministers. Second, that once again the maximum leadership was to be collectivized. Leonid Brezhnev took over the directorship of the Party and Aleksei Kosygin became the head of state.[1]

Whatever this shift in the Soviet command posts is taken to signify, one point stands out above all others: this change is a revolution and not a restoration in the forms of Soviet political life. At a recent international conference on world trade, held in Vienna, a Soviet economist and diplomat concluded his formal report with some rather remarkable informal comments: basically, that the fall of Khrushchev signifies changes in Soviet life even more profound than the shift from Malenkov to Khrushchev. Indeed, if the fall of Malenkov carried with it the collapse of Stalinism, it might well be that the fall of Khrushchev might entail the demise of Leninism—not, to be sure, as the saviour of mother Russia, but quite surely, as the author of Divine Truth and Providential Good.

[1] The information for the developments in post-Khrushchev Russia are basically derived from *The Current Digest of the Soviet Press*, Vol. XVI, Nos. 40-47, Oct. 28, 1964-Dec. 16, 1964. Additional information came from *The New York Times* of the same period, particularly the reports filed by Theodore Shabad and Henry Tanner.

Under Khrushschev the contents of Soviet policy dramatically shifted. Yet, the retention of traditional Communist Party forms of control and norms of discourse severely cramped the possibilities of a thorough breakthrough. Indeed, Khrushchev may be viewed as an "interim Pope," the leader who provided the bridge between Soviet totalitarianism and Soviet authoritarianism. This was precisely Khrushchev's historical mission, to have moved the Soviet Union out of the total terrorism of the Stalin era, into the sharply delimited elitism of today. Khrushchev had the ideological intelligence to denounce Stalin, but not the administrative skill to undo the machinery of the Stalinist system.

In every sphere of life, Khrushchev excoriated those who wanted to operate within traditional modalities, but he stopped short of instituting new, more modest norms of political behavior. Khrushchev was the very best product of the Stalin era: a believer in the goals of collectivization *sans* terrorism. That is why, while denouncing the "personality cult," Khrushchev did not find it possible to limit his own political power. Because Khrushchev still retained the Stalinist fusion of Party and government functions in one person, Bulganin's fall became inevitable. It is precisely this partial, incomplete aspect of Khrushchev's legacy which has been focused upon in the policy statements which have been forthcoming from the Soviet press since Brezhnev and Kosygin came to power.

The concern with style in Soviet politics is more properly a concern with maturity in human behavior. From the adulation and adoration of the Stalin period, to the capricious and even boorish qualities of the Khrushchev era, the new Soviet technical elite has had to wince, grin, and bear it. But with the Brezhnev-Kosygin regime, the term "business-like" has become the byword in Soviet political behavior. For example, in the closing session of the Supreme Soviet held in December 1964, Premier Kosygin spoke without the usual accompaniment of "thunderous ovation" or "stormy applause" so characteristic of Bolshevik politics. Also missing were the usual flamboyant phrases about the "building of Communism" and the "victories of socialist labor." So radical a departure was this, that *The New York Times* in its report was moved to point out that "Mr. Kosygin sounded more like the president of a big Western corporation than a Communist politician."

But the question of style, of the sophistication of Russian political behavior, has an authentic sociological content. The changes in the organization of Soviet life are far-reaching in their consequences, both for the Russian people and for the peoples of the whole world. It would be tragic were the rhetorical demands of the Cold War allowed to obscure these new beginnings. For the first time in Soviet history precise legal restrictions and limits have been placed on the political machinery. While there has existed since the "Stalin Constitution" of 1936 a formal recognition of the differences between government functions and the Communist Party apparatus, the differences were more observed in the breach than in observance. The leadership of the Party and of the government were fused at the very top of the political hierarchy, with the Party leadership also in charge of the principal (if not of all) administrative posts.

The new attitude is signified in two key words: *autonomy* and *exactingness*. Gigantic planning agencies, with their outmoded methods of production and distribution of goods, are giving way to a new autonomy. The critique of centralism, of the inability of centralization to determine volumes of output, changing consumer orientations, level of profitability, etc., in the early post-Khrushchev days has already been pushed into a wider critique of the politicalization of areas of economic life that are better left in the hands of knowing experts. This brought about a second word: "exactingness"—what might in the West be called "expertise." The demand for "high exactingness" was coupled by the Communist Party ideological organ with a "Leninist style of work." To be sure, every Soviet leader since the death of Lenin has demanded a style of work in keeping with the supposed demands of the founding father of Bolshevism. For Stalin, it meant primarily an "inner party struggle" with which to achieve a *Gleichschaltung*, a co-ordination of the various social sectors which would render unswerving (and uncritical) fidelity to the leader. For Malenkov, adhesion to Leninism meant adhesion and identification with the Party apparatus as a whole. During the Khrushchev period, Leninism signified an identification with the nation-state no less than with the Party. The present leadership marks a further development toward the liberalization of all that Leninism included. It has come to signify attention to details of administration and organization, and no less, to an avoidance of any linkage of personal achievement with political infallibility.

The new turn in Soviet politics emphasizes means no less than ends. It is no longer sufficient to "pursue the plan." The new, new Soviet Man must behave "correctly" in interpersonal relations. "Boorishness" or a "lack of composure," or "negative" psychological attitudes, attributed to the past leadership of the Soviet Party by the present leadership, are to be replaced by the technocratic virtues: "composure, discipline and industriousness."

These are not simply mandates for the behavior of Communist Party cadre, but more significantly, warrants for distinguishing between partisan political functions, and non-political technical functions. The various aspects of the planned economy require just this sort of separation of functions to mesh gears satisfactorily, which the words autonomy and expertise entail. In this respect, it is significant that traditional Communist clichés about Party loyalty have given way to demands for technical competence. This represents a considerable shift from personal styles to legalistic modes of judgment. "Moral judgment" has given way to "practical judgment." But this transition from charismatic to bureaucratic modes of rule entails serious limits upon the role of the Communist cadre.

The colossal changes in political structure are already widely reflected in changes in political ideology. True enough, these changes are being introduced cautiously and with circumspection—lest they become objects of the controversies now raging within the Communist sphere of influence. The main shift is from a "party of the proletariat" to a "party of the people." Yet it is difficult to imagine how such a phenomenon as the "Africanization" of the Soviet Communist Party can fail to come under critical gaze—even if this phenomenon of an all-peoples' party is veiled under the discussions concerning modernization of economic practices.

For a long while now it has become apparent that leaders of the Third World—Kwame Nkrumah, Sekou Touré, Abdel Nasser, Sukarno —have refused to accept the idea that their parties are class dictatorships, and therefore maintained that they are caretakers of transitional regimes and transitional economies. The ideological leaders of the Third World have insisted that their respective national liberation movements are "parties of the whole people," in this way fusing bureaucratic and charismatic features into a single dominant party.

Soviet intransigence on this point has, in the past, cost its leadership serious losses in the Third World—both with respect to the indigenous revolutionary high command, and also by advocates of the broad-based national liberation ideology adopted by the Chinese Communists in their overseas policies. Thus, the recent announcement in *Pravda* that: "The socialist state has ceased to be an organ of the dictatorship of the proletariat and has been transformed into a state of the entire people" serves a dual purpose. It serves to underscore the new Soviet policy of limiting the role and function of the Communist Party, and second, it serves to bring Soviet political ideology into line with the major "national liberation" ideologies of the Third World nations of Africa, Asia, and Latin America.

The internal affairs of the Soviet Union reflect this new focus on emergent nations. There is much current discussion in the Soviet Union on merging Communist Party organizations based on the principle of territory, and those based on industrial plants, and this represents much more than a criticism of Khrushchev's belief in regional-territorial councils, or multiplication in the number and costs of administrative agencies within the Party. In its most complete form this view is part of the process of decentralization; of separating Communist Party functions from administrative functions as such.[2] Nonetheless, the fact that for the first time in dim recollection a public *parliamentary debate* took place inside the Supreme Soviet, with the Party leader of Leningrad, Georgi I. Popov, actually speaking against the reorganization proposals, and for the expansion of industrial management councils set up under Khrushchev, is a powerful indication that the "state of the entire people" notion is already being put into substantial, albeit limited, practice.

The standard Soviet guide to problems of power and organization has been the principle of monolithic unity. This notion of single-party and single-purpose was supposed to insure against selfishness, opportunism, and deviant politics generally. It was on the basis of this dogma

[2] It should be noted that this position is not uniformly shared. More common is the "undulating" thesis in which Soviet politics is described in terms of power shifts rather than social changes. But such a view does little to resolve or to explain how the present Soviet leadership views the problem of succession or the larger problems of dictatorship as one of several forms of managing crisis. See on this problem, Myron Rush, *Political Succession in the U.S.S.R.* New York: Columbia University Press, 1965.

of the monolith that all forms of opposition, potential and otherwise, were eliminated with Stalinism. First, local party organizations (such as those which existed in Leningrad, Kiev, and Moscow) were deprived of their autonomy, in favor of an all-knowing Central Committee. Second, the potential threat of the Red Army to Communist Party leaders was minimized by professionalizing and, in this way, isolating the armed forces from the Party organization. Third, the Party elite periodically purged the military elite, thus insuring the allegiance of the soldier through the assignment of a cadre of political instructors. Fourth, the separate Republics which comprise the Soviet Union were deprived of their "States' Rights" in a manner different than in the United States, but without much difference in substance. Any show of a real thirst for local power, or of autonomous political decisions, was severely condemned as "bouregeois nationalism" and/or "petty-bourgeois separatism." Fifth, the Soviets, the actual council of workers, was devitalized in the early twenties, and never again became an effective countervailing agency. True, the Soviets were revitalized later in the decade—but only as an instrument of aiding higher production, as an instrument of the State, rather than as a spokesman of the Workers. Sixth, the leadership of the Bolshevik movement was badly fragmented organizationally and ideologically. The Lenin cult somehow made it unnecessary to pay attention to problems of succession. Thus, although the schisms between Trotsky, Zinoviev, Bukharin, and the other Politburo hierarchy served to enhance the magical force of Lenin during his lifetime, they created havoc afterwards—making possible the bureaucratic surge to power of Joseph Stalin.[3]

These various changes in the political structure may finally solve the problem of political succession—the central dilemma in the single party and/or single leader state. By emphasizing the separateness of Party and Bureaucracy, by going even further and emphasizing the technical requirements of Party membership, the Soviet political elite undoubtedly expects to create the internal checks and balances within the Party which can lead to pacific resolution of future political issues,

[3] The whole of volume six in E. H. Carr's A History of Soviet Russia can be interpreted as a study in the problem of succession under Communism. See Socialism in One Country: 1924-26 (Part Two). London: Macmillan & Co., 1959.

without leading to a multi-party system. The emergence of a science of government in institutes of higher learning, independent of an ideology of Marxism, is a clear indication that the problem of succession is foremost in the minds of the present Soviet ruling elite. The increasing attention to the social sciences, particularly social sciences such as sociology and political science which have a clear potential for policy statements but were formerly denounced as bourgeois, coincides with an effort to have every Party member resolve questions with precision. "The Party teaches boldness and daring. But it also calls for circumspection, a sober analysis of the pluses and minuses of every phenomenon, of the objective conditions, the real situation." This is a far cry from the "partiinost," the unthinking partisanship which undoubtedly had a divisive effect on the Communist Party apparatus. The *ancien régime*, which placed loyalty above truth, made every major bureaucratic shift in the power base a cathartic event.

It has long been apparent that in the trinitarian class world of "workers, peasants, and intellectuals" the last named have grown enormously with respect to the rest of society. A self-definition as "intellectual" has become an all-encompassing road to high upward social mobility. The term includes a broad sphere of government bureaucrats, engineers, professionals, scholars, and the technical expert as such. The demand for sophistication—in matters of culture as well as politics—stems from these diverse sectors. It might well be that the current developments in the post-Khrushchev era are a cross between pragmatic responses to practical exigencies, and a natural working out of bureaucratic requirements in industrial society.

Whatever the more distant meanings of the silent Soviet Revolution, some immediate consequences are evident. First and foremost, the new Soviet posture is a continuation of the struggle with Chinese Communism for the loyalties of Third World nations. Whereas Khrushchev conducted this struggle at an ideological level, the new Soviet leadership is conducting it at the technical level. It is attempting to solve some outstanding issues of the relationships between democracy and development, politics and economics, in a way that will enable the Soviet Union, like the United States before it, to reveal the "face of the future" to the new nations, that is, to serve as a "demonstration effect."

The Soviet Union's desire to "normalize" its relations with China, without at the same time altering its fundamental attitudes toward the Mao Tse Tung regime indicates that the present leaders, Brezhnev and Kosygin, perceive certain clear advantages in its struggle with China for pre-eminence in the Third World. The disadvantageous aspects have long been known and assessed: the Chinese were a people who endured classic and modern forms of colonialism, they are a colored people, an Asian people. Above all, they share in the general syndrome of impoverished "have-not" nations: a cycle of underemployment, overpopulation, food crisis, communication and transportation lags, etc. As against such "ascriptive" advantages for the Chinese, there are "achievement" advantages for the Russians in their struggle for worldly pre-eminence. The Soviet society cannot only claim to be a socialist state, but as the first and most successful socialist state it is a prototype of every other twentieth-century "revolution from below." Soviet society shows a concern with problems of democracy and total participation, which are close to the hearts of Third World militants, however much repressed. Above all, the Soviet Union is in a far better position to render economic and technical assistance than is China. And in a world of declining ideological loyalties and increasing nationalistic loyalties, the Soviets promise more in way of what the current situation demands.

With respect to the United States the new changes in the Soviet political structure will mean a continuation of "correctness" in diplomatic relations. It has long been plain that the Soviet Union is seeking a *détente* with the United States and is not in search of any *rapprochement* at the ideological or social levels. More than ever, the Soviets seem to believe that "history is on their side"; and that these new changes in political form and style only intensify the contradictions of the United States. The more attractive the Soviet Union becomes, the less appealing is the United States; or so at least the theory would have it. To be sure, the continuation of Soviet policy along present lines seriously weakens any outright control of its satellites. But this "turn to the West" has already gone beyond the point of recall. The Soviet Union is now so forcefully committed to the national style in politics and the regional style in economics, that the social transformations taking place in Eastern Europe, or even in Western Europe—in and out of Communist Party circles—may themselves serve as an insurance policy to the West that the Soviet Union has no future designs for a *Pax Sovietica*.

The word "revolution" with respect to current events in the Soviet political hierarchy might seem to be exaggerated. For those who view the word as a concept akin to revelation and redemption, this would be the case. However, in a world of political lag, of slow growth in administrative norms, the transformation from autocracy to technocracy is of considerable value. It illustrates the limits and even the reversibility of Lord Acton's famous dictum. For if "power corrupts, and absolute power corrupts absolutely," the really interesting question from the present viewpoint is the possibility of moving from absolute power to limited power. The Soviets have been at the abyss twice: with Hitlerism from the outside and Stalinism on the inside, they have seen the future, decided that while it worked, the principle of socialist survival is itself insufficient either to define the goals of a mass society or to delimit the immediate policies of that society.

Chapter 6

The United Nations and the Third World:
East-West Conflict in Focus

In the very process of a transformation in its size and character, the United Nations has become the locus for the emergence of the Third World as an organized, institutionalized bloc. Curiously, through the legitimizing functions of the United Nations, the Third World is no longer a loose confederation of ideological formulas, as was the case at the first Bandung Conference in 1955. Indeed, so far has this process evolved that the need for the United Nations has itself become minimized. Sukarno has taken the big psychological step of removing Indonesia from United Nations membership, and thus demonstrated that the Third World is somehow more significant than it. Conflict in the Congo has also served to expose the racial nerve separating the old colonialist powers, such as Belgium and Portugal, from the rising tide of African and Asian nationalism. Lesser strains are revealed in France's call for a summit meeting to revise and update the United Nations charter, in the Soviet Union's demands for a reorganization of the Secretariat, and in the incapacity of United Nations agencies to finance their peace-keeping efforts.

Perhaps the most powerful gap of all was revealed in the various postures evident at a little summit meeting on Trade and Development held in 1964. At this Geneva conference the United States found itself in splendid isolation on matters concerning the economic and social life-blood of the Third World. Few significant events in recent times have received so little journalistic attention. For what the conference reflected was not simply a mounting pressure for multilateral economic relations, but a deepening of American isolation from the world political economy. The profound schism between the Third World and the United States is reflected in specific areas. While the issues raised may in time produce a general schism between the Third World and the fully developed world, there is no doubt that at present the central focus of the animosity is the United States. What follows is a catalogue of grievances which form the background and prelude to the public rift which took place at the United Nations Conference on Trade and Development.

(1) *Bilateralism versus Multilateralism:* Third World commentators, like Raúl Prebisch of Argentina and Edmundo Flores of Mexico, claim that the character of United States aid is strictly bilateral, and that this aid often deteriorates into idiosyncratic assistance based upon tests of political allegiance. In addition to driving political bargains, bilateralism helps the advanced nation drive economic bargains as well, by setting up favorable terms of credit, shipping surplus goods in place of fluid capital, demanding certain raw material advantages, and determining with whom and under what conditions trade with others is to take place. Finally, the bilateral approach often limits recipient countries from extending their trade lines with others.

(2) *Modernism versus Structuralism:* It is the contention of many Third World nations that the basic posture of the United States is to discourage self-sustaining economic units in favor of heavy consumer-oriented economies. Thus, the United States lends its weight and prestige to nations securing finished consumer products, with little or no emphasis on the costs, in independence and growth, of such an arrangement. The hub of the argument is that the United States, in advocating modernism, in effect supports the relatively small elite within the developing nations able to pay for the import of manufactured goods, while it ignores the needs of the large mass who would be aided much more substantially if the country emphasized industrial goods for public use rather than commodity goods for private use.

(3) *Agriculturalism versus Industrialism:* In general, Third World nations dislike the role they are being assigned as agricultural and raw materials areas. At the present time most of the Third World is forced to import expensive finished consumer goods and export relatively inexpensive farm and mineral raw materials. Such a trade pattern saddles a nation with a deepening inflationary spiral due to the imbalance between

high-priced consumer goods and low-cost raw materials and with perpetual indebtedness, also because of the price differential. This trade pattern can only be broken if the United States gives meaningful across-the-board trade and tariff concessions. At the present time the United States appears reluctant to offer such assistance. Such a condition contributes greatly to social unrest in the Third World. It is ironic that the United States' very insistence on the present international division of production helps sustain social unrest which it feels compelled to treat as a military threat.

(4) *Private Sector versus Public Sector:* While the Third World recognizes that the United States, like every other dynamic economy in the world, is a mixed economy, it is still viewed as a predominantly private-sector economy. What is more, the United States does little to disabuse the Third World of this impression. Indeed, its official posture is private enterprise. This stands in profound contrast to the economy of most Third World nations, which are debating what type of public-sector economy they prefer rather than assessing the degree of public or private enterprise they should adopt. Third World nations are upset that the United States fails to understand their needs and demands an adhesion to an economic philosophy of private-sector pre-eminence which even the most highly industrialized nation can itself no longer pursue.

(5) *Economic versus Political Determinism:* The Third World views the United States as a parliamentary democracy. At the same time it considers the introduction of such a system into less developed regions an impossibility. The historical conditions which have given rise to the Third World, particularly the lack of a mature and self-sustaining polity as well as the demands for rapid economic acceleration, seem to imply the need for much more centralized authority than was present in the United States at the time of its take-off. The failure on the part of the United States to appreciate the need for political centralization is held to be a key abrasive in the situation.

(6) *Integration versus Fragmentation:* Third World nations tend to be racially homogeneous, have a high density of population, widespread illiteracy, and a relatively large rural population; and caste, class, and tribal sectors which make them fragmented and ascriptive societies. The United States does not sufficiently appreciate their lack of structural solidarity. The problems of the modern world presuppose partici-

pation in international relations; and this is hard to achieve in societies still bound by class, caste, and racial schisms. Yet it is true that Third World nations cannot obtain their legitimate role in the international arena while the United States hinders their efforts.

The basic premise of the "Prebisch thesis,"[1] upon which the whole United Nations Conference on World Trade and Development was based, was that the gap between rich and poor nations is widening. The reasons for this, it was stated, had to do with the intense fluctuation in the world price of raw materials, a fluctuation often manipulated by fully developed industrial nations. The increased cost of purchasing finished commodities from the fully industrialized nations is a primary consequence, not a cause, of the gap. This gap led directly to the formation of a "77" nation bloc within the Third World. Thus Prebisch directly challenges the classical assumption that progress resulting from technological innovation will automatically benefit industrialized and non-industrialized nations alike through the mechanism of free trade. The United States seems directly opposed to this thesis with Bismark's motto: "Free trade is the weapon of the strongest."

The group of Third World nations known as the "77" have termed this period the "development decade." They recognize the need for concerted international action to create prosperous growth in presently underdeveloped and developing nations. Emergence of the "77" indicates the extent to which the Third World countries have made their needs known to advanced industrialized nations, especially the United States and the Soviet Union. They have attempted to persuade the First and Second Worlds to treat them as a new international combination of powers, instead of as a loose network of easily manipulated subordinates, and to negotiate with them as legitimate nation-states. Much of the business of the United Nations is taken up with this bloc's quest for parity. In its efforts to meet the demands of the "77," in the form of proliferating conferences and studies, the major powers have left a pattern of votes and rhetoric reflecting their reception of the social and economic demands of the Third World.

[1] Raúl Prebisch, *Towards a New Trade Policy for Development.* New York: United Nations Publications, 1964 (E/Conf/46/3). For empirical confirmation of the widening gap between the economic growth of industrial countries in contrast to underdeveloped "primary producing areas," see Alfred Maizels, *Industrial Growth and World Trade.* Cambridge: Cambridge University Press, 1963.

In recognition of the "development decade" the United Nations General Assembly set a minimum target to be achieved by newly developing countries by 1970; a minimal annual economic growth rate of 5 per cent. The United Nations Conference on Trade and Development is designed to create an international trade environment which would offset the trade disadvantages to developing countries. It is first necessary to determine how developing countries hope to attain equality in trade. Though United Nations publications and numerous scholarly studies discuss this matter, it is still not clear what the Third World is demanding.

While underdeveloped countries have an increasing need to import industrial equipment, their exports do not earn enough to pay for basic capital imports. The result is a trade gap, which gold and foreign exchange reserves have not been able to bridge. The gap must be then filled by capital import. Neither foreign loans nor foreign investment provide a permanent solution. Eventually the richer nations will refuse to lend to or invest in nations with faltering economies. Even in the short run, the expenses incurred in servicing external debts diminish the stop-gap effect of capital import. Many developing countries are faced with declining prices for their exports of primary commodities at a time when the prices of their imports of manufactures, especially of equipment, have greatly increased. Their dependence on primary commodity exports has reduced their capacity to import. This trend represents a major obstacle to their efforts to diversify and industrialize their economies. Recognition of this trade pattern as a barrier to development led to the Conference on Trade and Development which convened at Geneva on March 23, 1964, and continued until June 16.

The 1964 conference was based on the following findings: (1) World export has more than doubled since 1950 through overall expansion of the "world economy" aided by socio-economic change and scientific and technological progress. (2) The countries of the world do not share proportionately in this expansion of international trade. Although exports of developing countries rose from nineteen billion dollars to twenty-nine billion dollars between 1950 and 1962, that is, by 50 per cent, the expansion of exports from these countries proceeded at an appreciably lower rate than that of developed countries. As a result, the share of developing countries in world exports declined from nearly one-third in 1950 to only slightly more than one-fifth in 1962. Concurrently, the developed market economies increased their share from three-fifths to two-thirds, and the centrally planned economies from 8 per cent to 13 per cent. (3) The rate of expansion of world exports declined from 8½ per cent per annum in the early 'fifties to rather less than 5 per cent in the early 'sixties. One reason for the decline is the inability of the developing countries to attain a higher rate of export expansion.[2] (4) The demand for the export products of underdeveloped countries is relatively inelastic. And they have little chance of gaining ground, not only because they are faced with artificial tariff restrictions, but also because raw material substitutes are being created, for example, the replacement of rubber, leather, and fabrics by plastic goods. (5) The monopolistic elements in developed nations channel technological innovation into higher profits, shorter working hours, and higher wages for their own populations. Thus, technological progress does not automatically become an advantage for the developing regions. (6) Finally, because their exports are not expanding significantly, developing nations are unable to increase their purchases of capital goods from the developed countries. The "development decade" looks more like a "stagnation decade."

World trade was aggravated by deterioration in the terms of trade between 1950 and 1963. "The slower growth in the quantity of exports of the developing countries and the adverse movement of their terms of trade were largely the reflection of the present commodity composition of their trade, consisting, as it does, predominantly of the exchange of primary product exports for manufactured imports whose relative positions in world markets have undergone significant changes. World trade in manufactures has been increasing at an annual rate more than twice that of trade in primary products."[3] This imbalance has produced widespread use of substitutes and synthetics, increasing technological efficiency in primary products in advanced countries, increased productivity there, and the low consumer demand for food compared to increases in consumer income, in the advanced countries where incomes and food consumption are already high. The gap between import requirements of Third World countries and their export earnings has

---

[2] *Final Act. United Nations Conference on Trade and Development*, E/Conf. 46/L.28, June 16, 1964, p. 8, Section III.
[3] Ibid., pp. 8-9.

been widening. "According to United Nations Secretariat estimates, this gap could be of the order of $20 billion a year in 1970, on the basis of a five percent per annum rate of growth set as the target for the United Nations Development Decade, assuming no change in the trends of the 'fifties upon which these estimates were based."[4]

Slowly, Third World countries have been turning to economic and social planning as a technique for accelerating growth, if only to keep pace with the developed economies. While planning carries with it a clear-cut responsibility to consider, impose, and carry out structural changes, they are hindered externally by the instability of the international market for primary commodities; and by restrictions on access to markets of the developed countries. If the developing countries are to succeed, there must be appropriate changes in the structure of international trade which will afford them an opportunity to earn adequate amounts of foreign exchange.

In spite of the risk of antagonizing the United States, Third World nations have turned to Communist bloc countries. At the present time, however, trade between Third World countries and centrally planned economies remains but a small part of the trade turnover of developing countries as a whole. "In 1962, $1,630 million, or 5.6% of the total exports of the developing countries went to the centrally planned economies, while imports from the latter into the former totalled $2,150 million and formed 7.3% of total imports. This trade has, however, shown a tendency to increase rapidly in recent years."[5]

There are obvious economic advantages in Third World countries trading with the centrally planned economies of the socialist bloc. The establishment of "normal relations" between these blocs becomes an important factor in the creation of an international push to improve the trade balance of developing countries with advanced countries in general. The General Principles of the United Nations Conference on Trade and Development underline this point: "There shall be no discrimination on the basis of differences in socio-economic systems. Adaptation of trading methods shall be consistent with this principle."[6]

The most striking aspect of the resolutions presented at the confer-

[4] Ibid., p. 9.
[5] Ibid., p. 11.
[6] Ibid., Second Part, Section I, Principles, p. 17.

ence is the voting patterns of the United States, tacitly supported by France and Britain (though they abstained from voting whenever possible and whenever they felt no direct economic stake), and of the Soviet Union. The United States consistently opposed the resolutions of the conference, even where it was the only nation at the conference to do so. The Soviet Union consistently supported the claims of the developing nations. It is therefore necessary to further explore the economics in back of these resolutions.

A 5 per cent minimum growth target is considered extremely good. But, even with such a growth rate, the real wealth of Third World nations will continue to lag behind the developed nations. Since the rate of increase of consumer imports continues at a 6 per cent rate, payments for these imports more than absorb any growth in the national economy. "One of the reasons for this is that any acceleration in the rate of growth requires additional investment; and the import content of this investment is normally higher than that of income as a whole. Consequently, it is not going too far to conclude that imports would have to rise at a rate somewhat higher than that of total income."[7]

It would also be necessary for exports of developing countries to increase by 6 per cent to pay for a volume of imports increasing each year at that rate. The income thus derived would help create the necessary capital formation for economic "take-off." Austerity policies, high taxation, and the creation of investment capital are fundamental for the realization of this goal. Trade is not considered a substitute for this responsibility.[8] Redressing the trade balance, however, is an important preliminary stage, one than cannot await the resolution of internal change.

The Third World has repeatedly emphasized, although judiciously and politely, that it opposes present trade associations and agreements such as the General Agreement on Tariffs and Trade and the Common Market. The first Trade and Development Conference, held in Havana nearly thirty years ago, took place in a context of a world economic crisis and impending involvement of advanced countries in World War Two. At that time the developing nations could not exert

---

[7] Raúl Prebisch, *op. cit.*
[8] Raúl Prebisch, *Towards a Dynamic Development Policy for Latin America.* New York: United Nations Publication (E/Conf/12/680/1), 1963.

sufficient pressure to produce trade agreements designed to encourage their economic development. The code of rules and principles of that conference are still, with slight modifications, embodied in the General Agreement on Tariffs and Trade. The GATT agreement, as it is called, is based on an abstract notion of economic heterogeneity, just as were regional protectionist measures before it. GATT simply internationalizes protectionism.

The GATT agreement does not take into account the considerable structural differences which exist between big industrial centers and peripheral countries. In particular, it fallaciously assumes full employment, complete elasticity of supply and demand, and homogeneity of economic systems. Regional or international trade agreements have not benefitted the Third World as they have developed nations. Structural economic change at the time of the GATT agreement was gaining momentum. The GATT negotiations were not designed to expand world trade but rather to develop the aggregate income of the Atlantic Community. It was reciprocal, based in the main on rationalizing trade between major centers. In the Common Market by contrast, the member countries grant each other, by means of industrial pooling, preferences which are expected to convert their reciprocal trade into higher industrial production. This preferential system therefore offers a powerful impetus to trade among member countries, whereas the GATT agreement does little to change the basic disequilibrium which obtains between "donor" and "recipient" nations. Third World countries have attempted to demonstrate that preferential trade systems need not conflict with one which encourages development in disadvantaged nations. But the developed sector's actual attitude toward the agricultural products of the Third World underscores the disparity between the interests of the two sectors. Western Europe's—especially France's—highly restrictive policy toward agricultural imports is one source of irritation.

> Agriculture is a declining sector in the Six, as it is in most countries. The level of agricultural income has not kept pace with other sectors of the economy. Moreover, the share of agricultural income in total national income is markedly lower than the proportions of people working in agriculture would lead one to suspect. This lag in agricultural income is due to two sets of factors, first the relatively low productivity of agriculture resulting from

such structural deficiencies as too many small holdings, the fragmentation of farms, the lack of available capital, and the poor mobility of agricultural manpower; and, second, the inelasticity of demand for agricultural products and the unfavorable relationship between the prices received for agricultural products and those paid by the farmer for his means of production.[9]

This conflict of interests is further heightened by a high degree of political participation of French agricultural groups. The same holds true for German agriculture. Trade becomes based on a preferential system between industrialized nations, and is very difficult to change because of political as well as economic reasons. The declining importance of agriculture in these developed economies may bode well for future agreements which can support a principle of an "international division of labor." But this rationalization in the world economy depends on a rationalization of economic systems as such. Presently constituted preferential systems—the European Six, the United States, and the Atlantic Community—have not been able or willing to liberalize terms of trade to take account of other "preferential systems."

Until developing countries have sufficient capital formation for economic take-off, preferential systems established on regional grounds will have limited value for them. Such attempts as the Latin American Federation of Trade Associations have value mainly for articulating economic claims in political terms. At best, Third World regional systems tend to allocate resources more efficiently. But their supply and demand, shortages and abundance, are similar to each other. They cannot satisfy one another's needs for the materials offered by developed countries. Hence regional organization cannot truly relieve economic pressure. As a result, aside from some minimal good effects, such associations serve to organize Third World business interests for the purpose of articulating their claims. And conferences sponsored by the United Nations, which present these issues as a matter of world concern, serve as a platform where trade and financial policy of all the great blocs can be compared and perhaps adjudicated. It is a way for Third World nations to take fresh initiative in making their multilateral image of the economic world a reality.

[9] Leon N. Lindberg, *The Political Dynamics of European Economic Integration*. London: Oxford University Press, 1963.

Western objections to such multilateralism of Third World economic aims seek, at the very least, to purchase time for favored nations. Such aims, whatever the moral implications, are quite specious. Nor can the underdeveloped and developing nations be assuaged with token aid measures. Multilateralist trade arrangement is considered by Third World nations to be a virtual model for slow and modest change since their governments and business classes wish to avoid total renovation of their social structures. Hence, Western objections based on accusations of haste merely reveal the speciousness of such opposition. Such a position fails to take into account the precipitous haste with which colonial empires were forged to begin with. It has been pointed out that "in the ten years 1880-1890 five million square miles of African territory, containing a population of over 60 million, were seized by and subjected to European states."[10] Furthermore, what appeared to be a "scramble" for colonies was, in fact, a relatively well-integrated program of the advanced European powers to adjust their "spheres of influence" to their actual economic and political roles. Thus, by the beginning of the twentieth century, Asia and the Middle East were quickly absorbed in the colonial fold, along the classical lines evolved in Africa.[11] If the processes of colonization were rapidly worked out, it is no wonder that demands for decolonization should now be insistently presented before the pivotal United Nations agencies.

Demands for preferential economic treatment and for multilateral decision-making in economic affairs have an obvious "anti-Western" political content. Yet, these demands also reveal a clear desire on the part of the Third World to avoid a policy of exaggerated economic self-determination which would make it too reliant upon the Soviet Union. This is done, particularly by the African nations, by extending invitations to major First World private enterprises to invest in their countries at favorable trade and exchange rates. Development may include an industrial base, but it is not defined by the presence of such a base. The satellite relation of Eastern Europe to the Soviet Union makes

[10] Leonard Woolf, *Economic Imperialism*, pp. 33-4, as quoted in Maurice Dobb, *Political Economy and Capitalism*. New York: International Publishers, 1945, p. 243f.
[11] On this subject, see Maurice Dobb, *Political Economy and Capitalism*, pp. 242-4.

it clear that economic development without political sovereignty leads to structural reform without a resolution of basic social tensions.

Despite the highly liberal tone of the general principles recorded at the Conference on Tariffs and Trade, liberalization to Third World countries means new preferential systems based on the profitable sale of their goods in the advanced sector of the capitalist economy. Unless this "liberalization" occurs, developing countries will turn increasingly to trade arrangements and exchange with the centrally planned economies of Eastern Europe. This in turn would help relieve the economic pressures the East feels from the West.

After World War Two, the centralized economies of the Soviet type had twin aims: reconstruction and industrialization. They were obviously designed to change the character of these societies and to solve their basic problems—surplus population in agriculture, accelerated investment rate, and the need to curtail private consumption. Certain priorities were set which ultimately produced unintended strategic imbalances. Industry as a whole was emphasized as against agriculture, heavy industry over other industry, and heavy machinery within heavy industry. East European countries increased their investments in industry by 50 per cent and placed very low priorities on light industry and agriculture.[12]

The countries of Eastern Europe were greatly harmed by the Soviet Union's dogmatic insistence on a heavy industrial base. Despite attempts to co-ordinate labor, serious inefficiencies and imbalances in output and trade developed within the bloc itself and even led to alarming food shortages. After Stalin's death, those nations sought a new economic course.

> The allocation of investments was to be shifted, up to a point, in favor of light industry and agriculture, which were to receive a higher priority than before. However, no sooner had these shifts started to be implemented than it appeared such a reallocation implied the abandonment of many projects foreseen by the early plans. New pressures started to build up, then, in the opposite direction and finally, by mid-1954, many of the allocations of

[12] Nicolas Spulber, "Planning and Development," in *Resources and Planning in Eastern Europe*, edited by N. J. G. Pounds and Nicolas Spulber. Bloomington: Indiana University Publications, 1957.

investment in favor of light industry were canceled. Cooperation in the sense of a broad division of labor still appears to be precluded by dogmatic adherence to the idea that each country "must develop its own heavy-industrial base."[13]

But from time to time, pressures to secure these "low priority" goods through trade mount and it is clear that to head off these pressures from finding Western channels, it is to the advantage of the Soviet Union that the claims of the underdeveloped bloc be used economically.

Because there is no rift in Soviet policy then, between its economic and political aims with respect to the Third World, it can afford to carry out common assistance programs. The Soviet Union has assisted developing countries not just with consumer goods, but with industrial equipment and technical knowledge. Vast numbers of Third World technicians and workers are currently studying in Soviet universities and technological colleges and learning industrial skills in Soviet factories. As Deutscher notes,

> This is the cheapest and most effective assistance. It costs less than does American aid in consumer goods; and it helps the underdeveloped nations to help themselves. The effect of American assistance is largely ephemeral. This is why it earns so little gratitude. The results of Soviet assistance are lasting; and those who receive it have the sense of being raised up from backwardness and dependence. The Russians say: "We can do all this because we are not afraid of foreign competition; we do not tremble for our markets; and we are not afraid of sharing industrial know-how. Western capitalists cannot afford to do this."[14]

Quite aside from the obvious political advantages of such moves, the Soviet Union also has much to gain from expanded trade with underdeveloped countries. It is in a position to allocate long-term loans and monies on a more efficient basis than the United States, since it is not faced with the "problem of perversity" from business or Congress as the United States is. But more important, the Soviet Union does not have a favorable trade balance with Eastern Europe. If Eastern Europe

---

[13] N. Spulber, op. cit., p. 93.
[14] See Isaac Deutscher, The Great Contest: Russia and the West. New York: Ballantine Books, 1961, pp. 117-18.

could import a large supply of foodstuffs, raw materials, and primary commodities from the underdeveloped countries instead of perpetuating its dependence on the Soviet Union, and if it could then ship its increasing surplus of "engineering products" to them instead of to the Soviet Union, Eastern Europe would obviously gain considerable economic maneuvering space. Such a policy would leave the Soviet Union economically freer, since it would reduce the present drain on its resources involved in directing the industrialization of Eastern Europe. Granick has pointed out that "The Eastern European countries would also gain, in the sense that they would have several eager trading partners instead of one reluctant one."[15]

Many development specialists of the United States have argued that American economic interests are compatible with the trade interests of the underdeveloped nations.[16] There is considerable misconception, among development specialists no less than among the general public, that aid to underdeveloped countries, whether given directly or in support of requested measures, represents generosity from the American taxpayer. But the funds made available are often smaller than generally believed. Aid figures often indicate commitments and authorizations rather than actual disbursements. Furthermore, amortization and interest payments must be deducted from gross aid figures. With respect to Latin America, disbursements are often in the form of Eximbank loans, "Whose funds are derived from the sale of Treasury bills to investors."[17]

> These loans have realized a profit for American investors. And with the aid of the Inter-American Bank potential investors are provided with new channels for development funds open to Latin American governments.[18]

Disbursement in part is made in the form of surplus commodities which would otherwise remain idle and be subject to storage costs or deteriora-

[15] David Granick, "Economic Relations with the USSR," in *Resources and Planning in Eastern Europe, op. cit.*
[16] Eugene Staley, *The Future of Underdeveloped Countries* (revised edition). New York: Frederick A. Praeger, 1961, esp. pp. 397-441.
[17] Irving L. Horowitz, *Revolution in Brazil: Politics and Society in a Developing Nation.* New York: E. P. Dutton & Co., 1964, esp. pp. 196-223.
[18] Tad Szulc, *Winds of Revolution.* New York: Frederick Praeger, 1963, esp. pp. 275-7.

tion. Furthermore, United States taxpayer-consumers often benefit from a decline in prices paid for import products; this is particularly so when wholesale prices of United States exports rise. This decline in prices is linked to the purchase of U.S. goods produced or marketed abroad.

The final report of the conference contains what might be called "historical" background. In it the origins are traced to the Havana conference of the 'thirties. Its "preface" placed the United Nations Conference within a setting of economic problems which represent a continuation of the Havana Conference. The rest of the proceedings consist of the General and Special Principles together with recommendations which press further the multilateralist implications of Third World claims.

The table on pp. 180-85 shows the voting at the conference. It makes plain what the actual "gap" between the United States and the Third World has come to. And it also provides a graphic description of the blocs within the United Nations.

Let us examine the United States voting response to the General and Special Principles of the Conference in more detail; particularly since the propositions as given in the chart have been condensed.

General Principle One states "Economic relations between countries, including trade relations, shall be based on respect for the principle of sovereign equality of states, self-determination of peoples, and non-interference in the internal affairs of other countries." The only vote against this proposition was cast by the United States.

General Principle Two: "There shall be no discrimination on the basis of differences in socio-economic systems. Adoption of trading methods shall be consistent with this principle." The United States voted against this.

General Principle Three: "Every country has the sovereign right freely to trade with other countries, and freely to dispose of its natural resources in the interest of the economic development and well-being of its own people." The United States voted against this.

General Principle Four calls for recognition of socio-economic development as the concern of the old community and co-operative policies among the nations of the world to enhance development. The only vote against it was cast by the United States. The United States, however, abstained on General Principle Five calling for measures to diversify and adjust underdeveloped countries to modern needs. This may well be because a portion of it, stating that "Developed countries should assist the developing countries in their efforts," is in keeping with unilateral and bilateral policies of the United States toward underdeveloped countries. Whenever independence, trade adjustment, expansion, sovereignty, economic diversification are called for, as for example in General Principle Six, the United States voted against acceptance. This is true for General Principles Seven, Eight, Eleven, Twelve. The United States voted for General Principles Nine, Ten, Thirteen, Fifteen, since "regional groupings" of underdeveloped countries pose no immediate threat to United States interests. Principle Nine calls for regional groupings among developed countries not to inhibit or injure Third World economies. Here the language was sufficiently clear-cut. "To insure that their economic integration does not cause injury to . . ." It could not really have been opposed. Indeed, no country at the conference voted against Nine. General Principle Thirteen was a matter of arranging the parts of the conference to include Principles relating to the transit trade of landlocked countries. Since nothing was at stake, no country voted against it. The United States also voted for General Principle Fifteen calling for recognition of the different stages of developing economies and measures adopted to take cognizance of these stages to insure growth. Again the Principle did not call for sovereignty, diversification, independence, freedom, or autonomy, and hence did not represent a challenge to American hegemony.

The vote on Special Principles followed the same pattern. Where the propositions implied multilateralism, the United States voted against them. Where bilateralism was protected or unchallenged, reflecting current United States relations, there were abstentions. Where tariff curbs on developed countries were called for in strong or clear-cut language, the United States either abstained or voted in favor of such a principle. Special Principles differed from General Principles in that the former covered more specific ground. They were more concrete and were concerned with suggestions for implementation.

The United States vote was preponderantly against most General and Special Principles because they called for the encouragement of independence, autonomy, free trade, and diversification of underdeveloped economies. Measures strongly inhibiting developed countries from acting against the interests of developing countries were supported by the

TABLE I—GENERAL PROPOSITIONS OF THE UNITED NATIONS CONFERENCE ON TRADE AND DEVELOPMENT

Propositions*	Asian Bloc	Latin America	African Bloc	United Kingdom	United States	Soviet Union	Eastern Europe	Western Europe	Vote Explanation**	Composite Vote Yea (+)	Nay (−)	Abs. (0)
(G.P. I) Economic relations between countries shall be based on respect for the principle of sovereign equality of states, self-determination, and non-interference in internal affairs.	+	+	+	0	−	+	+	+	Australia, Ireland, & New Zealand voted Yea. Portugal abstained.	113	1	2
(G.P. II) There shall be no discrimination on the basis of differences in socio-economic systems. Adoption of trading methods shall be consistent with this principle.	+	+	+	0	−	+	+	+	Germany & Canada Against. S. Africa, Spain, Monaco, Sweden, Switzerland, Netherlands, Norway abstained.	96	3	16
(G.P. III) Every country has the right to trade with others, and freely to dispose of its natural resources in the interest of the economic development of its own people.	+	+	+	−	−	+	+	+	Germany abstained. Nicaragua, Peru, and Japan abstained.	94	4	18
(G.P. IV) All countries will pursue internal and external economic policies designed to accelerate economic growth throughout the world, at a rate which would narrow the gap between developed and developing nations.	+	+	+	−	−	+	+	+	Belgium, Finland, France, Italy, Holy See, Japan, Luxembourg, Monaco, Peru, Netherlands, Nicaragua, S. Africa, Switzerland abstained.	98	1	17

* (G.P.) stands for General Propositions; (S.P.) stands for Special Propositions.
** When a given nation does not vote with its given bloc, it will appear in the vote explanation column.

Principle	Votes	Notes	For	Against	Abstained
(G.P. V) Economic policies should be directed towards attaining an international division of labor in harmony with needs for diversification of developing economies.	+ + o o + + +	As in vote explanation for G.P. IV, plus Canada and Spain abstained.	97	0	19
(G.P. VI) All countries should cooperate in creating conditions of international trade conducive to the achievement of the rapid increase in the export earnings of developing countries.	+ + + − + + +	Taiwan (China) abstained.	114	1	1
(G.P. VII) Developed countries shall progressively eliminate barriers that hinder trade and consumption of products from developing countries, and take steps to create new export markets for developing countries.	+ + − − + + +	Denmark and Switzerland Against.	87	8	19
(G.P. VIII) Developed countries should grant concessions to developing nations without extracting similar concessions in return. Special preferential arrangements presently in effect should be regarded as transitional.	+ + − + + o	Austria, Iceland, Sweden, Switzerland, Against. Brazil, Rwanda, Uganda, Venezuela abstained.	78	11	23
(G.P. IX) Developed countries participating in regional economic groupings should ensure that their economic integration does not cause injury to or adversely affect expansion of imports from developing countries.	+ + + + + + + o	Austria, Finland, Sweden, Switzerland did not abstain.	106	0	10
(G.P. X) All forms of economic cooperation should result in an expansion of intra-regional and extra-regional trade and encourage their growth and diversification with due regard to special features of each nation.	+ + + + + + +	Japan abstained.	115	0	1

TABLE I—(Cont.)

Propositions*	Asian Bloc	Latin America	African Bloc	United Kingdom	United States	Soviet Union	Eastern Europe	Western Europe	Vote Explanation**	Composite Vote Yea(+)	Nay(−)	Abs.(0)
(G.P. XI) Developed countries should increase net flow of international financial, technical, economic assistance to aid export earnings of underdeveloped countries. No political or military conditions.	+	+	+	−	−	+	+	0	Australia, F.R. Germany, Against.	92	5	19
(G.P. XII) Resources released as outcome of agreement on disarmament should be allocated to economic developing by the fully developed countries.	+	+	+	0	−	0	0	0		83	1	30
(G.P. XIII) (land-locked countries)	+	+	+	+	+	+	+	+		108	0	0
(G.P. XIV) Complete decolonization as in U.N. Declaration of granting independence & liquidation of all forms of colonialism is necessary for economic development & exercise of sovereign rights over natural resources.	+	+	+	−	0	+	+	0	Australia Against	90	2	22
(G.P. XV) Different levels of development to be recognized in individual developing countries & special attention to least developed countries to insure equitable opportunity.	+	+	+	+	+	+	+	+	Albania, Brazil, Canada, Iceland, Jamaica, Syria, Liechtenstein, Japan, Spain abstained.	101	0	12

Proposal	Votes	Remarks	For	Against	Abstain
(S.P. 1) Developed countries should cooperate with developing countries in setting targets for expansion of trade of the latter & in periodically reviewing measures taken for their achievement.	+ + + o − + + +	Canada Against.	99	2	15
(S.P. 2) Developing countries should modernize agriculturally and industrially. Developed countries should supplement these efforts through financing, training programs & expanding imports of processed & manufactured goods from developing countries.	+ + + + + + +		116	0	0
(S.P. 3) No action.					
(S.P. 4) Developing countries have the right to protect their infant industries.	+ + + o + + +		115	0	1
(S.P. 5) Domestic support for primary commodities in developed countries shall not preclude a fair proportion of the domestic consumption being supplied by developing countries.	+ + + o + + +	Australia, Austria, Belgium, F. R. Germany, Finland, France, San Marino, Greece, Holy See, Iceland abstained.	91	0	25
(S.P. 6) Developed countries should help developing countries promote new uses for products whose use has been reduced by synthetic innovations, by research, etc.	+ + + + + + + +		116	0	0
(S.P. 7) Whenever international measures taken are to stabilize primary product prices in relation to manufactured goods, equitable arrangements should be made in terms of facilitating the implementation of economic development plans.	+ + − − o o o	Australia, Austria, Canada, Denmark, F. R. Germany, Iceland, Japan, Norway, S. Africa, Switzerland, Liechtenstein, Against.	85	13	18

TABLE I—(Cont.)

Propositions*	Asian Bloc	Latin America	African Bloc	United Kingdom	United States	Soviet Union	Eastern Europe	Western Europe	Vote Explanation**	Composite Vote Yea +	Nay −	Abs. o
(S.P. 8) In the disposal of agricultural surpluses, developed countries should undertake to apply internationally agreed upon criteria of surplus disposal so as not to affect adversely export prospects of developing countries heavily dependent on the export narrow range of primary products. Criteria should also govern the disposal of all primary product surpluses and stockpiles.	+	+	+	o	−	+	+	+	Denmark, France, Iceland, France, Monaco, Sweden, S. Africa abstained.	106	1	9
(S.P. 9) Countries shall refrain from all forms of dumping.	+	+	+	o	o	+	+	+	Norway, S. Africa, Sweden abstained.	107	0	9
(S.P. 10) Scientific and technological achievements should be made accessible under favourable conditions to all developing countries and their application to the trade and development needs of those countries should be encouraged by an expansion of bilateral and multilateral programmes of technical assistance.	+	+	+	+	+	+	+	+		116	0	0

(S.P. 11) All countries should support an expansion of multilateral economic assistance to developing countries especially within the framework of the U.N. as well as bilateral assistance.	+	+	o	o	+	+	o	93	0	23	Japan, S. Africa abstained.
(S.P. 12) All countries should cooperate in devising measures to help developing countries build up transport for their economic development, to ensure the unhindered use of such facilities and to promote tourism in these countries in order to increase their earnings and reduce their expenditure on invisible trade.	+	+	–	–	+	+	o	92	7	17	Canada, Japan, Ireland abstained.
(S.P. 13) Mutually beneficial bilateral and multilateral trade and payments arrangements between developing countries constitute an essential element in the expansion and diversification of international trade.	+	+	+	o	+	+	+	111	0	5	Australia, Canada, Japan, Liechtenstein abstained.

major blocs. Fair pricing of primary commodities and technical assistance were also widely supported by all blocs.

Special segments of development concerned with *international commodity arrangements and removal of obstacles to, and expansion of, trade* were adopted without dissent. These recommendations were primarily concerned with ending the great trade advantages developed countries held over the underdeveloped countries. For example, there should be equitable disposal of surplus goods and a fair price on primary commodities, so that fair sales competition could exist. Here too, positive independence, low tariffs, free trade, and sovereignty were not at stake.

The propositions calling for a review and proper administration of the World Food Aid Program found no dissent; nor was any opposition voiced to competition from synthetics and substitutes. Because of the advanced nature of the goods involved, these tenets held little relevance for developing countries and great relevance for advanced countries. So none of the advanced countries offered dissent. On special legislation, the United States voted consistently. Where its bilateral arrangements were either left intact or promoted, it abstained or supported the measures. Where sovereignty and free trade were involved, it voted negatively. It supported only measures recommending studies, surveys, information gathering, and technical assistance.

Each of the countries was invited to explain its votes in a section called Observations. The United States explained its general opposition on two grounds: (1) The measures called for were not really going to provide efficient assistance to underdeveloped countries; (2) the recommendations prejudged the results of the proposed study, for it requested that a program of action be drawn up. United States objections sometimes reflected distaste for measures which encouraged trade with the "centrally planned" economies.

The following conclusions can be drawn from this welter of Propositions, Principles, and Observations. The Soviet vote was based on the union of its political and economic needs *vis à vis* the underdeveloped countries. The United States reflected the complications of its position. It would have been to its political advantage to support measures of the conference since they would be adopted anyway. But the internal political atmosphere of an election year affected political rationality. Economically, the United States has a policy of encouraging modernism at the expense of structural change for its own market needs. Thus far the United States is not prepared to consider its economic interests in a larger multilateral context. The latent mistrust of the capacity of Third World nations to guide their own destinies, or the implied competition involved, has led the United States to oppose measures which could enhance this process of development. This conference did shatter the myth that "development intellectuals" (who tend to favor measures such as those at the conference) are in charge of the nation's policy-making or diplomacy with respect to the underdeveloped world.

We tend to assume rationality in the decision-making process, particularly when it comes to questions of international relations. But this insistence on rationality has the defects of its virtue. In the case of the conference, for example, national explanations for the uniformly parochial and narrow reaction to Third World demands break down on the main point: that economists, political analysts, and scientific researchers from the United States were the *primum mobile* for the entire Prebisch position. Sociologically inclined economists such as Bert Hoselitz and Albert O. Hirshman, have for some time supported these same sorts of demands.

Thus, we reach the conclusion that the voting pattern of the United States in the United Nations at the Geneva Conference was partially inspired by outside factors strong enough to occasion United States opposition to the best opinions voiced by its own policy-makers. Chief of these "irrational" factors was the emergence of Goldwaterism as a political phenomenon during the early summer of 1964. The United Nations representatives were discouraged from any behavior which might be construed as precipitous, or as delivering ourselves into the hands of the socialist sector. Another is that the "hard line" with respect to Latin America had yielded major victories in Brazil with the April First *coup d'état*, with the collapse of guerrilla operations from Venezuela to Argentina, the election in Chile of Christian Democracy over the socialist opposition, etc. In short, the hard line was gaining points at the very time the developmental line was appealing for greater independence. And finally, American foreign policy in Southeast Asia became increasingly military and decreasingly political; so that it became less important to the United States to take the Third World voting bloc into account.

But these factors account only for low-order, immediately perceived irrationality. There exists, however, a higher irrationality. The United States, since entering international politics as a major force, has been confronted by a duality within its tradition. On one side, there is its revolutionary background, a belief in a democracy where each man counts as one, and no more nor less than one. On the other side, there is the United States of the manifest destiny, of the Monroe Doctrine, and of a general conviction that the fates of the world are determined by the march of American hegemony. But these political contradictions were no more a deterrence to American economic growth than was totalitarianism to Russia.

The confusions are well stated by Hans J. Morgenthau: "The traditional anti-imperialism of America was without a political objective either by virtue of its very nature or else because the radius of an active American foreign policy was limited to the Western Hemisphere." In contrast to this, "the new anti-imperialism can no longer afford to condemn the suppression of liberty from afar and limit its tribute to freedom to charitable deeds. Committed to the containment of communism, to the preservation of national freedom wherever it is threatened by Soviet imperialism, the United States can reconcile itself to this loss of national freedom only if it altogether ceases being anti-imperialistic."[19] In other words, anti-imperialism, by taking on anti-Communist pretensions, has become tough-minded instead of tender-hearted. But even Morgenthau shrinks away from the Realpolitik of this anti-Communist framework. He has to see United States interests as eternally linked to European allies in particular and to a "common civilization threatened by an alien and oppressive social system" in general. In other words, the classic stress between "interests" and "ethics" is seen as a uniquely American problem, and for that very reason, a certain jejune quality is manifested in United States international policies with respect to the Third World.

The United States of America, when faced with responsibilities and problems of world leadership, has shown that it is striving to be both powerful and ethical. It has not been, however, mature or wise in its attempts to reconcile power and morality, for it has not yet awakened to

[19] See Hans J. Morgenthau, "The American Tradition in Foreign Policy," in *Foreign Policy in World Politics*, edited by R. C. Macridis. Englewood Cliffs, N.J.: Prentice-Hall, Inc., 1962, pp. 206, 211.

the fact that in important ways the two aims are irreconcilable. It has striven for power to counterbalance totalitarian injustice, in addition to seeking self-enrichment. It has undertaken the "white man's burden" in order to extend the areas of what it conceived to be freedom. It undertook to build a counter-imperialism. The United States conceives the efforts of other nations to extend territorial influence as imperialistic; its own efforts to do so are often conceived as rescue operations. It is therefore blind to its own imperialism and considers the efforts to extend its own power as the height of justice.

With perfect moralistic consistency it can pursue policies which seek to extend its spheres of influence in the name of justice and deliverance from tyranny. The United States is an imperialistic democracy. But it cannot reconcile the nature of the terms. It could perhaps wield its power more ruthlessly in certain areas, but then it would not square with a democratic self-image. It could allow for the full autonomy of weaker nations, but then it would not be powerful. While it attempts both, it loses ground on both fronts. It cannot be frankly imperialistic as England and France were in earlier generations. Neither can it be truly just. It is ambivalent because it feels now the needs of one, now the needs of the other. Thus, it has never developed a satisfactory imperialistic style, nor a meaningful moral posture.

Every great nation has a sense of mission. It has often been noted that a great nation is both expansionist and imperialistic because it is in the nature of power that it be driven thus. The Soviet Union also has this divided self-image. It too is exporting democracy, economic if not political democracy. It also conceived the extension of its influence in the name of freedom from tyranny. It has sought to store immense power in its organs of government, and notions of its ethical mission have guided its foreign policies. It too has undertaken to solve the "white man's burden." It acts in the name of moral justice, often sincerely. The Soviet Union amasses power to extend the areas of freedom, though its conception of this term is largely economic. Like the United States, it is sensitive to reactions to its policies from those whom it tries to influence. It perceives itself as anti-imperialist.

The United States defines justice in terms of political liberty. The Soviet Union defines justice in terms of economic welfare. The latter best suits the needs of the Third World. The United States defines imperialism as a form of injustice. According to its political libertarian definitions of justice the Soviet Union is unjust and imperialistic, the former because of the latter. The Soviet Union defines injustice as attempts to practice political libertarianism without solving economic dilemmas of poverty. Injustice of this kind can only be engaged in legitimately by an elite. Hence efforts to spread this false democracy are imperialistic and unjust, the former because of the latter. The First and Second Worlds are therefore mirror images of each other's shortcomings.

The underdeveloped countries conceive it to be their sovereign right to make their own choice between the First and Second Worlds. And the United Nations is in an important sense their instrument for limiting the imperialistic variations of both worlds, while holding both accountable for their ideal claims. Efforts on the part of the United States to obstruct United Nations conference decision-making are seen as unjust and imperialistic. For the Third World shares with the Soviet Union an economic conception of democracy and justice. The successes of the Soviet Union in the economic sphere seem to be confirmation of this belief. Hence the Soviet Union does not seem to be imperialistic. The Soviet Union, like the United States, is seen as powerful, but United States power is viewed as necessarily restrictive of the sovereignty of underdeveloped nations. This is defined as imperialist. American attempts to combat the imperialist image, by such programs as the Alliance for Progress and the Peace Corps, have aimed at paralleling its interests with altruistic actions, but have never made a significant sacrifice of the former. The Soviet Union is not in a similar bind at the present historical moment. The United States can attend a conference at which the underdeveloped countries present a number of proposals and resolutions for implementing programs to relieve their economic distress, and out of the simple fact that the Russians can support these proposals without serious sacrifice to its positions, the United States seems peculiarly colonialist and, hence, unjust. To counter this imperialism the United States has to surrender some part of its own immediate interest. When the United States does not give support to the Third World, it gives the classical argument of the rights of power. The United States balances these factors "pragmatically," issue by issue. It cannot surrender any part of its interest, nor will it recognize other legitimate definitions of justice. It cannot see the temporariness of these given issues, and tends to stand therefore for "eternal truths" when it votes as when it fights.

That this "self-interest" doctrine is gaining support is shown by the tendency of at least one wing of American policy-makers to consider foreign aid in militaristic rather than in developmental terms. One authority has summed up this position most candidly: "American policies regarding aid and trade may legitimately be employed as strategic weapons in the Cold War, and that in such employment, flexibility is both appropriate and necessary."[20] In short, all trade and aid must be viewed in terms of enhancing the security of the United States, while any humanitarian concerns must be considered as a by-product of national objectives. The startling voting pattern of the United States, with respect to Third World trade demands, can be considered a response to the growing self-consciousness of America as a world power—something not in evidence during previous decades. The American dialogue between considerations of power in contrast to those of justice remains in evidence. It is also clear that the power factions within the political hierarchy now occupy command positions with respect to the issuance of foreign assistance.

The perverse voting pattern of the United States at the Conference on Trade and Development shows it to be combatting Soviet influence in the name of justice. It is, it believes, acting cautiously or out of principle. To the rest of the world, which does not share this dialectic of self-definition or self-interest with the Soviet Union, the United States is seen to be acting against its own interest. Hence, the United States is often looked upon as an imperialist which cannot extend the borders of democracy. The United States stands alone with irritating suspicions as to why, but with few explanations. This kind of political behavior, this incapacity to surrender anything but taxpayers' money for foreign aid, reveals it to be blind to the image cast. The United States cannot adopt colonialist positions as equivalent to justice. Modern imperialism is built into the American system of political democracy. This paradox cannot be easily removed by a new vocabulary or a new dedication to national purpose.

[20] James R. Schlesinger, "Strategic Leverage from Aid and Trade," in *National Security: Political, Military, and Economic Strategies in the Decade Ahead*, edited by David M. Abshire and Richard V. Allen. New York: Frederick A. Praeger (for the Hoover Institution on War, Revolution and Peace), 1963, pp. 688-9.

Perhaps the cruelest cut of all is that the political posture of the United States has itself become a unifying agency of Third World nations. What might easily deteriorate into national rivalries, regional jealousies, and social distinctions are prevented from doing so, in some measure at least, by the fear of United States policy formulators that a positive line toward the Third World is tantamount to a betrayal of national interests. Thus the purposes of United States moral aims are contradicted not so much by the Communist challenge as by United States political decisions.

THE THIRD WORLD IN DEPTH

"A backward country assimilates the material and intellectual conquests of the advanced countries. But this does not mean that it follows them slavishly, reproduces all the stages of their past. Although compelled to follow after the advanced countries, a backward country does not take things in the same order. The privilege of historic backwardness—and such a privilege exists—permits, or rather compels, the adoption of whatever is ready in advance of any specified date, skipping a whole series of inter-mediate stages. Savages throw away their bows and arrows for rifles all at once, without traveling the road which lay between these two weapons in the past...The possibility of skipping over intermediate steps is of course by no means absolute. Its degree is determined in the long run by the economic and cultural capacities of the country. The backward nation, moreover, not infrequently debases the achievements borrowed from out-side in the process of adapting them to its own more primitive culture. In this the very process of assimilation acquires a self-contradictory character ...The laws of history have nothing in common with a pedantic schemati-cism. Unevenness, the most general law of the historic process, reveals itself most sharply and complexly in the destiny of the backward countries. Under the whip of external necessity their backward culture is compelled to make leaps."

(Leon Trotsky in **History of the Russian Revolution**)

Chapter 7

Mending and Smashing: Economic Issues and Strategies

The main problem in the development process from the economic viewpoint is not the need to "break out" of stagnation. This is a politically inspired decision. The economic issues enter at that point where the initial political decision has to be sustained and upheld by economic action. The hub of the matter for Third World nations is this: how can they amass the savings necessary to bring themselves into the modern world?

Such savings can be created either through taxation or expropriation. Taxation can be called "forced savings," "guided investments," "reallocation of profits"; or expropriation can be called "land reform," "urban renewal," "popular control"—but the fact is that an economy can either be grounded in evolutionary principles of mending existing social structures, or upon revolutionary principles of smashing and replacing these structures.

In this chapter we will be concerned with the place of taxation, voluntary savings, and other fiscal measures in stimulating the economy. Second, we will consider types of expropriation—confiscation of land with the aim of establishing individual proprietorship or collectivist ownership. The decision to reform a society or conduct a revolution against it is presented from an economic perspective as a choice between whether to mend or to smash the social structure.

Various governmental and international agencies employ a convenient shorthand in describing development. Social development is indicated by such criteria as improvements in the fields of education, health, nutrition, housing, and social security. Economic development is indicated by such criteria as increases in production, in per capita national income, and in consumption measured as per capita use of electrical energy.[1] In point of fact the separation between the social and the economic only exists in the realm of academic analysis and governmental departmentalization.[2]

As the late Paul Baran well understood, economic development has always been propelled by classes and by groups interested in a new economic and social order. It has always been opposed and obstructed by those interested in, and deriving innumerable benefits from, an existing fabric of society, and from the prevailing mores, customs, and institutions.[3] Given the interrelation between social and economic development, we may begin the discussion of taxation and expropriation with an appreciation of the complexities involved.

I

Taxation is the transfer of real resources from the private to the public sector, and from personal consumption to social saving.[4] Moreover, taxation legitimizes the political apparatus by "rationalizing" the social system. Economic improvement carries with it the right and even obligation for the political apparatus to purchase or produce many goods and services, and to redistribute income among different sections of the community.[5] This perspective has further meant the crumbling of the older ideology that only the savings of the capitalists count.[6] The very extension of the principle of savings to include all economic sectors means that in some sense a model of development, which would be

[1] *Report on the World Situation.* New York: United Nations, 1961, p. 41. In this connection, see an earlier report on *Measures for the Economic Development of Underdeveloped Countries.* New York: United Nations, 1957.
[2] *Report on the World Situation.* New York: United Nations, 1961, p. 23.
[3] Paul Baran, *The Political Economy of Growth.* New York: Monthly Review Press, 1957, p. 3 et passim.
[4] *Economic Survey of Asia and Far-East.* New York: United Nations, 1961, p. 210.
[5] A. R. Prest, *Public Finance in Underdeveloped Countries.* London: Weidenfeld & Nicolson, 1962, p. 17.
[6] W. Arthur Lewis, *The Theory of Economic Growth.* Homewood, Ill.: Irwin Publishers, 1955, pp. 225-7.

liberated from the structures of any one sector, would, in part, be liberated from the restrictions of economic competition as such.[7]

A basic factor determining the rate of economic development is the ratio of investment to income, or the proportion of current income transformed into new productive uses. The strategy of increasing such investment capital is a political chore. Governments in the Third World survive or collapse by the decisions they take concerning the stimulation of development. To "tax" the poor through denial of wage increases or austerity programs is one way, to "tax" the rich directly through government collection of funds gained as a result of business profits, is another way. To do nothing results in stagnation. To burden the poor may stimulate revolution. To focus on the wealthy may lead to industrial demoralization and the flight of capital. Therefore to mend or to smash is at the basis of any taxation approach. The economics of development is thus linked to the politics of risk-taking.

To accomplish a mobilization of financial resources, governments often use fiscal manipulation. An important part of this program is taxation. An extensive and effective fiscal policy is indispensible to the acceleration of the "take-off" point. Government revenue and expenditure policies have a significant effect upon social and economic life, and upon the rate of economic development in particular. Such policies affect the allocation of resources, alter the distribution of income, promote capital accumulation, and restrain inflation.

In the Third World, government expenditure in a particular sector of the economy tends to attract resources, whereas taxation tends to repel them. Land and property taxes can affect the system of land tenure; tax exemption and tax discrimination can influence the direction of investment to particular sectors; taxes can serve as a break on consumer-oriented industries; and subsidies can encourage industries that provide prospects for wide social benefits.[8]

[7] A basic problem economists frequently encounter is that while they see the possibilities for moving beyond the laisser-faire assumptions in the idea that only capitalists save, they fail to appreciate the possibilities, even the likelihood, that when the state imposes universal taxation, it gives us a model of development which is no longer economic in character; that is to say, one which no longer relies on the free play of free market forces to amass savings. See Albert O. Hirschman, *The Strategy of Economic Development*. New Haven: Yale University Press, 1958, pp. 38-9.

[8] A. R. Prest, *op. cit.*, p. 27.

Fiscal measures alter the institutional environment which determines the distribution of income, or directly changes the resulting distribution. Government expenditures on health and education may increase occupational mobility and can upgrade workers; land taxes can alter the distribution of land ownership; and a system of taxes and subsidies can alter the degree of competition in various sectors of the economy. On the other hand, the distribution of income can be made more equitable through progressive taxation. This can be done by reallocating monies directly and providing government expenditures to lower-income groups.[9]

Fiscal measures (taxation chief among them) can serve to accelerate economic and social growth. These proposals, while basically mending ideals, when carried "too far," can bring about the demand for smashing tactics—and hence forestall the implementation of even modest reforms by the ruling economic elite.

To be effective in social development, fiscal measures of a newly developing area should satisfy the following conditions: (1) They must penalize non-essential consumption and encourage savings and investments. (2) They must channel an important proportion of the increments in national income to the public sector for further investment. (3) They must not promote inflationary spirals or curtail savings or investment. (4) They must not have any pronounced bias in favor of or against any particular economic class unless there is a socially recognized justification for it, such as wide gradations in wealth. (5) They must be administratively feasible for the country involved. (6) They must be capable of reducing and curbing economic inequalities without at the same time stimulating social chaos. If a fiscal policy of this type is to succeed, it is essential that the political powers be willing to risk nothing short of their own position.

The basic fiscal characteristic of Third World countries is that the largest proportion of national income exists in the agricultural sector. The majority of the population still gains sustenance through agriculture. But because of various reasons—illiteracy, primitive agricultural methods, overpopulation, overdivided lands, lack of transportation, and the lack of mechanization—farms are not economically productive. Agricultural cycles often accentuate the subsistence level of the economy.

[9] A. R. Prest, op. cit., p. 28.

Thus, the tax contribution of agriculture to the public commonweal is negligible.

The landlord classes of Latin America and Asia, and the tribal rulers of Africa, while small in size, own a substantial part of the land. But their contribution to the public revenue is even less than that of the small proprietor. In nations like Brazil and India the landlord class transforms its economic power into political power, and thus can avoid paying tax. In so doing, this class can influence fiscal policy as a whole, and determine the distribution of income, the direction of public expenditures, and the form of economic development. Recent United Nations data collected from 55 nations show that there is a very great difference in personal income tax between developed and underdeveloped countries.[10] In the United Kingdom and the United States, for example, from 30 to 40 per cent of the total population pays income tax each year. In the Caribbean territories, on the other hand, less than 3 per cent does. In Africa and Asia, a country is doing relatively well if 1 per cent of its population pays. Whereas income subject to personal income tax amounts to some 75 per cent of Gross National Product in the United Kingdom, it amounts to only 10 per cent in the Caribbean and 5 per cent or less in African territories.[11]

Taxation is made difficult by these factors: First, and most significant, is the disproportionate distribution of wealth. Second, most taxes are of the indirect variety (import duties, export taxes, excise taxes, sales taxes, and public utilities taxes) which affect the poorer classes disproportionately. Third, inflation, which is itself a form of taxation, increases the disparities between those who live on relatively fixed incomes, such as factory workers and lower-echelon bureaucrats, and those whose income is pegged to an informal sliding scale, such as shopkeepers and industrialists. Fourth, economic problems tend to become political problems.[12]

According to most current reports of the *International Labor Review*, in Venezuela, 50 per cent of the total wealth is in the hands of 12 per cent of the families; in Chile, a third of the national wealth is controlled by 5

[10] *Economic Survey of Asia and Far-East*. New York: United Nations, 1961, p. 211.
[11] A. R. Prest, *op. cit.*, p. 28.
[12] For a general account of the distinction between direct and indirect modalities of taxation, see A. R. Prest, *op. cit.*, pp. 27-79.

per cent of the population; in Colombia, 41 per cent of the national income was received by 5 per cent of the population; in Mexico, which has undergone considerable modernization, 16 per cent of the population receive 56.5 per cent of the total income (as late as 1957); while in Brazil, despite a huge public-sector orientation, 63 per cent of the wealth went to 17 per cent of the population.[13] Given this data, the relative weakness of the present tax structure is evident. It is a failure of underdeveloped regimes to collect and graduate the tax structure. It means that the very rich are even wealthier in relation to the rest of the population as a whole than even the damaging statistical information reveals.

Because of the unfavorable taxation schemes, lower income groups are responsible for a very high percentage of the fiscal expenses. As Luis A. Monge has declared: "The privileged minority groups have managed to guide fiscal policy along indirect taxation lines, largely to escape direct taxation."[14] Indirect taxation amounts to more than 70 per cent of the federal revenues in Brazil, Costa Rica, Ecuador, Guatemala, Honduras, and Nicaragua, while every other nation of Latin America, except Venezuela (which has a ratio of 58 per cent direct taxes to 42 per cent indirect taxes), has more than 50 per cent of its revenues collected from indirect sources. These indirect taxes are clamped on everything from the manufacture to the importation of goods. Such forms of taxation affect the poor much more than the rich, for the poor have even less opportunity to save than they would have under an equitable and direct tax structure.

The indirect effects of inflation are harder to verify statistically, but it is evident that those tied to a fixed wage scale are simply not in as advantageous a position to cope with the inflationary "tax" as merchants whose prices change when the market value of their currency changes, or the banker who adjusts his interest rates on a daily basis.

[13] *Economic Survey of Latin America.* New York: United Nations, 1957, p. 138; also see Celso Furtado, *The Economic Growth of Brazil.* Berkeley: University of California Press, 1963; and Albert O. Hirschman, *Journey Toward Progress: Studies of Economic Policy-Making in Latin America.* New York: The Twentieth Century Fund, 1963, esp. pp. 11-91.
[14] Cited in Luis Alberto Monge, "The Labor Movement and Economic Development," in Mildred Adams (ed.), *Latin America: Evolution or Explosion?* New York: Dodd, Mead & Company, 1963, pp. 185-6.

Thus, inflation, whatever its positive effects on the investment and circulation of funds by those who have large sums of money, has a deleterious effect on those who have no savings, or those whose savings are linked to insurance policies or pension programs. Hence, the revolutionary potential of the Latin American working class, and of the working classes throughout the Third World, does not result from ideological orientations or instinctive herd responses but represents a direct consequence of the underdeveloped economies as such.

Given these factors it may be unrealistic to expect that an economic development program can be financed to any large extent from taxation or from subsidiary forms of taxation such as import and export duties. As Paul Baran says, "For backward countries to enter the road of economic growth and social progress, the political framework of their existence has to be drastically revamped. The alliance between feudal landlords, industrial royalists, and the capitalist middle-classes has to be broken. . . . Such progressive and enterprising elements as exist in backward societies have to obtain the possibility of leading their countries in the direction of economic and social growth."[15] Otherwise the existing class system and power structure will again manipulate a debt policy advantageous only to the *status quo*. Foreign economic aid cannot substitute for domestic change. Such aid only postpones a settlement of the issues of mending and smashing—indeed, it makes any solution more wrenching than its consequences.[16]

II

Expropriation means the displacement of private ownership of lands and factories by public ownership or operation in the public interest. It is, like taxation, a form of social savings. Expropriation should be considered in two different aspects.[17] One is the case of land-tenure reforms to lessen the unequal distribution of real income and to relieve the

[15] Paul Baran, "On the Political Economy of Backwardness," in A. N. Agarwala and S. P. Singh (eds.), *The Economics of Underdevelopment*. New York: Oxford University Press, 1963, p. 90.
[16] Paul Baran, *op. cit.*, p. 91.
[17] A third case, the nationalization of foreign investment in newly independent countries, is not within the limits of this analysis.

peasantry from the burden of a land system which fosters inequitable and distinctly undemocratic conditions.[18] There is also what political authorities in some countries refer to as collectivization. Collectivism is not intended solely for agricultural sectors, but for the economy as a whole. In this sense, very high tax rates—such as 50 to 60 per cent of the production or income, differentially imposed—can be regarded as expropriation.

Since the economies of poor countries are largely based upon agriculture, the conditions of land tenure have great significance.[19] These conditions vary considerably. The ownership unit may be a tribe, village, family, or individual. Different types of ownership may also exist in combination, as in the Middle East. In many sections of the world, particularly Latin America, the land is in the hands of a few owners. In Brazil, Syria, and Iraq, for example, it is estimated that about half the land is owned by large landowners, and cultivated by small share tenants.[20] Where tenancy exists, the land is often fragmented into strip parcels and scattered holdings. Systems of inheritance, according to which every son receives a parcel of land, or every daughter is given land as a dowry, also make for a continual division and scattering of lands over wide numbers of already poor farmer-owners. Moreover, all tenure systems are custom-bound and semi-feudal. There are very few well-defined juridical rights and obligations between landlords and tenants. Feudalism regulates human relations through a system of custom and mutual acceptance of obligations. While most experts agree that land reform is an urgent need in the Third World, just what constitutes land reform is a complex matter. Land reform is an issue charged with political emotion, and it is often viewed as an economic panacea. It is vital that there be some evaluation of what it can and what it cannot accomplish.[21]

In the rural sectors of Japan and South Korea, efforts have been

[18] Parsons, Penn, Raup (eds.), *Land Tenure*. Madison, Wisc.: The University of Wisconsin Press, 1956, p. 44.
[19] See Gustav Ranis and John C. H. Fei, "A Theory of Economic Development," *The American Economic Review*. Vol. LI, No. 4 (Sept. 1961), pp. 533-8.
[20] *Land Reform*, United Nations Department of Economic Affairs: New York, 1951, p. 14.
[21] Arthur T. Mosher, "Research on Rural Problems," *Development of the Emerging Countries*. Washington, D. C.: The Brookings Institution's Publication, 1962, p. 86.

made to eliminate the abuses of the feudal social order. In these countries genuine attempts at land reform were made after the Second World War. The system of private ownership of land was not only retained but emphasized. In sharp contrast, the Communist pattern, which emerged in China and North Korea, viewed the reform movement as a means to abolish the existing land tenure system and collectivize the agricultural sector.[22] Japanese reform was externally guided by the United States, whereas Chinese reform was internally guided by the revolution.

In Japan and South Korea a modern land tenure system was achieved with a minimum of confiscation. In Japan the area under tenancy was reduced from nearly 50 per cent to approximately 10 per cent of the land under cultivation. As a result, owner-farmers and owner-tenants operated up to 50 per cent more land than before the war. On the small area remaining under tenancy, rents were reasonable, rental contracts were in writing, and local land commissions corrected any abuses and prevented a feudal backlash. This drastic change took place with relatively little disturbance to the existing farm management pattern, without interruption of farm operations, and without serious disruption of the psychological patterns of the farm population.[23]

The political disturbances caused by the reform were very significant. Japanese society was radically altered. Land reform, however smoothly it was carried off at the technological level, meant a drastic change in existing social relationships, traditional values, and vested interests.[24] The informal power structure of agrarian Japan was transferred from military overseers to middle-sized farmers. Land reform produced the following results: First, most of the farmers acquired the one thing that farmers the world over want—land of their own. This private property "instinct" proved to be the chief incentive for improving the land.[25] Second, the reform narrowed the traditional differences between

[22] Sidney Klein, *The Pattern of Land Tenure Reform in East Asia After World War Two*. New York: Bookman Associates, 1958, p. 189.
[23] Sidney Klein, ibid., p. 50-51.
[24] John W. Bennett and Iwao Ishino, *Paternalism in the Japanese Economy*. Minneapolis: University of Minnesota Press, 1963.
[25] Wolf I. Ladejinsky, "Land Reform in Japan: A Comment," in *Land Tenure*, edited by Parsons, Penn, and Raup. Madison, Wisc.: The University of Wisconsin Press, 1956, p. 225.

classes in the villages. The Japanese landlords who lost much of their affluence, also lost much of their influence. But land reform did not displace one class in order to put another in its place. Large- and small-scale peasant owners now serve on agricultural committees, co-operatives, and school boards.[26] Third, the distribution of land ownership among the multitude of farmers contributed to the foundation of a more satisfying rural life, and to the beginning of local control of the decision-making processes.[27] This was all made possible by a corresponding rise in the industrial sector and a broad trend toward urbanization and occupational specialization.

Taiwan and South Korea followed the Japanese lead, but with different results. In Taiwan, the area of land cultivated by owners increased by nearly 50 per cent, while the area cultivated by tenants decreased by more than 60 per cent. By 1954 only 16 per cent of the total cultivated lands was left to share-cropping tenancy. Significantly, land productivity did not show any noticeable increase. The conditions of tenancy were also put on a *de jure* foundation as in Japan. As for the South Korean experiment, the redistribution of land ownership seems to have been the sole achievement of the reform efforts of this country. The number of half-tenants and full tenants was reduced by 77 per cent, while the number of half-owners and full owners increased by 170 per cent. Ownership of approximately 26 per cent of all the cultivated land of South Korea was transferred to the tillers of the land.

Land reform in South Korea was essentially a failure. The conditions of tenancy were little improved. Rents remained high, paid in kind rather than money. Tenants were burdened with many expenses of cultivation which should have been borne in whole or in part by the landlord. Tenants were still insecure because landlords failed to put their leases in writing and to register them at the local Land Office. Tenants remained dependent upon the good will of their landlords. During the first three years of agricultural reform (March 1951-December 1954), some 235,000 farm families, who were unable to meet the payments due on 253,000 acres of land, had to give up their ownership rights and revert to their former tenant status. It seems certain that, unless some way is found for the new owner-farmers to meet their cash

[26] Sidney Klein, *op. cit.*, pp. 19-52.
[27] Ibid.

needs other than by the sale of their land, this reversion to tenancy will continue.[28] Thus, we see two different outcomes of externally induced land reform without land revolution.

While it is clear that great new advances in social life are now taking place in agricultural nations, and that problems of land, rather than problems of population, more nearly approximate the overall social situation of the Third World, the above discussion only provides a historical backdrop.[29] Land reform in the Third World can be defined as a series of strategies designed to break the mold of those land relationships as existed under the colonial period. In the main, when land reform is undertaken without reference to general industrial change, as in South Korea, the developmental process is abortive—even in the agricultural sector. When land reform is undertaken as a general consequence of industrialization, as in Japan, the development process is highly successful—even in the agricultural sector.

This does not mean that agricultural solutions are out of the question. Nothing could be further from the case. Such different nations as Yugoslavia, Cuba, and Malaysia exhibit precisely such an emphasis on food and mineral production. But it is much easier for a society to "sacrifice" the agricultural sector to the industrialization process than the other way around. And when the industrialization process is surrendered, it is usually done so as a "temporary maneuver," a "concession" to economic realities of size and strength, and not as an abandonment of the long-range ideal of achieving self-determination through industrial production.

Despite the urgent needs in most underdeveloped countries of Asia, Africa, and Latin America, land reforms either have not yet been undertaken or have not been satisfactory. To justify this failure, it is often said that there are technical difficulties in working with uneducated people, or that exceptional geographic features affect the programs. But Japan's experience leads one to the conclusion that agrarian reform

[28] The same situation has developed in Mexico's small farms where the absence of liquid assets often compels the independent peasants to resell their lands to the ever waiting large landowners. Often land is sold illegally, and just as often, small farmers are not aware of credits available to them from government sources. [29] For a brilliant examination of agriculture in developing nations, see Doreen Warriner, *Land Reform and Economic Development*. Cairo: National Bank of Egypt, 1955.

difficulties are more political than technical. In many countries land reform is thwarted not because there is any lack of technical knowledge but because the political apparatus is wedded to the economic *status quo*.[30] It is no accident that in both Japan and South Korea land reform was externally induced.

Under the political stimulus of a foreign military government, Japan succeeded in separating out, once and for all, military functions from landholding functions. Neither militarists nor landlords were "liquidated." They were simply provided with separate social roles. On the whole, land reform in Japan emphasized innovation rather than investment. In the past, other innovations had been undertaken; members of the functionless Samurai class became the business leaders of industrial Japan; students of literature were shifted to scientific skills by means of a clever manipulation of rewards and awards; economic efficiency increased through machine technology, and disciplined farm laborers formed the backbone of an enlarged migrant proletariat.[31] The growth of per capita income was not the result of rapid capital formation, for the growth of capital barely exceeded the rate of population growth. Hence, the role of innovation and the mode of utilizing savings in Japan goes far to explain why Japan succeeded where South Korea failed.

For the strategy of smashing as an answer to agricultural development, North Korea and China provide two interesting models. In the former, the property of landlords was confiscated and distributed. The peasants, however, did not acquire the rights of ownership but merely title to use the property. The redistribution of the land did not result in an increase in the income of North Korean peasants nor in a feeling of ownership. The tax rates set by the government on agricultural products effectively siphoned off revolutionary enthusiasm. All surplus production became state-owned, and subsistence became the norm. North Korean officials exercised a high degree of control over peasant co-operatives. The control and supervision of the peasants were excessive even by Soviet standards under Stalin. Given the constant threat of

---

[30] Parsons, Penn, and Raup (eds.), *op. cit.*, p. 228.
[31] Richard R. Nelson, *Growth Models and the Escape from the Low-Level Equilibrium Trap: The Case of Japan*. Santa Monica: The Rand Corporation, January 1959 (P-1537), pp. 1-23.

civil war and counter-revolution, this is perhaps understandable. But it is economically unsatisfactory, since production continued to stagnate.

China has become the focal model for take-over as the basic strategy of social development. The main impulse and support of the Maoist revolution have been the peasantry. China had its revolution in the countryside, the way Bakunin predicted, and not in the cities, the way Marx imagined. The special role of the Chinese landowner, who also had administrative power, made any formal scheme of taxation quite out of the question. The central government under the Kuomintang was supported by the wealthy landowners, and not the other way about. Under such circumstances, the Chinese Communists engaged in a policy of staged take-over.

The first period (1948-1952) saw an emphasis on private land ownership. The large peasant mass became enfranchised, albeit in an unprofitable economic maneuver. Parcels handed out varied from only 1.15 to .45 acres per person. This had the effect of uniting the peasants behind the revolution, but it did little to improve the productive capacities of agriculture. The second period (1952-1956) saw the introduction both of persuasion and coercion to move from individual proprietorship, first to mutual aid teams, then to elementary co-operatives, and finally to producers' co-operatives. The advanced co-operatives were based on the collectivization of the village economy. But each person was allowed to own, and people could voluntarily cultivate small properties. By the end of 1956, 96 per cent of the peasantry had pooled their co-operative shares. The state thus controlled the productivity of the land, without actually owning any of it. The third period (1957-1960), commonly referred to as the Commune period, sought to rationalize agricultural production by linking the peasant sector to the general life of the Chinese society. Mao Tse Tung is reported to have said: "It is better to run people's communes. Their advantages lie in that they can merge industry, agriculture, trade, culture, education, and military affairs into one entity, and make it easier for leadership."[32] The communes represented the final stage in the confiscation of private lands and private ownership, and the commune system also provided a case study in gentle terror— also known as the "Asiatic Form of Communism." The fourth period

[32] Choh-Ming Li, "The First Decade: Economic Development," *The China Quarterly* (London), No. 1 (Jan.-March) 1960, pp. 35-50.

(1960-1963) rescinded many of the harsher features of commune life by restoring personal possesions to their rightful owners; by putting a limit on the working day; and by returning to private dwellings as the basic mode of living, i.e. the three-generation system of housing.[33]

There can be no doubt that land collectivization in China, whatever its shortcomings, has made impossible a return to past feudal relations. But it is also clear that enforced communization, like other land tenure systems, must deal with the problem of taxation. In the case of China, the tax problem was dependent upon that part of production (translated into wages) held in reserve for state allocation. At present, each peasant brigade is guaranteed 60 per cent of its product. This guarantee still represents a "taxation" of 40 per cent of the yield. A central program of confiscation was to establish the ground rules of taxation. Thus, expectantly, the very phenomenon which causes governmental instability, the failure to collect and receive a portion of production or services for general allocation, is made possible in the post-revolutionary period.

The individualist solution in Japan and the socialist solution in China have worked with relative success not because of the unique advantages of private or public ownership of land but because of their unique ability to fuse nationalist values and peasant demands. This is borne out by the relative failure of the South Korean and North Korean economies alike—despite their structural and ideological differences. Thus, whether the strategies of taxation or take-over are adopted, the success of either depends upon the general processes of economic development, and not on any single policy-making decision.

III

In developed countries, there have been various degrees of governmental participation in the initiation and direction of the developmental process. In countries like Imperial Japan, Weimar Germany, and Soviet

[33] Edgar Snow, *The Other Side of the River*. New York: Random House, 1962, pp. 418-38. For comparable information of Chinese agricultural production during the first decade of Communist rule, see Ta-Chung Liu and Kung-Chia Yeh, "The National Income of the Chinese Mainland, 1952-59," *American Economic Review. Proceedings of the American Economic Association* (May, 1961), pp. 489-98.

Russia the political apparatus has played a large part in initiating and activating an entrepreneurial role.[34] By contrast, development in England and the United States occurred with much less deliberate governmental action.[35] The epoch of take-off, rather than the type of social order, determines the extent of political intervention.

Most observers agree that in the newly developing regions the very tardiness of the developmental process, coupled with the absence of a responsible economic elite, makes governmental intervention necessary for economic take-off. The situation in which the have-not countries find themselves is far different from the situation of those countries which developed during the nineteenth century. The obstacles for underdeveloped countries are now much greater than they ever were in developed countries—precisely because the developed countries in the past achieved their pre-eminence through economic and political imperialism, while developing areas today must rely exclusively upon their own population resources. Consequently, political action tends to unite around the theme of nationalism and anti-imperialism.

When we depart from the mending-smashing dualism and look at specific situations, vast differences arise. For a particular country, private-sector advocates suggest limiting the government's role to overall allocation of funds for research and development, where government intervention can easily be minimized. Public-sector advocates would have the government interfere directly with the market mechanism and exercise specific control over (and prepare for the eventual elimination of) private enterprise. In its more extreme form, this would mean that the market mechanism would be totally supplanted by central planning, and the state would replace private enterprise as the moving force in social development.

Differences in strategy generally arise when there are differences in estimates as to the sequence and tempo of development. Socialists maintain that obstacles to development in poor countries are so formidable that they can be overcome only by deliberate and immediate industrialization on the part of the state. The political apparatus should engage in

[34] Cf. Reinhard Bendix, "Preconditions of Development: A Comparison of Japan and Germany," in Nation-Building and Citizenship: Studies of Our Changing Social Order. New York: John Wiley, 1964, pp. 177-213.
[35] G. M. Meier and R. E. Baldwin, Economic Development: Theory, History, Policy. New York: Wiley, 1957, pp. 360-61.

programming and planning, assume most of the entrepreneurial activities, and attempt to achieve a high rate of capital accumulated as soon as possible.[36] Only then can the private sector be contained, if not confiscated. Capitalists, on the contrary, advocate gradual industrialization, which would limit the degree of specific planning, rely mainly on the market mechanism, and approach development problems in a step-by-step fashion.[37] In this way, the specific market mechanisms will not be aborted by arbitrary state planning; and industrialization will be both a stimulant and a response to increases in social mobility.[38]

Those who favor rapid and deliberate industrialization have two main arguments. *First,* in order to gather sufficient momentum, a development program must ramify widely in space and rapidly in time throughout the economy. Unless the program involves large changes in class relations and social structure, the development process can never be self-generating and cumulative. If rapid development is desired, certain steps must be taken. Regarding capital accumulation, investment must be on a scale, and of a type, that is only facilitated through the joint efforts of the underdeveloped country and large-scale investments from willing advanced countries. Socialists tend to believe that heavy industrialization in itself lessens both obstacles and dependencies on others. If ambitious capital and technical assistance programs are undertaken, social and cultural obstacles may disappear without being directly attacked. But industrialization will be obtained only if the scale of such assistance is large enough to provide a "shock treatment" for the traditional ruling classes, and flexible enough to turn present large-scale part-time unemployment into an asset.

Second, only through large-scale development can old distinctions between rich and poor be broken down. Unless class extremes are blunted, political agencies would be unable to regulate the total economy for social purposes. In short, if the strategy of forced savings is to be institutionalized, political power must supersede economic power. Thus, in the newly developing areas, confiscation is a necessary prelude

[36] Meier & Baldwin, *op. cit.,* p. 362.
[37] Meier & Baldwin, *op. cit.,* p. 363.
[38] See Gino Germani, "The Strategy of Fostering Social Mobility," *Social Aspects of Economic Development in Latin America,* edited by Egbert De Vries and José Medina Echavarría. Paris: United National Educational, Scientific and Cultural Organization, 1963, pp. 211-30.

to any real growth of the public sector. If rapid and accelerated development is to be undertaken, the nation must be prepared to rely on internal sacrifice instead of external foreign assistance.

"Mixed economies" such as India and Brazil have used a good deal of central planning to convert an agrarian economy into an industrial economy. But a more gradual and decentralized approach has gained increasing favor in these countries. Instead of seeking deliberate industrialization through direct political intervention, such nations tend to concentrate on agricultural improvements, the promotion of social services, the extension of public overhead capital, and the establishment of small-scale, dispersed light industry.

The rationale behind these more moderate programs are varied: First of all, the agricultural sector of the economy is predominant, and this is where extreme poverty exists. But the possibilities for rapidly increasing agricultural output are highly favorable, precisely because the disorganized state of farm labor makes the introduction of advanced machine technology easier than in the developed industrial sectors. Furthermore, welfare projects such as schools, hospitals, and disease control involve a relatively small investment in exchange for a high return in reducing human misery. Second, concentrated heavy industry is not immediately required because there are inadequate market opportunities, lack of capital, scarcity of skills and administrative capacity, and an insufficient supply of managerial expertise. Small-scale light industry may, on the other hand, be linked to local handicrafts. Small rural industry does not need many urban services and savings can be made in capital expenditure which would otherwise be applied to the cost of urbanization. A revitalization of the land must take place. It has the advantage of moving industry to the labor supply, which despite urbanization, remains largely immobile. This gradual approach to industrialization is characteristic of development plans in Latin America (such as the Alliance for Progress) and in parts of the Near East and Asia.[39]

Once a nation has achieved some kind of high-level industrial productivity in such areas as basic tools, iron and steel, automotives, etc., then the problem shifts from taxation to reinvestment, since the developed nation must shift from a reliance on borrowing capital, to a reinvestment of surplus. While it remains extremely difficult to extract taxes

[39] Meier & Baldwin, *op. cit.*, p. 365.

from industries in newly developed societies which have entered into an advanced phase of the industrial revolution, it may be even more difficult to get the upper classes to properly invest their profits. Thus, it is estimated that in Mexico, no less than in France, the collection of taxes has long been viewed as quixotic—with an estimated 25 per cent of the due taxes actually collected. But with extension of the franchise to urban working classes, as in Mexico today, it is possible to institute equitable tax reform. A new law of the Mexican Constitution will have the effect of giving workers 9 to 13 per cent of the profits of the companies for which they work. In short, bureaucratic capitalism, such as one finds in France and Mexico, is a political approach to economic change which involves planning without revolution.

Under the new Mexican law, profits must be made public, and every company's statement of profits will be subject to approval by its employees, who will have good reason to scrutinize it carefully, since it will determine their share. The tendency of monied classes in Latin America is to bank their profits abroad, rather than to plow them back into the business. In Mexico, reinvestment will be made virtually mandatory, for businessmen will receive a 30 per cent deduction in taxes if they invest in national enterprises. After further deductions for capital investment and labor costs, the remainder of the profits will be subject to a 20 per cent share for the workers.

It must, however, be borne in mind that such legislation came more than half a century after the commencement of the Mexican Revolution, and that its effectiveness is still largely subject to the wishes of the private sector of the economy. Legislation of this kind does indicate, however, that development can be "gradual" only after political and economic revolutions have taken place; and such development is largely managed by the political agencies so that a considerable public-sector economy will coexist with the private sector.

This gradualist approach has *prima facie* advantages over comprehensive planning. But social expectations are now very high, and the gradualist approach delivers results only over the "long haul." (1) By concentrating on agriculture it promises to increase national income and to distribute the increase to those people who need it most; however, it comes up against the established resistance of traditional landholding power. (2) This approach is less inflationary because the efforts to achieve full-scale industrialization are likely to encounter problems of capital absorption, and scarcity of raw materials. (3) It is not disruptive of the entire culture as is large-scale industrialization. It does not mean a rapid urbanization with its attendant social problems. And even if this approach should not achieve its ultimate goal, the cost of failure will not be as burdensome as would the failure of a grandiose industrial development plan. In terms of human discontent, the costs of abortive development programs would be much greater. However, urbanization is an ongoing process brought to a point of crisis by the constant pressures of industrialization. And the problems created by industrialization will have to be faced in any event—either in the short run or in the long run. (4) The types of government intervention required by gradualism have advantages over those required by large-scale industrialization. The latter implies centralized planning, comprehensive specific control over economic life, and government operation of industries. The gradual approach, in contrast, involves relatively mild state intervention. In limiting its activities to general allocations of resources, and to providing a favorable atmosphere for private entrepreneurs, the nation avoids the administrative problems, irreversible decisions, cumulative errors, and undemocratic controls associated with thoroughgoing industrialization. However, the gradual approach, precisely because it seeks to disarm opponents of industrial development, makes it possible easily to sabotage such development. Precisely because it leaves political agencies in a backward stage, the gradualist approach is not likely to nurture or promote those indigenous forces that are necessary to sustain economic development and allow the process to become self-generating and cumulative. Hence, the political agencies are in danger of collapsing before the rising tide of private property interests.

Even with the gradualist approach, rapid economic progress is not possible without painful adjustments. Inherited philosophies of life and colonialist institutions have to be scrapped; old social institutions have to be fought; bonds of caste, creed, and race have to be eliminated; and people who cannot keep up with the canons of development may find their expectations of a comfortable life frustrated.[40] In short, in so far as

[40] United Nations Publication, *Measures for the Economic Development of Underdeveloped Countries*, Department of Economic Affairs, New York, 1961, p. 15.

latifundism remains a force in traditional societies it generates tremendous social antagonism. Whether evolutionary or revolutionary techniques are utilized, the problems to be overcome remain the same.

The chief fact to be recognized is that very few "have" sectors of a society are willing to pay the full price for rapid economic progress. Thus, the policy of confiscation is not necessarily a spiteful insistence on ideological purity but often the quickest way to achieve rapid development, once there is a sufficient agreement in favor of development as such. Where economic and political power is concentrated in the hands of a small group, whose main interest is in the preservation of the *status quo*, prospects for economic progress are very slight unless a social revolution effects a shift in the distribution of income and power.[41]

The argument that only a policy of democratic consensus can be sanctioned has to be rejected. This argument greatly oversimplifies the problem of development by assuming that development hinges on constitutional norms rather than on a more rational allocation of resources. In any expanding society the political system must cope with a wide range of conflicting demands. Even an authoritarian regime must recognize such demands. Significantly, most demands do not entail reform of the political system but are concerned with the allocation of material resources.

Development may prove to be a basic demonstration of the viability of mass democracy. The emergence of mass democracy may be a long-range consequence of the failure of authoritarian rule. A one-party system primarily oriented to economic development may find that it can satisfy demands only in areas affecting the use of economic resources. Under such conditions all aspirations must be translated into party terms, and thus an excessive political strain is placed on the limited resources of the country. Totalitarianism remains a clear and present danger. It is also true that mass terror is not as powerful a method of extracting loyalties as mass persuasion. The sociological theory of groups demonstrates that a developmental consensus based upon force does not provide the same degree of individual or group motivation as recognition of status to outstanding persons within the group.[42]

[41] United Nations Publication, *op. cit.*, p. 16.
[42] George C. Homans, *The Human Group.* New York: Harcourt, Brace and Co., 1950, esp. pp. 288-312. For a more recent extension of this view, see Peter M. Blau, *Exchange and Power in Social Life.* New York: John Wiley, 1964.

There can be no rapid economic development unless the various groups within a country—politicians, teachers, engineers, business leaders, trade unionists, religious figures, journalists—support economic progress and are willing to sponsor a successful take-off. This in turn entails the elimination of traditional class privileges and a maximum allocation of social savings. Given powerful political leadership and public willingness to accept such leadership, few problems of economic development are insoluble. People take their cue from those in authority only if authority poses no threat of a confiscatory force, a force ready to smash as well as mend. If leaders are reactionary, selfish, and corrupt, the masses are, in turn, dispirited and disenchanted. If the political leaders win the confidence of the country, which they can only do by vigorous elimination of class privileges and racial inequalities, they can inspire the masses with an enthusiasm for development. The problem before the political leadership of the developing countries is not so much mass support (which it already has), as it is class support. In Latin America the unwillingness of the old classes to share political power with new social elements has created the conditions for revolution and for the strategy of expropriation. This conflict did not occur in most of Africa and Asia, because the "enemy" was clearly the "foreigner," the outsider.

The Third World increasingly has to choose between types of take-over, not between taxation or take-over. Traditional landed classes have thus far never accepted a progressive tax structure. But as speculation on scarce goods rises, as excessive profiteering takes place, as consumer spending rises, the capacity for self-imposed limits sharply declines. The wealthy classes become incapable of the sort of effort necessary to impose economic rationalization since they are themselves caught in the inflationary spiral. The growth of intermediate classes and intermediate elites, such as the military or white collar, has the effect of further isolating the very rich—and making confiscation a broad-based and necessary strategy for the nation's political survival.

Confiscation has been successful because the process of industrialization depends on the rationalization of production as a whole, and on the elimination of social classes that make such planning mechanisms impossible. In Japan, planning agencies were externally introduced as a result of the collapse of the Empire in World War Two; in China such agencies came about as a result of the Civil War. Nonetheless, from a

Western frame of reference, confiscation goes against the grain of economic morality and economic interests. And the resort to direct take-over is usually a sign that weaker forms of restraint on private drainage of public wealth (such as taxation) have failed.[43]

IV

The obstacles to confiscatory policies in the agricultural sectors of the Third World are considerable. Factors impeding confiscation stem not simply from the latifundiary character of much agricultural ownership but also from the international ramifications of such bold measures. Furthermore, most land tenure systems of the Third World generate lethargy, backwardness, suspicion, and the inability on the part of the huge peasantry to distinguish its interests from those of the ruling classes. The romantic image of the peasant fighting for possession of the land is, it must be remembered, the exception. The peasant is suspicious of new forms of production, fearful of innovation and crop rotation, and opposed to government intervention. Thus if there are "natural" reasons in support for confiscation and collectivization of the land, there are equally powerful *social* reasons for moving with caution and circumspection in the direction of take-over.

But in the industrial sector matters are quite different. Here, where it would seem that taxation and the promulgation of a private sector would fulfill the norms of development, there are powerful *social* reasons for confiscation. If the class adversaries of confiscation are potent, so too are the class agencies which support it. We might cite three basic categories of production which, in their very nature, are highly socialized:

(1) Monopolistic and oligopolistic enterprises attract the attention of the state, the "guardian" of the public sector, because they are usually engaged in a highly critical enterprise (such as machine and electric products). Since competition is conspicuously absent, the traditional laisser-faire argument of free enterprise is inadmissible.

(2) Those basic commodities or creature comforts necessary for

[43] M. Bronfenbrenner, "The Appeal of Confiscation in Economic Development," *The Economics of Underdevelopment*, edited by A. N. Agarwala and S. P. Singh. New York: Oxford University Press, 1963, p. 487.

community wants naturally fall into the public sector. Hence, forests, roads, water supply, dams, canals, post and communications systems tend to be placed under public directorship. The character of public control may vary from local-township control to large-scale state control, but even where basic utilities are privately run, they are very heavily supervised and controlled by the state. The very complexities of a modern supply system make a powerful argument for public ownership. In countries under colonial domination the initial action is often to attack foreign ownership and control of utilities—the telephone systems in Brazil, natural gas and oil in Argentina, electric power in Algeria—for on such matters, a clear consensus exists among the various classes of the country, which is not the case in agriculture or commodity production.

(3) Defense establishments and military production also tend toward public ownership, because the function of such production is directly tied to the policies of the national state. In addition, research and scientific technology in this area tend to be profitless unless they are under state supervision. Investment in military hardware may sometimes be politically necessary but at the same time it is a drain on the economy. In any case, the higher the degree of economic rationalization, the more a society is able to engage in military production. But this is simply part of the larger truth that modern technology is intrinsically "socialistic." Hence, the advantage accrues to that power which can bring its rhetoric in line with reality.

The arguments against increased emphasis on the public sector come down to the following: First, an absence of the profit motive leads to waste and results in inefficiency and sluggishness in production. Second, efficient working is hampered by bureaucratic red tape. Third, there is a tendency to make appointments to major positions from political considerations extrinsic to job qualifications.[44] The interesting aspect of each of these three objections is that they are basically arguments concerning efficiency and management, and not arguments in favor of private enterprise. As such, the counter to such arguments is not an increase in profit incentive or private capitalization and funding, but scientific management procedures. Such procedures are consonant

[44] For a cogently argued modern critique of expanding the public sector see Wilbert E. Moore, *The Conduct of the Corporation.* New York: Random House, 1962.

with healthy organization—whether public or private; and therefore cannot *legitimately* be employed as an argument against expropriation or public operation or ownership. The achievements of "private socialism" of the sort to be found in any major corporation in the United States are not dependent upon private ownership of the instruments of production and distribution. They are a direct consequence of the rise of mass production techniques in the early part of the century and automation in the middle part of the century. In other words, the problem of organizational management is directly tied to the level of technology a society has achieved and not just to class relations within a society.

V

No discussion of the political economy of mending and smashing would be complete without some historical accounting. First, in the last days of the old colonial regimes the rulers of these regions became increasingly intransigent and corrupt. They were drawn from a class of landowners who had hardly any interest in developing an industrial base, but who did consume on a large scale commodity products manufactured by foreign nations. Second, once the colonial economy snapped, old solutions became dysfunctional. Laisser-faire and marginal adjustments through a private enterprise system could not, in most instances, cope with problems of development, since what was needed was not marginal but fundamental growth. Third, the process of take-over was directed by a revolutionary and nationalist regime, whose first action was to curtail the political influence of the rich.[45] It limited in the first place their wealth and their incomes, and then later, expropriated them. These stages are rarely simultaneous. Indeed, they may take decades to coalesce. And it is at this historical level that national differences make themselves felt, and give peculiar shape to expropriation policies throughout the Third World.

One must not overlook the marginal advantages of expropriation,

[45] Cf. R. C. Agarwala, *State Enterprise in India*. Allahabad (India): Chaitanya Publishing House, 1961. This work contains extremely valuable materials on the process of nationalization in India after the 1948 independence period. The chapters on industrial enterprises owned by the government, and the problems of administration and financing that they create, clearly reveal the managerial level at which the problem of the public sector is encountered.

advantages which oftentimes determine the time-table of development, if not the structural changes in a society as such.

(1) In many of the developing regions, particularly in the Middle East and Asia, there exist long-established traditions of strong central governments. Given material conditions of poverty and inequality of opportunity, state authority increases, if only to prevent the unleashing of economic competition and the pursuit of self-interest which could lead to a breakdown of society. Of course, the permanent threat of mass violence will prevent the middle classes from abandoning national economic policy.

(2) The Third World can dramatically show its independence by trading with the socialist nations of Eastern Europe and Asia; this is particularly true for such states as Egypt, Algeria, Indonesia, and Cuba. In dealing with the centrally planned economies of Communist countries, Third World nations have to gear their own planning activities to those of the Communist bloc in order to make such dealings effective. Thus, government organizations tend to adjust their dealings to socialist techniques so that the problems of trade and commerce can be adequately handled. The pressure for such adjustments depends in part on Third World political affinities to the socialist bloc, and upon the extent of trade agreements with the Western bloc. The coexistence of capitalist and socialist features should not be overlooked as a factor which paves the way for any easy transition from confiscation to state socialism.

(3) Many Third World countries have been drawn closer to socialist bloc countries on the basis of a common *political* rhetoric: nonalignment in the Cold War, the development of nuclear-free zones, common strategies for dealing with larger states, etc. Thus, the political postures of such countries as India, Yugoslavia, Egypt, Algeria, Indonesia, and others are not very intense. The sharp dichotomy between capitalist and socialist worlds has given way to polycentrism in the socialist sphere and pluralism in the capitalist sphere. The existence of mixed economies even within self-declared capitalist and Communist countries has proved stimulating for the Third World. By absorbing the latest techniques a society can achieve new combinations and variations on the development theme.

(4) Civil and international wars have also accelerated the drive

toward confiscation and public-sector domination. The immediate consequence of the Suez crisis and its aftermath led to the "Egyptianization" of the large British and French economic holdings.[46] The conclusion of the Algerian conflict brought about a similar confiscation of foreign landholdings and industrial wealth which was then followed by a declaration of the socialist character of the Algerian Revolution. The settlement of the Civil War in Vietnam, which was hardly an all-out decisive victory, nonetheless made possible the development of a socialist economic sector in those areas "liberated" from the old regime. In short, the outcome of warfare has served to stimulate socialist public-sector economies where none before existed, or to consolidate such a public-sector economy where it may have existed in a shaky condition.

What these economically marginal factors suggest is that the strategy of confiscation blends invariably with an immense outburst of state activity leading to consolidation of the public sector.

(5) Confiscation may produce such economic advantages as higher production through standardization of manufacturing procedures, decentralization of the centers of production, an orderly shift in the transition from rural to city living, etc. The total capital requirements are kept to a minimum, while the percentage of national income held over for development is brought to a maximum. The judgment of the economist Henry Villard is particularly instructive in this respect. In comparing the advantages of the Chinese approach, based on total confiscation, to the Indian approach, based on partial and differentiated confiscation, he notes that the fear of Western politicians and sociologists that Communist development rests on perpetual coercion may be exaggerated.

> It may well be that, when starting from a low level, an initially larger amount of resources devoted to development will "pay off" very rapidly indeed even in terms of available consumption, so that it is not certain that the present Chinese generation will be "exploited" for very long. In fact, the reluctance of the Indian government to reduce present consumption, which presumably explains why it is unwilling to devote a larger percentage of the national income to development, could conceivably mean that

[46] Saiah El Serafy, "Economic Development by Revolution: The Case of the UAR," *The Middle East Journal*, Vol. 17, No. 3, Summer 1963, pp. 215-30.

the present Indian generation will receive, over its lifetime, *less* consumption than the present generation in China.[47]

We have already seen the large extent to which the "democratization" procedures in the Soviet Union followed hard on the heels of peacetime on one hand and a degree of material abundance on the other. Thus, the traditional dialectic of personal "costs" versus social "gains" in development may be less significant than has usually been estimated.

(6) The following remarks, made by Isaac Deutscher, must undoubtedly have been used on many occasions in Third World nations, especially those which aspire to some sort of political and military "greatness." The central point—that a private-enterprise economy is inadequate to meet the challenges of the East-West struggle, that in fact, the West has had to become socialized in some measure—cannot fail to impress factions advocating evolutionary approaches in the Third World.

> The new technology tends to outgrow our inherited institutions and to render obsolete the frameworks within which we have been accustomed to act, think, and live our lives. It grows above the head of private property. Even in the West atomic power has not been the child of private enterprise. It has been the child of State enterprise. Henceforth nearly every act of the technological upheaval is likely to strengthen the trend towards public ownership and enterprise; the gigantic scale of the new inventions and scientific ventures puts these beyond the resources of private investment . . . The more rational and concentrated use of resources in a nationalized economy follows from the organic integration of its elements.[48]

If the Third World learns from the Soviet Union that absolutist government, rather than a spark to development, is an impediment, it learns from the United States that its system of private enterprise may prevent Third World nations from making the most effective and con-

[47] Henry Villard, *Economic Development* (second edition). New York: Holt, Rinehart, and Winston, Inc., 1963, pp. 200-201. Compare this with Paul Baran, *The Political Economy of Growth*. New York: Monthly Review Press, 1957.
[48] Isaac Deutscher, *The Great Contest: Russia and the West*. London and New York: Oxford University Press, 1960, pp. 110-12.

centrated use of their economic resources. Destruction of the middle classes may therefore create a *prima facie* advantage for a public-sector economy. It rests on the logic of economy, not on the exhortations of morality.

(7) A powerful "international" reason for confiscation is that the intermediary classes of the economy are unlikely to advocate anything more effective than budget surpluses to fill the gap resulting from increased taxation of the wealthy. A policy of inefficient taxation inevitably invites foreign investments for the wrong reasons, that is, for keeping the social system "going." The savings derived from taxation, even under optional circumstances, can scarcely pay for necessary social services, much less stimulate new investments and capital plant expantion. In so far as foreign capital is needed for economic expansion and not for maintaining a political equilibrium, the arguments in favor of confiscation are strengthened. This is because money agreements, particularly as they affect interest charges, can be negotiated more advantageously by independent states than by nations under foreign control. A policy of inefficient taxation invites foreign investment, and such investment adds to the instability of the economic situation for it drains off the nation's wealth.

(8) A public-sector economy has no difficulty in appropriating much of the fruit of economic development for capital accumulation rather than for increasing consumption demands. As long as some areas of capital formation are in the hands of large-scale entrepreneurs, it is inevitable that there will be an outright struggle between the monied sector and the rest of the society. There is no simple way of resolving this conflict to satisfy both private interests and provide for a proper distribution of income among the people at large. Hence, from an economic position, a choice must be made between mending and smashing.[49]

(9) Confiscation also has certain political and sociological advantages. But it does not necessarily provide a license for authoritarian modes of politics. Indeed, it may take more of a dosage of totalitarianism

---

[49] See the following papers on this necessity of choice: N. Belshaw, "Economic Development as an Operational Problem," *Civilizations*, Vol. II, No. 2, 1952, pp. 159-60, and I. G. Patel, "Mobilization of Domestic Resources for Economic Development," *Civilizations*, Vol. II, No. 4, 1952, pp. 487-95.

to induce the wealthy sector of the economy to pay taxes than it would to induce the poor to march on the latifundists. By the same token, it would be a mistake to equate confiscation with the appeal of socialism —since very often land take-over represents a delayed mopping-up of feudal sectors under the aegis and sponsorship of the national bourgeoisie. Nationalism and radicalism ought not to be equated—either by friends or enemies of the Third World.

(10) Confiscation also unites a sizable portion of the population in a common historic endeavor; mobilizes the masses behind the political system over and against the entrenched economic system; makes it possible to introduce changes such as urbanization and rapid mobility which have been thwarted by conditions of economic and monetary polarization. It is easy to see why confiscation has become a principal feature of the national revolutions of our age. That such policy directly affects foreign credit arrangements and threatens existing securities is a small matter when put against the country's need to "close the gap" and enter the modern world. The *ideological* advantage of take-over is based on the mobilization and integration of anti-imperialist forces; the economic substance of such take-over is basically anti-traditional. This strategy produces political independence from the old ruling classes and creates a nationalism which serves to unify the popular classes.

Confiscatory policies cannot of course in themselves solve the "social question," that is, the relationship between social classes. Economists, particularly those with orthodox left-wing biases, tend to overestimate the role and function of agrarian confiscation and redistribution, and to minimize drastically the nature of the obstacles which face a nation attempting to advance toward an even partially functioning industrial economy.[50]

Most countries are not economically self-sustaining, and indeed tend to be single-crop economies. The sale of this crop and the use of the cash surplus thus realized for industrial expansion depends heavily on who controls the international market price of the crop involved. Thus, sugar prices can, without too much effort, be manipulated by the former colonial country long after actual colonial status is dissolved. An

[50] See Paul A. Baran, *op. cit.*, esp. pp. 271-83; and Edmundo Flores, *Tratado de Economía Agrícola*. Mexico City: Fondo de Cultura Económica, 1961, esp. pp. 300-345.

agrarian reform policy based on confiscation which is not followed by crop diversification is likely to run into serious difficulties. Problems arise in particular if the crop cannot be exported in its entirety, and if the pricing of the crop cannot be externally manipulated by the colonial powers. Yet, diversification is costly. In itself it may act to delay industrialism rather than accelerate it. The degree of actual national sovereignty, while in part demonstrated by the ability to redistribute the national wealth, may be limited by other factors—such as the degree of external control of the over-all economy. It may be that subsidization and cash grants are still required—and that whatever the sources of such foreign loans, the actual political indebtedness is great enough to cast doubt on the ability of the nation automatically to move from land confiscation to a socialist revolution. I am not asserting that such a transition cannot or should not be effected, but only indicate that the transition cannot be effected by any one master plan for agriculture—and indeed it may be necessary to reverse the process and move from industrialized centralization to agricultural decentralization. While Cuba represents the centralization process, Yugoslavia is a case of the decentralization process. Nonetheless, both can be included in the radical socialist wing in the developmental race. All of this indicates that, while taxation and expropriation are both techniques for guaranteeing the stability and well-being of a society, the ability of a nation to make its own choice is in itself the best index of its own stability and well-being.

Chapter 8

Party Charisma: Political Practices and Principles

It is a democratic dogma that the two-party system, with a legally sanctioned change-over of political power, is not simply functional in certain Western cultures, but organic and universal to any definition of democracy. True enough, this is more of a populist than a professional view; yet academic sanction is not lacking. Perhaps the most direct expression of this position was made by Maurice Duverger, when he wrote that "the two party system seems to correspond to the nature of things, that is to say that political choice usually takes the form of a choice between two alternatives."[1] This proposition contains two distinct and not necessarily connected premises. First, that the two-party system is "natural" because contradictory interests tend to polarize. Second, that political choice entails a choice between alternative party organizations.

Since *Political Parties* was written, a great deal has taken place which would indicate that, while politics does indeed involve choice, and while the "myth" of a centrist focus in politics is just that, this offers little warrant for the necessity of a two-party system. In fact, political gamesmanship, and even democracy, is just as adaptable to a single-party apparatus representative of the major interest groups and factional elements as it is to different parties.[2] There is increasingly pointed evidence that even in such a classic two-party nation as the

[1] Maurice Duverger, *Political Parties: Their Organization and Activity in the Modern States* (second edition). New York: John Wiley & Sons, 1959, p. 215.
[2] See on this John H. Kautsky, *Political Change in Underdeveloped Countries: Nationalism and Communism*. New York: John Wiley & Sons, 1962, pp. 116-17.

United States there is probably more difference between factions within each party than between Democrats and Republicans as such.[3] Indeed, astute commentators have taken to speaking of the American "four-party" system—with liberal and conservative groupings within each political party.[4]

The number of parties does not necessarily determine the presence or the absence of democracy—the word is being used here simply to denote the extent and impact of public opinion on policy decisions. This asymmetry between democracy and the party system is essential to any discussion of political behavior in Third World nations; in such "one-party democracies" as Mexico (*Partido Revolucionario Institucional*) and India (Congress Party), no less than in such "two-party dictatorships" as Morocco, the Union of South Africa, and Paraguay.[5] Thus, to examine seriously political principles and practices in the Third World requires a radical shedding of parliamentary preconceptions in the study of democratic and totalitarian processes alike.

Max Weber went far toward anticipating the instability of personal rule, or pure charisma. Because of the caprice of "god-like" rulers, bureaucratic institutions, which represent the routinization of political life, become necessary. While Weber did allow for the charisma of office, he did not apply this concept to political systems, in the present context of bureaucratic regulation and rationalization. For him, there was an ultimate choice between "the sovereignty of the charismatic man" and the "superordination of the institution." While Weber notes that the "conflict between discipline and individual charisma has been full of vicissitudes," the polarities between discipline and individual charisma remain hard and unyielding. Discipline, "like its most rational offspring bureaucracy, is impersonal," while charisma, which often reveals itself in military or semi-military situations, "uses emotional means of all sorts to influence followers through 'inspiration' and, even more,

[3] See Hugh P. Williamson, "The Two Party System, Its Foibles and Follies," *The American Journal of Economics and Sociology*, Vol. 23, No. 1, January 1964, pp. 85-93.
[4] See on this James MacGregor Burns, *The Deadlock of Democracy: Four Party Politics in America*. Englewood Cliffs, N.J.: Prentice-Hall Inc., 1963, pp. 280-322.
[5] For a useful discussion of this question of multiple parties and singular dictatorships, see Fred R. van der Mehden, *Politics of the Developing Nations*. Englewood Cliffs, N.J.: Prentice-Hall Inc., 1964, pp. 61-2.

to train them in 'emphatic understanding' of the leader's will."[6] What has become apparent, but thus far remains relatively inexplicit in the literature of political sociology, is how discipline and charisma, rational authority and personal appeal, are fused in the political party which is at the same time the national party. This party, which embodies both the charismatic leadership responsible for making the national *revolution of independence* and the bureaucratic directors responsible for guaranteeing the follow-up national *revolution of development*, in effect transforms the Weberian duality into a search for a "higher unity"—into what is herein called party charisma.

There is scarcely a Third World nation which is not caught up in a political bind. This is becoming clear only now, after liberation. On one side, nearly every nation in the Third World exhibits a powerful leader principle, a *Führerprinzip*, in which power is seen to reside first and foremost in the leader, since he contains within his person the sum and substance of the aspirations and sentiments of the whole people. There is thus a powerful tendency in the direction of charismatic authority—particularly since the leader is identified in the minds of the people with liberation from colonialism. But at the same time the people themselves have become greatly interested in participating in the existent apparatus. Socialist rhetoric has only heightened the mass appeal of such participation.

In the light of the tensions produced by these contrary trends, unique political forms have evolved in the emergent states. This new form, however "transitional" it may turn out to be, can be summed up by the phrase *party charisma*. Yet, the number of new states reflecting the crystallization of party charisma would indicate that it is anything but a passing fancy. The single party assumes the "god-like" features of leadership, which in the medieval world belonged to a series of Popes, in the seventeenth and eighteenth centuries belonged to a series of monarchs—some enlightened, but all absolute—and which, in the present century, have been raised to a new level by such secular rulers as Hitler, Stalin, and, on a lesser level, Mussolini and Perón. Nonetheless, in the past charisma was most often lodged in living rulers rather than in the

[6] H. H. Gerth and C. Wright Mills (editors), *From Max Weber: Essays in Sociology.* New York: Oxford University Press, 1946, pp. 254-5; also see their introduction, pp. 51-5.

institution per se. Although, as Weber showed, the Catholic Church attempted to lodge charisma in the institution rather than in the person.

I

Every social institution has an ideological rationale. As long as the colonial powers held ultimate power, they could support the growth of European types of institutions against the pressures exerted by the internal society to resist such institutions with stubborn parochialism. The civil service ethos increased steadily under the sponsorship of colonial powers.[7] Indeed, as in India, the bureaucracy is often considered a colonial achievement in the underdeveloped areas. But with the completion of the anti-colonial phase, we find what seems to be a curious political reversion to traditionalist ways of sanctioning public authority. This is especially noticeable in Africa.[8] Thus, the new leaders, who may appear as demagogues to Westerners, are often considered democrats by their own peoples. The Maximum Leader is someone whose authority is permanent, personal, pervasive, and, above all, "legitimized." It is a power not necessarily destroyed by being out of office, as is made clear by the career patterns of men like Patrice Lumumba and Jomo Kenyatta, and to lesser extent by Juan Perón and Getulio Vargas. Indeed, it might be argued that political exile aids resistance to new political leadership and may actually prolong the life-span of obsolete political institutions.[9]

Recently James S. Coleman has divided party systems into three distinct types—one-party dominant systems, comprehensive nationalist parties, and competitive party systems—but they seem more academic

[7] See Irving L. Horowitz, "A Formalization of the Sociology of Knowledge," *Behavioral Science*, Vol. 9, No. 1, January 1964, pp. 45-55. Paul P. Van Riper, *History of the United States Civil Service*. Evanston, Ill.: Row, Peterson and Company, 1958, esp. pp. 533-64.
[8] See on this clash of universalist and particularist political norms, David E. Apter, *The Gold Coast in Transition*. Princeton: Princeton University Press, 1955; and James S. Coleman, *Nigeria: Background to Nationalism*. Berkeley: University of California Press, 1958.
[9] The idea that there is a correlation between the growth of charisma and the decline of colonialism was first put forward to me by my colleague Alvin W. Wolfe. This idea is being further developed by him in a work in progress on African Conceptions of Authority.

than real.[10] First, most of the big nation-states fall into the category of one-party dominant systems; second, comprehensive nationalist parties are functionally one-party systems, only without the protective gloss of minority parties. Third, even competitive party systems are rarely competitive, since the dominant parties invariably have more than 65 per cent of the total electoral vote, the minority parties rarely more than 25 per cent. Hence, only in rare instances can sub-Sahara Africa be said to exhibit a genuine two or multi-party system. Thus, party charisma accounts for more fundamental characteristics than can be appreciated by an examination solely of the political doctrines or organizations apart from the men behind them.

It is significant to note that this phenomenon of pseudo-competitive parties is by no means strictly African. The Mapai, ruling party in Israel, has maintained an unbroken rule, despite ostensible "competition" from other parties. More recently, the Mapai has withstood the onslaught of its own charismatic founder—David Ben-Gurion. He was only able to muster small support against an "organization" candidate. The Congress Party in India has clearly become an omnibus ruling party, despite the tolerance of other political parties. The P.R.I. in Mexico encourages the widest differences and divergences of opinion—but only as long as they occur within the party. Hence, the shift from multi-party to one-party domination is a world-wide phenomenon. The end of traditional society, the rise of modernization, has been accompanied by a decline in competitive party politics.

Charisma, however vague a concept it may be, is a factor in the "national liberation struggle." We must satisfactorily explain what takes place after this revolutionary phase. On the whole, the social functions of charisma radically shift after the successful conclusion of the national liberation effort. The revolutionary period is characterized by a heightened personal charisma. The revolutionary leaders take advantage of the weakness of the established social order by intensifying the mass sense of bewilderment and helplessness and by terrifying the popu-

[10] See James S. Coleman, "The Politics of Sub-Saharan Africa," *The Politics of the Developing Ideas*. Princeton: Princeton University Press, 1960, pp. 286-95. It should be noted that Coleman's paper makes explicit reference to sub-Saharan Africa, but he leaves no doubt that his categories can be extended to other regions of the world.

lation through the specter of innumerable dangerous enemies. In this way the new set of leaders can establish their credentials.[11]

Charisma in the post-revolutionary period must respond to an entirely different set of needs: (a) it entails a response to the need to make order out of revolutionary chaos; (b) it fuses the social sectors rendered antagonistic during the revolutionary period; (c) it must resurrect the disintegrated personality by welding it to a higher collective purpose. Through the process of symbolic identification of the masses with the leadership, the individual can realize his sense of fulfillment. For such reasons, charisma in the new nations of Asia and Africa increasingly takes on depersonalized qualities—with the *mystique* of charisma residing in the leading office, not in the person. This kind of political charisma makes the fusion of mass aspirations with leadership demands much simpler, if for no other reason than that party charisma is a more stable and reliable guide to action than personal (and inevitably capricious) leadership.

Charismatic authority is not only a stimulus to change; it may also act as a brake on social change. As Hirschman has shown, the idea of change may be a prime obstacle to development.[12] The charismatic leader develops an ego-focused conception of progress which hampers economic development by placing the responsibility for it on the political means rather than the technological. In the United States, development has historically been accomplished in a "human engineering" light, whereas in many of the emerging nations struggles for political popularity tend to reinforce charisma features of rule. To summarize this point, a highly accentuated charisma is dysfunctional in that it puts tremendous weight on fate, fortune, and the skills of leadership to make capital of each, but it underestimates political skills based on use

[11] A serious deficiency in the sociological literature is that while "pure" charismatic leadership and bureaucratic structures have been well described, the intermediary, transitional systems have not been appreciated. On pure charisma, see Leo Lowenthal and Norbert Guterman, *The Prophets of Deceit.* New York: Harper & Brothers, 1941, and Erich Fromm, *Escape from Freedom.* New York: Farrar E. Rinehart, 1941; on pure bureaucracies, see Robert K. Merton, "Bureaucratic Structure and Personality," and Alvin W. Gouldner, "Introduction," to *Studies in Leadership,* edited by Alvin W. Gouldner. New York: Harper & Brothers, 1950, pp. 3-49.

[12] Cf. Albert O. Hirschman, *The Strategy of Economic Development.* New Haven: Yale University Press, 1958, pp. 16-18.

of exact information, and defeats development of a mass educational and political socialization apparatus.

Charismatic leadership often degenerates into personal tyranny because intrinsic to its practices is a heavy reliance on the symbolic value of the ends sought, with little consideration for the means necessary to achieve such ends. The charismatic leader, in order to make good his pledges and promises, is forced to turn to terroristic methods or run the risk that his followers will quickly turn from disillusionment to disaffiliation. Party charisma is a synthesis of practical political considerations and symbolically laden personalist leadership. While it is unappealing to those reared in a culture stressing constitutional norms, it is an outgrowth of pressures to limit the excesses of pure personal charisma. What is more, party charisma can more readily absorb defeat, or a series of defeats, than can the individual leader. The Church long ago understood that the fallibility of Popes had to be separated from the infallibility of the Papacy if the charisma invested in Catholicism was not to deteriorate into sectarianism.

II

Party charisma is hardly a new phenomenon. While it has achieved considerable refinement in African nations, many of its aspects can be seen in the revolutionary movements of Latin America. Here the "science" and "art" of leadership are dedicated to moving beyond the legacy of Western parliamentary democracy and socialist centralism. Capitalism and socialism, mass action and creative leadership, worker and peasant, male and female, etc., are all summed up in the party of the "whole people." In Argentina it bore the name *Justicialismo* under Perón. The party became the "mediating power." The party is also the "perfect organization." For whatever the defects of the maximum leader may be, such "human defects" (as Perón called them) do not carry over to tarnish the party. Unlike Africa, however, old and well-established political parties do exist in Latin America. But the charismatic party claims that these traditional parties are riddled with self-interest and fraud, and are too weak to integrate the nation. The "politicos" go nowhere; they lack a sense of destiny—which is what *Justicialismo* claimed to have. For it is not simply an "old-fashioned party," but a movement—an activity going somewhere, responsible to somebody, headed by someone.[13]

The extent to which Peronism is a party phenomenon, rather than a simple charismatic condition, is made clear in the survival of the party, even though the leader is scarcely likely to resume power, since he has been in exile for a decade.[14] Personal leadership does not by any means disappear. The Revolutionary *Party* persists even though the Revolutionary *Government* may be overthrown. And this is a significant fact—since party charisma seems also to be evident in such diverse conditions as the *Apristas* of Peru and the Brazilian Labor Party (PTB) of Brazil. Signs of this are now taking place in Cuba, where despite the monumental personal authority of Castro, the elevation of the United Party of the Cuban Socialist Revolution (PURSC) to a supreme place necessarily means that Castro has been willing and able to place himself under its authority.[15] Perhaps this is the only way to prevent factionalism from openly breaking out.

Strangely enough, the Peronist movement in the Argentina of the 'forties is more a prototype of what took place in Africa a decade later, in the 'fifties, than an imitation of fascist Italy of the 'thirties. Peronism was directly linked to the transformation of a rural society into an urban society; it served as a catalyst for the industrialization of the nation; it served to give the drive toward economic development a base in a socially revolutionary doctrine and ideology.[16] But perhaps the most perfect symbol of charismatic authority is the unique relationship the

[13] See Juan Perón, *Conducción Política*. Buenos Aires: Ediciones Mundo Peronista, 1952, esp. pp. 205-12, 295-7.
[14] See on this dichotomization of Perón and Peronism, Irving Louis Horowitz, "Modern Argentina: The Politics of Power," *The Political Quarterly*, Vol. 30, No. 4, October-December 1959; in this connection see Gino Germani, "El autoritorismo y las clases populares," in *Política y Sociedad en una Epoca de Transición*. Buenos Aires: Editorial Paidós, 1962, pp. 127-46.
[15] See the report by Richard Eder on Castro's urging of an easing of tensions between Cuba and the United States, in which Castro's plans for a "constitutional regime in Cuba by 1969" are reported. *The New York Times*, July 6, 1964.
[16] For contrasting views of the significance of Peronism as an ideology of development, see Marcos Merchensky, *Las Corrientes Ideológicas en la Historia Argentina*. Buenos Aires: Editorial Concordia, 1961, esp. pp. 215-30; and Jorge Abelardo Ramos, *Revolución y Contrarrevolución en la Argentina*. Buenos Aires: La Reja, 1961, esp. pp. 435-45.

"leader" is said to have with the "people," a uniqueness underscored by the "anguish" of the past and the "joys" of the present. Eva Perón wrote:

> The Argentine people does not forget those days of anguish and death. Why should it not celebrate the First of May, now that it can do so without fear and anxiety? Instead of screaming with clenched fists in front of the closed doors of Government House, the Argentine working people now celebrate May Day with a magnificent festival, at which their Leader presides from the balconies of Government House in his character of the first Argentine worker, the title which, without any doubt, Perón appreciates most. And the marvelous thing is that, instead of fearing death on that day, the people are wont to offer their lives, yelling a chorus which always moves my soul: "Our lives for Perón."[17]

The role of the leader is to purify the hearts and cleanse the minds of his followers. There is always much to purify and cleanse! The culture of poverty is difficult to celebrate when it is realized that its asking price is the surrender of the political processes to the benevolence of wealthy classes. Up close, within sight and touch, the culture of poverty evaporates into a poverty of culture. For want of a resistant and sophisticated political system, the mass of the poor is prey to promises of deliverance. For this reason, the leader can be charismatic, can appear god-like in his presentation of self to the undifferentiated mass. But when the poor are newly mobilized, uprooted from older patterns and former life styles, then "working class authoritarianism" becomes a factor. The process of development cannot be judged by whether it avoids charismatic appeals, but only by its achievements. Hence, the real measure of party charisma is, first, in the successful execution of the tasks of social development and, second, in its ability to satisfy the claims of the masses.

This "role confusion," in which the leader identifies with the nation in an almost tautological fashion, has been carried to perfection in Latin America. We have the most "perfect" illustration in the suicide of Getulio Vargas, who in his suicide message[18] declared he would enter

[17] Eva Perón, *My Mission in Life*, trans. by Ethel Cherry. New York: Vantage Press, 1953, pp. 101-2.
[18] Getulio Vargas, "Farewell Message to the Brazilian People," *Revolution in Brazil: Politics and Society in a Developing Nation*, by Irving L. Horowitz. New York: E. P. Dutton & Company, 1964, pp. 132-3.

history by this act of identification with the "people." "My sacrifice will maintain you united, and my name will be your battle flag. Each drop of my blood will be an immortal call to your conscience and will maintain a holy vibration for resistance . . . I fought against the looting of Brazil. I have fought against the looting of the people. I have fought bare-breasted. The hatred, infamy, and calumny did not beat down my spirit. I gave you my life. Now I offer my death. Nothing remains. Serenely I take the first step on the road to eternity and I leave life to enter history." One can see here, as in the words of Evita Perón, the powerful strain of messianic fervor, a fervor which gives rich substance to the charismatic aspect of this ostensibly altruistic identification of person with nation, and through this identification, with the gods, with immortality.

From the less sacred and more profane side of things, it is evident that this "old-fashioned" Latin American personal charisma is not easily transferred into party charisma. In the case of Perón, through *Justicialismo*, and in the case of Vargas, through the *Partido Trabhalista Brasileiro*, the image of the personal leader was a handicap rather than a help to party charisma. In the absence of any *authentic social* revolution, the mystique of charismatic leadership cannot readily be transferred to a party as the bearer of "principle." Therefore, when personal charisma collapses under such circumstances, there is a return to traditional political processes. This shows that, in Latin America at least, traditional politics may yet house modernist economics—at least until the question of structural reform is pressed to the limit.

Political party leaders often see themselves as the "vessels of universal truth" while manipulating their party machinery "as simple mechanisms with which to gain power."[19] But in fact, this approach is more common to the "old" underdeveloped nations of South America than to the "new" underdeveloped nations of Africa. In Latin America, the artificial grafting of a libertarian political code onto a soft underbelly of feudal socio-economic relations often accentuated pure charisma, just as it also accentuated pure bureaucratic norms. It is precisely the kind of per-

[19] See Kalman H. Silvert, "The Costs of Anti-Nationalism," in *Expectant Peoples: Nationalism and Development*, edited by K. H. Silvert. New York: Random House, 1963, pp. 355-6. Also see his article on "National Values, Development, and Leaders and Followers," *International Social Science Journal*, Vol. XV, No. 4, 1963, pp. 560-70.

manent crisis of dependency evident in Latin America which many of the new nations of Asia and Africa have sought to overcome through party charisma. In those cases in Latin America where more or less successful changes in the social structure have been brought about—Cuba, Mexico, Chile, and to a lesser extent Venezuela—the party apparatus becomes the vessel of universal truth, while the leadership draws its inspiration from the claims of the party. Developing nations tend to become the model—replacing that of the most developed "first new nation," the United States, and avoiding the well-advertised problems of the Soviet Russian bureaucratic state.

In Brazil, precisely because its present military leadership is charismatic without party, political parties often follow the ways of United States politics by stressing electoral function and providing bureaucratic careers for popular leaders. In these instances the leadership often turns to the bureaucracy or military to build up power reserves. This intensifies the political character of the bureaucracy and makes it subject to political seizure. Control of the "bureaus" at the administrative levels and important alliances with military and other sectors become the real power bases. The direct power relation is between personal leadership and the state machinery. The Brazilian political party is the leader's vehicle, but it does not become enmeshed in government as such or enjoy the mass following of a "movement." It lies outside the state to a greater degree, and control of it is only peripheral. It does not become fused with charismatic dimensions except in revolutionary "movements." Even then, party organization, being essentially "non-ideological," is likely to overpower or modify charismatic party tendencies. It is a commonplace for the Brazilian intellectual to decry the opportunism of Brazilian parties and their lack of solid ideological lineage and loyalty. Because of the tenuous connection between leaders of the party and those of the state, political reorganization may be stifled. Politics may then be fragmented into many parties' representative interests.

III

One of the peculiarities of authority in the Third World is that the party ideology is generally much more inflexible than criteria for party membership. While the ideological features of the political apparatus are often highly centralized, the actual organization allows for a wide variety of ideological types. Lipset has recently noted that "such parties tend to be loosely structured, more like a *rassemblement* than a party of ideology or interest. They combine a number of interests and strata, either through the charisma of the leader or through the original need for unity in the struggle for independence. Charisma is necessary if the system is to survive in its early stages, and the absence of opposition may prove beneficial if it preserves the often frail mystique upon which authority depends."[20] It is not so much the "frail mystique" which determines the situation, since it rests on the frailties of power, but rather the inability of any one social sector to dominate the political context. The foundations for legal authority are strengthened when one well-defined social-economic sector is in control of the state. The American bourgeoisie in the nineteenth century (notwithstanding the rubrics which may be employed to show the aristocratic tastes of that class) gave legal shape to society because they were able to generalize their class interests so that they became identified with the national interest. Since the emergent nations of Latin America, Asia, and Africa have never witnessed a complete crystallization of modern class relationships, there has not been a properly installed rational-legal superstructure. The irony is that in many nations of Latin America law has been revered rather than obeyed. On the other hand, in those nations where the national movement was initially based on charismatic force, such as Mexico and Cuba, there are strong grounds for anticipating the long-range success of rational authority, as was the case in the United States between 1775 and 1865.

If we take Japan between 1860 and 1940 as typical of the "pre-Third World" developmental process in Asia, we find that disillusionment with multi-party processes does not necessarily resolve itself in party charisma but may result in personal charisma, which in this context meant the emperor.

> Despite growing popular participation in elections and extensive parliamentary experience, a politically mature middle class, with demands and expectations, did not develop. There was not enough time for this adjustment: rather, politicians came to be regarded

[20] Seymour Martin Lipset, *The First New Nation: The United States in Historical and Comparative Perspective*. New York: Basic Books, 1963, pp. 314-15.

as corrupt, parasitic, somehow un-Japanese, and "politician" took on a pejorative ring in prewar Japan. Essential power remained entrenched in a small elite, civilian and military, with the latter having direct access to the Emperor and able to use him to sanction its objectives without reference to the wishes of the popularly elected Diet.[21]

The tension between the needs of a mass society and a neo-feudal economy did not have to be resolved by party charisma. Stability was supplied by custom and tradition, the hierarchical rigidity of Japanese political leadership, and its close identification with military order and religious sanction.

This sense of hierarchy is precisely what is absent in most Third World nations, where there is extreme fluidity in both the definition and execution of leadership. Charismatic leaders are often under pressure to establish a principle of rule that is based on the political party as such. In Kwame Nkrumah's Convention People's Party (CPP) in Ghana, this transference of charisma from the person to the party is nearly total:

> The party must become at once the symbol and the focus of the national consciousness towards which loyalty can be directed above and even irrespective of loyalty to particular persons. Thus the agents of the party's authority may be acknowledged to fail or defect and ministerial heads may be seen to roll, but this must never be equated with any failure by the party as such. When the source and agency of authority are successfully separated in this way, it can then become true that *le parti regne mais il ne gouverne pas*. Charisma will become successfully routinized once the separation of the source from the agency of authority immunizes it against the failure which would bring about the collapse of a "pure" charismatic system.[22]

Even where personal charisma is exceptionally powerful, as in Cuba, we find direct appeals to party charisma. In an address delivered in May 1964, Fidel Castro said: "If the imperialists should invade this country,

[21] Lawrence Olson, "The Elite, Industrialism and Nationalism: Japan," in *Expectant Peoples: Nationalis mand Development*, edited by K. H. Silvert. New York: Random House, 1963, pp. 409-10.
[22] W. G. Runciman, "Charismatic Legitimacy and One-Party Rule in Ghana," *Archives Européennes de Sociologie*, Vol. IV, No. 1, 1963, p. 159.

you would have to realize that the majority of the leaders of today would die in the struggle. But the people will remain, and the party would remain. There would be no need to ask for names or for men. Each one of us would do his duty in the way demanded of him and do it well."[23] There is no question of the sincerity of the emotions herein expressed. It is obvious that under stress and duress the appeal to the rank and file is made in the name of the people and the party. The rhetoric does indicate a clear distinction between transient elite and permanent mass. Cuban leadership displays a passionate involvement rather than an Olympian detachment. In this fashion the party serves to solve the succession of leadership without destroying personal charisma. To say that this is simply a clever and modern way of reinforcing personal charisma misses the point that the cult of the party is quite commonplace. If we examine the history of the Soviet Union, it will be found that the extreme cult of personality came, not at the outset of the Revolution, but only at a late stage when the goals of political revolution hardened and became goals of economic development; and only at that point when the fight over control of the party apparatus became uppermost.[24]

One of the chief functional byproducts of charismatic leadership is that traditional economic sectors are made subordinate to state decisions. The kinds of independent class struggles engaged in by trade unions and business associations in the highly developed capitalist nations are intolerable for the Third World. They are viewed as obstructions to the task of social development—and in this way, the conduct of the union or the corporation has to become subordinate to state power. This is perfectly expressed by the African leader Tom Mboya. Speaking of both union and management separatist tendencies, he writes:

> The lesson they have to learn is that if their beliefs are to be respected in our new countries, they will need to show a response to government and nationalistic requirements. If their stand appears to be negative and unnecessarily obstructive, then it is inevitable that, with this sense of urgency in our new countries, they will be overridden and completely set aside. If they show

[23] Quoted by Dave Dellinger, "Cuba: Seven Thousand Miles from Home," *Liberation*, Vol. IX, No. 4, June-July 1964, pp. 11-21.
[24] See Myron Rush, *Political Succession in the U.S.S.R.* New York: Columbia University Press, 1965.

they are cooperative and become partners in the urgent need for development, then they will survive.[25]

This is a way of pointing out that, in the Third World, economic power is not equivalent to political power.

IV

Class competition is replaced by the doctrine of the "whole people." This doctrine makes multiple parties superfluous, since the whole people can obviously be represented by the whole party.[26] Yet, the conception of the whole people, or the myth of the mass, imposes severe limitations on totalitarian possibilities in the Third World. For any party which is compelled to make appeal by crossing class lines has clearly limited its cohesive potentialities. Yet party charisma is also the product of a relatively unstable equilibrium, an instability created by the fact that the very social forces which contributed to the formal political independence of the emerging nation are not compelled to choose between socialism and capitalism. Since experimental attitudes do prevail, they create a political atmosphere that is far from rigid or totalitarian.

Many Third World countries tend to place great emphasis upon the mobilization of the working classes and union movements in support of the national leadership. In this, the nations of the Third World have incorporated selective features of other radical movements to further consensus between the various classes in the society. Unionism becomes the most powerful bulwark of the nationalist elites. The working classes thus believe they have attained power rather than acted as a mere factor in the power arrangement. This variety of "national socialism" is made possible by the rational division of the economic spoils. Since large-scale capital is held by foreigners, internal economic fissures between classes will be dissolved, or at least drastically minimized. In this form, the *development ideology* of national unity replaces the *socialist ideology* of class struggle.

[25] Tom Mboya, *Freedom and After*. Boston: Little, Brown & Company, 1963, p. 197; also pp. 56-7.
[26] The most impressive study of this phenomenon of the whole people, and its effects on political processes in the new nations, is Emile R. Braundi, "Neocolonialism and the Class Struggle," *International Socialist Journal*, Vol. 1, Number 1, January-February 1964, pp. 48-68.

The formal independence of many Third World nations makes possible greater economic penetration by the older colonial powers. Formal freedom liberates the ex-colonial powers of the necessity of rule, and insures greater productivity, greater output, and greater interaction with foreign powers. The new middle classes which emerge in post-colonial situations move in the direction of the kind of formal authority which characterizes advanced middle-class societies elsewhere; but they are thwarted by the overt sentiments of the revolutionary leadership. More important, middle-class political consolidation stands in contradiction to the stated socialist objectives of many emergent nations. Therefore, the political elite must continue to exercise the special prerogatives of office, lest the middle class and proletariat jeopardize through social conflict the thorough mobilization and integration of the nation.

Party elites are shrewd enough to avoid making exaggerated claims for themselves as purveyors of universal truths; they now prefer to invest such claims in their party. In a new nation like Mali, for example, the Political Bureau of a dozen men make all decisions, and these decisions are binding for all Malians. It is the *Union Soudanaise* party which "holds in its hands the destiny of the country and has absolute power." The danger in this situation is that it fails to "surround the party with guarantees of popular agreement." There is a genuine concern about keeping connections to the mass, and this is resolved by an unnatural consensus—a demand for collectivity as a way to avoiding errors. But this often leads to an avoidance of decision-making.[27] Party charisma enables the new nation to combine maximum organizational efficiency with the greatest mobilization of the masses. It becomes a way of establishing the paradoxical claims of a consensus built upon mass participation and of a coercive apparatus built upon elitist drives toward development. And to the degree that such paradoxical claims are matters of ultimate interests and are "non-negotiable," then party charisma may turn out to be an unstable and temporary equilibrium. But then again, the entire Third World may be in this position in relation to the advanced industrial-military complexes of the world.

The new nation-states are an extremely fertile area for observing

---

[27] See on this subject William J. Foltz, *From French West Africa to the Mali Federation: The Background to Federation and Failure.* Unpublished Ph.D. dissertation. Yale University, 1963.

party charisma. The problem might be posed in the following way: Why is there a need for charismatic rather than rationalistic types of political authority? First, there are very few educated people in the new African states; very few whose background and qualifications alone could help create non-charismatic rule. Second, people feel frustrated that development has come so late and been so difficult; party charisma therefore serves as a ready-made tool to accelerate this process. Third, most African states have a long history of acceptance and response to raw power. In both British and French former possessions the lines of authority were clear, however much they were hated.[28] With the departure of the colonialists, this clear demarcation between ruler and ruled also ended. Party charisma thus overcomes the problem of political succession in the most feasible way possible within a context which exhibits a high degree of traditionalism amongst the masses and a no less marked modernism amongst the elites.

In response to the cry of treason which has been heard with increasing stridency from socialist elements in the Third World and Western Europe alike, the leadership of many emerging states has asserted that the national liberation phase has not yet been concluded (at least this is held to be so in Africa); only when nations like Angola and South Africa are liberated from white domination will it be possible or desirable to focus attention on internal imbalances between social sectors within the continent. It is further stated that for relatively advanced nations such as Ghana and Nigeria to intensify the conflict between the new urban proletariat and the new urban bourgeoisie would only postpone a settlement of accounts with the remaining imperial powers. Thus, the spokesmen of these new nations claim that a class struggle would prove to be sectarian and self-defeating—at least at this historical juncture. This concept has come to define not only the whole people, but has been enlarged into one for the whole continent. It seems to underly the insistence on the unique properties of African socialism.

The growth of party charisma in the Soviet Union was thwarted by two important factors; one practical and the other theoretical. On the practical side, the Soviet Union inherited a relatively complex, if not especially well-organized, bureaucratic apparatus from the Czarist regime.

[28] Cf. Aidan Crawley, "Patterns of Government in Africa," *African Affairs*, Vol. 60, No. 240, July 1961, pp. 393-4.

Unlike the post-colonial situation in the new nations of Africa and Asia, the technical functions of this pre-revolutionary bureaucracy were left intact. From the outset, it was a distinctively Russian entity, and not a colonial import which could be expanded or withdrawn at the pleasure of the foreign governing body. It was not necessary for the Bolshevik Party to incorporate unto itself all the features of organizational life. On the theoretical side, the separation of power between Government and Party was a Leninist canon. It represented the Communist Party way of establishing a one-party system of checks and balances. The fact that under Stalin the role of government was profoundly weakened, and federal and party functions combined, made possible the kind of personal charisma which sapped the strength of Soviet organizational life. One may characterize, therefore, the Khrushchev and Kosygin eras as a time of restoration—the re-establishment of lines of authority which are in some measure traditional, while, in other respects, legalistic and rationalistic.[29] In any event, at no point in past Soviet political history has there been any real unfolding of the party charisma phenomenon.

V

The underlying assumption that "man" will eventually assert his individuality in the face of tyranny takes for granted that people of the Third World share the Western cultural conception of "man against state." There is no evidence that the powerful disposition in favor of constitutionalism exhibited by the British working class in the nineteenth century is a valid guide to action for the recently liberated colonial working classes. To assume that a mobilization system is undemocratic while a reconciliation system is democratic simply turns constitutionalism into an article of religious faith.[30]

Until now constitutionalism, when employed in underdeveloped na-

[29] Irving L. Horowitz, "The Second Soviet Revolution," *The Correspondent*, No. 33, Winter, 1964-65.
[30] For a conventional "Western" position on this, see David E. Apter, "Political Religion in the New Nations," *Old Societies and New States: The Quest for Modernity in Asia and Africa*. New York: The Free Press of Glencoe, 1963, pp. 57-104. It is interesting that the very abstracts and quotations Apter uses to prove the existence of personal charisma and "political religion" demonstrate an impersonal or, better, depersonalized charisma lodged in the authority of the party and not the person.

tions, has not operated to create or broaden the consensual base but became a basic instrument for popular wants and needs. The role of party charisma is therefore to establish a basis of authority which is at one and the same time personal and legal—one that focuses on the party and not on either the individual or the law as such. It should not be assumed that the Third World is one in which personal authority is exclusive and dominant. This is, as a matter of fact, rarely the case. Party authority is not simply a rhetorical device used to disguise the fact of personal power. It is itself a limitation on personal power, though not yet legal or universally acknowledged. The actual transitory character of political parties stands in the way of the complete rationalization of the social systems in the Third World.

Party charisma does not do away with problems of bureaucracy and formal organization. On the contrary, such problems are multiplied to the degree that authority takes on multiple social roles: a portion of power remains with the leader, and another portion with the party directly, and yet a third in the technical requirements of leadership and organization. Historically, a greater measure of power has been invested in the personal leadership *prior* to the revolutionary period and a greater measure of power invested in the technical-professional elite *after* the revolutionary phase. The charismatic party functions as the clearing house for ideologists and technologists alike, deriving its own momentum from the unstable equilibrium they create. The ability to perform a particular task may appear to rest on "rational" grounds, while the choice and allocation of such tasks may appear to rest upon "irrational" political grounds. Actual political interaction is far muddier, since as a matter of course, the line between task and decision is constantly shifting, and it is in the areas between that friction arises.

The problem becomes particularly acute because so many of the new nations have one-party arrangements. All major decisions and tasks must be funneled through this single-party channel. The battle for control of the party apparatus becomes especially bitter. To lose control of this apparatus may mean to lose out in the overall sense, to forfeit the opportunity to move the nation. Thus, the battle for control is not only severe, but invariably subversive.[31] Seen in this way, we can understand

[31] See on this Colin Legum, "What Kind of Radicalism for Africa?" *Foreign Affairs*, Vol. 43, No. 2, January 1965, pp. 237-50.

how personalism and constitutionalism are tactical responses to an unstable historic situation, and not historical stages in the unfolding of nationhood.[32]

There is a growing literature dedicated to proving that not all of the emergent nations fit this pattern. Sir James Robertson has recently cited Nigerian "exceptionalism" based on the long precedent of compromise, the slow maturation of political responsibilities under the Crown, and the development of three strong parties.[33] This sounds more like an apologia for the superiority of British imperialism than an example of significant differences between Nigeria and other new African states. There is also the literature attempting to prove that constitutional monarchy resolves the problems of Middle Eastern bureaucracy. The argument is that, given the background and context of Middle Eastern history, a cultivated, Westernized notion of democracy can only be brought about by the modern counterpart of the eighteenth-century benevolent despot. This seems to place Middle East nations, like Iran, in a more backward political condition than even that reflected by party charisma. The latter at least has the advantages of depersonalization of the political machinery, and the legalization of the bureaucracy over and above kings and monarchs.[34]

VI

Ideology has become a particularly powerful force of rationalization in the newer African states. It can be seen with striking voice in Sekou Touré's explicit rejection of the classic struggle in favor of the anticolonial struggle—even after the successful conclusion of the national liberation phase of the revolution. He speaks of unionism in Guinea as "specifically African . . . an authentic expression of African values."[35]

[32] The various papers in Gwendolen M. Carter (ed.), *African One-Party States.* Ithaca, New York: Cornell University Press, 1962, provide a solid basis for my judgment that charisma and bureaucracy ought not to be viewed as historical stages in the unfolding of nationhood, but simply as dialectical poles, between which choices are constantly made and unmade.
[33] Cf. James Robertson, "Sovereign Nigeria," *African Affairs*, Vol. 59, No. 239, April 1961, pp. 145-54.
[34] Mohammad Reza Shah, *Mission for My Country*. New York: McGraw-Hill, 1963.
[35] Sekou Touré, *L'expérience et l'unité africaine*. Paris: Présence Africaine, 1959, pp. 390-91.

This means that European socialist standards of labor relations are to be replaced by the ideology of development as such. Speaking for Senegal, Leopold Sedar Senghor says that this Africanization of socialist ideology will eliminate the "one-sidedness" of European socialism and Communism. Actually, it is an instrument for making socialism and nationalism problems of social development. This development is to take place through "Community Development Centers." In this the Senegalese Party (UPS) is to be the "echo of the popular aspirations" and also the "scientific expression" of peoples' needs. In this apocalyptic vision of socialism and negritude, the party of the whole people may even become the party of the whole race.[36] The Third World has produced a party ideology as well as a political strategy. However mythic the synthesis of European socialism and African nativism may be, it would be foolish at this early stage to assume that the doctrine of the whole people led by the single, unified peoples' party, headed by the knowing and responsive leader, who is furthermore the choice of the whole people and the unified party alike (the two are not always distinguishable), is either transitory or lacking in practical application. For whatever else they are, the leaders of the emergent African states are sharp-eyed and razor-tongued, and above all practical men, concerned with political survival in extremely rugged social-economic circumstances.

Party charisma also represents a response to the division of power between local or tribal units and national units. Speaking of Ghana, Dennis Austin makes precisely this point. "If one asks how such an aim [of resolving the cosmopolitan-local duality] is pursued, the answer is clear—through the party, which dominates the contemporary scene. It remodels the State in its own image—reducing the power of the chiefs, centralizing the trade unions, legislating against tribal and regional parties, and centralizing power within the constitution."[37] According to Kwame Nkrumah: "There must be no stress on local, separatist loyalties . . . in Ghana, in the higher reaches of our national life, there should be no reference to Fantis, Ashantis, Ewes, Dagembas, etc., we should call ourselves Ghanaians—all brothers and sisters, members of the

[36] Leopold Sedar Senghor, *On African Socialism*, trans. by Mercer Cook. New York: Frederick Praeger, 1964, pp. 154-9, and 165.
[37] Cf. Dennis Austin, "The New Ghana," *African Affairs*, Vol. 59, No. 234, January 1960, pp. 20-25.

same community, the State of Ghana."[38] We can see that, contrary to present-day European socialist ideology, ethnic heterogeneity through the "self-determination" principle vanishes after the period of national independence.

However reluctant the inherited oligarchical system is to surrender its traditional power, and however desirous the political rulers are to avoid a direct confrontation with these traditional classes, the introduction of an industrial system compels these rulers to fight the oligarchy. The two forms of legitimation inherited from the past—personalism and constitutionalism—are historical and structural at the same time. Personal charisma, while a mechanism of transition from colonialism to independence, is not something which yields automatically to rational authority. While party charisma may be unstable, with the leader having to choose between absolute dictatorship and benevolent despotism, it remains an ongoing force in every Third World nation—long after some system of rational-legal authority has been created. The dialectic of the situation dictates that a charismatic figure must stay in power long enough to permit the crystallization of those opposing factions which can debate the character of the legal system. Charismatic parties thus make possible discussions on laws of political succession, divisions in the power structure, and relations between social and economic sectors. The growth of rational authority should allow for the kinds of innovations by the leadership that will not produce rigidly opposed political factions. There should be enough fluidity to permit the existence of highly personalized relations between leaders and followers in the revolutionary movement for national development. This is the proper function of party charisma.

[38] Ibid., p. 21. See also Kwame Nkrumah, *I Speak of Freedom: A Statement of African Ideology.* London: Heinemann, 1961.

Appendix C

Part 1—The Ideological and Institutional Bases of Party Charisma in the Third World*

ARGUMENTS JUSTIFYING
PARTY CHARISMA

COUNTER-ARGUMENTS
UNDERLYING PARTY CHARISMA

1. Political parties sabotage national unity and even when differences are honest, they sap the nation of a meaningful direction.

1a. National independence is often directly linked to a specific leadership, which, since it defines what a meaningful direction is, carries within its party the wisdom necessary for honest rule without a multiplicity of party systems.

2. The nationalist organization, which summed up the collective aspirations of the people prior to the national liberation period, is uniquely charged with the responsibility of realizing the fruits of

2a. Groups outside the nationalist organization are viewed as disruptive and disloyal to the basic aims of the revolution, and hence are not believed to enhance the post-liberation position of the new na-

* I am greatly indebted for the contents of this chart to several recent works on the ideology and structure of political parties in the Third World. In particular, Paul E. Sigmund, Jr. (ed.), *The Ideologies of the Developing Nations*. New York: Frederick Praeger, 1963; Fred R. van der Mehden, *Politics of the Developing Nations*. Englewood Cliffs, N.J.: Prentice-Hall Inc., 1964; Gwendolyn Carter (ed.), *African One-Party States*. Ithaca, New York: Cornell University Press, 1962; Gwendolyn M. Carter (ed.), *Five African States: Responses to Diversity*. Ithaca, New York: Cornell University Press, 1963.

victory in the post-liberation period.

tions. The idea of party competition is considered bourgeois rather than democratic; and in political contexts party charisma increasingly defines national aspirations as identical with socialist aspirations.

3. Multiple parties waste valuable manpower and time; and anyhow, the existence of multiple parties is no guarantee of democratic norms of political behavior.

3a. There is a technological-managerial void which tends to drain off talent from directly political ends. Nonetheless, the argument that multiple parties create a waste tends to reveal a strong bias in favor of the cult of efficiency, rather than of democracy. And these canons of efficiency tend to reward precisely that professional sector which garners the rewards of political organization far out of proportion to its numbers. Hence, the only forces capable of meaningful political opposition are in this way co-opted.

4. The system of multiple political parties is not suited to emergent nations where mutual assistance rather than mutual competition is the order of the day.

4a. One institutional weakness making multiple political parties hard to establish is the absence of a neutral bureaucracy, without which the functioning of the modern state is extremely difficult. Because of this, a consensus ("mutual assistance") must be developed within the political infra-structure, since in the absence of a neutral bureaucracy, multiple parties would indeed occasion a high degree of dissensus ("mutual competition").

5. Competition between political parties is a metaphysical rather than a sociological need. It is based on the principle of the selfishness and interest-bound character of political life, something uniquely true for capitalist states, and not characteristic of the new states of the Third World.

5a. This argument of the dysfunctionality of political parties is largely spurious. As a matter of fact, there is a great deal of selfishness and interest-boundedness within a single party system, i.e. the competition for control between ideologists. And, in the older, more mature conditions of political charisma (often where the original leaders have died, as Gandhi and Nehru in India), there are powerful institutional provisions for channelizing conflicting interests through the dominant party to avoid the necessity of multi-party solutions.

6. Multiple party states arose at a time when the economy sponsored the fragmentation of society into different and antagonistic social sectors; since the economy is itself politically directed, and the Third World societies are not fragmented in either structure or purpose, there is no need for multiple party units.

6a. The institutional structure of Third World nations is the farthest from being united as to structure or purpose. Conflicts between urban and tribal interests in Africa; between racial strains in Latin America; between peasant and bourgeois in India and in other parts of Asia attest to the disparity of economic structure. The single party state, when it is in effect, only serves to compel these economic interests to funnel their demands through political channels, making the state the biggest "business" of all in many of the emergent nations.

Appendix C

Part 2—Intra-Country Variations in Party Charisma

There exist certain intra-nation, or even intra-continental, variations in one-party charismatic patterns which, while they do not disrupt the validity of the root premises, do materially affect the operational phases of Party Charisma. Naturally enough, when these variances are pushed to their limits, the forces cementing Party Charisma dissolve, and give way either to a classic political structure—of either a straight bureaucratic or charismatic variety—or to entirely new political structures.

LATIN AMERICAN BLOC (examples: Argentina, 1945-55; Brazil, 1930-46; Mexico, 1948-64; Bolivia, 1952-64)

AFRO-ASIAN BLOC (examples: Ghana, Indonesia, Egypt, Algeria, India, etc., all in post-colonial period 1945-64)

1a. With few exceptions—the early stages of the Mexican and Cuban Revolutions—Party Charisma in Latin America was formed on the basis of the landholding or middle classes. In addition to this, there is only a partial severance of colonial relationships.

1b. In the main, Party Charisma is formed in terms of the modern classes, particularly the peasantry and the urban sectors, both white collar and proletariat. Even though the middle sectors show a steady rise in post-colonial strength, the party directorate is still committed to lower-class, socialist solutions.

2a. Single-party states are formed in social environments which are highly heterogenous in terms of population composition, i.e. racial, ethnic, and linguistic differences tend to weaken the cementing properties of Party Charisma. Regional, local, and immigration factors add to these difficulties.

2b. Single-party states are also formed in environments which are —as in Latin America—heterogeneous with respect to the indicators of race and ethnicity.

3a. In Latin America, the historical development of the middle classes, however impeded and frustrated by the traditional classes, was relatively independent of political domination. Indeed, in nations like Mexico and Bolivia, the economic classes really "won out" over the political directorate which forged the revolution. Hence Party Charisma, which requires a relatively powerful political directorate and no less weak socio-economic classes, comes upon the existence of well-formed classes that are not easily subject to state pressures. Hence, the Latin American Party Charisma has "mediative power."

3b. In the Afro-Asian bloc, despite the growth of a middle sector and a large urban population as such, there is the continued strength of the state to curb any propensities to independence or class separatism on the part of any one element. In many African nations, the state is the biggest of business, and hence a reinforcement of Party Charisma. In this way, through the combination of political and economic functions, the state comes to have "dominating power" and not, as in Latin America, only "mediative power."

4a. Latin American intellectual and ideological traditions are long-standing. They stem from the bourgeois enlightenment. Hence it is extremely difficult for any leader to justify or to rationalize his control in terms of the absolutism of his claims. But the fact that Latin

4b. The Afro-Asian bloc continues to reveal a strain between national and local-regional-tribal power. The contact with enlightenment ideologies of the West in this bloc has been through the colonial-imperial powers. Hence, the bourgeois tradition has come to be perceived as

America contains old nations and classic ideologies may aid the formation of Party Charisma as a half-way house between the bureaucratic and the charismatic states. It need not serve just to reinforce democratic patterns or norms of political behavior.

being alien to popular democracy. In such contexts, it may be simple to develop Party Charisma. Indeed, as in the Congo, when the single party state was not allowed to function, it was replaced by mass chaos and not mass democracy. It may however be that Party Charisma is too sophisticated a political form to work in many of these newly independent nations.

5a. The Latin American political pendulum has moved between personalism and constitutionalism; and hence solutions have been demanded in terms of these choices, rather than a compromise decision. Leaders must appear as human, constitutions must provide real safe-guards. There are entrenched political factions which have a vested interest in the politics of personal connections on one side, and the legal superstructure on the other. Party Charisma might resolve these long-standing dilemmas, but at a price that is held to be too high by the contrasting parties.

5b. The Afro-Asian bloc is not plagued by alternative solutions, but by an organizational vacuum. The leadership in these nations tends to fill the vacuum in terms of Leninist principles of organization. But in an "underdeveloped," non-European context, such socialism drastically moves into an elitist posture. Party Charisma enshrines the politics of social distance. Politics in the parliamentary sense becomes the expression of select pressure groups rather than the expression of the popular will or an electoral decision.

6a. Perhaps the most basic aspect of Party Charisma in Latin America is its instability. The political structure is such that no one sector can dominate or control all other sectors for any length of time. Hence, in such a fluid political uni-

6b. In the Afro-Asian bloc, Party Charisma tends to be quite stable, and institutionally reinforced by the absence of any countervailing sources of authority. As a matter of record, where Party Charisma has been established it also has

verse, the rate of elite turnover, as expressed primarily in "palace revolutions," is exceedingly high. This in turn has the effect of continuing instability, but, at the same time, of minimizing undemocratic and anti-democratic tendencies in political rule.

been successful. In such a firm political universe, the rate of elite turnover is exceedingly low. This in turn has the effect of minimizing political and social instability, but, at the same time, of maximizing undemocratic tendencies in political rule.

Chapter 9

The Military Pivot: From Revolution to Nation-Building

I

The national independence of nearly every Third World nation—the old nations of Latin America and Asia, as well as the newer nations of Africa—has been insured through revolution and secured through the organizational skills of revolutionists. The mass character of these revolutions can hardly be ignored. It is certainly not helpful to conceive of these movements in terms of insurgency and counter-insurgency, as so many recent strategists have done. In this way, the lofty rhetoric is preserved at the expense of the mass character of revolution.[1]

Actually within the Third World itself such revolutionary action is not seen as civil warfare between the nationals, but as the struggle of the underprivileged and underdeveloped areas against the direct military might or indirect economic interests possessed by the old colonial powers. Even in a "marginal" case such as the Congo, the people do not consider the conflict civil warfare but the final stage of anti-colonialism. For this reason "wars of national liberation" frequently take on an "anti-imperialist" content. To term such struggles insurgent uprisings minimizes the national scope of such military activities, and no less debases their mass revolutionary content. While there is by no means a direct correlation between national liberation movements and radical revolu-

[1] See, for example, David Galula, *Counterinsurgency Warfare: Theory and Practice*. New York and London: Frederick Praeger, 1964, pp. xiii-xiv. Mr. Galula does not want to admit the revolutionary nature of military movements in the Third World; moreover he is unwilling to surrender the term revolutionary. He necessarily ends by making the terms "insurgency" and "revolution" equally meaningless.

254

tionary ideologies, the confusion on this point, fostered by colonial apologists no less than by revolutionary romantics, tends to drive nationalists into radical channels.

For modern mass revolutions to be successful, they must assume a military character: this may take the form of a conventional military apparatus turning "leftist" as in the case of Nasser's Egypt. It may take the form of a peasant-based counter-military force, brought into existence by the continuing adhesion of the existing military establishment to the old social-political order, as in the case of China. It may be a peasant guerrilla army pressed into existence to do battle with a foreign controlled army, as was the case of Algeria. But whatever the precise form, it is clear, perhaps axiomatic, that the success of a social revolution, whether dedicated to a particular class or consecrated in the name of the entire people, depends on the level of military organization. Like the old political system, the conventional military establishment does not disappear with the revolutionary consolidation of power. Quite the contrary, its prestige and its power grow in direct proportion to the nation's growth. There is no recorded case of a nation that has achieved its independence since 1945 voluntarily and consistently reducing the role or the size of its military apparatus. Any attempt at developing an operational model of disarmament or arms control must take this into consideration.

To gain some appreciation of how radically different the shape of modern warfare has become since the rise of the Third World, we need only examine basic studies of military power made in the pre-World War Two period. Even the most far-seeing of them fails to reveal even a faint appreciation of Asia, Africa, and Latin America as centers of military affairs.[2] In less than a quarter century, the military pre-eminence of Europe—of Germany, Italy, France, and England—has given way to the pre-eminence of the United States and the Soviet Union. Just as these two evolving goliaths stood on the periphery of power during the first decades of the century, so now the leading nations of the Third World stand at the entrance of military power in the last decades of this century.

The chief reason that the military might of the Third World remained unexplored in the pre-World War Two period was that the na-

[2] See, for example, Max Werner, *The Military Strength of the Powers*. London: Victor Gollancz Ltd., 1939.

tion-state, which is an essential prerequisite for the growth of a military, hardly existed in Asia and Africa. In the main they were colonial or semi-colonial areas. Once national sovereignty was established, particularly if that sovereignty was recently gained with the aid of revolutionary mass movements, then the role of the military tended to increase in proportion to the growth of industrialization and urbanization. There have been minor exceptions: the pacifism of India's rulers prevented a big military build-up for several years after independence (a situation which has now been "corrected"), while the military expenditures of countries like the Philippines and Indonesia are more swollen than the threats to their sovereignty, real or imaginary, warrant.

In considerable measure, the pivotal role of the military in the Third World stems from the importance of military engagements in the transitional "war" period. Perhaps the case of China is the "classic" model of the formation of an army from below. But not even Maoist Communists claim that guerrilla and peasant insurrections are caused by anything other than the breakdown of conventional rules and habits in the old regime. The leading general of the Chinese Revolution, Chu-Teh, noted that

> in a semi-feudal and semi-colonial country like China, the simplest democratic rights for people had to be fought for with guns in hand. In Shanghai, Hankow, Canton, and other cities, workers and intellectuals were being beheaded in the streets for demanding free speech, press, assembly, and the right of organization, and for demanding the right to defend themselves in court when arrested. The eight-hour day, increased wages, and the abolition of child labor were all branded as Communist banditry, as was the idea of free trade unions.

Because of this, Chu concludes, it was evident "that the Chinese people could win democratic rights only by the armed defeat of the counter-revolutionary henchmen of foreign imperialism."[3] Guerrilla action was thus said to be a response to three factors: (a) misery of the masses; (b) the inability to settle conflict in a parliamentary or legal way; and (c) foreign control of the domestic economy and polity. But above all,

[3] See Agnes Smedley, *The Great Road: The Life and Times of Chu-Teh*. New York: Monthly Review Press, 1956, p. 254. For a more recent account of China's turn to "military determinism," see Lin Piao, "China's Grand Strategy," *Current*, No. 64, October 1965, pp. 6-9.

such guerrilla action took place when the old colonial powers were intransigent.

These items are true for China as for Cuba. That is why it would be a profound mistake to describe *all* military action in the Third World as "revolutionary," or correspondingly, all revolutionary processes as military. Indeed, most of Latin America illustrates a different situation. After new nations pass through their initial consolidation stage, the military establishment remains nationalistic, while often becoming politically conservative. National revolution and social revolution are radically different phenomena. That is why the distinction between revolution from above and from below is significant. There is a direct correlation between revolutions made "from above" having national orientations, and revolutions made "from below" revealing social orientations. One might say that "national" revolutions appeal to present-day values, while "social" revolutions appeal to specific interests and utopian longings.

Militarism in the Third World can be studied in terms of key variables which define the role of the military in the political sphere. This may extend from peripheral or even non-existent policy-making roles to paramount decision-making roles, such as control of the government apparatus. We might analyze the military by isolating the elements of a professional and political army. We might then differentiate between these professional or political types.[4] I have chosen to divide the military establishment into component roles which are at the same time illustrative of the structural characteristics of the armed forces. There is no exclusive rationale for any approach, except that the manner employed here better accounts for the similarities in the Third World military than any other. Not until a full-scale analysis of military budgets, hardware, war-making potential, etc., is undertaken will it be possible to make a definitive choice of one set of measures over another.

II

The emergence of the Third World, both in the form of newly independent nations and revitalized old nations, has created new elites, the

---

[4] I am grateful to John Lovell, who raised many of these points in his paper on "A Study of the Involvement of the Military in Political Problems of Achieving Conceptual Clarity," presented at the Special Operations Research Office Conference held in Washington, D.C., between May 26 and May 29, 1965.

most outstanding of which are the party bureaucracy and the military. Often indeed these post-colonial political leaders are also military heroes of the liberation period. Only in Africa below the Sahara is this military-bureaucratic combination absent.

The military elites of the new nations function in radically different ways from conventional European military forces and yet have many structural similarities to them. New nations require new armies. And the sources of these new armies are often the popular classes. Hence these armies were in origin often radical as well as national. Membership at all levels was drawn from formerly dispossessed sections and from elements demanding rapid social mobility. This latter group supplied the intellectual fuel which triggered mass resentments. Thus the formation of a new army in such places as Algeria, Cuba, and Indonesia was at the same time a pronouncement in favor of rapid economic development and revolutionary political structures.

Military power exists in its relation to state power. It is geared to defend a well-defined geographic terrain and a certain body of people having a common set of economic, psychological, and linguistic elements within this terrain. The function of the armed forces at the very outset of nation-building is to preserve and make visible national sovereignty. They "defend" and "project" the national entity into the international arena. And once actual sovereignty is obtained, they acquire a critical role with respect to the internal affairs of the state. The military revolutionists thus come to power against colonialists, but maintain power against internal threats.

The relationship between government and the military is no less intimate than the connection between control of power and control of violence at the more general level. But whatever the main role of the armed forces at any given moment, whether toward the maintenance of the state against external enemies or against internal terrorists, the military leadership alone is assigned the right to use physical violence. This exclusive source of the right to use violence does not, however, extend to legal authorization. The ambiguity in civil-military relations often resides in the separation of the use of violence (a military function) from a definition of the limits of violence (a legal-social function). Such exercise of violence in the absence of complete legitimation also remains a constant source of tension between the military and the civil apparatus.

The military, when functioning properly, quickly acquires a sense of the nation and becomes hostile toward vested interests and sectional enclaves. Military organizations recruit from disparate groups and classes within the society. By minimizing the class base of membership through a heterogenous recruitment policy, the armed forces can function as an important socializing agency.[5] This trans-class role can be performed despite the relatively pronounced class base of military leadership. In nations such as Egypt, Iran, and other Middle Eastern states, where the class formations remain relatively diffuse and weak, the corresponding importance of the army as a national and even a class-welding agency becomes manifest.[6]

Unlike the formation of either the United States or the Soviet Union, the armed forces in the newly emergent nations are not so much absorbed into the civilian society but they tend to become partners with the society. It was one of the hallmarks of the first United States administration, that of George Washington, that it made the military subject to political control.[7] Curiously enough, in the Russian Revolution, despite urgings of the permanent revolutionists, the military was placed under the rule of the political elites.[8] In the United States civilian control had democratic consequences and in the Soviet Union autocratic consequences, but in neither case did it make much difference in terms of the functional efficiency of the armed forces. In both the First and Second Worlds the military served as a professional source of political strength and developmental orientations rather than as a ruling directorate. The same cannot be said for most Third World nations, where, as a matter of fact, the political functions are oftentimes militarized from the outset of independence. Due to this early identification with the

[5] See Joseph La Palombara, *Bureaucracy and Political Development*. Princeton: Princeton University Press, 1963, pp. 31-2.
[6] See on this Manfred Halpern, *The Politics of Social Change in the Middle East and North Africa*. Princeton: Princeton University Press, 1963; and George E. Kirk, "The Rise of the Military in Society and Government: Egypt," in *The Military and the Middle East*. Columbus: Ohio State University Press, 1963.
[7] See Seymour Martin Lipset, *The First New Nation: The United States in Historical and Comparative Perspective*. New York: Basic Books, 1963, pp. 16-45; and William N. Chambers, *Political Parties in a New Nation*. New York: Oxford University Press, 1963, pp. 21-7.
[8] See Klementi Voroshilov, *Fifteen Years of the Red Army (Russia)*. Moscow, 1933. Quoted passages in Max Werner, *The Military Strength of the Powers*. London: Victor Gollancz, 1939, p. 36.

national cause, the military is transformed from a symbolic badge of sovereignty into a decisive partner in the composition of the state.

The function of the military establishment as the mark of sovereignty is well exemplified by post-liberation India. Given its strong traditional bias against force and violence, India represents a good test case. Under the reign of Nehru, the Gandhian approach to pacifism was severely modified in the name of expediency. According to Gandhi, the key to real victory is the doctrine of *Satyagraha*—the force which is born of truth and love, rather than error and hatred. Non-military, non-violent social action was pitted against all enemies.[9] But the actual conduct of foreign policy after the British left compelled a quick and uneven modification of this policy. With reference to the early stages of the Kashmir dispute, Nehru considered it his "misfortune that we even have to spend money on armaments and that we have to keep an army, a navy, and an air force. In the world one is compelled to take those precautions."[10] While the rhetoric remains pacifist, the actual chore of strengthening the military was well under way no more than two years after independence. And, by the end of the 'fifties, Nehru abandoned even the pacifist rhetoric. He noted that "none of us would dare, in the present state of the world, to do away with the instruments of organized violence. We keep armies both to defend ourselves against aggression from without and to meet trouble from within."[11] India responded to the increased military determinism of all worldly situations. And in so doing showed Gandhism to be a practical "dead-letter" in India.

The increase in military spending in India has kept pace with the general militarization of the Third World. From 1960 to 1964 alone, the increase in military allocations has been threefold.[12] The percentage of

[9] See Joan V. Bondurant, *Conquest of Violence*. Princeton: Princeton University Press, 1958; W. H. Morris-Jones, "Mahatma Gandhi: Political Philosopher?" *Political Studies*, Vol. III, No. 1, February 1960; Irving Louis Horowitz, "Tolstoi and Gandhi: The Pacifist Dream," in *The Idea of War and Peace in Contemporary Philosophy*. New York: Paine-Whitman Publishers, 1957; and Arne Naess, *Gandhi and the Nuclear Age*. Totowa, New Jersey: The Bedminster Press, 1965.
[10] Jawaharlal Nehru, *Speeches: 1949-1953*. New Delhi: Publications Division, Ministry of Information and Broadcasting. Government of India, 1957, p. 357.
[11] Ibid., p. 211.
[12] See Ministry of Information and Broadcasting, *India, 1962*. New Delhi: Publications Division, Government of India, 1962, pp. 72-4; and *India, 1963*, pp. 21, 64, 180.

India's budget has gone from 6 per cent of the Gross National Product in 1961 to 17 per cent in 1964. The national military cadet corps, the breeding ground of the future officers, has gone from 150,000 in 1958 to 300,000 in 1964. Slowly also, the military mix of army, navy, and air force is changing to reflect the tactical nature of modern conflict. The air force has grown steadily at the expense of the other branches. And with the increasing military hardware sent in by both the Soviet Union and the United States, India has been transformed from a leader to a buffer zone of the Third World.

The military build-up is continuing. The rise of Communist opposition to Congress Party rule in Kerala and elsewhere and the pressures from China and Pakistan explain only partly this increase. For, as in other Third World nations, national greatness is becoming ever more linked to military grandeur. And no country of the Third World, even one conscientiously dedicated to pacifism, has been able to withstand this formula of a civil-military partnership—what can be controlled is the degree of military involvement (as in some parts of Africa) but no longer the fact of involvement.

III

The capacity of the military in Third World nations to help establish a political system depends upon three main factors: its control of the instruments of violence; its ethos of public service and national identity instead of private interest and class identity; and its representation as an articulate and expert group.[13] In the Third World the military alone combines these factors, which may be generalized as technical skills combined with an ethic of national purpose.

These factors also help to explain why the elite of the armed forces is no longer aligned with the traditional upper classes. As long as the military maintained such alignments with the aristocracy and with religious groups, it was difficult, if not impossible, for the nation to become developmentally oriented or for the military to perform in terms of public service or its technical or professional skills. This shift has been most pronounced in those nations where the military underwent a trans-

[13] See Morris Janowitz, *The Military in the Political Development of New Nations.* Chicago: University of Chicago Press, 1964, pp. 27-8.

formation from within; especially in Latin America and in Egypt, where the inherited military establishment had to break with this oligarchical notion of service to the upper classes in order to function as a redeemer of the popular will.

The military becomes concerned with internal security when a national revolution becomes a class revolution. Since most Third World societies are highly stratified, according to class, race, caste, or area, the possibilities, even inevitabilities, of class conflict persist. Thus the military establishment, whether it so desires or not, is compelled to align itself with either traditional social classes or modern social classes. In a concrete sense, the role of the military in maintaining internal security is impaired by the very existence of class forces, for it is subject to pressure from both sides. It is possible to overthrow military establishments as part of a general upheaval against traditional class. At the same time, if the military is identified too closely with the popular classes, it tends to bring about an oligarchically inspired counter-revolution.

The role of the military is impaled upon the horns of a structural dilemma. In the very act of serving as an instrument of national redemption, it finds itself aligned against traditional class forces that have a great deal to lose in terms of wealth as well as prestige. At the same time, the use of the military as an instrument of suppression for riot control and secret police action has the effect of aligning the military against the popular class forces it is ostensibly serving. This problem is more acute in the Middle East and in Latin America than in most parts of Asia or Africa—where the military has not been replaced in the course of revolutionary action so much as found its roles transformed in the course of the developmental process.[14] Interestingly, these former areas also contain nations where there is high tension and low stability.

The political leadership in the Third World tends to be drawn from the military corps. Therefore, in the "Egyptian socialism" of Nasser, or in the "guided democracy" of Sukarno, there is extreme emphasis on providing adequate policy-making roles for the armed forces. The tendency of political leadership in the Third World to simulate military

---

[14] See Dankwart A. Rustow, "The Military in Middle Eastern Society and Politics," in *The Military in the Middle East*, edited by S. N. Fisher. Columbus: Ohio State University Press, 1963, p. 11; and more generally, P. J. Vatikiotis, *The Egyptian Army in Politics*. Bloomington: University of Indiana Press, 1961.

models, and at times to adopt even the dress, manners, and bureaucratic norms of the military establishment, underscores the close kinship and partnership between military and civilian elements.

The only countervailing power to the charisma of party is the bureaucracy of the military. These are the two major pivots of domination in the Third World, and they often act as partners in moving their nation from colonial rule in independence or from constitutional to one-party control. Involvement by the military in the political system can take place by promoting developmental programs or by consolidating or stabilizing the popular revolution. But whatever the mechanism, the fact of involvement in the maintenance of the social structure is clear.

The strength of the military often reflects the absence of strength on the part of the middle or working classes. This is particularly true in the new nations. When the popular classes are too ineffectual in changing obviously bankrupt social relations, the elite of the armed forces perceive themselves as capable of filling a social vacuum. The army is thus able to guarantee an equilibrium between classes through military might. The army, in virtue of its national liberation character, may not have the capacity to crush opposition, but it may prevent any successful attempts at overthrowing the new regime. It is remarkable how few *coups d'état* have occurred in Asian and in African single-party states during the postcolonial epoch. On the other hand, in such multi-party states as the Congo, where there are no fewer than two hundred political parties and three different military directorates, there is far more instability than in the one-party political-military condition. Nearly all the leaders who were in charge when independence was attained in Africa are still heads of state or of the party: Nyerere, Touré, Nkrumah, Balewa, Kenyatta, Senghor, Banda, and others. Even when this original leadership collapsed, as in Algeria, the new leaders were chosen from an alternative faction of the original revolutionary group. This indicates how well the strain in the system is managed by the present power hierarchy.

The military in the new nations can oftentimes exercise international power. The Egyptian and the Algerian military see themselves very much concerned with problems of the unification of all North Africa, including the training of Palestinian Arabs for the reconquest of Israel. The same kind of regional pattern is to be found with Indonesia in Southeast Asia, where it too hopes to function as a homogenizing force in the whole of the area, especially in the Malaysian peninsula. But thus far, the international role is more regional than truly world-wide. The internal role predominates.

Nevertheless, the search for regional, if not international, roles cannot simply be dismissed as artificial. The annual regional meetings within the Third World provide a show of force no less than a show of political principles. The collective military might of the Third World determines its strength in relation to the First and Second Worlds. At the same time the individual might of each nation within the Third World determines its position in relation to the other nations within that world. Even nations who are debtors before the International Monetary Fund may act as creditor nations within regional blocs. Thus, a nation like Egypt may be a borrower of funds, but it is a distributor of arms to other Middle Eastern nations. As long as the First World and Second World were organized against each other for the purpose of making nuclear exchanges, the Third World could not be considered militarily significant. With the widespread acceptance of war as a game, the rise of insurgency and counter-insurgency, and the nuclear standoff created by First and Second World competition, the conventional military hardware of the Third World has come to function as a more significant variable in international geopolitics than it did a decade ago.

The character of the military of the Third World is often shaped, symbolically at least, by the military power or powers which trained or occupied the territory during the colonial period. Thus in Indonesia one finds a Japanese and Dutch combination; in Egypt there are English and German types of models; in many parts of Latin America there is a combination of French and German as well as United States prototypes. In other words, the actual organizational charts which describe these military organizations are based upon prototypes brought over from the former imperial power.

Even though the military in the Third World may think of itself as distinct and distinctively nationalistic, it still carries on the traditions of the old colonial armies. This is not just a cultural inheritance, but a consequence of the complex nature of modern warfare, especially the complicated technology of advanced combat and the problem of training human forces so that they become a significant military asset. Thus there is rising tension between the need for autonomy and the necessity for seeking out models and materials from the advanced blocs. One way Third World nations attempt to overcome this contradiction is by the process of "spin-off," by relying on one major power for technological and military hardware and on another for its military organization charts. Many African nations, such as Ghana, Nigeria, and Sierra Leone, which exhibited total military dependence on the British style at the outset of the independence period, have moved to counteract this by arrangements with advanced countries as disparate as West Germany, France, and Czechoslovakia.

Another reason for the diversification of military programming derives from local factors. Thus the strength of Ethiopia compels Somalia to accept Russian military missions. Pressure from China leads India to diversify its forces by using both Soviet and United States tactical and strategic weapons. A limiting problem is that the debtor nation faces the same problems in military terms that it does in economic terms. The credit line is not irrevocable. This serves to place an economic impediment and limit to the problem of political management in the Third World. Military assistance becomes a focal point in maintaining exclusive relations with the former imperial power. For example, the fact that France remains the exclusive distributor of military hardware to most of its former African colonies can undermine the purpose of independence as much as it is undermined by exclusive trade arrangements.[15]

There is less apparent ambiguity in the military's role on the international side than its role as an internal agency. Military organizations directly influence social structure by their allocation and distribution of power. The military decides how much violence should be used in any internal situation. But a military establishment often feels freer to use violence in foreign than in domestic matters. Not only is the military reluctant to compete with civilian authority, but positive factors contribute to this situation. First, institutions subject to comparison, such as an army, are tested against other armies. It can never be wholly judged in terms of maintaining internal security. The military thrust cannot completely avoid international considerations. Second, because of a long-range aspect to foreign affairs, armed forces are immune to

---

[15] For a significant discussion of this point, see William Gutteridge, *Military Institutions and Power in the New States*. New York: Frederick Praeger, 1965, pp. 117-29.

pragmatic tests of economic efficiency. They are not subject to the pressures of private enterprise or to the rules of business and investment. They can function as a planning agency even within a "free enterprise" social order. Third, an armed force generally has a style of its own. It is not subject to or limited by ordinary standards of behavior or legal canons.[16]

These distinctive features also have negative byproducts. The role of the army as an international agency requires a highly professional group of men, capable of making and rendering decisions on strategic issues, whereas an armed force concerned with internal security requires a much more politicized orientation in which considerations of bureaucratic efficiency or separation of functions may be secondary. Hence, the multiplicity of roles for military establishments in the Third World may involve structural incompatibilities. As Andrzejewski indicates, "Modern military technique produced two contrary effects. On the one hand, it strengthened the centripetal forces by making subjugation of distinct regions easier; but on the other hand, it fostered a disintegration of multi-nation empires, because universal conscription became an unavoidable condition of military strength, and armies raised in this way were of little value unless permeated by patriotism."[17]

IV

When armed forces participate in nation-building, they are involved in the whole gamut of political processes—internal versus international, political versus professional, and democratic versus repressive roles. Nation-building is also dedicated to resolving social stress—to control, if not eliminate the cleavages of class and of status.[18]

The capacity of the armed forces to act as a nation-building instrument is inherent in its structure. It is often the most "modernized" and

[16] Lucien Pye, *Armies in the Process of Political Modernization*. Cambridge: Massachusetts Institute of Technology, 1959, pp. 12-13.
[17] Stanley Andrzejewski, *Military Organization and Society*. London: Routledge & Kegan Paul Ltd., 1954, pp. 83-4.
[18] In this capacity, the role of the military is not much different than it was during the industrialization process of Germany and Japan. See on this Reinhard Bendix, *Nation-Building and Citizenship: Studies of Our Changing Social Order*. New York: John Wiley & Sons, 1964, pp. 177-213.

most highly refined organization in Third World nations. This does not simply mean that it is technologically proficient. The armed forces offer the individual a conspicuous channel for advancement based on achievement and merit rather than on background or ascribed status.

The army has had an historical role as a nation-building device, particularly in Japan under the Shogunate and in Germany under the Kaisers. They both provide significant cases of how a military modernizes a society in the midst of the predominance of feudal sectors. Since the jump in most Third World nations is from some kind of latifundism to some kind of socialism, the army can act as a surrogate for the bourgeoisie in the classical Western process of development under capitalism.[19] Hence from an historical as well as a functional point of view, the army serves in this developmental capacity.

In societies where everyone is tardy, the military is prompt. Where the population is ragged, the soldiers are neatly uniformed. Where indecisiveness reigns supreme, the military can take direct action. This enables the armed forces' leadership to claim a mystique about its role in the developmental process. But this mystique is no mystery! Since, in such nations as Turkey and India, the mystique of civilian supremacy is even more powerful than any military metaphysics, it becomes plain that only when the military has something better to offer in enhancing social cohesion than other social forces can this mystique obtain. When it does produce this unifying effect, when the nation is finally solidified, it is just as likely to be anti-military as pro-military; the popular resolution is likely to be made in terms of relative inefficiency of the military and the civilian and not in terms of their respective rhetoric.

The military establishment can also be seen as an instrument of continuity in a context where violent breaks with the past are unsettling. In nearly all the countries of the Third World, Westernization has produced the deterioration and the breakdown of traditional societies. Oftentimes the one institution that was preserved from the old order, and indeed reinvigorated, was the armed forces. This surely must rank as a key factor why the armed forces serve as a socially cohesive element

---

[19] To see how this works out in a nation such as Turkey, see Dankwart A. Rustow, "Turkey's Second Try at Democracy," *Yale Review*, Vol. LII, June 1963, pp. 518-38; and by the same author, "The Military in Middle Eastern Society and Politics," in *The Military in the Middle East, op. cit.*

in the new nations. They can embody at one and the same time traditional values and modernist goals, and still contribute to stabilizing the political situation.

The rapidity of the developmental process guarantees the absence of well-organized, popularly controlled political parties. In the absence of such parties, and at times of crisis, the armed forces may be the only group capable of maintaining political order or preparing the ground for further economic breakthroughs. Thus the military tends to perform all sorts of omibus functions, paramount of which is direct political rule.

But this situation often produces a widespread condition of atrophy. The military, powerful enough to cancel democratic norms, is not powerful enough to maintain social order over a long period of time. By temperament and by training, the military is more capable of preventing the exercise of political rule than of exercising such rule itself. Thus the armed forces have the ability to cancel democratic norms but not the political knowhow or the mass support to retain power in their own hands.[20] The wear and tear of prolonged governing is likely to reduce the armed forces to the level of just another political group in the eyes of the country. The very sectionalism, or schismatic quality, fostered by military directorates would destroy the prestige which gives to the army its exceptional role in the Third World. Even where military men do rule, as in Egypt and Algeria, a process of "civilianization" has set in.

The role of the armed forces is not just dependent upon the level of industrial technological achievement. In itself the army promotes such achievements; it demands the newest technological apparatus. To function comparatively—with respect to other armed forces—it must be at the technological level of these other armed forces. Hence the army makes great demands upon the economy. The army demands a highly efficient economy, while it insists on remaining the touchstone for determining the character of economic production.

---

[20] I have documented this point in several different ways in a series of articles on Argentina. See Irving L. Horowitz, "Revolt Against Political Mythology: Storm over Argentina," *The Nation*, Vol. 194, No. 13, March 1962; "The Peronista Paralysis," *The Nation*, Vol. 195, No. 10, Oct. 1962; and "Militarism in Argentina," *New Society*, Vol. 1, No. 39, June 1963. This same phenomenon has been described for another area. See Josef Silverstein, "First Steps on the Burmese Way to Socialism," *Asian Survey*, Vol. IV, No. 2, Feb. 1964, pp. 716-22.

In this way a point is reached at which the army serves not only as a mark of political sovereignty but as a strong influence on the economy. It may use the industrial technology for its own purposes. It may sustain a certain portion of the industrial base by its contracts and purchases (and this is just as true for the "public sector" as for the "private sector"). It may underwrite certain industries which are weak or non-competitive either in the domestic market or in the world market, if it is convinced that such industries are militarily useful. For these reasons, the impact of the armed forces on the economic sector of Third World nations is likely to increase greatly in the forthcoming period. To some degree, the public-sector character of many Third World economies will make them more subject to military pressures than would be the case were industry to remain in the hands of even a powerful private-economic sector. In a public-sector economy, the factory and shop managers have a special relation to other portions of the state, of which the military is most immediately appraised. And since decision-making is in the hands of the state, the ability of private industry to perform a countervailing power role is severely circumscribed. Thus, we can observe how the military reduces the threat to itself from "alien" class forces not by destroying such classes but by embracing them in an overall national consensus based on the "needs of the whole people."

V

There are a number of contradictions in the role played by the military in the Third World. The nation-building potential of the military may in itself be a response to external prodding from more radical sectors, or the military may itself be a prod to other groups. In either event, this nation-building potential must be correlated to the costs of maintaining a military establishment. In many Latin American nations, the military represents a constant drain on the national economy—anywhere from 5 to 40 per cent of the total budget. It might well be that the idea of a Latin America demilitarized, denuclearized, and protected by the United Nations directly, far from creating chaos, may actually stimulate social and economic development. But this possibility remains quite remote, since such a solution would also confirm the role of many Third World nations as permanent satellites. This may prove to be an inescapable dilemma. It may be that a permanent contradiction remains between the military as a drain on processes of economic development and in its role in the development process.

The military is geared both to national redemption and to the international expectancies of big foreign powers. This is as true of Eastern European nations with respect to the Soviet Union as it is of Latin America with respect to the United States. In other words, there are competing claims of autonomy and heteronomy: the international demands of the leading powers in contradiction to the nation-building role of the military in the secondary powers. This contradiction may in time prove a more serious drag on disarmament negotiations than any of the present schisms between the United States and the Soviet Union.

The actual military strength of new nations is obscured by the fact that the definition of a military budget, while often put in terms of the Gross National Product, is in fact subject to immense contributions from foreign military missions, defense agreements with the major power blocs, and technical training provided by these external power blocs. The actual militarization process in the Third World is therefore far more extensive than is usually realized. And because military aid tends to be packaged and bracketed along with other kinds of aid, the difficulties in developing statistically significant devices for understanding the actual size of a military establishment are compounded.

The military in the new nations derives its power from the degree to which it can be welded together into a common front against the older traditional powers of Europe and North America. On the other hand, the only significance of this power is the relation of Third World nations to each other. This may simply be another way of saying that the Third World is hardly a unified, solid phalanx. But this very contradiction between national independence and international dependence helps to accentuate these rifts.

Many of these military establishments, particularly in Africa or Asia, function in terms of the new classes in emerging nations, while others, in Latin America, function in terms of the needs of traditional classes. Thus, in describing the Third World military, one is describing a military forged both in support of traditional class interests and in support of contemporary developmental classes. This has often produced great confusion in big-power foreign aid programs, for there has been a tendency to treat the military as either reactionary or revolutionary without evaluating the historical context of area development.

Ultimately the problem is whether the military sector of the Third World—any more than military establishments elsewhere—can function as a modernizing democratic force. The organizational and structural characteristics of the military are fairly universal: bureaucratic standards, chain of command, authoritarian traditions, sharp distinctions between enlisted men and officer corps, etc. Whether such an apparatus, geared to a system of superordinate and subordinate units, and particularly one unchecked by other sectional interests, can ever function in terms of democratic values or developmental needs—or can ever do so for any extended period of time—is indeed questionable. Even the most democratically organized military organizations with the most obvious popular bases, such as the Algerian army or even the Cuban army, will have great difficulty in maintaining both a democratic structure and a developmental orientation. One or the other, or both, must eventually give way to the military politics of *status quo.*

To turn the matter around, can there be real development in the Third World without a military establishment committed to development? A trade-off of democratic values takes place not simply at the level of economic production but also at the level of military dominion. While the general trend is in the direction of more development and less democracy, this decision in itself does not guarantee successful development. The same is true of the military. While the existence of a large armed force may enhance development, it is more likely to hinder it. East European nations who endured the Stalin era will attest to this.

In short, the military of the Third World presents us with a set of contradictions which have not been resolved in fact and therefore cannot be resolved in theory. What we are entitled to say is that the Third World is contributing its share to the rise of a military determinism, or at least to the military determination of the conduct of social affairs. Further, it has been proven throughout the Third World that as long as there is a nuclear stand-off between the First World and Second World, conventional arms can serve quite readily to continue to define each and every crisis in terms of military might. Thus, the militarization of the Third World may be as large a threat to the peace of the world as the nuclear stockpiles of the advanced industrial powers. The world may be divided in three, but the military dilemma remains the same.

Appendix D

The Organization and Ideology of Hemispheric Militarism

Several things we do know and several things we don't know about the organization and ideology of the military in the contemporary period. First, let us consider what we know, or at least what we know to be wrong. For this in itself constitutes a kind of necessary prelude and background for discussion.

First, we know that the nuclear stand-off, far from creating any delicate or indelicate balance of terror, in the absence of any peace-keeping parameters only creates the basis of a more sophisticated conventional arms race.

Second, we know that the rise of a scientific military technology does not in itself lead to the "civilianization" of the military in industrially advanced societies, but rather to the militarization of the civilian population.

Third, we know that the central dynamic in present-day war-making is constituted by the relationship between the fully developed (and over-developed) nation-states in contrast to the semi-developed (and under-developed) nation-states.

Fourth, we know that the "rule of Law" which was to replace the "rule of force" is no more a reality with the United Nations than it was with the League of Nations. Indeed, regional and inter-regional military blocs constitute the major legitimate forms for intervention in the affairs of other sovereign states.

Finally, we know that while the potentiality for total destruction is far greater than at any previous time in history, the actual types of destruction now taking place as a result of military engagements are "minimal," and have not necessitated anywhere near the sort of total mobilization evidenced in World War Two.

There are, doubtless, many other factors and items not herein taken account of. But these do help set a framework for coming to terms with our more pressing problem: What don't we know about the military structure of Latin America, and perhaps of the Third World generally, that makes analysis a hazardous, if not a downright dangerous, undertaking?

First, perhaps the most serious shortcoming in the study of Latin American military establishments is the absence of a significant body of empirical information concerning their internal performances or perceptions. Unlike studies of the United States military, such as those by Stouffer[1] and Janowitz,[2] we have no comparable studies of the actual mechanisms of command and consensus, of bureaucracy and ideology, in the Latin American military.

Second, what we know tends to be restricted to general studies on the interaction of military rulers with government functions, and some crude data on the size of military budgets, the allocation of these budgets to various branches of the service, and the number of people engaged in military service. But even here, our knowledge is for the most part more official than real.[3]

Third, we know very little of the rivalries between military factions or the separate services, at either the organizational or ideological levels. We know, for example, that as a general rule, the army will be more liberal in its position than either the air force or the navy; however we don't really know why this is the case. It might well be that this liberal-

---

[1] Samuel Stouffer, Edward A. Suchman, Leland C. DeVinney, Shirley A. Star, and Robin M. Williams, *The American Soldier: Adjustment During Army Life*, Vol. 1; and *Combat and Its Aftermath*, Vol. II. Princeton, N. J.: Princeton University Press, 1949.

[2] Morris Janowitz, *The Professional Soldier: A Social and Political Portrait*. New York: The Free Press of Glencoe, 1960.

[3] Several efforts at collecting basic information on a regional level have been recently undertaken. On the Middle East, see Morris Janowitz, *The Military in the Political Development of New Nations*. Chicago: The University of Chicago Press, 1964; and on Latin America, Irving L. Horowitz, "United States Policy and the Latin American Military Establishment," *The Correspondent*, No. 32, Autumn 1964, pp. 45-61.

conservative dichotomy has nothing to do with Third World characteristics, but is simply a function of the land-based nature of both army and
civil functions, giving to their policies a realism perhaps less present in
other branches of the armed forces who are geared to operate in "unnatural" environments such as air or sea.[4]

Fourth, while studies are now underway to determine the recruitment practices, class, religious and ethnic backgrounds, types of educational systems, etc., relevant to the Latin American military, these have
thus far not been linked to political behavior.[5] We can hardly be sure
that such sociological information is even relevant to an understanding of
schisms within the armed forces that now are evident in nearly every
nation of the hemisphere, including our own.

I propose to do two things here: first, discuss the national and international characteristics of military relationships; and, second, develop a
meaningful typology which, in bypassing certain conventional issues such
as the relationship between different branches of the armed forces, gets
at the core of the issue—the relationship between different types of military systems and military situations.

Since this raises problems rather than solving them, perhaps I
should begin with a brief note on the stereotypical attitudes of military
analysts and sociological analysts. Perhaps the different goals sought prevent a complete fusion of both kinds of expertise, but certain conventional bits of mutually held nonsense could be removed so as to rid
ourselves at least of self-inflicted reasons for ignorance.

The problem of generating internal analysis of Latin American military establishments is made very difficult because of the differences of
opinion and contrasting stereotypes held by militarists and sociologists.
The military often thinks about the sociologist as a kinsman to the socialist, while the sociologist oftentimes harbors a flattened view of the military as a collection of committed, purple-sashed reactionaries. Like most

---

[4] See the studies by Mario Horacio Orsolini, *La Crisis del Ejército*. Buenos
Aires: Ediciones Arayu, 1964; and José Luis de Imaz, *Los Que Mandan*. Buenos
Aires: Editorial Universitaria de Buenos Aires, 1964.
[5] While a number of recent studies have called attention to the socio-economic
aspects of military recruitment, to my knowledge none has thus far linked the
service rivalries with differential status or mobility rates. For some first attempts,
see John J. Johnson, *The Military and Society in Latin America*. Stanford:
Stanford University Press, 1964, pp. 102-33.

stereotypes, these have some basis in truth. It is the case, particularly in underdeveloped areas, that sociologists tend to be politically leftist, and tend also to have a view of the military which is less than flattering. It is also true that the military oftentimes do perform right-wing roles, and tend to protect and save rather than advance or build. However, it is also the case that with the introduction of new tools of scientific analysis, the sociologist, whatever his values, is in a good position to examine problems of the military. Similarly, the rise of a new type of military man, whom for want of a better expression we will call the national redemptive type, are becoming more operational than they formerly were. This is not to say that there has been a complete about-face or that the stereotypical view has no basis in truth. It is both quite easy and convenient to overestimate the conservatism of sociologists, and no less the radicalization of the military. One must walk a thin line to reach a meaningful perspective with respect to social scientists and military decision-makers.

I

Aside from this competition between military experts and social scientists, which translated into practice means misunderstanding between militarists and sociologists, we might list the reasons for an absence of internal study of the military under four headings. In so doing it will perhaps become clearer why raw statistics on the Latin American military are often unreliable even when they are available; and also why obstacles to the study of militarism are rooted in circumstances beyond the control of the social scientists. For a sufficiently accurate index of military determination of political events, we have to examine the structure of military establishments with far greater exactitude than has thus far been displayed.

(1) *The Problem of Splendid Isolation.* In Latin America there is neither a particularly pronounced militarization of the civilian population as there was in Nazi Germany, nor is there any attempt at a "civilianization" of the military population, as there was in India. In Latin America separation of military elites from civilian functions is underscored by the proximity of the military encampments from civilian population centers. Barracks are often close to the main cities, but rarely are

they actually part of the main cities. This symbiotic relationship tends to underscore the watchdog properties of the military, its constant surveillance over the political situation. While on the surface this would enable one to study the national military more readily, their furtiveness, their fear of negative publicity, and their bureaucratic discipline at the officer level all serve to make the study of national military establishments quite difficult, particularly in times of peace. And the irony of the Latin American situation is that the continent is strangely continuing in its traditionalist ways. For the most part, barracks revolts and *golpes* are rare enough and of short enough duration not to upset this self-imposed Olympian isolation.[6] The ecological proximity serves to reinforce Bonapartist attitudes so that even radical military sectors tend to be highly elitist and undemocratic in character.

(2) *Problem of a Rose by Any Other Name.* The definition of what actually constitutes a military apparatus is shifting. The military uses of militia, of gendarmes, and even traffic police for military duties is one ploy used in nations such as Costa Rica, where its civic militia was strong enough to be sent into battle against the Dominican rebels during the Civil War of 1965. In Buenos Aires, for example, city police are more feared by the political extremists for their riot prevention techniques than are the ordinary, ill-kempt, misshapen military men. Indeed, the distinction between the police and army officers in Buenos Aires begins precisely with the physical appearance of both groups. It is plain to see that the smartly styled police are far more feared by the civilian population than are the ragged army troops, for quite sound reasons. The existence of legally sanctioned but localized paramilitary units raises the problem of what actually constitutes an army. Since the civilian functions of the police are subordinate to its military functions in terms of such things as riot control, it is quite difficult to know the actual distribution of military power even within orthodox uniformed troops in charge of defending law and order.

(3) *The Problem of the Private Army.* As a remnant of feudalism, there are privately controlled armies run by large latifundists, often in co-operation with the local heads of power or state governors. This was

---

[6] Indeed, when outside foreign interference occurs, these barracks revolts are capable of being transformed into civil wars, and escalated far beyond the original intentions of the competing factions.

made particularly plain in the Brazilian *coup* of April 1964. Unlike the United States, the state militias of these countries are basically uncoordinated with each other or with any of the national armies. Their actual military activities may be much like those of a Reserve Corps—resolved in terms of weekly drill patterns, while the rest of the week they function in relation to the plantation economy. But their presence is felt beyond a doubt. They constitute a shadow military force. How forceful they can be is reflected in Adhemar de Barros' command of 40,000 privately controlled troops during the uprising which deposed the Goulart regime.[7] Thus the feudal sector of the economy itself has generated a feudalistic pattern of armed establishments. To the best of my knowledge, these private armies have never been studied, nor accounted for in the literature of social science.

(4) *The Problem of a People's Army.* There are also, of course, insurrectionary forces. The rise of guerrilla insurgency in Cuba, Venezuela, Paraguay, and even in countries such as Argentina and Brazil, may also be considered a remnant of feudalism or at least a response to backwardness. These guerrillas are not so much paramilitary as they are semimilitary. Like the private armies run by the big landholding estates, the men in these forces often function in terms of peasant activities and peasant modes of production. Like the private armies, they too tend to be unconcerned, unintimidated by the stable armies mobilized around the big cities. People's armies differ structurally from private armies in several important details. Private armies oftentimes have their leadership recruited from local sheriffs and police officers who control the rural areas. The leadership of people's armies tends to be drawn either from city intellectuals who completely submerge their old personalities into the needs of the People's Front and who oftentimes manage to work out arrangements with local potential leaders among the peasant masses. Without intending a parody, the search in people's armies is for high achievers, men who may be frustrated in their present style of life, but who prefer to fight rather than to migrate. The membership of these people's armies have only the barest capacity to engage in sustained conventional wars. Their military training is ragged and at the worst simply an informal assignment of rank. Training oftentimes

---

[7] Cf. Irving L. Horowitz, "Revolution in Brazil: The Counterrevolutionary Phase," *New Politics*, Vol. 3, No. 2, Spring 1964.

can initially take place with brooms, mops, or local agricultural implements, indicating a lack of weaponry no less than of discipline. The strength and élan of a people's army oftentimes derive from the extended process of stealing weapons from the regular armed forces. Thus, the actual build-up period of a popular army is in some sense determined by the amount of weapons which can be siphoned off from regular armed forces. Weapons of North American manufacture are in particular demand, since their parts are interchangeable and standardized. An arms cache invariably yields a high proportion of United States manufactured weapons.

To determine what constitutes a "people's army" is a complicated issue. There are times when people's armies may originate or even become bandit armies. Such is the case in the backlands of Colombia.[8] These outlaw armies may be adjuncts of either private or people's armies and their form is oftentimes quite obscure until the final phases of a conflict. The same was the case with the Algerian civil war, where similar outlaw armies flourished before independence; as indeed they did in Texas during the period of statehood struggles. The ambiguous status of a "people's army" is a strong reason for avoiding a definition of the situation, which is more rigid and universalistic than the actual context permits or than is analytically worthwhile.[9]

These then are the four structural types of armed forces one encounters in Latin America: (1) The regular national army under official control. (2) Paramilitary units sometimes known as civic action groupings which are also officially sanctioned and are distinguished from the regular army by their regionalism and by their ostensible internal rather than international functions. But since it is clear that all military activities in Latin America serve an internal purpose, this distinction is merely formal. (3) The private army under the control of a local or regionally powerful latifundist supplied by the estate and responsible to his leader, or at the most to a regional governor, but generally irresponsible with respect to federal laws or federal troops. (4) Finally, there are the peo-

---

[8] Germán Guzmán-Campos, Orlando Fals Borda, and Eduardo Umaña Luna, *La Violencia en Colombia: Estudio de un Proceso Social*, second edition. Bogota: Ediciones Tercer Mundo, 1962.
[9] For a sensitive essay on the need to select variables so as to highlight differences in military response to specific circumstances, see Davis B. Bobrow, "Soldiers and the Nation-State," *Annals*, Vol. 358, March 1965, pp. 65-76.

ples' armies, the guerrilla insurgents, whose leaders may be drawn from urban sectors, but whose mass battering ram is composed of the rural peasantry. In brief, each of these armed groups serves distinct interests.

CHART 1

NATIONAL CHARACTER

	FEDERAL ARMY	GUERRILLA ARMY	
LEGAL SANCTION	Sponsored by the state	Sponsored by subordinate class, race, or ethnic group	CHARISMATIC SANCTION
	REGIONAL ARMY AND LOCAL GENDARMES Sponsored by local sub-government units	FEUDAL AND PRIVATE ARMY Sponsored by the superordinate class, race, or ethnic group	

REGIONAL CHARACTER

II

A large-scale problem is what precisely constitutes a military budget in Latin American terms. One can state the budget in terms of gross national products exclusive of foreign aid and hence get a peculiarly, indeed a deceptively, low budget figure for military expenditures; or one can state the problem in terms of an overall national budget which includes foreign aid sources, and this gives a more realistic picture of spending procedures of the underdeveloped areas. Even this is not a true estimate of the size of the military establishment. Very often there are foreign troops stationed in these countries, and their expenditures are not listed on the budgets of the nationals. Hence, if there are a large number of United States Air Force troops stationed in a foreign country, they in effect constitute a military force which has a great deal of bearing on political decisions and outcomes, yet they are not accounted for in estimating the strength of that national military establishment. Beyond the difficulties of ascertaining the size of the military budget are the problems related to figuring out expenditures directly linked to the maintenance of armed forces at full strength. In the United States, for instance, while 10 per cent of the Gross National Product is devoted to military purposes, these same purposes consume 50 per cent of research and development activities.[10] While there is far less research and development in Latin America, the proportion of the civilian-military allocations is probably similar.

The middle classes, including a large and remarkably inept bureaucracy, often support the military out of a fear that any civilian regime which hoped to establish permanence would have to fundamentally overhaul economic policies to gain stability. With such a shift, and with any sizeable reduction in the government payroll, the swollen ranks of the middle sectors would be drastically reduced in size and scope. Military careerism and bureaucratic advancement are basic forms of middle-class mobility. At the other end of the spectrum, urban working-class and socialist elements see in the military an ambivalent force, and possibly a positive one, for national redemption. They seem to await a military messiah who can perform for the Latin American area what President Nasser has achieved in Egypt or what Premier Ben Bella has achieved in Algeria; namely, to impose a socialist construction from above.[11] As a result, the pivotal role of the military cannot be seriously challenged because it does have, contrary to sentimental belief, a broad base of popular support. And undergirding this support is a vast network of armed soldiers and officers' corps who deflect a considerable portion of the national budget and national manpower (through conscription) to solidify the military establishment.

The size and budget of armed forces in Latin America are conservatively estimated. One expert has said that "in most of the Latin American countries the military receive 20 per cent or more of all the funds expended by the respective governments in a given year." And as cases, Argentina, Chile, Peru, and Venezuela are cited as nations having mili-

[10] See Committee on Foreign Relations, United States Senate. *United States Foreign Policy: Compilation of Studies.* Washington, D.C.: U.S. Government Printing Office, 1961, p. 815.
[11] Cf. Gino Germani and Kalman H. Silvert, "Politics, Social Structure and Military Intervention in Latin America," *Archives Européenes de Sociologie,* Vol. 2, No. 1, 1961, pp. 62-81.

tary budgets of between 25 per cent and 50 per cent.[12] In addition to such direct military allocations, there are the private armies under the direct aegis of local, regional, and state leaders which are not calculated into the national budgetary allowances. We can only point out that in every Central and South American nation there exist such security and paramilitary forces directed toward maintaining internal "order."[13]

III

Behind statistics stands policy. And behind the size and strength of the military in Latin America stand the policy decisions of the United States. It has been shown that (a) in good measure, the entrenched military establishments of Latin American countries are underwritten by the United States; (b) that such underwriting is made in the name of international or hemispheric security, irrespective of the actual uses of the military for internal repression; (c) that the United States foreign loan policies have increasingly shifted from a civilian to a military base; and finally (d) that such policies are basically of recent derivation and do not represent a long-term orientation. Hence, they are subject to re-orientation.[14]

While foreign aid may not be directly used for repressive ends, it at least supports the military elites in the style to which they have become accustomed. Of course, certain intangibles cannot be measured in statistics, such as the ideological allegiances developed by mechanisms like the Mutual Defense Assistance Pact and the International Treaty of Reciprocal Assistance. The loyalties of old military elites to the established regimes are a function of their economic support, no doubt; but the extent or efficacy of such loyalties is questionable. The strategy of

[12] Robert J. Alexander, *Today's Latin America*. New York: Doubleday-Anchor Books, 1962, pp. 183-4.
[13] For more information on this see the collection of papers edited by John J. Johnson, *The Role of the Military in Underdeveloped Countries*. Princeton, N.J.: Princeton University Press, 1962, RAND Corporation Research Study.
[14] This is not to deny that the United States, at the turn of the century, had a full-blown imperialist policy—see for instance the papers reprinted in *The Imperialist Reader: Documents and Readings on Modern Expansionism*, ed. by Louis L. Snyder. Princeton, N.J.: D. Van Nostrand Co., Inc., 1962, pp. 385-413. However, this policy was abandoned by Franklin Delano Roosevelt in favor of the Good Neighbor Policy.

"evolution from below" often entails a political strategy of "hyper-nationalism," since to eliminate the established military elite is to eradicate a prime recipient of American financing. This strategy places the Latin American military structures in a policy bind; for they are confronted with the choice of supporting the United States policy of using the military for counter-insurgency purposes and thus jeopardizing their self-created image of national redeemers, or supporting national redemption and jeopardizing their foreign aid. This dilemma helps to explain why most of the military south of the border contributes to the continued state of political unrest in these nations.

The most significant contribution a sociologist can now make to the study of military establishments in the Third World, especially in Latin America, is a close scrutiny of conventional arguments for the necessity of present military postures. We learn painfully that there is a huge gap between science and policy. We must also learn about the gap between conventional norms of politics and present realities of military policy-making. *Only* if military men are prepared to enter serious and open discussion of these points can a dialogue be scientific rather than ideological. The sociologist may have to relinquish his hallowed vision of a world *without* war, but he would be a fool to surrender his right to indicate the costs and casualties of a world *with* war. The physician in government service cannot ignore his primary calling; to make society a better place to live in. Unfortunately, the "calling" of the sociologist is far less secure than that of the medical man or the military man, and hence he is more likely to say what is expected rather than what is needed. That as it may be, we must turn to the typical arguments and rationalizations of extensive military aid.

Boomerang Thesis: It is argued that if the United States does not supply arms to Latin America this will prompt Latin American rulers to turn elsewhere for weaponry and we will have made "enemies" out of "friends." This is the most frequently applied rhetoric and to the best of my knowledge has been openly challenged within government circles only by Senator Wayne Morse.[15] What advocates of this position fail to recognize is that the command position of United States non-military

[15] See Wayne Morse, *Report on a Study Mission to the Committee on Foreign Relations, United States Senate.* Washington, D.C.: U.S. Government Printing Office, 1960.

assistance could easily curb any propensity to purchase arms elsewhere—by forfeiture of all economic assistance.[16] It should also be noted that it is by no means the case that Latin American elites are thirsting for additional arms. Over the past several years, such erstwhile leaders as Juscelino Kubitschek of Brazil, Jorge Alessandri of Chile, and Lleras Camargo of Colombia have made strong appeals to the United States to direct more funds into economic development programs and less into military assistance programs. Thus, the boomerang argument is without support even amongst those whom it is intended to preserve.

Bulwark Thesis: It is argued that the Latin American military is the best defense the United States has against Communism. The argument has been put most recently and most forcefully by John J. Johnson, who maintains that without the military, every government in the Latin American orbit would be further to the left than it is now.[17] Ignoring the assumption that this resistance to any and all left tendencies is a good thing, what real evidence is there for this statement? Very little. Military tyrants such as Fulgencio Batista, Pérez Godoy, Juan Perón, and Rafael Trujillo had little trouble with the Communist left. Nor did the Communists have difficulties with the military regime.[18] It is the non-Communist left, men like Juan Bosch of the Dominican Republic and Miguel Arrais of Brazil, who most often suffer at the hands of the entrenched military. On the other hand, as we have already pointed out, there are cases on record in Guatemala and in Chile where the military stimulated left tendencies as part of a Nasserist or Bonapartist ideology. Thus, the "bulwark" argument lacks weight, either as science or as policy.

Hemispheric Thesis: It is argued that the arms supply and training of military cadres are part of the overall United States strategy for defense of the Western hemisphere in the event of attack. This argument

[16] This is the argument by two former State Department officials in their recent book on Latin America. See Karl M. Schmitt and David C. Burks, *Evolution or Chaos: Dynamics of Latin American Government and Politics.* New York: Frederick Praeger, 1963, pp. 36-8.
[17] Johnson, *The Military and Society in Latin America, op. cit.,* pp. 143-4. See on this my critique of this position, "The Military of Latin America," *Economic Development and Cultural Change,* Vol. XIII, No. 2, January 1965, pp. 238-42.
[18] Cf. Robert J. Alexander, *Communism and Latin America.* New Brunswick, N.J.: Rutgers University Press, 1957.

is heard with increasing frequency. However, since no Latin American military establishment could withstand a major conventional invasion, much less a thermonuclear attack, it is plain that the military are being trained for internecine counter-insurgency attack. This is obvious from the types of armaments shipped to Latin America by the United States— and from the rise in ideological "training."[19] This makes the notion, cherished by many hemispheric-minded government officials, that the military can be uniformly relied upon as a stabilizing agency, simply preposterous. The "hemispheric defense" argument is the old "spheres of influence" doctrine spruced up to meet the increasing amount of guerrilla activities.

Developmental Thesis: It is argued that the military can perform all sorts of civic action. The army, by virtue of its unique level of discipline and organization, can take part in essential projects for economic and social development—everything from public works to health and sanitation programs. The further aim of civic action is to counter-claim that the army is, by nature and function, an anti-popular instrument. "As the interdependence of civil and military matters is increasingly recognized, the social and economic welfare of the people can no longer be considered a non-military concern."[20] Even a superficial look at Latin American military history will show that civic action often turns into anti-civil action, into conspiratorial acts against legitimately constituted governments. But there are other more weighty grounds for declaring this latest and most sophisticated approach pernicious as well as unrealistic. First, the costs of the military are exorbitant with respect to their minimal possible effect. Second, the character and structure of the conventional armed forces of Latin America are peculiarly ill-suited, in size and training of the officer corps, in temperament of the enlisted men, and in the outlook of the entire military organization, to perform legitimate economic roles. They are what they are by virtue of their political roles; it is difficult to understand why or how or under what compulsion they should become developmentally oriented. The myth of middle-class salvation has given way to the myth of military salvation.

[19] Cf. Karl M. Schmitt and David C. Burks, *op. cit.,* p. 38.
[20] See United States Department of Defense, *Armed Forces Information and Education: For Commanders.* "Civic Action: The Military Role in Nation-Building," Vol. III, No. 14, January 15, 1964, pp. 1-3.

But as long as either sector remains structurally unaltered, the developmental hopes pinned on either force are pipe dreams. Finally, civic action, developmental programs, have the effect of making the military more political and less professional in their concerns. To the extent that they become policy involved, they must become policy oriented. And this means a deepening cleavage between the army and the people; between political and professional roles.[21]

In considering these four rationalizations for maintaining and expanding militarism in the hemisphere, one clearly sees they are weighted differently. While each of the Latin American military establishments might employ such theses to justify their own behavior, basically they represent supposed United States needs in the area. This supposition in itself is the most decisive aspect of the present situation—namely, the breakdown of neo-colonialism, and its replacement with imperial politics of a more classic vintage. Simply put, the present turn to counter-insurgency as a style of politics marks a return to military solutions for economic problems, rather than economic solutions for military problems. The form of colonialism may be classical, but the content is quite new. The Marxian notions concerning the economic bases of imperialism seem quite outmoded and farfetched given the economic costs and penalties to the present military actions undertaken or underwritten by the United States, with scant chance for an economic "pay-off" even in the distant future. Thus, while the form of imperialism has gone back to an earlier model, its substance is political rather than economic.

The age of Latin American *coups d'état* may very well have come to an end. They are no longer allowed to unfold naturally, because even the most conservative of them may have unanticipated political consequences unfavorable to the metropolitan center. What has taken place in increasing degrees is the external, foreign management of internal conflicts in Latin America. The study of this transition requires a supple methodological approach—one able to control for the degree to which the current "four-fold" military division within Latin American countries is either autonomous of or dependent upon external intervention.

To be sure, conflicts are still likely to be generated by the internal conditions within each of the Latin American states. But they can rarely,

[21] For a critical evaluation of the developmental thesis, see Mario H. Orsolini, *op. cit.*

if ever, remain local any longer in character. The tendency is increasingly to transform such local conflicts into international relations of power. Prior *golpes* were shaped by both internal and external forces. National and imperial forces performed a vital service of mutual reinforcement in overthrowing the regimes of Pérez Jiménez, Juan Perón, Fulgencio Batista, Manuel Odría, etc. But it was clearly understood that the external influence had self-imposed limits, that is, the internal interests would be responsible for providing the "ideology" and the "organization" of the new system of government.

With the rise of overall strategies on a grand scale, with the assertion that the basic purpose of American national policy is to promote and secure a structure of world relationships compatible with the values of the United States and the Free World, local control, idiosyncratic regimes, and classical Latin strongmen can no longer be considered compatible with this projected *Pax Americana*. This emphasis on overall design has also led to higher degrees of planning and co-ordination of hemispheric military activities. For this reason chinks in the armor of design become intolerable. The Dominican Republic obviously poses no threat to the United States or the Free World per se; it does threaten the *Gestalt* of the grand design. And after all, the much feared domino effect can take place only when there are those wishing to build complete stable edifices on unstable ground.

Prior to the occupation of the Dominican Republic, the Department of Defense issued a statement to President Leoni of Venezuela requesting permission for the installation of naval bases at Paria and Goajira, both sites in Venezuela. The statement provides the sort of global military determinism which is becoming increasingly standardized as policy. "The grave fact that a considerable sector of the Armed Forces has been seduced by ideologies dangerous to the national interests of Venezuela compels us to look forward to that time in the future when our own forces will have to guarantee the defense of the country; in support of perhaps that weak and small sector of the military which has not succumbed to the seductive voices of oppositional sirens."[22]

[22] Department of Defense, "Request to the Commander of the Venezuelan Navy To Install Naval Base," p-2, 16-2-65, Series 009, printed in *Marcha*, Vol. 26, No. 1248, March 26, 1965, p. 15. In this same issue see Gregorio Selser, "El Pentágono conmina a Leoni."

United States policies of military globalism tend to make obsolete earlier efforts at a standard typology of Latin American military styles and forms based exclusively on internal political affairs. The decisive variable has become foreign rather than domestic, centralized power rather than autonomous authority. Perhaps this is what Juan Bosch, the former President of the Dominican Republic, was thinking about when he poignantly said of the Dominican crisis: "This was a democratic revolution smashed by the leading democracy of the world, the United States. That is why I think my time is over. I belong to a world that has ended politically."[23] The purpose of these remarks has been to attempt an initial explanation of the world that replaced it.

Just as the four-fold table above illustrates the "internal" characteristics of the Latin American context, the following nine-fold chart will clarify the "external" characteristics of North American involvement in Latin America. The key item in the internal chart is political *sponsorship*; the key item in the external chart is economic development.[24] In other words, the doctrine which asserts the legitimacy of "limited war" also, and, parenthetically, asserts the need for unlimited intervention. It is here that the issue of colonialism and development is joined in its full fury.

To say that we live in an age of rapid development is more of a truism than a significant observation. What is of critical importance is the exact character of the transitional process—not only in the sense of where we were and are now heading—but no less how will we get there? To favor "indeterminism" is not to take seriously the possibility that some factors are more important than others in the development process.

Without wishing to indulge in philosophic debate over the nature of determinism or causality, it is evident that from the social science perspective there are some variables which can explain a greater degree of variance than others. The political apparatus of sixteenth-century Italy, the eco-

---

[23] *The New York Times*, Saturday, May 8, 1965, p. 8.
[24] For the final design of this ninefold table, I am indebted to the work of Seymour J. Deitchman, whose model of a limited-war matrix is surprisingly parallel to my own attempts at linking modern non-nuclear war and the level of the developmental process. But given the priority of publication of Deitchman's book, no less than its formal precision, I have adopted his model, with some serious modifications. See *Limited War and American Defense Policy*. Cambridge, Mass.: M.I.T. Press, 1964, see esp. pp. 103-7.

CHART 2

TYPES OF PHYSICAL ENVIRONMENT (E)

TYPES OF PROSPECTIVE OPPONENTS (O)

O E 1:1
War against enemy who has much the same technical sophistication as the United States, in an environment with extensive industrial development and highly developed transportation facilities. Cross-country movement of mechanized forces is flexible.

O E 1:2
War against enemy who has technical sophistication, in an environment with high industrial development, but with only moderately to poorly developed transportation and communication. Cross-country vehicular movement is possible, but difficult.

O E 1:3
War against enemy who has technical sophistication, in an environment with high industrial development, has little or no development of transport and communication facilities, and where surface cross-country movement of mechanized forces is impossible or possible only in local areas.

O E 2:1
War against enemy able to organize and operate armed forces using fairly modern weapons and equipment. Artillery; tactical air force; in an environment with extensive industrial development, highly developed transportation facilities. Cross-country movement is flexible.

O E 2:2
War in an environment with some industrial development, but only moderately to poorly developed transport and communications. Cross-country vehicular movement is possible, but difficult. The enemy in this war is able to organize armed forces using fairly modern weaponry.

O E 2:3
War in any environment which may have some industry, but little or no development of transport and communication facilities, and in which surface cross-country movement of mechanized forces is impossible or possible only in local areas.

O E 3:1
War against primitive forces most likely to engage in guerrilla warfare. Lack of technological sophistication; no aircraft; no radar; rudimentary communication system; in an environment with extensive industrial development, including highly developed transportation facilities.

O E 3:2
War against guerrilla forces in an environment with some industrial development but with poorly developed transportation and communication. Cross-country vehicular movements possible, but difficult.

O E 3:3
War against primitive guerrillas in an environment which while it may have some industry, has little or no development of transport and communication facilities. Surface cross-country movement of mechanized forces is impossible or possible only in local areas.

nomic foundations of eighteenth-century England, are obvious cases in point. It is my belief that the military apparatus of twentieth-century civilization has the same kind of "deterministic" properties—to be sure, like any system of determinants, it has its limits and perhaps even its deficiencies as an explanatory system.

But the basis of my remarks, and of my standing concern with problems of the military is that the rise of military establishments throughout Latin America, as well as the vigorous pursuit of counter-insurgency techniques and weapons amongst the major powers, represents a readiness to generate social and economic advances through military means rather than through conventional industrial processes. The sheer capacity of military power to cancel any and all "processes of history" by canceling society gives weight to the term "military determinism." Again, it should be noted that this is not an attempt to deny multi-causality. Without a certain level of industrial production, modern armies are impotent. But even this basic shibboleth may be restricted to national armies. It does not seem so for guerrilla forces. Furthermore, unless legal codes are sanctioned, armies tend to militarize civilian populations. But is this true in developing Third World regions?

The Latin American complex offers an excellent laboratory for showing the extent to which the military determine the game of politics in the Third World. In the present decade, eight countries have experienced one or more military *coups* (Argentina, Peru, Ecuador, Guatemala, Dominican Republic, Honduras, and Brazil); three more in which the military has continued its pre-eminence from the previous decade (Nicaragua, Paraguay, and Haiti); one country in which a guerrilla army has been constituted into the regular army (Cuba); and one country which has tranformed its essentially pacifist civilian-oriented militia into paramilitary, counter-insurgency units (Costa Rica). There are also nations in which the military perform back-stage pivotal roles—an omnipresence rather than a simple presence (Venezuela, El Salvador, and Colombia). Mexico, Chile, and Uruguay are the only nations in which the military determines policy only minimally. They also are probably the only ones in which guerrilla insurgency units are non-existent.

The rise of guerrilla activities throughout the Third World has been spectacular. Yet, it might well be the irony of hemispheric affairs that counter-insurgency units precede in time the formation of insurgency units. This, at any rate, seems to have taken place in the Dominican Republic. When the legitimate aspirations of the people are frustrated by military action, and when newly formed, foreign-sponsored counter-insurgency units spearhead the ouster of legitimate regimes, then a rise in guerrilla action is likely to follow. The exact causal sequence is important. If it is the case that counter-insurgency precedes the formation of insurgency units, then the self-fulfilling prophetic aspects of United States foreign policy may well turn into self-destructive actions.[25]

It might well be that for ecological, sociological, and political reasons, insurgency forms of revolutionary activity will either be unsuccessful or simply unfeasible. Its patent failure in the big nations of the hemisphere, particularly in Brazil and Argentina, makes it clear that insurgency warfare, as outlined by Mao Tse Tung or Ernesto Guevara, is not necessarily operational in highly urbanized and industrialized sectors. Given the concentration of Latin America's population and resources (not to mention political power) in the urbanized coastal regions, it is unlikely that the strategy of surrounding the cities with a peasant mass would be successful. On the other hand, it must also be borne in mind that the deployment of regular troops, either of a home-grown or colonial-imported variety, does little to resolve fundamental demands made by revolutionary movements. If it takes between twenty and thirty thousand troops to maintain a cease-fire agreement in one small Caribbean nation, it becomes evident that it would take at least one hundred times that number to maintain an equilibrium in the face of revolutionary tides and sentiments. All of which should provide sober food for thought to those devotees of *Realpolitik* who still believe that those who rely on international, legally sanctioned organizations are dazed romantics.

[25] See on this the recent work by Edwin Lieuwen, *Generals Vs. Presidents: Neomilitarism in Latin America*. New York: Frederick Praeger, 1964, esp. pp. 7-9, 126-9, 136-41.

Chapter 10

The Mental Set of Developing Man: Cultural Lag and Utopian Longings

I

The main fact about the mental set of developing man is that he uniformly blames his shortcomings, his failings, and his condition on society rather than on himself as in former times. Unquestionably, some men are more anxious than others to increase their standard of living, while others are more deeply rooted in the world of their ancestors, childhood, and kinship ties. But it is safe to say that most men are complicated enough to represent, in their persons, a combination of achievement and ascription—that is, personally sought for gains and advantages derived from birth. It may have some value to determine which type of men can be galvanized into social mobility, but it is more pertinent to examine how all such men have come to expect from their societies answers to dilemmas which in past ages were viewed as purely personal or determined by a supernatural force.

The distinction between social and personal responsibility is not confined to the industrial epoch. In early Christianity there was a great debate between those who saw in the scriptures a mandate for the militant pursuit of justice in the world and those who saw private renunciation of the world.[1] In Greek culture, competition pervaded all aspects of

---

[1] Despite the vigorous critique by Kurt Samuelsson of the Weber thesis, based on the view that "no matter what the church or sect, the guiding principle is the renunciation of the world," there is the other strain of involvement with, no less than estrangement from, things temporal. In truth, what particular version of Christian doctrine prevails is contingent on non-religious events. But for a religion to make an appeal to the sacred through a negation of the profane

the social life. The mutual acceptance of a hierarchically arranged system which had obtained in Egyptian society was broken by the city states. The evolutionary process may be considered in the following way. The allocation of responsibility in traditional society relied upon institutions which functioned only to satisfy the needs of masters. Classes were deeply separated from masses. In the process of development, the search for identity becomes pronounced and the classical distinction between classes and masses dissolves. In a very advanced stage of development discontent becomes channelized along altogether new lines. Problems of class membership give way to problems of professional association. The link in this process is the growing responsibility of government to rationalize the social system.[2]

In bureaucratic societies, individual intelligence and initiative are easily thwarted. The individual is rarely permitted to select his ends—particularly if there is reason to believe that such ends are in violation of the fundamental rules of the "game." Knowledge is reduced to expertise. This instrumentalization of man makes it difficult to blame any one person; hence the individual thinks he can forget about self-blame or self-loathing. If man may turn his self-doubts and self-loathings toward an impersonal object of discontent, such as the organization, the party, or the state, his own shortcomings become transformed into the general ills of society. This emphasis on depersonalized ways of solving problems, on automatic operations in production, on maximizing formal rules and roles, compels each individual to engage in a struggle for self-reclamation. The rise of social movements which are anti-bureaucratic and anti-organizational indicates that psychological problems persist, whatever the level of economic productivity.

The bureaucratic strain is particularly prevalent in classical capital-

---

would doom it in an industrial-urbanized complex. And Christianity shows no signs of such a form of ascetic death. On this topic, compare and contrast Kurt Samuelsson, *Religion and Economic Action: A Critique of Max Weber*, edited by D. C. Coleman. New York and Evanston: Harper & Row (The Academic Library), 1964; and Ephraim Fischoff, "The Protestant Ethic and the Spirit of Capitalism: The History of a Controversy," *Social Research*, Vol. II, No. 1, February 1944, pp. 53-77.

[2] See on this an interesting statement by Richard Korn, "The Private Citizen, the Social Expert, and the Social Problem," in *Mass Society and Crisis: Social Problems and Social Pathology*, edited by Rosenberg, Gerver, and Howton. New York: Macmillan & Company, 1964, pp. 576-93.

ism: its industrial output is nearly always less than its actual capacity. Personal savings are liquidated through market fluctuations and inflationary spirals, and the capitalist as an entrepreneur is unable to survive without direct assistance from the bureaucratic organization. The image of the capitalist as a swashbuckling investor with a devil-may-care attitude has given way to the cautious manager who can only be induced to take risks with government assistance, and whose sense of the social commonweal and its needs is rarely more elevated than that of his employees. Even the entrepreneurial class has taken to blaming failure on the government, on the impersonal laws of the market, on the inequities of the tax system, rather than on the corporate self or the corporate image.

Under such conditions it is little wonder that freedom and liberty have increasingly come to mean security for the person. When such security is not forthcoming, the situation becomes ripe for social rebellion. This is particularly so in industrial society. Here sectional and sectoral imbalances are at their maximum. Educational advancement can be very high and social mobility relatively stagnant, as in Argentina. An urban complex may advance at the expense of the rest of the nation, as in England. A program for agrarian reform may be promoted by civilian government, but carried out under militaristic rule which leaves the democratic aspects of this reform unachieved, as in Brazil. A nation may achieve high political integration, yet continue to be economically stagnant as a result of military over-commitment.

The developmental process is itself a cause for discontent and not just a response to a deterioration in the traditional ordering of things. This discontent is in turn blamed on the society rather than on the self. For this reason the need to stimulate achievement motivation is far less significant than the need to channelize already existing discontent. In the economic system the industrial states show to the emerging nations the psychological face of their own future.[3]

Discontent with the present is first encountered at the level of the thinking process. There must be dissonance observed between general economic growth in contrast to one's own comparative stagnation. There

---

[3] An exposition of the problem of channelizing discontent is in H. H. Gerth and C. Wright Mills, *Character and Social Structure: The Psychology of Social Institutions.* New York: Harcourt, Brace and World, 1953, pp. 456-80.

must be a *cognitive* awareness of the gap between advancement at one end of the social scale—say, education—and stagnation at the level of economic opportunity. There must be a conception of a social order, not only different, but morally superior and politically more inclusive than the one men presently live under. These psychological states cannot be induced. Disequilibrium in the fabric of society must precede any widespread demand for reorganization. Induced discontent may boomerang. It may result in a deep insulation from social realities.[4]

Retreatism is a negative response to the frustrations inherent in social change. There is a growing tendency to devalue *both* the traditional position of the poor and the conventional life styles of the wealthy. Retreatism not only erodes the values of traditional society; it also disputes and then destroys the familiar relations which are almost omnipotent in maintaining traditional patterns of authority. The retreatist himself may prove incapable of mustering the effort needed to show an achievement orientation, but the next generation, aware of the discontent their parents have suffered, may develop a strong achievement orientation. The drive for achievement does not necessarily guarantee that alienation will not take place. To be sure, such neo-Freudian syndromes may not work out in many cases, but what is important is that the forms of dissonance and disequilibrium, whether they yield aggressive involvement or retreatist isolation, are less important to the development process than the existence of such forms themselves.[5]

Just as retreatism may be an aid in development, overdedication to development may actually work against its requirements. A man may make a great deal of money quickly but still have no idea of social savings and investment. This process has been described in any number of novels about post-revolutionary Mexico. In Bolivia, after the 1952 popular revolution, the mine workers retained their arms and used their populist control as a demonstration of their power, not as a symbol of hard work. The working time in the mines was drastically cut and the actual mineral wealth produced dipped far under what it had been

[4] See David C. McLelland, *The Achieving Society*. New York and Princeton, N.J.: D. Van Nostrand Co., Inc., 1961, for a perfect illustration of the confusion which can exist in the investigator's mind between achievement and development orientations, esp. pp. 36-61.
[5] See E. E. Hagen, *On the Theory of Social Change*. Homewood, Ill.: The Dorsey Press, 1962, pp. 175-85.

during the previous rightist dictatorship. These illustrate the complexities in the relationship between an achievement orientation and a developmental orientation.[6] An achiever can remain egoistic, and a promoter can remain rooted in traditional values. Indeed, this is usually the case, which is why the role of the state ultimately supersedes the free actions of private individuals in the developmental process.

The psychological characteristics of developing man directly affect the economic take-off point. It is commonly recognized that development takes a certain type of man who is dissatisfied with his existential condition and demands something else in its stead. What that "something else" is, and how "it" can be induced in others and extended to future generations, is the real problem. One economist recently reported that in order to induce the peasantry of the northeast Brazil to work hard at long hours, he had to retain, and even reinforce, the methods of exploitation used by the latifundists.[7] It is manifestly untrue that to reveal to a person his "true interests" guarantees his participation in the mass participation in the mass society or in the modernization process. The line between action and interests is far from straight. Even if we ignore the dilemmas arising out of a direct correlation of actions and interests, there is a policy issue involved: namely, the degree of social unrest necessary to stimulate a person to think along developmental lines without creating complete revolutionary upheaval.[8]

A myth has been propagated that external stimulants are necessary to place the masses of Third World nations into a "take-off" posi-

[6] On this range of questions, see Kalman H. Silvert, *The Conflict Society: Reaction and Revolution in Latin America.* New Orleans: Hauser Press, 1962.

[7] This was reported by the Brazilian economist, Celso Furtado, who as the Director of SUDENE, the Northeast Redevelopment Program in Brazil, found that the method of democratic persuasion yielded fewer results and was more widely mistrusted than traditionalist methods of authority. This is a kind of empirical confirmation of Charles Sanders Peirce's famous declaration that of the three methods for fixing belief, none is more satisfactory for mass consumption than authority. See Charles S. Peirce, "Method of Fixing Belief," *Collected Papers of C. S. Peirce*, Vol. 5, edited by Charles Hartshorne and Paul Weiss. Cambridge, Mass.: Belknap (Harvard University Press), pp. 233-48.

[8] Rex D. Hopper has raised the interesting proposition that revolution-making is inevitably in the control of socially displaced and marginal people. And that the process of automation, insofar as it accentuates the distinction between integration and marginality, accelerates the revolutionary process. See his paper, "Cybernation, Marginality, and Revolution," in *The New Sociology*, edited by Irving L. Horowitz. New York and London: Oxford University Press, 1964, pp. 313-30.

tion. While there are certainly great differences between levels of achievement and aspirations, the poor do not require much motivation for change beyond their own existential situation. If we take the "case histories" of two slum people—Carolina Maria de Jesus in the Saõ Paulo *favelas* and Jesús Sánche~ in the Casa Grande of Mexico City—what emerges is a picture of dislocated, no less than developing, people in changing circumstances. We might outline the common characteristics among the poor who are part of the development process:

(1) Ability to move from a rural society to an urban society, and also from a society based on barter and property to one based upon money and contract.

(2) Discontent with low-grade economic status, which is expressed in a variety of ways—shifts from house to house and from job to job, concern with the education of children, willingness to postpone immediate gratifications.

(3) Politicalization, as expressed in voting, concern with candidates and party issues, and even membership in organized political groupings.

(4) Secularization of personal values, as expressed in "free" love patterns, a lessening of the bonds of religious fervor, or even sometimes conversions to other faiths, and a general acculturation to the impersonal, anomic life of the large industrial city.

(5) Above all, an unwillingness to return to the agricultural communities from which they have immigrated.[9]

Nonetheless, despite the similarities of these case histories, Carolina de Jesus did not escape from the *favelas* from whence she emanated. The elder Sánchez, for his part, held firm to his desire for personal advancement, and for the success of his children in the new urban world of Mexico City. Even when there is an achievement motivation in common, it is difficult to distinguish between those who succeed in making the great ascent and those who return to the source of their discontent. Indeed, this is further complicated by the fact that the second generation offspring of Papa Sánchez turned out to be far more uprooted and

[9] Carolina Maria de Jesus, *Child of the Dark*. New York: E. P. Dutton & Co., 1962; and Oscar Lewis, *The Children of Sánchez: Autobiography of a Mexican Family*. New York: Random House, 1961.

anomic than the original pioneer to the outskirts of Mexico City. Displeasure with the old way of doing things does not guarantee successful adjustment to the new way of doing things. It may be a necessary ingredient in social development, but it alone is not sufficient.

II

The classical traditions within economics and sociology give little insight into the solution of such development problems as generational disputes, marginality, transitional stages, norm deviations, and *anomie* as a form of social discontent. Yet, they have set the stage for an independent variable. Earlier discussions of the mental set of developing man have emphasized class and status, imaginary and real.

Prior to the rise of the Third World, the psychological aspects of development were embedded in a maze of sociological and economic doctrines. Within Weber's sociology of religion, for instance, an entire series of psychological criteria, what might be termed his notion of the psychic economy, were evolved. Protestantism was made to appear more as a strategy for capitalist development than a religious revolution. The concepts of delayed gratifications, trust in fellow religionists, and salvation through hard work rather than otherworldly faith, were introduced in such a way as to demonstrate the unique connection of capital formation and religious salvation.[10] In Werner Sombart, writing at approximately the same time, the Jews were made to appear as the "original Calvinists," as having possessed in perfect combination those psychological characteristics of frugality, thrift, conservatism that gave them a "positive attitude" toward development in the capitalist economy.[11] In Georges Sorel and the Franco-Italian school of power sociology generally, the notion of the capitalist as a "Creative Apache" was used to show that the Robber Barons were actually the heroes in the

[10] Cf. Max Weber, *The Protestant Ethic and the Spirit of Capitalism*, trans. by Talcott Parsons. New York: Charles Scribner's Sons, 1958; and "The Protestant Sects and the Spirit of Capitalism," in *From Max Weber: Essays in Sociology*, edited by H. H. Gerth and C. Wright Mills. New York: Oxford University Press, 1946.
[11] Cf. Werner Sombart, *The Jews and Modern Capitalism*, trans. by M. Epstein. Glencoe, Ill.: The Free Press, 1951, esp. pp. 157-90.

developmental drama, and not the villains portrayed by the muckrakers. Their "constructive violence" made them the elite of economic development. Unlike the European bourgeoisie, they retained their energies, their will to victory, and their characteristic class interests.[12]

The economists came earlier, but they have persisted in rendering clumsy service to the psychological basis of development throughout. In the world of Adam Smith and his moral economy, it was not "benevolence" but "regard to one's interests" that prompted economic growth. Indeed, the desire for such growth was so great on the part of "men of inferior wealth" as well as "men of superior wealth" that they always joined forces when the sovereign order as such was threatened.[13] Marx still retained a psychological insight toward social change, even though his vision of class struggle in industrial society prevented him from perceiving the grounds of class compromise. The mass rather than the class came to be the carriers of economic rationality. The will of the people imposes a socialist construction; the wealthy classes are too corrupt to behave rationally; while the middle classes are too beholden to the wealthy to behave independently. Thus, only in the poor is there a congruence of interests and rationality. Indeed, the degree of altruism necessary to realize socialism is not one whit less important, or imaginary, than the degree of egotism necessary to realize capitalism.[14] Nor has interest in the psychological aspect of economic growth lessened since the classical period. Indeed, if anything, there has been a strong tendency to recognize and accept the psychological as a necessary, if inexplicable, factor in any economy. Thus, we are told about the necessity of "confidence" in a stable economy—whether there is an objective warrant for such confidence or not. We are told of how irrational commitment to style changes promotes general innovation—without being told how such emphasis on style apart from function is manipulated.

[12] Cf. Georges Sorel, *Reflections on Violence*, trans. by T. E. Hulme. Glencoe, Ill.: The Free Press, 1950.
[13] Cf. Adam Smith, *The Theory of Moral Sentiments*, in *Adam Smith's Moral and Political Philosophy*, edited by H. W. Schneider. New York: Hafner Publishing Co., 1948; and *An Inquiry into the Nature and Causes of the Wealth of Nations*, edited by E. Cannan. New York: G. P. Putnam's Sons, 1904.
[14] The materials of Marx on the social psychology of economic behavior are widely scattered. Perhaps the best sources are contained in *Karl Marx: Selected Writings in Sociology and Social Philosophy*, edited by T. B. Bottomore and M. Rubel. New York: McGraw-Hill, 1964.

Consumer spending becomes equated with faith in the economic system itself.[15]

The rise of psychological theories of society, therefore, is not simply an effort to evolve an "applied" approach to achievement motivation, but in the larger sense, and on the theoretical side, a reaction against a deterministic view of history, which assumes the primacy of a single factor in individuals who make up any given group.[16] The emphasis on individual psychology also serves to minimize any faith in hidden mysterious forces operating behind men's backs.

The psychologists working in the field of development have pointed out that it is not sufficient just to *declare* that social mobility and high aspirations exist or are important or that they differ from person to person. Some men are blind to the values of literacy, while others will give up all comforts to learn how to read and to write. Some men could not care less about the length of time it takes to repair or replace commodities in a backward region; while others react with impatience and demand high efficiency. Some women find their traditional roles comforting, while others view them as repressive and oppressive. In short, to locate the main sociological variables in the developmental process is not the same as explaining *why* some men are ambitious, driving, and adventurous, while others are not.[17]

III

Societal Man and Natural Man

We have mentioned that all developing men appear to place responsibility for achievement on society rather than on themselves. In a

[15] See R. F. Harrod, *Economic Essays*. New York: Harcourt, Brace & Co., 1952. His studies on the ethics of imperfect competition are an excellent summary of Keynesian economics, particularly its psychological network.
[16] For a useful summary of the controversies between "sociologism" and "psychologism," see Alex Inkeles, "Personality and Social Structure," in *Sociology Today: Problems and Prospects*, edited by R. K. Merton, L. Broom, and L. S. Cottrell, Jr. New York: Basic Books, Inc., 1959, pp. 249-75.
[17] Perhaps the most resourceful, and still impressive, presentation of these problems is contained in H. G. Barnett, *Innovation: The Basis of Cultural Change*. New York: McGraw-Hill, 1953.

deeper sense, the traditional orientation toward self-resignation and away from social responsibility represents a fundamental commitment to "nature" as something to be accepted and lived with, rather than a series of hurdles to be overcome. Traditional culture in Latin America has frequently been identified with putting off until tomorrow what can be done today. Traditional men suffer from a poverty of wants as well as from a poverty of ideas for satisfying them. This represents a fundamental attitude common to pre-industrial styles of living rather than a special religious or ethnic property. The same point is made in contemporary Korea. One study points out that in "East Asian culture, man typically has not been so concerned with gaining mastery over his enivronment as he has been with living in harmony with it. Mountains that might obstruct travel and rivers that might be impassable during certain seasons have not been viewed as merely frustrating inconveniences. Rather, these are historical facts to which man must discipline himself."[18] The same attitude was expressed during the classical Greek period. The philosophy of Epictetus and of the Stoics in general reveals a resignation in the face of Nature.

Equally significant is the traditional attitude toward Time—both as an empirical measure of change and as a moral measure of worth. In the first case, the attitude toward Time is distinctly a creation of our own culture, where "time is money." In underdeveloped regions, however, things do not run "on time," but only "more or less on time." Centralized planning is viewed with suspicion, not simply because it is usually connected with totalitarian political slogans but also because it disrupts traditional patterns. In Italy, the Fascists made much of their boast that under their regime the "trains ran on time." Under such conditions, it is easy to see how the opposition might well argue against being on time.

The industrial attitude toward Time, Motion, and Nature differs even within the First World. The search for high achievement indices has obscured the different work habits in European and American industrial plants. The best response to this issue was made by Samuel

[18] Don Adams, "The Monkey and the Fish," in *Dynamics of Development: An International Development Reader,* edited by Gove Hambidge. New York: Frederick Praeger, 1964, pp. 362-3.

Gompers in 1890, when he gave testimony to the United States Industrial Commission on Capital and Labor. He noted that in

> every mechanical trade, when European workmen come over to this country and stand beside their American fellow workingmen it simply dazes them—the velocity of motion, the deftness, the quickness, the constant strain. The European bricklayer, the European carpenter, the European compositor-printer, the European tailor comes over here and works in the shop, or factory, or office, and he is simply intoxicated by the rapidity of the movements of the American workingmen, and it is some months, with the greatest endeavor, before he can at all come near the production of the American workingman.[19]

Gompers was no theorist; in trying to explain the reasons for this gap, he went into everything from climatic conditions ("The changes in weather make the people more active, more nervous; accelerates their motion, accelerates their thought") to the absence in America of a hereditary condition of slavery and serfdom. But above all, it was his contention that the gap is best explained by the superior condition of the American workingman. He was the arch advocate in labor ranks of class co-operation. Like his counterpart, the enlightened capitalists, he insisted that more wages and better conditions make for greater output and superior quality. This direct confrontation of American experience with European traditions is surely a prime factor in understanding the different psychologies of development between the two capitalist spheres.

In terms of the ethics of Time, we often find a profound psychological nostalgia reinforced by religious observances. The Good Life is defined in terms of living in the past, especially at a time when man was closer to Nature. Respect for ancestors is common in the East, while in the West there is an equivalent notion of redemption in the next world. Indeed, such attitudes have always had great pull and magnetism, for all societies have identified virtue with events in the dim past: "Good

[19] See Samuel Gompers, "The Philosophy of Organized Labor," in *The Nation Transformed*, edited by Sigmund Diamond. New York: George Braziller, 1963, pp. 206-17.

old days" that never were, and "Men who were men" in contrast to an effete culture of the present. These frequently uttered banalities clearly show that such habits of mind are not the property of any single religion or culture.[20]

An orientation based upon the inviolability of Nature involves at least an implicit commitment to the idea of stability. In judging human affairs, this orientation rests on the theme of "eternal return"—a changing world without growth, lacking in novelty or even chance. Like seasons in the year, human change is said to follow a principle of steady recurrence. Nature affords a spectacle of change within repeating cycles. Growth tends to be measured in geological terms: the layers upon layers of striated rock which form the age of the universe. The societal orientation, for its part, often involves some commitment to the idea of history in the sense that changes which occur are fragmented, non-repeating, and under at least partial control of human agents and agencies. Society offers the unique spectacle of change which is constantly being evaluated for its "worth," that is, for its developmental properties. It may be that the view of nature as a stable entity is itself metaphysically conditioned by social norms and expectations. Be that as it may, this classical vision of "living close to Nature" involves results which are sharply different from those which start with a societal bias.

The Nature orientation offers slender inducements for taking high risks, since the "natural history of men" is part of an enormous cycle of *corso* and *ricorso* that rewards the high risk-taker and the low risk-taker in the same way—by destruction, dismay, and death. By the same token, the societal orientation, since it is a view which sharply demarcates man from other animals, and certainly from inanimate nature, offers reasons for taking risks. The notion of human uniqueness is so welded into the major Western religions that cautions and prohibitions against excesses of materialism become the foundation of Western theology. One of the essential properties of Western religions is their

---

[20] See on this subject of the contrast between underdeveloped and developed Charles J. Erasmus, *Man Takes Control: Cultural Development and American Aid*. Minneapolis: University of Minnesota, 1961; and for a more specific study, Kasum Nair, *Blossoms in the Dust: The Human Factor in Indian Development*. New York: Frederick Praeger, 1962.

utopianism. This longing for a perfect future is the basis of what has been called "positive mysticism" in Western society-oriented religions.[21]

Developing man has a great propensity toward taking risks. He has a great gambling instinct as compared with non-developing peoples, rooted as they are in Nature. He also believes the world is imperfect as it is; and further, he believes that he can better himself or better the world as such. In the very notion of society there is the idea that it is imperfect and exists in time and that the world order can be improved. Optimism or pessimism do not necessarily have a connection with taking risks. One might be optimistic about the possibility of changing the social world, and on the other hand, one might be pessimistic about the chances of success. Nonetheless, the willingness to take risks is stimulated by a faith in the perfectability of man.

This same attitude is reflected ecologically in the willingness of a person to risk his position and possessions and move elsewhere to an unknown place. The stimulus may be materialistic or religious. The religious factor may become an important surrogate for an ideology which justifies risk in terms of ultimate rewards. People might move from comfortable surroundings, as immigrants on the eastern seaboard of the United States did when they headed west to frontier lands. Such people may brave many hardships and take all kinds of risks as the result of a theological commandment. Thus, a belief in the perfection of a heavenly order does not necessarily entail a belief in the necessity of improving the temporal world. But, as in the case of Judaism or Christianity, it sanctions a search for perfectability of man in this world.

Those who take risks are oftentimes spurred on by a strong theological sanction against failure. There may be a lesson in this for developmental theory. It might be possible to stimulate risk-taking by minimizing the advantages of standing pat; by penalizing, in effect, those who do not take risks. In the Soviet Union this has been a particularly important aspect in the colonization of the relatively unpopulated "virgin soil" territories of Asian Russia.

The major difficulty of risk-taking is that the more developed may be penalized on behalf of the less developed, and the more urbanized

[21] See David C. McClelland, *The Achieving Society.* New York: D. Van Nostrand Co., Inc., 1961, pp. 367-88.

on behalf of the less urbanized; hence there is danger that those already engaged in the developmental process will become alienated and disenchanted. But, still, high risk-taking does indeed seem characteristic of rapidly developing areas. And whether this spills over into threats or coercion against those unwilling to make sacrifices of comfort or unwilling to take the risks necessary for achievement of rapid and high development is an administrative question, not a problem for psychology or religion.

We need to emphasize that the mental set of developing man includes a philosophical (no less than a religious) component. One could call this a nominalistic or empirical metaphysic. In some sense even the religious divines exhibit a belief in the material, scientific world as primary rather than other-worldly gratification. Here we immediately face the contradictory situation where, under the early Protestantism of Luther and Calvin, rapid *social* development seems to be connected with the rewards of the *spiritual* world, the rewards of Paradise. But, on close inspection, these notions are not incongruous since the idea of betterment is really the secular expression of the idea of the calling. The concept of betterment is a definition of what the good man strives for in this world. It has not yet been resolved whether or not there is a theological sanction, or whether the theological ballast has to be overthrown entirely along with other traditionalist residues. Algeria is described as both Moslem and as socialist, whereas Ghana is called by its leader materialist in philosophy and socialist in economy. The fact remains that the emphasis on scientific measurements is part of the societal orientation of developing man. He needs something "objective" and impersonal that can be measured so that he can determine what is or is not developing.

The nineteenth century of progress, which has been so severely criticized, was a perfect illustration of a material scientific orientation. One measured development by the number of buildings that went up each year; the amount of money one had in the bank account; by the size of the population of the industrial center; by the size of the political apparatus. Such quantitative measuring of social entities became extremely important to the mental set of societal man. Progress became not only a subject for liberalism, but an object for scientism. This is seen most clearly in the matter of numbers. Developing societies exhibit a fetish for numbers: the size of the gross national product; the amount of money in the personal bank account; the height of a sky-scraper; the rent paid and rooms had in one's house; the number of automobiles in one's garage; and so forth. These all may serve as indices of wealth and power. There is an equation between numerical size and rates of development. Some theorists have even taken to speaking of symbolic power "banks" as analogous to real economic banks.[22] Often-times this assumes a grotesque giganticism, a desperate search for the bigger and better. This was typical of nineteenth-century United States and reached its culmination with phenomena like the Empire State Building, the highest building in the world. The same phenomena are now being reproduced and replicated in the Soviet Union with the largest rockets, having the highest payload, providing the maximum thrust into outer space. Thus, the quantification of science serves as a guide and a measure for social development.

Perhaps the question of second thoughts ought to be considered. What happens when and if upon inspection the social "contract" no longer meets one's needs? Should rules then be violated? In taking risks, one must have some end in view. Such risk-taking must not become disengaged from economic rationalism.

Attitudes Toward Traditionalism and Modernism

Even where a people is already committed to the idea that society can be brought under greater control, there is often still a strong commit-ment to traditional social patterns. Far from collapsing in the presence of modernist ideologies, traditionalism retains its vitality, not only among the aristocratic classes but also among large segments of the working classes.

The poor argue that by working longer hours they are doubly ex-ploited. They are exploited by the amount of time they work and their inability to enjoy what leisure time they have. A more sophisticated version of this is that the notion of savings is not so much an alien con-cept as it is a foolish one, given the inflationary spiral of most underde-

[22] Talcott Parsons, "Some Reflections on the Place of Force in Social Process," in *Internal War*, edited by Harry Eckstein. New York: The Free Press of Glen-coe, 1964, pp. 33-70.

veloped economies. Also modernism, far from releasing human energies for creative acts, reproduces the anomie and alienation so typical of advanced nations. Hence, the arguments in support of modernism by developmentalists are unrealistic in terms of behavioral patterns and plans among the working classes.

Traditionalist arguments are better known; they have been uttered for longer periods of time. Essentially, they too claim that the equation of that which is modern with that which is good is illogical. The displacement of conventional myths, mores, and mysteries with modern science and technology only substitutes a higher form of mythology. Modernism replaces one form of superstition with another, but by no means eliminates the gap between the haves and the have-nots. It is further reasoned that the displacement of aristocratic exploitation by middle-class or even proletarian exploitation shows little evidence that this vast social change has succeeded in its intended effect of reducing man's inhumanity to man. Thus, the argument concludes, the conflict between traditionalists and modernists is essentially ethical rather than economic—one which takes place between permissive (traditional) and coercive (modernist) factions. That the bourgeoisie is on one side, and aristocratic and laboring sectors on the other, it is held, represents but a momentary accident of history.

The difficulties in equating the developmental process with the presence of modernism or modernization may be due to lack of precision in the term. Even accepting the idea that to be modern is a positive asset, every attempt to define modernism in terms of an operational set of variables results in the introduction of new ideas which have relatively little to do with the original concept. A standard definition of modernization usually includes at least the following: a belief in the primacy of science, or at least in the products of applied engineering; belief in a secular way of conducting affairs; and belief in the need for continuing changes in society and economy. But beyond that, it often means the intensification of the destruction of local and regional cultures in the name of a national culture, and the elimination of native language clusters in the name of national identity. Thus modernism may be science for some and internal imperialism for others.[23]

[23] See on this question the perceptive essay by Charles F. Andrain, "Democracy and Socialism," in *Ideology and Discontent*, edited by David E. Apter. New

Let us summarize the objections to modernism thus far introduced. First, faith in scientific causality is no different from faith in providential teleology, whatever differences the consequences of these beliefs may have. Second, the materialism reflected in the worship of commodity goods is hardly different now from what it was a hundred years ago —the kind and cost of consumer items may be different, but not the psychological motivation. Third, the components in secularism are hard to define. Is secularism the reduction of religious worship and church attendance to one day per week, or the transformation of the church into the social center for seven days a week? Fourth, and of a different magnitude, modernism may be present in one sphere and not in another without impairing the quality of development. A father may be traditionalist in child-rearing, beating his children as a regular part of their growing up, and yet be quite daring and modern in his business or managerial decisions. The same person may also be daring and radical in business practice, and an arch-conservative in his political orientation. The concept of modernism tends to lose its explanatory character in such a situation. Contradictory attitudes are customary: the Chinese peasant may refuse to spare his son for the educational process, since he wants the additional farm labor; yet this same man will insist on calling the Chinese Revolution his own. The American businessman who denounces the size of the federal budget may be first in line for federal contracts and government allocations.

It is not always clear how modernism replaces traditionalism. Frequently, it is a surrogate for the maintenance of traditional class patterns by the infusion of modern techniques of distribution and trade. In economic terms, modernism stands for the primary exchange economy, for the importation of commodity supplies and the export of raw materials and farm goods to pay for them. This "international division of labor," while ostensibly a move toward greater economic rationalization, in fact strengthens the economic and political position of the supplier nation. Modernism is thus often little more than an injection into the traditional agriculturally dominated society. It provides the gloss of contemporaneity and of self-determination without its substance. The social

York: The Free Press of Glencoe, 1965, especially on the psychological expression of independence, pp. 189-91.

structure remains what it was, while the economic system of exploitation changes its locale.

Interestingly, where modernism has been extensively applied, industrialization has had little success. Far from serving as a demonstration effect of the advantages of industrialization, modernism serves to reinforce the existing social structure by showing how it is possible for a small section of the population to share in the goods of the scientific-technological world, without altering the forms of human relations or the character of social production. Thus, modernism may serve, ironically, to underwrite traditionalism and not to displace it. The United States has often fostered this sort of modernism as a way of curbing the marked propensity of Third World nations to seek industrial identity through economic autonomy. Many sections of the Third World have become veritable cornucopias of up-to-date goods. Such sectors satisfy the craving for modernity and, not incidentally, function as a solution to overproduction within the United States. Thus, the international division of labor continues to work to the disadvantage of the Third World, for while the instinct for modernization seems to be satisfied, no real social structural change takes place.[24]

Actually traditionalism is just as consonant with revolutionary approaches to social problems as modernism. Perhaps more so, since science and secularism may turn men away from holistic and mythical solutions and toward pragmatic and partial solutions. The modernist drive lacks a cohesive ideology, and hence tends to minimize revolutionary potential. Traditionalism, especially in newly emerging nations, may function to stimulate revolutionary action. For example: Kwame Nkrumah refers continually to a traditional "African personality," which in turn is defined by a "cluster of humanist principles which underlie the traditional African society." This "African personality," in its search for revolutionary principles, chooses socialism over capitalism because the latter "might prove too complicated a system for a newly independent country," not to mention the added fact that capitalism would be "a betrayal of the personality and conscience of Africa."[25]

[24] See William Paddock and Paul Paddock, *Hungry Nations*. Boston: Little, Brown & Co., 1964.
[25] Cf. Kwame Nkrumah, *Consciencism: Philosophy and Ideology for Decolonization and Development*. London: Heinemann Educational Books, Ltd., 1964, pp. 79, 74-5.

Here one can see clearly how traditionalist orientations, far from handicapping revolutionary sentiments, may in fact serve to stimulate them much more than modernist orientations. Revolutionary groups are "social inventions" which arise as a response to an immediate crisis situation. Their political character is independent of their social functions—at least to the degree that "left," "right," or even "center" revolutions are possible in a traditionalist or in a modernist framework. The "blockage" of social change, not the nature of the social values, ultimately determines the size and the extent of revolutionary sentiments. And the transformation of these sentiments from personal protest to organized acts determines the effectiveness of the revolutionary situation.[26]

The "Spirit of Work" versus the "Spirit of Revolution"

The variables of revolutionary upsurge often differ from development. Revolutionary movements based on "rising" new classes invariably come after the first phase of the economic development thrust is well under way. This was the case in France, which witnessed the triumph of the economic bourgeoisie long before its political ascendancy, and in Russia, which witnessed the steady growth of industrialization from late in the nineteenth century until the 1917 Revolution. There are few cases on record in the classical epoch where this has not been the case. In the Third World nations, particularly of Africa and Asia, however, there is often a political preliminary to economic take-off. Indeed, it might be said that the more backward a country, the more likely it is to have a political revolution which precedes efforts to carry out economic development.

It is after an initial economic spurt that revolutionary sentiments are crystallized and mobilized.[27] The condition of the peasants in France was worse in 1788 than in 1789. The condition of the factory proletariat in Russia was worse in the opening years of World War One; by

[26] See Paul Meadows, *The Masks of Change: Essays on Development Roles and Actors.* Syracuse, N.Y.: Center for Overseas Research (Publication No. 13), 1964, pp. 66-74.
[27] See on this the study by Alexander Gerschenkron, "Reflections on Economic Aspects of Revolution," in *Internal War*, edited by Harry Eckstein. New York: The Free Press of Glencoe, 1964, pp. 196-7.

1917 it was improving. The condition of the American tradesman was superior in 1775 to that of 1773 or 1774. King George had agreed to rescind much of the oppressive taxation legislation when the colonists assumed insurrectionary measures. What this means is that if development is encouraged successfully, a revolution may not be avoided or even delayed. Quite the contrary, development often makes the chances of revolution higher, and the chances of successful revolution higher still. In each of these cases, we have a striking illustration of rich societies with impoverished governments.[28]

The making of revolution does not guarantee rapid growth. The "spirit of work" is bound in a dialectical relation to the "spirit of revolution." Where the spirit of revolution prevails in the post-revolutionary period, and where the spirit of work does not replace these revolutionary energies, stagnation can easily occur.

The Hungarian Revolution of 1919 and the Bolivian Revolution of 1952—an admittedly unlikely comparison on any number of counts—are nonetheless highly instructive. The regimes of Béla Kun and of Víctor Paz Estenssoro created post-revolutionary situations in which "direct worker control" was immediately translated into workers' establishing their own norms of work, controlling the armed forces, and disregarding established technical personnel and bureaucratic elites. The result in both instances was a curtailing of production, a heavy increase in inflationary spiraling, and monetary speculation. The collapse of the Hungarian Revolution took place in less than a half year. The collapse of the Bolivian Revolution was delayed for over a decade—but only by an incredible pump-priming that made the Bolivian worker the most heavily subsidized person in the world. While there are many factors involved in the collapse of each revolution—the thorough non-cooperation of the bourgeoisie with the Béla Kun regime, the incomplete way in which traditional military was controlled in Bolivia—it remains the case that in both Hungary of 1919, and again in Bolivia of 1952, the spirit of revolution never was transformed into the spirit of work.[29]

<hr />

[28] See on this point, Crane Brinton, *The Anatomy of Revolution:* (1938). New York: Vintage Books-Random House, 1957, pp. 30-31.
[29] On the Bolivian situation, see Robert J. Alexander, *The Bolivian National Revolution.* New Brunswick, N.J.: Rutgers University Press, 1958; and the interesting "reactionary" document written by Gonzalo Romero, *Reflexiones Para Una Interpretación de la Historia de Bolivia.* Buenos Aires (privately printed),

The First World is still guided by concepts of the French En- •
lightenment, namely, that each person, following his own self-interests,
will mysteriously serve the goals of society. This doctrine asserts that
self-interest maximizes profits. The businessman would produce at the
lowest possible cost and sell at the highest possible price, while the
laborer, for his part, would work the longest possible hours for the highest
possible salary. In this way, the operational classes would contiguously, if
not co-operatively produce the largest amount of goods in the best possible society.

The Soviet variation of the enlightenment theme served only to
transform the theme of ego-gratification from a personal level onto a
public plane. Self-interests were found embedded in the social interests.
In this way, personal striving would produce an automatic rise in the
welfare of society. This Second World variation, based upon Marx,
fused the French Enlightenment notion of social interests to the English economists' notion of personal welfare. But it came to terms with
the ego-drive as being essential to the study of social processes.

While significant distinctions in the social psychology of the First
and the Second Worlds exist, in neither of these previously emergent
nation-areas does one find any fundamental questioning of the positive
values toward work and money. At the economic level this has been reflected in the emphasis on thrift, savings and banking, and fear of
inflation, while at the sociological level it has been reflected in an automatic assumption that the purpose of making a revolution is to establish the basis of independent sovereignty which would at the same time
make the citizens wealthy. In the United States, economic reasons were
in the forefront of the desire to end its colonial status. In Russia, similar economic reasons were put forth to end the Czarist dependence on
the European West. In both nations the revolutionary period soon gave
way to a high-energy output period. Now much of the Third World
must choose between revolutions which yield chaos, like Hungary in
1919 and Bolivia in 1952, and those that create a higher social system,

---

1960; and on the Hungarian Revolution, see Arpad Szelpal, *Les Cent Trente-
Trois Jours de Béla Kun.* Paris: A. Fayard, 1959; and Leo Pasvolsky, *Economic
Nationalism of the Danubian States.* New York: Macmillan Co., 1928, esp.
Sec. 5.

like Mexico and Russia after 1910 and 1917. There is strong pressure in the Third World for gratification through leisure rather than through work—through having "enough" money for survival of self and family, rather than through savings, increased labor output, and efficiency. In each case, a set of counter-desires for independence from colonial powers and for rapid national development. Whether the same rates of growth can be achieved depends in some part on the capacity of people to adopt or transform this persistent psychology of ego-gratification to larger social needs.

There is a general ethical cast of mind in sectors of the Third World, especially where traditionalism prevails, which considers accelerated development an evil. This is so, the argument goes, precisely because development accentuates the drive for personal, worldly possessions. To work at fulfilling ego demands is sinful, a substitution of worldly possessions for spiritual redemption. In addition to which, such material goods are thought of Pyrrhic value, useless in the long run. The drive to possess goods creates a *new* man but not necessarily a *better* man, one responsive to permanent verities. Extreme traditionalists promote the sort of spiritual "inner tranquility" which makes even the enjoyment, much less the production, of material goods difficult. This argument—enunciated by tribal leaders, religious elders, university thinkers, and a host of middle and higher echelon elites—serves to corrupt and confuse the masses eager for the rewards of industrialization. Traditional classes, typically connected with rural life, often want development without incurring either the risks or penalties of industrialism and urbanization.

Even without the urgings of such leaders, there may still be widespread hostility to greater output and increased savings. In certain instances, those who are members of the urban proletariat may see little reason to earn more money, since such earning power may actually result in a decline of status within the "member group." The local manufacturer, for his part, may see little reason to reinvest his profits in capital goods. His drive for self-gratification can be met without fulfilling the relatively abstract demands for socially useful investment in the national economy.

Since the First and Second Worlds have insisted on reading the history of development in terms of either the private accumulation of great fortunes or the public acquisition of such fortunes, it should occasion little surprise that this insistence, reinforced as it is in a barrage of advertisements, periodicals, pictorials—in short, the entire cultural apparatus of mass society—would serve to stimulate the drive for increased social control over the use of personal wealth, and for greater productivity within the entire society.

The leading international powers not only want to define the character of development but also insist upon setting forth the proper ground rules for development. Thus, the United States will have foreign-language editions of its leading weeklies flown to every village and hamlet in the Third World, and expect the "achieving orientation" to take only acceptable—that is capitalist and parliamentarian—forms. But a psychological imbalance pervades Third World politics. What occurs is in the nature of a boomerang effect: the goals of Americanization, material wealth, and quality merchandise do indeed become internalized, but the means for achieving these goals remain highly traditional and even authoritarian. This is one psychological basis for the seemingly strange economic and political combinations scattered throughout the Third World, especially the combination of developmental ends and coercive instruments, and industrial values and paternalistic norms.

The development process itself is placed in jeopardy by the heavy human costs involved and by the confusion and chaos often produced by modernization procedures. The conflict between immediate gratification and hard work is resolved by social pressures to maintain at least the same level of life styles that exist prior to a revolution. The rapidly declining death rate and the stabilization of the birth rate have combined to produce a population increase which can only be held in check by greater economic productivity per person. Furthermore, the desire for more goods and more education has stimulated huge shifts in family and kinship patterns. Old patterns of marriage and family collapse; respect for elders is turned into competition with them; the nuclear family replaces the extended family in importance; the general society performs more of the roles once played by the immediate family. These trends, admittedly set in motion and stimulated by the advanced nations, impinge directly on the everyday life of Third World peoples and produce a conflict between traditional values denigrating hard work and celebrating subsistence life styles.[30]

The Makers of Development: Managerial versus Mass Types

People are engaged in the developmental process in different ways. Some individuals in a sleepy rural town desire to move to big cities; others do not. But which ones? Some members of the business community have the capacity for disinterested investment for the good of the nation; others do not. Which ones? Some factory workers are content with their "station" in life; others desire higher remuneration or "cleaner" work. Which ones?

Unfortunately, the literature seems more concerned with demonstrating the entrepreneur's, theologian's, or revolutionist's role in development than in settling upon criteria to be used in solving the knotty issue of the kind of person who contributes to development. This may simply represent a long-standing gap between "personality" and "systematic" explanations of human events. Or it may be that to single out developmental "types" involves the researcher in the kind of "intervention" which may be viewed as interference with the sovereignty of a community or a nation, or may be considered as adding to the stress and strain of a given situation.[31] But we must still answer the question —what special class is most concerned with development?—before taking account of the kinds of people within these classes who are most likely to concern themselves with development.

Modernism is often an argument for middle-class elitism. The First World bias has often tended to consider industrial development as a function of managerial pre-eminence. Originally, this was done in a critical spirit by James Burnham.[32] Then more recently, the same thesis

[30] The most useful information on the question of attitudes toward work and money is contained in the economic literature. See in particular Robert Theobald, *The Rich and the Poor: A Study of the Economics of Rising Expectations.* New York: Clarkson N. Potter, Inc., 1960; and at a more technical level, Peter Bauer, *Economic Analysis and Policy in Underdeveloped Countries.* Durham, N.C.: Duke University Press, 1957.

[31] For excellent papers on research problems of this type, see *Reflections on Community Studies,* edited by Arthur J. Vidich, Joseph Bensman, Maurice R. Stein. New York: John Wiley & Sons, Inc., 1964.

[32] James Burnham, *The Managerial Revolution: What Is Happening in the World.* New York: The John Day Co., Inc., 1941, esp. pp. 71-138.

was asserted as a positive and necessary correlation of industrial development.[33] Aside from how correct it is to speak of a managerial "revolution "[34] the decision to invest in managerial talent definitely presupposes a competitive social system. There are no Harvard Business Schools in the Soviet Union. For better or for worse, education of engineers, physicists, and mathematicians was given top priority, and these men began, with increasing frequency, to fill managerial assignments. Thus, while it is an indisputable fact that development requires a high educational input to gain industrial take-off, there is no significant evidence that emphasis on managerial training is a necessary component of the developmental formula. The decision to invest funds in managerial training is clearly one which must weigh the level of inefficiency resulting from poor management against the level of the production gained from mass scientific training.

From the psychological viewpoint, one must ask what kinds of innovation can be expected from what manpower sources. Here the Soviet experience is quite relevant. The decision to invest in natural and engineering science personnel resulted in all kinds of managerial errors: giganticism, arbitrary norms, bookkeeping mistakes, industrial cheating on goods, misallocation of raw materials.[35] Furthermore this approach dehumanized the industrial pattern and produced anomie far beyond the levels reached in Western countries. Industrialization is in its essence a process of dehumanization.[36] These factors notwithstanding, Soviet industry was a success by all standard economic measurements. The policy question is actually the amount of non-essential investment which should be tolerated in the drive toward development. The real issue is to what degree can alienation and anomie be checked. The

[33] See, for this interpretation, Frederick Harbison and Charles A. Myers, *Management in the Industrial World*. New York: McGraw-Hill, 1959, esp. pp. 21-4; and Clark Kerr, John T. Dunlop, Frederick H. Harbison, and Charles A. Myers, *Industrialism and Industrial Man*. New York: Oxford University Press, 1964.

[34] See H. H. Gerth and C. Wright Mills, "A Marx for the Managers," in *Power, Politics and People*, edited by I. L. Horowitz. New York and London: Oxford University Press, 1963, pp. 53-71.

[35] See Naum Jasny, *Soviet Industrialization: 1928-1952*. Chicago, Ill.: University of Chicago Press, 1961.

[36] See on this subject Norbert Wiener, *The Human Use of Human Beings*. Boston: Houghton Mifflin Co., 1954; and more recently, *God and Golem, Inc.* Cambridge, Mass.: Massachusetts Institute of Technology Press, 1964.

long-range problem is to what extent can machine labor replace human labor without creating mass unemployment, fear, and panic. By so doing, advanced industrialization makes possible new forms of creative work.

The sophisticated notion that there are "industrializing elites" does not take seriously enough the possibility of working-class or peasant elites. All elitist theories fail to take into account the social psychology of the masses as a chief agency in promoting revolutionary development. Too often the assumption is made that development is a process moving from top to bottom.[37] In this way dynastic reactionaries come to be linked to intellectual revolutionaries in a sophisticated way. All men become part of the "elite" through which the impulse to development is asserted. Managerialism is broadened to include every form of elitist sentiment, and thus comes to be identified with development as such. Managers "create" and workers "respond" to the industrializing process. The idea of revolutionary change is neatly divorced from that of industrial change. Even worker protest, when it is mentioned at all, is discussed in terms of how elites can harness such protest to the industrialization process. The mass unrest is converted into a problem of "industrial strategy." The problems posed by socialist parties, guerrilla warfare, and revolutionary ideologies simply fall by the wayside. Managerial doctrines treat mass unrest as "unsponsored decisions," which is another way of saying not treated at all.

Development is a function of managerialism and reveals "class consciousness" not one whit less assertive than the Marxist notion of development as an exclusive function of the revolutionary. Indeed, at the psychological level, scholars like Hagen, McClelland, and Kerr are seeking to provide the kind of "non-Communist" manifesto which W. W. Rostow provided for the economic realm. For Hagen, there are two personality types: the "authoritarian," which prevails in present economies, and the "creative outsider," found in advanced industrial economies. In this system, change is induced from the outside, from marginal creative elites.[38] In McClelland, achievement motivation is directly related to entrepreneurial types. "High-achieving mystics" are to be found among these business-oriented types, while "low-achieving

---

[37] See Clark Kerr, John Dunlop, Frederick Harbison, and Charles A. Myers, *op. cit.*

[38] Everett E. Hagen, *On the Theory of Social Change*. Homewood, Ill.: The Dorsey Press, Inc., 1962.

traditionalists" are to be found in the peasant sectors.[39] In the work of the Kerr group, development occurs through the interaction between industrializing elites and managerial types. This relationship is held to be the creative force underlying development.[40]

It has been succinctly and convincingly pointed out that managerial elite doctrines fail to account for several critical variables: (1) Economic development is a highly selective and uneven process. A developing region may exhibit a marked growth in one sector of the economy—transportation and communication, let us say—but not in heavy tool-manufacturing industries. Is this a function of creative elites being present in one sector of the economy and not in the other? Or is it not more likely that prohibitions imposed by the strength of colonial powers are responsible for this "creative imbalance"?[41] (2) Managerial elites tend to be conservative in their economic policies for underdeveloped regions. The assumption that such elites are high achievers omits the critical variable—that is, the different notions of achievement that can be entertained. (3) Personal aggrandizement may be a reflection of high achievement, but it certainly is not necessarily conducive to high development. One ought not to confuse a *petite* bourgeoisie with an *haute* bourgeoisie and drown both in the language of creative "types."[42] There are other objections to the elitist formulations. The main point to note, and drawn most recently by McCord, is that latent entrepreneurial talent exists in almost every region and in every economic class.[43]

The conflict between managerial and mass types is more than an intellectual plaything of social scientists. It is a reflection of crucial differences which exist. The problem of class stereotype contributes to the imbalance between social forces. The middle classes, when questioned about their attitudes toward the urban proletariat (of Chile and

[39] David C. McClelland, *The Achieving Society*. Princeton, N.J.: D. Van Nostrand Company, 1961.
[40] Clark Kerr (ed.), *op. cit.*
[41] For criticism of Schumpeter's doctrine of development, see Arthur Lewis, *The Theory of Economic Growth*. Homewood, Ill.: Richard D. Irwin, 1955, and Benjamin Higgins, *Economic Development*. London: Constable & Co., Ltd., 1959.
[42] Thomas Bottomore, *Elites and Society*. New York: Basic Books, 1965.
[43] William McCord, *The Springtime of Freedom: Evolution of Developing Societies*. New York: Oxford University Press, 1965, p. 143.

Mexico), uniformly answered that the workers were good-hearted and lazy, indifferent rather than shiftless. When the same workers were polled as to their attitudes toward the middle classes, their attitudes were vague and undefined. Nonetheless, they possessed a self-definition of themselves and of the nation that was more optimistic than was that of the middle class. They held to a hard-working, virtuous self-definition, and to a mobile, dynamic vision of their society.[44]

Stereotyping has blunted consideration of important aspects of society such as demography. Most middle-class people interviewed in one sample felt that the problem of overpopulation rested with the absence of restraint on the part of the working class, when in fact, in a nation such as Mexico the middle classes tend to be less concerned, and consequently more tradition-bound, than the poor.[45] It may be that the formula that the "rich get richer" while the "poor get babies" is preferred by the rich. It is evident that the psychology of development is unevenly spread in a nation or in a community. More important, it is not self-evident that middle classes and entrepreneurial sectors are a genuine vanguard in the reorientation of attitudes toward industrialization. But, like the bourgeoisie of Victorian England, they frequently tend to equate poverty with indolence, and, correspondingly, wealth with wisdom.

The emphasis on linking social achievement to individual motivation is itself representative of a large-scale ethnocentricism characteristic of Taylorist (First World) and Stakhanovite (Second World) styles of work introduced by the managerial castes in the United States and the Soviet Union. Each culture has a different way of socializing responsibility for achievement. In the United States, social security, old-age pensions, privately administered health programs, check-off plant insurance programs, and unemployment compensation systems serve, each in their own way, to underscore and to underwrite the responsibility of society

---

[44] I owe this information to Raúl Benítez, who is working on this material concerning class stereotypes. At the same time, Benítez's findings corroborate similar early findings made by Eduardo Hamuy. See Eduardo Hamuy, *Educación Elemental, Analfabetismo y Desarrollo Económico*. Santiago de Chile: Editorial Universitaria, 1960.

[45] See Joseph Kahl and J. Mayone Stycos, "The Philosophy of Demographic Policy in Latin America," *Studies in Comparative International Development*, Vol. 1, No. 2, 1965.

for the individual. In Japan, the system of socialization is considerably different. Japanese workers rarely, if ever, are fired. Promotions are made on the basis of seniority rather than of efficiency. Pay is determined by a complex set of social factors in which the number of dependents and length of service are prominent. In the Japanese system, the industrial decision-making process is socialized through a vast paternalistic set-up. All decisions are made on a group basis—this allows for no one to lose face or be ashamed.[46]

The forms of social responsibility may differ from culture to culture. But given the fact that the rate of growth of Japan has been equal to that of the United States throughout most of the twentieth century, it should be clear that these forms of social control may be different and yet yield the same overall productivity. The "peculiar" characteristics of development in Japan are not explained by the "inscrutable" oriental face-saving mind. A more ready explanation is that in Japan the lower nobility absorbed capitalist businesses. In the absence of a productive and independent middle class, this traditionalist sector assimilated the corporate phase of capitalism to the feudal ways of the noble and military elite.[47]

Imitation and Innovation

The process of development which relies upon foreign assistance can never be the same as the process of autonomous industrialization of the past. Models of an earlier period have not so much grown spontaneously in new environments as they have been adapted to non-Western conditions. Third World social or cultural systems build upon each other in symbiotic fashion. This is clear even in the imitative element present in the basic vocabulary of development, i.e. "demonstration effect" or "combined development." What formerly was a product of chance now becomes a matter of planning.

The notion of Western democracy became important in Third

[46] See James Abegglen, The Japanese Factory. Glencoe, Ill.: The Free Press of Glencoe, 1958. For a keen anthropological study, see John W. Bennett and Iwao Ishino, Paternalism in the Japanese Economy. Minneapolis, Minn.: University of Minnesota Press, 1963.
[47] See E. Herbert Norman, Japan's Emergence as a Modern State. New York: Institute of Pacific Relations, 1946.

World thinking by its accepting some improvisation in its own ideology, and, second, because it demanded that the West adhere to Western political codes. The Third World has very consciously embarrassed the West by calling attention to the latter's failures to live by the principles it advocates.[48] Consider the following report given by Malinowski:

> Nationalism is the sense of a conservative reaction, and the recognition of the integral value of its own culture by each nation is spreading like wild fire all over the world. We, the members of the white race, are primarily responsible for that, and we have been giving our religion, our education, and many other spiritual boons to other races and peoples, with an implied promise that once they accept our civilization, they will become our equals. This promise has not been redeemed. We are beginning now to see how dangerous it is to speak about the white man's burden, and to make others shoulder it and carry it for us. We give all the promises implied in our concept of human brotherhood and of equality through education, but when it comes to wealth, power, and self-determination we refuse this to other people.[49]

Furthermore, even the use of the military to bring about colonial domination created a boomerang effect. Those that came with the gun did indeed conquer. But in turn, the colonizing powers created the basis for a new consciousness, which is dramatically described by Ndabaningi Sithole.

> World Wars I and II helped the cracks of the white myth to widen. Thousands of African soldiers went abroad on active service . . . They were ordered by the white commanders to kill white enemy soldiers. The African soldiers from Southern and Northern Rhodesia, Nyasaland, French Equatorial Africa, the

[48] One must appreciate the fact that this psychology of embarrassment can work both ways. It may inhibit the use of totalitarian forms of development deemed feasible in times of lower levels of communication transmission. See on this the perceptive paper by R. P. Dore, "Japan as a Model of Economic Development," *Archives Européennes de Sociologie*, Vol. 5, No. 1, 1964, pp. 138-54.

[49] Bronislaw Malinowski, *Freedom and Civilization*. New York: Roy Publishers, 1944, p. 219; also see Irving L. Horowitz, "Crime, Custom and Culture: Remarks on the Functional Theory of Bronislaw Malinowski," *International Journal of Comparative Sociology*, Vol. III, No. 2, December 1962, pp. 229-44.

Gold Coast, and Nigeria, found themselves at the front line of war with one purpose in view: to kill every white enemy soldier they could get hold of. Many German and Italian soldiers fell victim to shots fired by African soldiers. The African soldiers saw white soldiers wounded, dying, and dead. The bullet had the same effect on white and black alike. This had a very powerful psychological impact in the African. He saw those whom he used to call his betters suffer defeat, though not conquest, at the hands of the Germans and Japanese, and once more he was impressed by the fact that it was not being white or black that mattered but the necessary training in these things. The veil between him and the white man thinned to a point of transparency, and at other points it disappeared altogether. After suffering side by side with his white fellow soldiers the African never again regarded them in the same light. After spending four years hunting white enemy soldiers the African never regarded them again as gods.[50]

Thus what was provided, in the instance cited by Malinowski, was the political ideology and, in the example given by Sithole, the military cast of mind. In both cases it was indicated that the colonial exploiters were not simply hypocritical, but subject to the same laws of nature as black and yellow peoples, or of people in general.

Work styles and living styles were imitated and adapted to new environments. But this absorption was always accompanied by an assertion on the part of the colonialists that they be produced and developed under humanizing circumstances. In short, innovation, whether large or small, is a necessary part of the ideological re-armament which the Third World undergoes. The way in which the Russians adopted American techniques of industrialization represents an outstanding example. It was never done by applying simple mimetic principles, but with the idea that adaptation is innovation.

The extent to which the early founders of the Soviet Union kept the United States as their model of development has been underestimated. It was manifested not only in "electrification" and "mechanization," but also in Soviet emphasis on American work styles. Stakhano-

[50] Ndabaningi Sithole, *African Nationalism*. New York: Oxford University Press, 1959, pp. 155-7.

vism is little more than an adaptation of Taylorism—programs of scientific labor management or manipulation—to Russian industrial conditions. Lenin indicates that "the Taylor system, without its initiators knowing or wishing it, is preparing the time when the proletariat will take over all social production and appoint its own workers' committees for the purpose of properly distributing and rationalizing all social labor. Large scale production, machinery, railways, telephone—all provide thousands of opportunities to cut by three-fourths the working time of organized workers, and make them four times better off than they are today."[51]

The only hitch in Lenin's prediction is that this automation has not exhausted its possibilities within the framework of capitalism. Whatever modifications had to be made by capitalism—whether equal to or less than the modifications required in the Stalinist system of Stakhanovism—the system of private ownership proved equal to the innovative challenge. Taylorism was understood as a managerial device from the outset. Stakhanovism was not so clearly understood. Indeed, it was presented as a response to worker initiative. What is interesting is the extent to which labor opposition to Taylorism, to piece-work payment, and to managerial determination of working conditions not only failed to slow up but actually promoted increased labor output in capitalist centers.

It becomes increasingly apparent that there is a geat deal of tension between imitation and innovation in the "take-off" period. Innovation is based upon the existence of political and cultural variety, coupled with technological needs and capacities to absorb novelty. Collective resistance to social change is first manifested by the reluctance of individuals to accept novelty. These may come about in several ways. First, the introduction of a new product or tool may completely disrupt traditional relations between men and women. Consider this example cited by W. Arthur Lewis. "The introduction of central mills for extracting oil from the oil palm fruit doubles the yield of oil, but it also deprives the wives of West African farmers of the perquisites they get when they extract the oil for their husbands, and is therefore strongly and effectively resisted by them; it also alters the division of labor between husband

---

[51] See V. I. Lenin, "The Taylor System—Men's Enslavement by the Machine," in Collected Works, Vol. 20. Moscow: Foreign Languages Publishing House, 1964, pp. 152-4.

and wife, and anything which does this has far reaching and unforeseeable consequences."[52] The "Luddite Syndrome" of resisting innovation in the name of maintaining social order is repeated endlessly and everywhere. Sometimes such resistance is individualistic, as in the case of aristocratic intellectuals; sometimes collectivistic, as in the case of whole agricultural settlements moving from one nation to another, such as the Kurdish Jews' migration to Israel. But the problem of resistance to change is not simply traditional; it is increasingly modern—a fear that development in itself is not a justification for uprooting traditional ways.

The success or failure of an innovation may well hinge on its source. One can mimetically reproduce the behavior of "rich foreigners" if they are admired, or "powerful elders" if they are feared. But this imitation is severely restricted, or dissolves entirely, if foreigners are loathed as imperialists, or if elders are viewed as obstructionists or internal colonialists. At some critical juncture either imitation is replaced by innovation, or the latter is rejected and falls into disrepute. Thus, the mechanism by which an imitation is transformed into an innovation itself constitutes a special form of development.

Innovation is the near-exclusive property of advanced nations. Technological novelty is a function of technological proficiency. Third World nations continue to remain imitative in technology, however innovative they may be in adapting new styles of work and industrial relations. The special drive for innovation in fully developed regions has multiple sources: the desire of entrepreneuers for social success, the hope of big profits or large wages, or, negatively, a fear of economic loss if innovative schemes are not used. The newly emergent states have serious problems providing substitute stimulants. They have instilled the ideology and ethos of equality. This cuts down or eliminates entirely the hope of quick profits or high wages. Further, social prestige is not usually measured through entrepreneurial activities; thus the impulse to innovate in the economic realm is weakened. The fear of economic loss is eliminated through the socialist system of production, but so too is the hope of great profits. Public subsidy can save failing or ailing industries, but it creates problems of motivation.

Thus Third World nations have specific problems with innovation

[52] See W. Arthur Lewis, *The Theory of Economic Growth*. Homewood, Ill.: Richard D. Irwin, 1955, pp. 178-9.

incentives in addition to their difficulties about imitation. It is almost impossible for them to restore competitive, laisser-faire norms, and even if possible, such norms might create even worse social imbalances. Hence, the task is to stimulate innovative behavior despite the absence of direct monetary rewards. One way this is done is through political, bureaucratic, or cultural payoffs. The case of the Soviet Union with its Stakhanovite movement indicates that such non-monetary payoffs can be effective. But this non-economic approach seems to become decreasingly effective with the passage of time and the growing affluence of the society involved. Thus, the maturation of the socialist system may witness the increase in "capitalist ego-incentives" to maintain work norms and to stimulate further innovation. At the same time, capitalist nations are witnessing a growing socialist trend in their innovative processes—i.e. the rise of automated machinery has made plain the need for central planning procedures on a vast scale. Automation has increased efficiency requirements, and with this a demand for more and not less planning.

Innovation serves to fuel the arguments about, instead of for, socialism. In the developing states, demands for innovation seem to trigger utilitarian solutions at the economic level and command approaches at the political level. The dialectics of development are such that the transformation of imitation into innovation is essential to the Third World. While limits to innovation remain cultural, technology and economic organization in the Third World are badly suited to innovative work styles. At the same time, in the competition between the First and Second Worlds, the arguments for capitalism and socialism both come to rest on their innovative potential. Perhaps the destiny of the Third World will be to resolve this outstanding antinomy between competitive and co-operative doctrines of economics, or at least to tip the scales decisively one way or the other.

Developing Man as a Personality Type

For development to take place, growth must be desired. We have attempted to fill in the substance of this mental set: scientific attitudes of mind, societal orientations, achievement motivations, etc.; but people themselves must be committed to development. There may even be an "irrational" decision to support development although the private sector is thwarted. And "gratification" may be derived from co-operative rather than competing acts. In all societies non-conformity has limits beyond which a series of explicit punishments are established. Non-conformity is the psychological reflex of the developmental process, and it may lead not only to disorganization but to social re-organization.[53]

Where there exists a large number of "positive-oriented" deviants, there is also generally a high developmental impulse. It is hardly accidental that crime rates have increased, rather than decreased, as the economy of the United States has expanded. Similarly, the extent of mobility in Soviet society may better be tested by the increased extent of "normal" crime, and the minimization of punishment for such crime, than by the organized channels of legal expression. Many basic forms of crime, such as professional and white-collar crimes, become legitimized business enterprise after a time. Waterfront activities, trucking, and, earlier, railroads are examples of industries in the United States which went outside the law to expand rapidly. Later, they became legitimized in terms of their social standing by virtue of their economic importance.

Criminal behavior and radical political behavior are often consonant with efforts toward rapid development. Part of the institutionalization of marginal groups in a nation such as the United States represents a wide tolerance of non-conformity. There is a deep recognition that everyone is deviant with respect to some other outside group. Thus the degree of movement from a member group, the amount of discontent within a member group, and the availability of other reference groups to which one can move are useful indicators of the psychological components in development. There is an absence of development as such when there is no division of organizational life and where there are no voluntary organizations of different persuasions with contrasting social functions or representing conflicting economic interests. Therefore normative standards, no less than deviations from such standards, interact with one another to define the psychic economy of developing man.

Not only is there a process of socialization involved in the division of labor, but the need for specialization produces a corresponding recog-

---

[53] On this distinction between deviance and disorganization, see Robert K. Merton, "Social Problems and Sociological Theory," in *Contemporary Social Problems*, edited by R. K. Merton and R. A. Nisbet. New York: Harcourt, Brace & World, Inc., 1961, pp. 718-28.

nition of the role of the individual. The individual begins to act as an agent for himself, setting up *agencies* over and against a backward and stagnant society. The developmentally oriented "deviant" has a highly refined sense of goals. He accepts allegiance to professional groups rather than to society as a whole. The developing man thus has a basic affiliation to the particular kinds of activities he engages in, rather than to the locus or the place where these activities occur. If someone is a machine-tool operator, what is important is that he have the expertise needed for maintaining his position, not that he works for a particular tool and die company. Small companies oftentimes slow down the rates of mobility by committing the loyalties of the employees to personal factors.

The transition from corporate loyalty to professional loyalty has to be seen as part of a twentieth-century collectivism. Associations based on professional affiliation increasingly displaced the web of association traditionally identified with the place of work.[54] This is one of the big changes between the mid-nineteenth and the mid-twentieth century. Collectivism increases; planning increases; allocations of materials and of men also increase. These events, while giving an indication of the growing breakdown of the traditional forms of social control, compel a growth of anti-organizational attitudes. The degree of resistance to collectivism has now shifted from the factory to the profession. Social interaction increasingly takes place outside the work environment. In the struggle for achievement, mobility is stimulated to the extent that social life is professionalized. Greater individuation depends on extending socialist forms of work.

In speaking of the mental set of developing man, we are dealing with intangibles—items which go under the name of self-sacrifice, altruism, dedication, purpose, and even "divine madness." These are not the same things, of course, but in sum they add up to a willingness to submit the personality to (and for) some abstract principle, a socially accepted rather than privately defined good. However much such noble sentiments can be traced to "base" motives, the fact remains that a truly developing society exhibits them while an underdeveloped society *does not* and the "overdeveloped society" *can no longer* do so. The charge of

[54] An excellent anthology covering this theme is Sigmund Nosow and William H. Form (eds.), *Man, Work, and Society.* New York: Basic Books, Inc., 1962.

naïve optimism was made only when the indices of progress as such had ceased to be meaningful to men. That ours is an age of cynicism, that indeed, as Camus put it, cynicism is the *only* possible sophisticated confrontation with our reality, is a sign not of maturity but of overdevelopment—of a time when "the standard of living severely limits the style of life."[55]

Nothing strikes the "Westerner" as more perverse than the longing after paradise which goes by the name of fully developed society. Do not the peoples of Asia, Africa, and Latin America realize that problems of life persist, indeed deepen, in the post-industrial age? Do they not realize the turmoil that exists within the mind of a person subject to the bureaucratic will?

They do indeed realize these problems. But the quest for development persists because, bluntly put, problems of the mind are less urgent than problems of the stomach. Further, there is no evidence to prove that every malevolent industrial practice must be reproduced in all its ghastly details. The terrors of development often turn out to be imaginary. The failure to put discovery and invention to the good of the commonweal is after all a human failing and not a failure of science. It only offers the Third World a greater challenge—to harness the sciences for human ends. But the human uses of the natural sciences involve a deeper appreciation of the scientific uses of the human sciences, and a further appreciation that democracy, like development, is a process and not a fact. The inordinate sacrifices made by peoples in emergent nations—years of civil war, famine, separation from families, sacrifice of material comfort—attest to the existence of a transcendent factor, a binding psychological commonality in development.

If such superordinate goals were not present, the actual process of development would be slower and far less meaningful. Famines in China, civil war in Algeria, blockades in Cuba, blunders of management, investment, and allocation—these are typical of all newly emergent societies. On strictly "rational" grounds any one of these factors would be enough to topple many, if not all, revolutionary regimes. But such collapses are infrequent. Where genuine "movements from below" are in

[55] C. Wright Mills, "The Problem of Industrial Development," in *Power, Politics and People*, edited by Irving L. Horowitz. New York and London: Oxford University Press, 1963, pp. 150-51.

control, adverse conditions may often create renewed effort and lead to a sense of rededication. The case of China is typical. The post-revolutionary period was filled with hardships, but also with commitment.

> At no stage in its history has the Chinese Communist party had a more positive popular appeal than during the first six years of its rule. There is of course no doubt about the significance of 1949. During that year there was a drastic acceleration in the collectivization of land, which seems to have quantitatively changed the relationship between the regime and the majority of the peasants. In the late forties and the first two or three years after the establishment of the new government, Communist party members and cadres urged or compelled the peasants to expropriate the landlords and to punish them often by death. Their land was then distributed among the poorer peasants. Therefore, in China, unlike Russia, the Communist Party could claim credit for having distributed the land.[56]

There are of course dangers and obstacles in these sentiments of self-sacrifice, altruism, and patriotic feelings. The examples of Nazi Germany and Stalinist Russia stand as a steady reminder of this. And, further, these "psychological factors" are often euphemistic ways of taking account of irrational and abnormal elements in development. To cite a few examples: nations as confined in their culture and traditions as Canada, Belgium, the Philippines, India, and Puerto Rico view bilingualism as an imperialistic hangover rather than as a novel opportunity. Language becomes a basic vehicle for expressing the ultimate in nationalistic sentiments. This is so despite the fact that the double-language system actually provides a decided cultural advantage. Another case of irrationality is the immense movement of people into cities, a movement all out of proportion to actual economic opportunities available in the cities. Indeed, families are often willing to endure all sorts of personal privation and even starvation to participate, however marginally, in the vast benefits of urban living.

A final example of such irrationality is the population boom, which

[56] See Martin Bernal, "The Popularity of Chinese Patriotism" (a review of A. Doak Barnett's *Communist China*), in *The New York Review of Books*, Vol. IV, No. 2, February 25, 1965.

is encouraged by traditional patterns of extended kinship ties. These no longer can effectively compensate for the profound economic loss occasioned by large families. In short, farming patterns, where children were significant units of economic production, continue to promote the population incline despite the changeover to industrial production. This "lag" is just as evident in contemporary China as it is in Puerto Rico. Thus, the psychological study of development must be in good measure a study of irrational elements in the stagnation and acceleration processes, and not just operational definitions of how to provoke or induce greater output per person. The lag here has been intensified by the complete schism between "experimentalists" working in laboratory conditions and "practitioners" working out in society. At the theoretical level, it has divided social scientists into competing schools.[57]

Noble sentiments are fragile. Those ready to betray such sentiments, to substitute pieties for ideals, must surely be aware that they run the risk of upsetting the developmental process as such. This very knowledge enables, in fact compels, the elites of developing nations to continue to be responsive to the mass demands of their own nations. When this is not the case, the slightest disturbance in the economic process causes friction. When mass participation in developing nations exists, then all sorts of blunders can be absorbed. This is another way of saying that mass social changes "from below" can absorb error, while elitist revolutions can crumble at even slight strain.

In the modern epoch at least, commentors have recognized that development takes a personal toll. As Freud put the matter: "civilization obeys an internal erotic impulse which causes human beings to unite in a closely knit group." But this group existence can only be achieved "through an ever increasing reinforcement of the sense of guilt." And when the individual moves from the family to society at large, he suffers "a loss of happiness through the heightening of the sense of guilt."[58] This fact is confirmed by sociological literature, which indicates that suicide rates vary directly, and homicide rates inversely, with urban and

[57] See on this, Alvin W. Gouldner, "Explorations in Applied Social Science," in *Applied Sociology: Opportunities and Problems*, edited by A. W. Gouldner and S. M. Miller. New York: The Free Press of Glencoe, 1965, pp. 5-21.
[58] See Sigmund Freud, *Civilization and Its Discontents*, trans. by James Strachey, in *The Standard Edition of the Complete Psychological Works of Sigmund Freud*, Vol. XXI. London: Hogarth Press Ltd., 1961-62, pp. 96-101.

industrial development. To be sure, whatever suicide is to be found in underdeveloped nations is centered chiefly among the middle and upper strata of the population.[59]

Development, however much we would like to subject it to scientific control, produces unanticipated results. Indeed, for the romantic tradition of Freud, the losses outweigh the gains of development, since the maturation of civilization carries with it not simply the threat of increased guilt feelings for the individual but the annihilation of civilization itself. Whether this extreme outcome predicted by psychoanalysis is accurate or not, it remains clear that development affects personality structure even more decisively than personality structure affects developmental decisions. Perhaps this very fact may help ease the destructive potential in social change. From this vantage point, personality is not simply a critical factor in development, but may often turn out to be the sacrificial offering to the "needs" of the developmental process.

Conclusions

We opened our discussion of the mental set of developing man by indicating that its main feature was the shift in responsibility for welfare from the individual to the collective society. In closing, we must also indicate another radical change which characterizes developing man—his replacement of ethical problems with strategic problems. He does not ask, as men before him have asked, whether economic growth is desirable. He takes for granted the negative features of retardation or stagnation—which from a comparative economic standpoint is the same. His thoughts are now firmly fastened on another line of reasoning: since change cannot be prevented, at what rate should it be accelerated, and at what costs, and who must bear the primary burden of this "transitional" period—which might be called the "interminable" period?

W. Arthur Lewis has tried to explain why this displacement has

---

[59] See Richard Quinney, "Suicide, Homicide, and Economic Development," *Social Forces,* Vol. 43, No. 3, March 1965, pp. 401-6; and Leo F. Schnore, "Social Problems in an Urban-Industrial Context," *Social Problems,* Vol. 9, No. 4, Winter 1962, pp. 228-40.

taken place—why indeed men of the Third World do not seem to raise with any urgency the question of the value of development as such. He locates his answer in two items: first, as a result of the rapid communication of information and ideas, human aspirations have grown faster than economic production. Second, death rates are falling faster than birth rates. These factors therefore create the need for rapid economic growth, if for no other reason than maintaining present life styles.[60]

To this might be added a third item—a value question. Men are always faced with making choices between what they determine are good things. At certain times, the redistribution of property arrangements is deemed important enough to justify revolutionary turmoil. It is not that revolution in itself is good, but that the objects desired override normal social inhibitions. The same wish holds true for the developmental race. Men want the commodities which result from development rather than a part in the ownership of these products. In this sense, socialist demands are a means of gaining such ends as desirable commodities. That in the process of development certain precious political or ethical standards, such as free elections or the rotation of elites, may be sacrificed is merely viewed as the price one has to pay for higher goods. In any revolutionary situation, the death of certain innocents, or the excessive application of curfew laws and food rationing, are viewed as a necessary byproduct of the revolutionary process. That such "aberrations" may come to be permanent features of the new social order is only one further risk inherent in the development process. They only emphasize how arduous and painful development now is; but they do not invalidate the ends development seeks.

What we have tried to do in this chapter, then, is not so much locate a psychological explanation for the facts of colonialism or "deficiencies" which are purported to be a function of underdevelopment, for these facts are economic, political, and social in nature. Rather, we have offered some guidelines to the psychological consequences of colonialism—for the developmental process as a whole, no less than for the imperial and colonial publics in particular.[61] If the mental set of devel-

---

[60] W. Arthur Lewis, op. cit., pp. 420-35.
[61] This distinction is well made by O. Mannoni, Prospero and Caliban: The Psychology of Colonization. New York: Frederick Praeger, 1964, esp. pp. 197-209.

oping man appears to us to be excessively focused on feelings of inferiority based on racial differences, we must remember that the highly developed societies have brought this racialism down on themselves through their own peculiar notions of superiority. The marks of oppression remain implanted on the "liberated" peoples of the Third World, but in some measure this is because the habits of the oppressor remain implanted on the peoples of the "enlightened" First and Second Worlds.

IV

TOWARD A GENERAL THEORY OF DEVELOPMENT AND REVOLUTION

"It is true that men have themselves made this world of nations, but this world without doubt has issued from a mind often diverse, at times quite contrary, and always superior to the particular ends that men proposed to themselves; which narrow ends made means to serve wider ends, it has always employed to preserve the human race upon this earth. Men mean to gratify their bestial lust and abandon their offspring, and they inaugurate the chastity of marriage from which the families arise. The fathers mean to exercise without restraint their paternal power over their clients, and they subject them to the civil powers from which the cities arise. The reigning orders of nobles mean to abuse their lordly freedom over the plebeians, and they are obliged to submit to the laws which establish popular liberty. The free peoples mean to shake off the yoke of their laws, and they become subject to monarchs. The monarchs mean to strengthen their own positions by debasing their subjects with all the vices of dissoluteness, and they dispose them to endure slavery at the hands of stronger nations. The nations mean to dissolve themselves, and their remnants flee for safety to the wilderness, whence, like the phoenix, they rise again. That which did all this was mind, for men did it with intelligence; it was not fate, for they did it by choice; not by chance, for the results of their always so acting are perpetually the same."

(Giambattista Vico in **The New Science**)

Chapter 11

Dilemmas and Decisions in Social Development

The rise of new states in old regions of Africa and Asia and the growth of new industrial complexes in old states, especially in South America, have proven to be the most volatile and vital fact of the modern age. Economic development on an international scale has not only created new varieties of social and political differentiation but is already providing channels for action in the developing societies. The stratification of future societies is clearly being shaped by the decisions taken now. Development acts to redistribute political and economic forces and determines the form that modern nationalism and internationalism take. Political control, economic growth, and social structure are "plugged" into one another as never before. The consciousness of development has revolutionized the structure of development. For this reason, certain long-standing roadblocks can be cleared away, while newly emergent issues can be satisfactorily posed.

The Uneven Nature of Development

Neither continents nor nations develop. What do develop are specific geographic areas which have particular ecological patterns, economic properties, and psychological orientations. In short, sectors develop rather than societies. One might speak of the rapid development of the Brazilian or Indonesian economies; but what is really more to the point is the growth of São Paulo and Jakarta—growth measured by the stand-

335

ard economic indices of real wealth, capital growth, improved living standards, changed conditions of existence, and changed relationships between social groups.

At the same time, the "costs" of development are not an abstraction. Generally, what suffers most in this process (comparatively) is the agricultural sector, and the people who suffer most are the peasants. Even if we were to choose as our model the relatively advanced Soviet Union, we would find agricultural technology and farm production lag badly. And if this is true for the advanced Soviet Union, it is still more so for such recent entries into the development race as Brazil—where the contrasts between the industrial and agricultural sector are sharp and taut. On the unevenness of development, on this "sectorial phenomenon," a recent United Nations survey is most instructive.

> Ideally, productivity in agriculture would rise at a rate meeting the cities' growing demands for food as well as the demands of export markets, while permitting the release of agricultural workers at a rate meeting the rising demand for labour in industry and services. In practice, of course, the transition does not proceed so smoothly, and in many countries today something quite different is happening: productivity is hardly increasing at all, while masses of rural workers come to the cities looking for jobs that either do not exist or from which they are barred by illiteracy and lack of skills.[1]

Thus, even during the transitional phase, when a country is shifting from rural to industrial patterns, differences between the sectors only become highlighted.

Such disparities produce friction. Farm labor is more difficult to come by and farm profits are lower than the condition prevailing in the industrial sector. But if this is indeed a friction-producing condition, it is also a situation which produces change. An entirely new phenomenon, "transitional man," has come into existence.[2] The English peasant was rapidly absorbed into the industrial life of Manchester and London be-

---

[1] United Nations, Department of Economic and Social Affairs. *Report on the World Social Situation, with Special Reference to the Problem of Balanced Social and Economic Development.* New York: United Nations, 1961, pp. 19-20.
[2] Cf. Oscar Lewis, *The Children of Sánchez.* New York: Random House, 1962; and William McCord, "Portrait of Transitional Man," in *The New Sociology,* edited by Irving L. Horowitz. New York: Oxford University Press, 1964.

cause development was a national event and there were common features making for social solidarity—ethnic, religious, and racial. The cross-over from rural to urban economic and social patterns occurred with minimum delay and without foreign impediments. The conflict between agricultural and industrial sectors in the newly developing nations often produces the sharpest kinds of differences in social norms, cultural patterns, and personal habits. Marginal, unabsorbed elements in the transitional periods tend not to disappear but to become a permanent fixture. Thus marginal sub-societies form outside Mexico City, Rio de Janeiro, and Buenos Aires which are permanent.

While many economists have pointed out the "advantages of coming last"—that is, the ability of current underdeveloped countries to profit by the experiences of other civilizations—too few have dealt candidly with the disadvantages of coming last. And it is precisely these disadvantages which are most apparent when one examines underdeveloped regions. We have already alluded to one: the fantastically wide gap between wealth and poverty.

Other examples come quickly to mind: (1) The intensification of the features in modern labor which produce alienation, as when "transitional man" must confront and cope with automatic assembly-line techniques. (2) The gap between skills of handicraft or agricultural labor and the highly refined knowledge necessary to participate in advanced industrial life. (3) The jarring effects of the depersonalized, bureaucratized forms of "modern" existence on the traditionalist value systems of the impoverished. (4) The rise in competition between peasant and proletariat.

Clearly one of the major problems of development is how to extend its advantages to the greatest number of people. In a world of divisions between a barter sector, a money sector, and a public planning sector, it must be seen that the costs of development are higher because the number of people adversely affected by development is much higher. These costs themselves are not subject to debate—yet are a consequence of development in a post-capitalist world. What is of moral concern is whether development is worth such costs. To enter the modern world at this late period means that a nation must pay a heavier price. The "advantages of being last" will produce a Pyrrhic victory unless a society is ready and able to absorb the disadvantages of being last.

The Irreversibility of Development

People in highly developed nations are fond of thinking about social questions in terms of human will. Even those committed to social determinism are generally hesitant, if not unwilling, to rule out the existence of options and choices—at least within a certain sphere. But the fact remains that, once the conscious (and perhaps volitional) act of setting in motion the wheels of guided social change occurs, little can be done to halt the process.

Bluntly put, no known society has ever consciously accepted a lower standard of living as a permanent feature of social existence. Indeed, a primary cause of social revolution is the incapacity or inability of an established set of rulers to maintain or accelerate the growth rates of a society. The movement from ruralism to urbanism may appear as simply a matter of change to social scientists, but for the mass of people it is a matter of emancipation. Women are emancipated from domestic obligations; children are emancipated from the work force; laborers are emancipated from the vagaries and tyrannies of the land; and human relations as such are emancipated from strict economic necessity.

What then happens to human will under the stress of automation and rapid development? Certainly, it is a part of the growing rupture between advocates of traditionalism and modernism. To be "reactionary" in this sense implies that even though one knows that social development is irreversible, one must still do battle against the forces of development in the hope of maintaining traditional values. It is therefore no accident that conservatism has become increasingly strident, and perhaps obsolete, as it becomes increasingly frustrated by the irreversibility of developmental patterns.

There may be very sound reasons for opposing rapid development. After all, every "emancipation" is also a "hardship" for some social sector or class. The loss of domestic servants may represent a genuine deprivation to those who have been used to an "aristocratic" life in a pre-industrial world. And the utility of washing machines may offer slight consolation to those who either were or still are in the position to employ human washing machines. Nonetheless, there is little point for anyone to shed crocodile tears over the social costs of development to essentially parasitic groups. Development, in being irreversible, tends also to sharpen the competition between sectors within a nation rather than to lessen such conflicts. In this sense the unilateral direction of development is joined to the sectorial nature of development to increase social pressure, and hence increase social revolution as a means toward rapid change.

Actually, development today may succeed in accomplishing what often repeated political slogans of the past were not able to accomplish: namely, to create the basis for the theory and practice of permanent revolution. It is becoming increasingly evident that to desire rapid socio-economic development means to accept the realities of permanent social transformations on a deep and wide scale.[3] This is not to say that no options are left—indeed, they may well increase—but they all must operate within the framework of the developmental pattern. Nostalgia in its own way reflects an inability to cope with the realities of the revolutionary process.

Necessary Coercion versus Internecine Terrorism

Although inherited models of development may not be applicable to a developing nation, there remains the question of relevance in these inherited ideologies. One writer has seen the choices as between totalitarian models, in which there is a total appropriation of power by a single group, and authoritarian models, in which the formal apparatus, however repressive, admits of a considerable latitude at the level of informal life. This distinction has the advantage of delineating between public and private spheres, if nothing else. Now while this model has much to recommend it, it does not quite face the issue.[4]

The main issue is not the institutionalization of legal safeguards. Such a legal superstructure is simply a consequence of development without deformities—*in vacuo*. Such restraints may well involve the aban-

[3] Cf. Marion J. Levy, "Some Sources of the Vulnerability of the Structures of Relatively Non-Industrialized Societies to Those of Highly Industrialized Societies," *The Progress of Underdeveloped Areas*, edited by Bert Hoselitz. Chicago: The University of Chicago Press, 1952, pp. 113-25.
[4] Cf. Lewis Coser, "Prospects for the New Nations: Totalitarianism, Authoritarianism or Democracy?" *Dissent*, Vol. 10, No. 1, 1963, pp. 43-58.

donment of the revolutionary impulse toward development. In any comparison of economic growth rates between China and India, one notices a direct ratio between the rate of industrial growth and the presence of coercive mechanisms. When Baran points out that India's stagnation is due to its being "neither able nor willing to accept that challenge [of breaking the hold of the property-owning strata] and to provide the leadership in breaking the resistance of urban and rural vested interests," he has in mind the willingness and/or the capacity of the Chinese to do just that.[5] It serves no purpose to recoil in horror or employ disparaging slogans about oriental despotism and authoritarianism.

Therefore, legal safeguards are clearly going to be violated whenever a high priority is placed on rapid industrial development. It is a relatively simple matter for a citizen of an advanced country, which has long since "internalized" the necessity for judicial restraints or witnessed no serious repressive parliamentary forms, to be outraged by authoritarian measures in the nations of Africa and Asia which are now entering the modern world. To be sure, what complicates growth patterns in Latin America is precisely this long history of parliamentary cretinism, the mystical regard for formal restraints to expropriation or land redistribution that suited the interests of the vested classes.

The real issue is to distinguish between necessary coercion—i.e. those forms of coercion which both suppress vested interests and also ensure the normal functioning of the productive classes—and politically inspired terrorism—i.e. that form of coercion which spends itself on the maintenance of state power and the prevention of free criticism and free choice by the citizenry. Whether we start with Lord Acton's formula that power corrupts and absolute power corrupts absolutely, or a more specific sociological variation such as Roberto Michels' theory of the oligarchical tendencies of organization, or Max Weber's concept of a rise in the bureaucratic sector as a direct response to the rationalizing agencies of state power, we are still confronted with the problem of distinguishing necessary coercion from internecine terrorism.

The Soviet Union and China represent classic examples of the failure to maintain a distinction between these two factors. Once rapid industrialization was decided upon, it was also decided that to oppose

[5] Cf. Paul A. Baran, *The Political Economy of Growth*. New York: Monthly Review Press, 1957, pp. 225-6.

this process in any size or shape was tantamount to betrayal, treason, and "wrecking." Indeed, if any useful definition of Stalinism is to be made, it must emphasize its liquidation of the distinction between "class struggle" and "party struggle." The Stalinist period in Russian industrialization rested not simply on coercion but on terrorism. And the distinction between these two words is not inconsequential—the former may involve persuasion, education, relocation, as well as expropriation, while terrorism as an exclusive principle involves the liquidation of all private existence and the replacement of the private man with the thoroughly "integrated" industrial man.

It is in this sense that a concept of law (what is at times ignorantly called "liberalism") might well prove fundamental. For without rules for the "circulation of elites," without rules for leadership as well as for membership, the impulse for coercion to become terror is almost irresistible. This is particularly so in those newly emerging nations where the "basic industry," and at times the exclusive lucrative industry, is the maintenance of the state as such. This is not to say that terrorism is without pragmatic value for growth. No one has proven that terrorism and development are incompatible. One might argue that from the Communist point of view the two are mutually exclusive; and therefore that the Revolution is "betrayed." But this is an argument which begins with the absolute need for an ideology to deliver "the goods" down to the final prophecy. However distasteful to Western opinion, the position expressed by E. H. Carr and Isaac Deutscher—that Soviet society has indeed satisfied the requirements of a growing society, however deformed its method of doing so—can no longer be doubted.

From the standpoint of development the most dysfunctional feature of coercion turned inward, turned terroristic, is that the revolutionary social process thus unleashed will be aborted.[6] The "great leap forward" in Communist China, the suppression of the "hundred flowers" doctrine, had a profound boomerang effect on the developmental process. Even so sympathetic a reporter of China as Edgar Snow[7] criticizes the bad effects brought on by the extreme pressures to "catch the

[6] Cf. John J. Johnson (ed.), *The Role of the Military in Underdeveloped Countries.* Princeton: Princeton University Press, 1962.
[7] Edgar Snow, *The Other Side of the River: Red China Today.* London: Gollancz, 1963.

West" in the shortest possible time. The slipping of coercion into terror demonstrates only the political efficacy of violence, not its value for development. In this connection it is significant that the Chinese have avoided the technique of the general political purge and the internecine factional strife that played such havoc with the evolution of Soviet Russia between 1927 and 1953. Khrushchev's own denunciations of Stalinism, whatever else they signify, are a clear announcement that "inner party struggle" has little to do with "class struggle," and that since the latter has been resolved in favor of the combination of a worker-peasant state, development will be through "consciousness" and "harmony," or what in the West is referred to as consensus. And it is here that we can see the increasing similarities of the functional pre-requisites of growth in Russia and the West—however distinct the goals of these societies may remain.

The "models" for the developing nations remain paradoxical. West-ern liberal styles do not seem to "deliver the goods." And while the social and political traditions of many new nations remain Western-influenced, their great needs for economic and technological development make them move from Western liberalism in favor of "oriental des-potism." In this context the strongest argument against terrorism can be made by an authentic socialism, which fully recognizes the needs for main-tenance of a coercive apparatus but at the same time seeks to sharply distinguish class struggle from party struggle and necessary suppression from politically inspired terror.

Coercion is often necessary because private industries either fail to accelerate developmental patterns or are unwilling to alter conventional patterns of development. Even if one were to assume the sufficiency of available resources, the private investor will undertake to make invest-ments which are profitable and directed toward short-run return on the investment rather than costly (such as explorations in the technological uses of nuclear power) and directed toward the long run. The private sec-tor in underdeveloped economies generally has neither the means nor the will to interest itself in those industries that require a large initial invest-ment with the prospect of low returns for an immediate future. In a pri-vate-sector economy, the uncertainties attached to any given combina-tion of factors of industrial production tend to inhibit growth patterns. Thus given the fact that in an underdeveloped country risks are infinite and the task of capital formation complicated by intervening social variables, some form of coercion will undoubtedly be required. Coercion would thus be used to rationalize productivity, avoid excessive expenditures on consumer goods, create the basis of support for unprofitable but necessary lines of scientific industrialization, curb speculative spending, and minimize the exercise of power by the former ruling classes. Coercion in this sense is actually the reverse of naked power—since the former may imply a wide use of persuasive devices, while the latter eschews persuasion in favor of raw power—often used ignorantly and maliciously.

Achievement and Ascription in the Developmental Process

The developmental take-off is connected with a strong emphasis on achievement values. As a matter of fact, there is a powerful sense of achievement, of getting ahead in the status race by one's own efforts, implied in the developmental process. But if achievement is not to be taken as a synonym for development, it must also be recognized that this achievement motivation by no means rules out traditional values and judgments. If the right to "get ahead" within a social system is part of a developing society, it is no less the case that the social class, race, or nation also has the right to get ahead. The self-awareness of development therefore implies, at the personal level, the abandonment of ascriptive factors in favor of achievement factors.

The ease with which national liberation efforts spill over into anti-white crusades is symptomatic of the fact that an ascriptive element not only is present in the developmental process, but, in its earlier stages at least, may well be the essential catalyst. Nor does this necessarily represent an ideology foisted on the masses from above. The following striking interview with a Vietnamese peasant shows this:

> The other day I [an American reporter] visited a small farmer near Saigon. Through my interpreter I asked him to tell me what he thought of the Americans coming to Indochina. He said: "White men help white men. You give guns to help the French kill my people. We want to be rid of all foreigners and the Viet Minh . . . was slowly putting out the French." I said: "Don't you know there is a white man behind the Viet Minh?

Don't you know that Ho Chi Minh takes Russian orders?" He said: "In Saigon I have seen Americans, and I have seen Frenchmen. I have never heard of any white men being with the Viet Minh."[8]

The apocryphal remarks attributed to Mao Tse Tung to the effect that in Asia and Africa, at least, the race war is the class war symbolizes the powerful role of ascribed status.

If the central issue of development at the take-off point is an acute *definition* of friends and enemies, rights and obligations, then the central issue at the stage when (or if) development is undertaken is how a society attempts to *consolidate* its initial successes.

It serves little purpose to argue for the best of all possible worlds, in which political democracy and economic growth march hand in hand. Such a view is predicated on the willingness of backward social forces to accept their demise peacefully and legally. Classes simply do not accept their demise with grace, nor do new ruling groups spring into being with a full appreciation of the craft of political leadership. The mark of an authentic and democratic revolution is not the maintenance of traditional canons of law during periods of dynamic change in economic and political relations; but rather, the degree to which the transitional stages in social development can be shortened and the amount of coercion minimized, without inviting a breakdown of the processes of social change as such.

Breakdown can thus occur from two directions: either through the excessive use of terrorism or through the absence of a regulatory machinery for enforcing developmental norms. Once the take-off stage has passed, the central issue becomes how to get people to work more efficiently and with greater purpose. Development depends not so much on high productivity as on a reduction in the expenditure of human effort *without* any corresponding loss in material productivity. It is clear that by *developed* most people mean simply (and rightly) the degree and the extent to which human energy is displaced by machine technology. And in fact, highly developed societies reveal just such an ongoing process.

[8] This statement, reported by Fred Sparks, is quoted in Hans J. Morgenthau, *Politics Among Nations: The Struggle for Power and Peace*, third edition. New York: Alfred A. Knopf, 1960, p. 341.

One need simply recollect that in the 1860's the average factory work in Western Europe was 14 hours per day, while today it is between seven and eight hours and steadily diminishing.[9]

What is of even greater consequence is that factory laborers—the paid proletariat—are a constantly diminishing social class. New standards of machine technology not only shorten the work day but eliminate the need for a large undifferentiated labor supply. Georges Friedmann has even suggested that "some word other than 'worker' will be needed to characterize the duties and responsibilities of automatic operators." Development in this sense means that manual labor is likely to disappear in terms of social needs, however useful it may prove as a "therapeutic" device.

This long-range process has given rise to a third stage in development: the revolution of achievement as a standard index of social and personal worth. It is not *who one is* so much as *what one knows* that comes to govern wages, political influence, community standing, and other types of rewards. What seemingly has gone by the boards in this stage is a judgment of worth or "ratings" based on race, class, nationality, or ethnic and religious affiliation. Throughout the "classical" industrial period of development there has been a "status revolution" based essentially on intelligence or "know-how" as a measure of the degree of social worth. This does not mean that class conflict has been absent. The fight for higher wages and better conditions of labor still remains a primary task of unions and worker organizations. Nonetheless, even in the unions there has been a perceptible shift away from traditional concerns toward the wider implications of automation. Thus unions have become much like any other "business" protective organization—concerning themselves with retraining members for higher skilled work, protecting their members with wise and prudent investments, and guaranteeing their members some priority in available positions rather than concerning themselves with new recruits or with the non-affiliated portion of the work force.

Labor organizations, like business organizations, tend increasingly to

[9] Cf. Georges Friedmann, "Leisure in an Automated World," *The Nation*, Vol. 195, No. 5, September 1962, pp. 89-92. For a general useful estimate see W. Lloyd Warner and Norman H. Martins (eds.), *Industrial Man: Businessmen and Business Organizations*. New York: Harper & Row, Inc., 1959.

have shared problems and hence shared values. Managerial concerns in automated factories supersede traditional schisms along class lines—and the forms of the division of labor do not so much disappear as alter. The skilled technician of "labor" and the trained engineer of "management" have more in common with each other than either has with their traditional classes. This process of redefinition of work roles is far from complete, and may even be said to be in a nascent stage. Nonetheless, the traditional systems of stratification have proceeded far enough along revolution for some general features of yet a third stage in development to be examined.

As for the new features of development, they seem implicit in what has already been said. Emphasis is now placed on redefining social relationships in terms of "functional" ties rather than "class" antagonism. But more than that, the achievement process is accompanied by a rise in autonomous relations between people rather than integrated factory or office relations. The place of work becomes an accidental property of urban living, rather than the reason for the urbanization process. Urban life does not consolidate class affiliation; rather, it relates the individual worker to matters outside his work. Workers are linked to one another, and develop what Durkheim called solidarity, not through factory life as such but in terms of their skills. Scientists exhibit a concern for their profession, and not for the institution in which their work is carried on. What this means is that the advanced stages of development reveal professional competence as a prime condition of work mobility. The higher the degree of professionalization, the less the attachment to any particular place of work; and, conversely, the fewer the professional skills individuals possess, the greater their institutional concern. The degree of movement resulting from a change of job is indicative of the acceleration of social *mobility* in the advanced stages of development. Marginal affiliations are characteristic of the modern period.

What then happens to invidious distinctions in a world where "achievement" values prevail? This is a highly speculative question. The answers, however tentative, appear quixotic. There seems to be a return to a fourth "saturation" stage. Problems which were supposedly transcended at earlier stages of development reappear. The process of social mobility has clearly not eliminated social stratification. Indeed, the stratification of men through skill and "knowledge" becomes increasingly difficult to maintain and gives way to stratification through ascription.

To an extraordinary degree the search for status differentiation falls back on racial and religious dimensions. In an advanced stage of industrial development, Germany was witness to an incredible outpouring of religious hatred that led to mass genocide. The United States now exhibits problems between Negro and white that would seem to make most class struggles appear tame by comparison. In short, industrialization is not a homogeneous item acting on all other variables.

What is more, the achievement of industrial abundance is not an automatic guarantee that all sectors of society are going to share it equally. That is why political struggles become sharper than ever. The choice between capitalist and socialist sectors is essentially reduced to a decision as to who can best manage the affairs of state. Economic production is increasingly subject to political control. Who then is to manipulate whom? The political platform concerned with management rights or workers' salaries simply misses the point at this stage. Parties increasingly come to win support through their public attitudes on racial equality, religious toleration, immigration policies, etc. Social mobility increasingly depends on the political manipulation of the symbols of ascription. Questions of achievement cease to be points of friction. This then is the paradox. The developmental process has gone far enough to upset new found individual attitudes. It can add a new variety to old ascriptive systems by intensifying group competition and shattering the individual seeking a "solid place" in the established system.

The persistence of values of ascription once achievement standards are more or less realized may be indicative of the general state of normlessness in the advanced nations. There is a growing search for forms of political control that can be said to overcome the inherited forms of stratification systems. The change from a natural market economy to a planned economy may help settle problems of achievement motivation, but it scarcely touches the rationalization of society in terms of ascriptive values. For that reason, it must be said that development is basically an ongoing process rather than a fact. Development is no panacea. Industrialism does not put an end to human conflict. An increase in the velocity of change will accelerate conflict.[10] It is utopian in the extreme

---

[10] For a most interesting speculative thrust into the special "phases" and "multiple levels" (double orientation) of development, see Alain Touraine, "Sociologie du développement," *Sociologie du Travail*, Vol. 5, No. 2, April-June 1963, pp. 156-74.

for a nation to embark on the path of industrial development in the hope of ending social struggle and political rivalries.

It is necessary to realize that the "risks" of development remain firmly intact, while there is a great increase in the number of people willing to take risks to achieve social status. The risks are worth the price only if a higher premium is placed on social transformation than on stability. The enthusiasm for the new is a contemporary Western value. It ill behooves us therefore either to condemn others for over-throwing their forms of traditionalism, or to sanction only those models which have been tried (satisfactorily or otherwise) elsewhere.

Risk-Taking and Policy-Making

It would be an oversimplification to view risk-taking exclusively in terms of willingness to upset inherited culture patterns. For instance, there is the question of the relative ease with which Cuba resolved the "religious problem" and Hungary's relative difficulty. Catholicism in Hungary has been a long-standing force and deeply embedded in the nation's traditions, while it has never gained a strong foothold in Cuba because the Vatican sent Spanish priests unconnected with the problems of Cuban society. Hence, the risks must be measured against tolerable loss.

Soon after a new nation has obtained relative independence from the old colonial power, it is faced with a number of policy-making alternatives: (a) maintenance of a favorable balance of trade with the former colonial overseer—which carries with it the danger of aborting social development and hence creating instability; (b) pursuance of a thoroughly independent financial and trading policy, which means entering the Third World—which can abort social development through denying the country the capital goods and basic technological needs which can only be supplied by the fully developed areas; and (c) passage over into the "socialist bloc" directly (or conversely, from the "socialist bloc" into either a neutralist or capitalist bloc), which can abort social development through external military aggression or the prospects of further civil conflicts. The alienation of sectors within the newly formed national units is increasingly under the weight of industrial and commercial specialization.

The "simple" process of development runs grave risks no matter how smoothly internal transition takes place. For the very entrance of a new nation into the developmental race is bound to have serious consequences for established power and trade equilibriums. That is why the Third World slogan appears to be: seek ye first the political kingdom and the rest shall follow. It is not possible to understand the rise of a Third World as such without realizing that this is a melange of nations arriving in a world turning on American-led or Soviet-led blocs.

Thus a series of Third World nations have attempted to enter the modern economic world by minimizing political risks. The fact is, of course, that variations of capitalist and socialist patterns are quite possible given the historic peculiarities of Asia and Africa. Bureaucratic militarism (Nasserism in Egypt, Sukarno in Indonesia) imposing a custodial socialism from above is an increasingly growing trend. On the other hand, a "semi-private" agricultural sector in Yugoslavia exists within a largely socialist framework. But these are interregnums, intermediary conditions which move in the direction of basic public-sector or private-sector economies. The question of risk-taking and policy-making entails fundamental decisions as to the direction of a social system.

The greatest confusion seems to result from failing to distinguish differences between political strategies and economic structures. Too many Third World leaders tend to make pious declarations about having created new forms of "national" economic behavior; and too few are prepared to admit the actual economic character of their regimes. Such an "admission" may itself entail serious risks. When Cuba announced its goals as governed by Marxism, or when Egypt, India, and Guinea made similar pronouncements about being socialist, each nation ran the risk of being excluded from traditional trading and loan privileges. It must be concluded that development in underdeveloped areas tends strongly to be socialistic because planning is itself a consequence of the self-awareness of development.[11] But the need to avoid internal political upheaval ensures non-involvement in East-West struggles as a long-term fact of national development in the new nations.[12]

[11] Cf. Karl Mannheim, *Freedom, Power, and Democratic Planning.* New York: Oxford University Press, 1950, esp. pp. 41-76.
[12] Cf. Kwame Nkrumah, *Building a Socialist State.* Accra: Government Printer, 1961; and also, *I Speak of Freedom.* New York: Frederick Praeger, 1962.

The extent to which a new nation is willing to take risks is directly related to its social wealth. It is increasingly clear that a rough equation can be used: the greater the wealth of a nation, the fewer risks it feels necessary to take; while the lower the level of development, the more risks are necessary to reach parity with others. This high-low risk ratio is subject to modifications. For example, it appears that, despite the bellicose language of the Chinese Communist regime, its actual political policies have been quite cautious in relation to the off-shore islands, i.e. Taiwan. Nonetheless, it is generally valid that the poorer a nation is the more it is likely to resort to force and violence, and even war, to reach parity with surrounding states.

Because of this the struggle for development no longer shapes up as a struggle between capitalist bloc and socialist bloc nations, but rather a conflict between have and have-not nations—that is, between nations which have a great deal to lose in any international conflict and those which, though they might prefer pacific solutions, would risk outright conflict rather than stagnation. The virtues of battle are enhanced over those of rule. Albert Hourani has put the matter well:

> The new States find themselves faced with the interests and pressure of the Great Powers, and also with neighbors who, although no Great Powers, in the strict sense, may still be great in proportion to them. What is more important, they are touched by new ideas, by that new ideology of economic and social development which is taking the place of the ideology of nationalism, or else giving it new content. It is only through economic development, the modern world believes, that nations can be strong and economically united; only a developing State can be morally healthy and united. So the problem is still that of strength, and of the social and political virtues which are inseparably connected with strength.[13]

In addition, the rapid nature of development tends to postpone settlement of issues relating to war and peace or capitalism and socialism; a type of national egoism comes into play which connects political invincibility with economic development. The remarkable recovery of the

13 Albert Hourani, "Revolutionary Nationalism," in *History and Hope: Progress in Freedom*, edited by K. A. Jelenski. London: Routledge and Kegan Paul, 1962, pp. 106-7.

French economy between 1955 and 1963 did not necessarily lead to lowering the risks—since development is comparative in all things. France sought parity in the thermonuclear race no less than in the industrial race. Thus, the paradox is that the simple quantitative growth in national productivity and styles of life is hardly an assurance of international security. The Third World has been in the forefront of efforts to pacify the thermonuclear balance of terror. Whether this is a temporary condition, occasioned by the military powerlessness of the new nations, or a permanent part of developmental ideology, remains a question for the future.

Imbalance Between Life Styles and Industrial Styles

The disparity between levels of personal living and levels of industrial productivity is a complex matter of marketing. There is an increasing disparity between the domestic and foreign markets for industrial goods produced in Third World areas. In the take-off period, the industrialization process is sustained by the high needs of the internal population, but as the market expands there, the country often finds itself unable to sell off its excess to foreign markets—particularly to advanced countries. The economy sinks into a condition of stagnation, while the population becomes increasingly conditioned to higher living standards as something coterminous with the evolution of the industrial process as such. Thus, at the very point when the industrial population is conditioned to high levels of production and consumption, the industrial plant is compelled to make cut-backs in its productivity.

Lacking this momentum for sustaining a high rate of productivity, the Third World nation is compelled into a cycle of borrowing capital on a large scale, if for no other purpose than to sustain the levels in life-styles already achieved or to satisfy expected, but unfulfilled, demands placed upon the economy by its population. In brief, where capitalism exists there is extreme competition for markets. Under free enterprise conditions, the disadvantages of coming last are most apparent. And given the fact that the population is not geared to sacrifice for "the next generation," nor willing to be coerced as in the process of socialist development, the contradiction between the levels of social living and those of industrialization become increasingly severe. Under such circumstances the nation is likely either to return to a heavy emphasis on the agricultural sector or to seek economic aid and commercial markets outside of the leading capitalist-bloc nations. In either event, complete self-determination is implausible as long as external markets determine the character of social production.

This process—combined as it is with continued agricultural backwardness, inadequate investment in public-sector enterprises, and the over-emphasis on one part of the industrial base (the consumer-oriented) —brings the economic system to an impasse. The ways to break this impasse are discussed elsewhere. We need note, however, the ways in which advanced capitalist nations might be of service: vigorous efforts on the part of the United States and Western Europe to open their markets to trade exports from the Third World countries, foreign technical assistance in the modernization of plant operations, but without strings, and a self-imposed screening by the leading powers of their own private-enterprise foreign holdings. All of these assume a degree of economic free will which is nowhere to be found, except in economic textbooks. Whether or not it is theoretically possible to construct a model in which the advanced capitalist states surrender part of their economic monopoly on international trade is quite beside the point. The point is that they simply do not operate this way; whether because of "laws of the market" or of subjectively perceived interests is immaterial. The effect on the Third World countries of their economic monopoly is to increase the gap between levels of personal living and levels of industrial output— tailored for an internal market, and funded by foreign capital. A problem inevitably arises when repayment of debts comes up on the agenda—as it invariably must. A choice has to be made by both contracting parties (the advanced and the underdeveloped nation) as to what should be done.

As long as the answer from the advanced nation is to extend the credit line, the *status quo* can be maintained. But when some monetary crisis (or other crisis) occurs, no more credits are forthcoming until the underdeveloped nation agrees to co-operate with the creditor nation. Then the Third World nation can either acquiesce and run the risk of revolution from below (since such downward mobility is often unacceptable to the urban proletariat and to certain bureaucratic and middle sectors as well); or resist such pressures, issue a debt cancellation notice, and provoke (or induce) a revolution from above—which runs the risk of foreign invasion, warfare, blockades, etc.[14] In either event, it is clear that as long as the present gap between consumer demands and production potential continues to widen, there can be no stabilization in the Third World—and certainly no stabilization based on the simple expansion of technological innovation and industrial growth.

The Imbalance Between Industrial Availabilities and Educational Achievements

Public opinion in the advanced nations holds that revolutionaries and Communists are bred by poverty and ignorance. They therefore strongly believe that educational achievement is a necessary precondition for genuine social change. Indeed, the entire Alliance for Progress has as its chief goal the manufacture of social content through higher levels of educational achievement. Actually, such educational orientations have the reverse effect. As a result of higher and more specialized education, there is a corresponding rise in expectations. And the inability of most underdeveloped societies to fulfill these expectations creates an acute awareness of the gap between work capacity and work available.

What has developed in the most literate portions of Latin America, especially in Argentina and Brazil, is that educational levels have increased significantly in each generation, while at the same time there has been relative stagnation in the economic and productive centers. The lack of fulfillment in career expectations thus creates a revolutionary climate. For in the cultures of poverty there is a relative balance between life expectations and life-styles. Those who reside in the *favelas* in Rio or in the *Villas Miseria* outside of Buenos Aires may have to face untold hardships and horrors. But since skilled labor remains relatively content, there is small hope for any link between the skilled classes and the lower classes.

---

[14] For an extremely interesting account of this phenomenon of structural gap between living styles and industrial exports, see David Felix, "Monetarists, Structuralists, and Import Substituting Industrialization." Prepared for the Rio de Janeiro Conference on Inflation and Growth, January 3-11, 1963. *Studies in Comparative International Development*, Vol. 1, No. 10, 1965, pp. 137-53.

On the other hand, where work possibilities far outstrip educational levels of achievement, the bottleneck thus created leads to a frustration which can only be solved by a revolutionary overhauling of the social structure. Plans for massive educational reform are best realized in societies capable of mobilizing and integrating vast sectors of the "masses." A high productive capacity without a corresponding broad program of education leaves the society without the skilled personnel for the conduct of its affairs. Thus, the production and education spheres must be meshed with one another.

Actually imbalance as such not only serves as a bottleneck to social development but as a trigger for redressing this condition. Indeed, it is evident that structural imbalance is a causative base for revolution-making. In the developing areas it is the university students (in conditions of low productivity and occupational stagnation) and bureaucratic officials (in conditions of low educational standards and massive illiteracy) who form the backbone of radical and revolutionary movements. This is not merely a phenomenon native to any social class or occupational group; it is not a manifestation of "working-class authoritarianism" or "middle-class revolutionism."

The presence of high illiteracy rates or the absence of work opportunities for the would-be professional cannot be isolated from the special kind of "mis-education" that occurs in many underdeveloped countries, especially those of long standing who have been influenced strongly by aristocratic tastes and philosophic concerns. This produces an anti-industrial bias; education too is not geared for industrial concepts of professional training, still harkening back to educating a conversationally stimulating, cultivated leisure class. This deepens the crisis of using "manpower" with advanced degrees.

One writer on Latin American affairs, William S. Stokes, has singled out the *pensadores* (the thinkers) as particularly responsible for, and reflective of, this mis-education. While the problem can probably not be pinpointed so specifically, his information should give pause to those who think that educational growth is indispensable to economic growth. He devised a sample which included thirteen universities from eight Latin American countries, plus the figures for all colleges and universities of Brazil, for the years 1950 through 1952. His findings were as follows:

The total number of students in all of these universities was 82,135, out of which 45,540 or almost 66½ percent were in law, medicine, and engineering. Law, medicine, and engineering were the top three choices in Brazil (composite figures for 115 colleges and universities) and in 9 out of the other 13 universities in the sample. There were 30 schools of law in Brazil with 11,455 students and only 12 schools of agriculture with 1,188 students, a ratio of almost 10 law students to each student in agriculture. There were only 539 students studying veterinary science in all of Brazil. Argentina depends on agriculture and stock raising for a large part of its national income, yet at the Universidad Nacional de la Plata, there were in 1956 2,169 students in Juridical and Social Science and only 62 students in agronomy and 42 students in Veterinary Science.[15]

The educated classes in many Third World nations with a long tradition of independence combined with fixed class and status composition have an expressed belief that leisure is superior to work and that abstract ideas are more important than technical ability. In this way, entire communities are keyed to seek sinecures, to obtain shorter work schedules without any corresponding improvement in work styles, and in general to avoid heavy labor whenever and wherever this is possible. Persistent inflationary spirals, the absence of any reasons for savings, and the unstable character of political behavior all serve to reduce the effectiveness of the educated classes.

Having established standards for living the life of ideas and eschewing the life of labor, the intelligentsia is faced with a growing demand for the products of the latter, without any desire to participate in their creation. Thus, there is an effort to capture the developmental process as a whole and hope that Providence will provide what the educational elite cannot—an advanced and modern form of industrial life in an intellectual climate of pre-capitalist techniques and post-capitalist ideologies. Unfortunately, the elite is ensnared by a double-bind of traditionalism and utopianism.[16]

[15] William S. Stokes, "The 'Pensadores' of Latin America," in *The Intellectuals*, ed. by George B. de Huszar. Glencoe, Ill.: The Free Press, 1960, p. 426.
[16] Cf. Irving Louis Horowitz, "The Philosophy of History in Latin America," *History and Theory: Studies in the Philosophy of History*, Vol. 11, No. 1, 1962, pp. 85-9.

Latin America is not unique in its emphasis on the relatively low status of manual labor or business pursuits. The same is true of such Moslem nations as Turkey, Syria, Iraq, and Iran. Despite the resourcefulness of these peoples, their educational leadership undermines efforts at development by assigning a special priority to ideas separated from technology. The fact is that the Middle East did have a long tradition in the practical sciences throughout the medieval period. Once Western concepts of mechanization reached Middle Eastern society to be promulgated by the educational elite, then the attitude toward manual labor changed. Tragically, the gap between scientific technology and the educational vistas of the leisure class grow further apart, rather than closer together. Bernard Lewis has put the matter in the following manner:

> Medicine, engineering, and other useful sciences were taught at the very first military schools; scientific treatises were among the first Western works translated into Turkish and Arabic—but many medical graduates preferred to become administrators rather than soil their hands with patients, and the scientific schools remained alien and exotic growths, in need of constant care and renewed graftings from the West. There has been no real development of original scientific work, such as exists in Japan, China, or India, and each generation of students must draw again from the sources in the West, which has meanwhile itself been making immense progress. The result is that the disparity in scientific knowledge, technological capacity, and therefore of military power between the Middle East and the advanced countries of the West is greater now than a hundred or fifty years ago, when the whole process of Westernization began.[17]

That every major twentieth-century revolutionary regime has found itself moving away from ideological orientations to technological application and that such reorientations have often taken on the bizarre form of a struggle between the humanistic and scientific traditions can be attributed to the historic process of mis-education.

We might sum up this point as follows: the initial problem in most Third World countries is an ignorance bred of illiteracy and a lack of

[17] Bernard Lewis, "The Middle East versus the West," *Encounter*, Vol. XXI, No. 4, whole number 121, October 1963, p. 28.

training. The second problem is that, once a basic educational framework has been established, the forces of ascription and the general low state of social mobility serve to impede the utilization of education to the fullest extent possible. And the final point is that the process of education is often impeded by the value structure and favorable social position of the educator—who imbues the entire society with an orientation and ideology which is at once revolutionary in phraseology and reactionary in content; that is, it serves to prevent the development of a sound and balanced technological development, while at the same time demanding revolutionary changes which presuppose a relatively abundant material culture.

The Imbalance Between Political and Economic Development

Development of a mature political structure does not necessarily entail economic development; and similarly, there are many cases of economic development taking place in a stunted polity. Argentina, for example, has the highest per capita output in Latin America. It is the only nation in Latin America which can be said to have relatively few feudal "hangovers." Yet Argentina suports a political structure in keeping with much of Latin America. It has a strong centralized military authority which functions as a political "stabilizer" and "formulator," much as it does in parts of the non-developing portions of the hemisphere. On the other hand, Bolivia, which until recently had a relatively democratic political structure exhibiting direct worker participation in the decision-making process, remains the poorest of nations, only exceeded by Paraguay in low productive yields, and exceeding all other nations in the amount of foreign aid per person it receives from the United States.

Coalescences of political maturity and economic development are unusual. This destroys the idea that economics is a "base" and politics the "super-structure." If anything, the recent Third World pattern is to develop a political apparatus which is in a position to impose order and independence on the economy. Only through political agencies can planning commissions be organized; only through the exercise of political coercion can economic expropriation and redistribution be initiated. It will be noted that political maturity is not equivalent to political coercion—indeed, dependence on the coercive apparatus of a state demonstrates the absence of voluntary reorganization and of a common consensus.

This whole problem can be seen most clearly in the victory of Bolshevism, a political victory in an underdeveloped nation.

Stalinism identified socialism with internationalism only in theory. In practice, socialism and nationalism were celebrated. Communism became anathema in the West not through its intrinsic concepts—for such beliefs were ancient and honorable even in the United States throughout the nineteenth century. The animus was derived from assuming that building state socialism in one backward nation was synonymous in itself with socialist ideals and values. On the other hand, capitalism is not anathema in itself, but rather in the assumption that capitalism and the interests of the United States (and earlier Western Europe) are synonymous. Thus, any defense of capitalism as an economy clearly has come to signify a defense of the United States. And this is not an easy defense to make, given the history of United States diplomatic and economic relations with the new nations.

The matter of the relationship between nationalism and socialism is most delicate. To say the "simple" truth, that they are not the same and may require different agencies and instrumentalities for their respective realization, does not say much about their interaction.

As a rule, the early stages of developmental impetus can and usually do elicit the whole-hearted support of all major sectors of the underdeveloped area involved. When the focus is on eliminating foreign capital and turning a heterogeneous mass into a homogeneous nation, it is politically superficial to raise the dangers and threats of nationalization to the socialist polity, or for that matter, the dangers of socialism for nationalization. At this level, the "common enemy" is external, and hence the imbalance between economic and political development hardly manifests itself. The problem for the political leadership is one of *animating* the total population rather than *coercing* any one sector of the people.

After the successful conclusion of this initial stage, no guarantees exist that the political apparatus will be marshaled to support any particular economic system. Indeed, the tendency toward an economic mix between capitalist and socialist formations is quite strong. Israel, which gained its independence in 1948, and which also at that time had a powerfully socialist-oriented (if not dominated) labor and agricultural sector, has since then moved increasingly toward promoting private investments from abroad, and in manufacturing a domestic bourgeoisie— all in the name of national security and strength. Indonesia, which also gained its independence after World War Two, has shown a different pattern—one which has increasingly moved toward the socialization of the nation—through military intervention from above more than through mass political pressures from below. The fact remains that Indonesia shows that socialism is much more a goal to be striven for *after*, rather than before, the nationalistic revolutionary phase is concluded.

Clearly, one central reason why the Third World is not under constant attack or criticism from the major power blocs, East and West, is the simple fact that the nationalist phase of the revolution is still incomplete, and hence the new nations are potentially compatible with either capitalist or socialist economic formations. But one thing will not do: for socialist or capitalist supporters to identify the process of national liberation as belonging to them by definition. The *ralliement* necessary for national revolution is something quite different from the class differentiation entailed in a socialist revolution.

The question of how one "approaches" the developing nations of Africa, Asia, and South America is therefore a good deal more complex than it initially appears. "Men of good will" might cheer the rise of national sovereignty, but these same men might be genuinely apprehensive about the "Balkanization" of Africa. Would "men of good will," who are also men of capitalist enterprise, appreciate the rise of anti-imperialist and anti-bourgeois spirit in the new nations? And might not "men of good will" deplore the displacement of foreign capital investment by an inferior, and possibly harsher, domestic bourgeoisie, willing to seal off the new nation from foreign competition and willing to minimize the country's industrial nationalization program?

In part the problem is not quite as insoluble as it first appears to be. In the first place, nationalism and socialism are in fact linked in many of the new nations. Hence the imbalance between political ambitions and economic structure is not quite as pronounced as might be the case were socialists to adopt an "internationalist" or "one-world" ideology prior to the completion of the national liberation period. In the second place, certain archaic forms of economic production are simply not feasible for new nations with low levels of capitalist accumulation— the state must by necessity if not by choice have to go into "business." It may have to nationalize petroleum, coal, oil, and chemical industries, if it is to have such industries at all. The likelihood is that only the political apparatus can command the degree of capital and human wealth necessary to enter the modern industrial world—and in this sense, the politics of nationalism may very likely promote socialist economic structures. Mali's Minister of Development, Seydou Kouyate, has put the matter crisply:

> As a matter of fact, the political organization has been the melting-pot where the peasant and the city dweller have met. It has pulled the former out of his isolation, cured the latter of his disdain for the bush, and achieved practically the national unity from which it was drawing its strength. Thus, the gap which existed between the city and the countryside has been filled up and the various strata of the population have been unified into one single stream oriented toward the political objectives.[18]

In the third place, nationalism itself has an "open sesame" effect; that is, forms of economic experimentation are possible after a revolution that are not possible without one or even during one. Economic determination is quite out of the question. The issue is not which form of economy can best promote development, but the nationalization process which will allow development to take place at all.

It might well be that development is another word for internationalism—for the co-operation between states and regional clusters which can only be completely realized when nationalism has broken down. But since to phase in a developmental take-off in the first place means to have gone through some kind of national revolution, the nation as symbol attains an importance which makes impossible its supercession to more rational international organization. To move from colonial status to being part of the comity of liberated men simply through a process of self-liquidation on the part of the established imperial powers is pleasant but wishful thinking. It is a paradox that nationalism, which is the

---

[18] Seydou Kouyate, quoted in "Dakar Colloquium: Search for Definition," *Africa Report*, Vol. 8, No. 5, May 1963, pp. 15-16.

supreme protagonist of internationalism, is at the same time its necessary precondition. On the other side, it might be that stage-skipping is not possible in the economic sector either. An extensive period of national exploitation may well replace the period of colonial exploitation—through the development of a powerful political apparatus which extracts a higher productivity from the labor force (usually in the name of socialism) than was possible under colonial conditions.

Nationalism as such makes possible a degree of self-exploitation that is out of the question in the colonial period. As the brilliant Frantz Fanon has pointed out:

> The colonized bourgeoisie which comes to power uses its class aggressiveness to take over the positions previously held by strangers. It brandishes energetically the notion of the nationalization of cadres . . . On their side, the town proletariat, the mass of unemployed, the small artisans, side with this nationalist attitude.[19]

They side with the national bourgeoisie because, in some special sense, the bourgeoisie itself is highly "socialized." Just as in the West there is the "bourgeoisification" of the working classes, so in the new nation there is the "proletarianization" of the bourgeoisie. Africa has had a noticeable absence of the classic view of class struggles, and hence believes that coercion can be minimized in the process of development. Socialism itself is redefined to include the national bourgeoisie. The word comes to mean "an appeal for a common effort."[20] Even if we discount the rhetorical aspects of such a definition, it must be appreciated that the newer nations see that the imbalance between politics and economics can be eliminated by a common identification with social development as such. As Sekou Touré put the matter in relation to Africa: "There exists only one and the same class, that of the dispossessed."[21]

At the empirical level development depends heavily on the extent

[19] Frantz Fanon, *Les Damnés de la terre*. Paris: Maspero Cahiers Libres, 1961, p. 118. On this same subject, see Manfred Halpern, *The Politics of Social Change in the Middle East and North Africa*. Princeton: Princeton University Press, 1963.

[20] Cf. A. Fenner Brockway, *African Socialism*. London: Bodley Head, 1963.

[21] Cf. Sekou Touré, *Expérience Guinéenne et Unité Africaine*. Paris: Présence Africaine, 1961.

to which economic and political forces can be mobilized in a common effort to free a people, a community, or even a continent from traditional imperial fetters. And we must not forget that by being willing to await events the more developed areas may provide immeasurable aid to the newly developed areas in the settlement of the latter's policy questions and economic structures.

The Contest Between Liberty and Equality

Perhaps the ultimate duality in the Third World as it is now constituted is the deadly competition between liberty and equality. The French Enlightenment and the French and American Revolutions announced the fusion of these two concepts, of the principle of personal liberty and of mass equality. Utilitarianism was to supply the ideological cement through which the one and the many, the person and the society, were to act as mutual reinforcements.[22]

The international schism within the democratic tradition expressed itself through the contrary roads taken by two economic systems, capitalism and socialism. The "moral economy" of each was hardened into an ideological controversy over man's essential nature: the "natural egotism" of men became identified with the forms of capitalist production, while the "altruism" of "socialist man" became identified with socialism. The fact that neither egotism nor altruism had much to do with the development of either capitalism or socialism—that in fact, all sorts of emotional components entered the picture—was forgotten in the process. A veritable barrage of moralistic rhetoric cascaded forth, as if private appropriation or commodity production was in itself the guardian of personal egotism, and as if the state appropriation of commodity production was itself the ultimate in socialism. The appeal to "human nature" became encased in the respective industrial ideologies of the East and West—and what was lost was the common problems faced by industrial societies.

[22] On this contest between liberty and equality see J. L. Talmon, *The Origins of Totalitarian Democracy*. London: Secker & Warburg, 1954; Hannah Arendt, *On Revolution*. New York: The Viking Press, 1963; Irving L. Horowitz, *Radicalism and the Revolt Against Reason*. London: Routledge and Kegan Paul Ltd., 1961; and Alvin W. Gouldner, *Enter Plato*. New York: Basic Books, 1965.

This schism between egotism and altruism, between capitalist and socialist ideologies, initiated the present competition between liberty and equality—between liberalism and socialism, and between John Stuart Mill and Karl Marx. It was the modern myth of the eternal return, fused with the metaphysical problem of the one and the many—the individual and the collective as contrasting styles of judgment. What the late nineteenth-century debates disguised was the essential similarity at the economic level between industrial societies. The problems faced by the American and his European counterpart are after all quite similar: the kind of allocation desirable, the need for horizontal or vertical industrial integration, the problem of forced spending and forced savings, etc.

The growth of the Third World has finally put all these problems into perspective. Indeed, it has been the Third World which has made plain the fact that the socialist system of economy is not a consequence of advanced capitalist production but a direct path from backwardness to modernity, unmediated and unencumbered by the baggage of industrial history. It has been the Third World which has made the leviathans of both East and West realize that the way they had divided the world ideologically was no longer universally acceptable. The conflict between capitalism and socialism gave way, under the steady push and pull of new nations, to a new definition of the competition between liberty and equality—one based on the differences which still exist between rich nation-states and poor nation-states. Each new nation has faced the same dilemma between libertarian and equalitarian modes of life. The only clear point now known is that there are no automatic solutions. Liberty is not a consequence of voting privileges, nor is equality a consequence of affluence. Voting rights and economic abundance may prevail in an atmosphere sorely lacking in both liberty and equality. This is the sobering reality each new nation must face as it enters the period of industrial acceleration.

Chapter 12

Consensus and Dissensus in Social Development

I

Symmetry is the decisive word for the big nuclear powers. Asymmetry is the decisive word for the non-nuclear Third World powers. War remains as real in the nuclear era as in the pre-nuclear era. The dangers may be greater since many of the Third World nations act on the assumption that they can move freely in full confidence that the nuclear stalemate guarantees unlimited action. When neither optimism nor fear is mutual, when a real advantage would accrue to the agggressive nation, then the very condition of military disequilibrium is itself a factor in war-making. And no factor would create a politically unbalanced condition more rapidly or completely than an abandonment of prudence and intelligence on the part of some Third World nations—who, from the viewpoint of the Cold War, are potential nth powers. Yet, what can a nation like India or Algeria do? Forfeit its national sovereignty? The main foreign policy dilemma of Third World countries is how to maintain independence and sovereignty in a competitive nuclear context which views with suspicion and alarm any noticeable shift in the international balance of power.

Social development, involving the destruction of traditional power relations and power matrices, necessarily raises with increasing urgency the question of conflict and conflict resolution. While there is a broad recognition that international peace is a basic requirement of social development, it is less well understood that the price of one is sometimes purchased at the cost of the other.[1] However "inter-related" world de-

[1] Cf. Thomas C. Schelling, *The Strategy of Conflict*. Cambridge: Harvard University Press, 1960.

364

velopment and world peace may be, they are neither historical nor conceptual equivalents.

Rapid social development has in the past been accompanied not only by widespread economic and political upheaval, but also by wars affecting large numbers of people. The demand for social change in the Third World has been materially assisted by the transfer of the locus of military action to their sphere. The very fact that power now "cancels out" is a stimulant to further extensive social change.[2] In other words, dissensus, while dysfunctional with respect to the ruling powers, is quite functional for the newly emergent nations.

While social development has become more greatly desired than ever before, warfare has become a less viable instrument for producing changes.[3] In its most fundamental meaning, war has become obsolescent, since the possibility of one side emerging victorious has been obviated by the fact of massive retaliation—by the capacity of each side to annihilate the other. Thus, the problem of social development urgently requires a reconsideration of the basic forms of human co-operation, or, in the language of military analysts, human bargaining.[4] It takes little imagination to construct a utopia in which war could be eliminated. All that is required is a consensual picture of the world in which there are no "sides," but only one side—enthusiastically underwritten by the whole of mankind. The really complicated problem is how to live in a world of "sides," in a world in which the power equilibrium is constantly changing through the creation of yet new "sides."

The problem can be stated as follows: when there is little or no active social development, and if a single power can impose a widespread dominion, then a Caesaristic consensus obtains in the absence of abrasive and fragmenting forces. When there is rapid social development, and no single power can assert a "universal" dominion, then an intense conflict pattern obtains. When there is rapid social development, and if the major powers can agree upon the rules for the conduct of international affairs, then a co-operation (programmed conflict + programmed

[2] Cf. Kenneth E. Boulding, *Conflict and Defense: A General Theory*. New York: Harper & Row, 1962; and Anatol Rapoport, *Fights, Games and Debates*. Ann Arbor: University of Michigan Press, 1960.

[3] Cf. Irving L. Horowitz, *Games, Strategies and Peace*. Philadelphia: American Friends Service Committee, 1963.

[4] Cf. Hannah Arendt, *On Revolution*. New York: Viking Press, 1963.

consensus) pattern obtains. Hence consensus, or an internal agreement in principle on the forms of social action, is most unlikely in its present form. But any further social development through armed struggles is no less unlikely, since conflict patterns on any large scale are likely to prove mutually destructive and hence mutually untenable. This leaves us with the problem of how the world is to co-operate or bargain when some nations insist on the absolute primacy of social change *even at the expense of life itself*. Neither conflict nor consensus has been able to contain the impulse toward development—for both are total concepts and total commitments in a world of partial commitments.

The idea that world hegemony can be achieved, either through pacific or military means, must be placed in the context of the uneven nature of development.[5] Even if the world were unified into an international economy, peace would not be assured. The increasing military competition of capital nations for the last three hundred years substantiates this point. And now we have the additional evidence that the socialist bloc is no less competitive among its members. Even if the world were uniformly socialist in nature, peace would likewise not be assured. This classic claim of socialist theorists has been snapped decisively by the rise of polycentric forms of Communism. The competition between China and the Soviet Union is clearly quite as intense as any in the capitalist world. Indeed, the very fact that socialism claims it can create a new and tolerable world hegemony makes the conflict within the Soviet bloc even more bitter than anything in the West; for here many divergencies do exist if only because capitalism is based upon competition and freedom in trade, commerce, and politics.

As patterns of consensus and conflict have mutually canceled one another out, there remain great possibilities for planned co-operation. The right to be different has become as necessary to a nation as it once was to the individual. And this right to be different, once institutionalized in world law and in agreements covering such matters as travel in outer space and off-shore limits, makes possible unimpeded social development which emerging societies require, and which the past concentration on consensus and/or conflict patterns has seriously stifled.

[5] Gino Germani, *Política y Sociedad en un Época de Transición*. Buenos Aires: Editorial Paidós, 1962, pp. 98-109.

II

There are at least seven shades of meaning which currently attach to the term "consensus" beyond the common-sense usage of the word as a proper synonym for agreement among people. First and perhaps most commonly, it is defined as "adjustment of social dissension." This usage is borrowed from the present psychoanalytic definition of normality as social adjustment and neurosis as the failure of adjustment.[6] The second view begins with role theory. Consensus is seen as an accord between role behavior and role expectation.[7] The third position, while having a point of contact with an adjustment approach to consensus, lifts it out of the individual realm into a cultural framework. "Where an opinion is very widely held and cuts across all groups in society," there you have consensus.[8] The fourth theory sees the term as affiliated to a hedonistic impulse, as "possible only when two or more parties want to maintain a relationship which each regards as in its own interest."[9] A cognate definition is offered by the same writer in terms of game theory: "Two parties or groups are playing to gain a maximum, but they are prepared to settle for less within the recognized limits."[10] The sixth theory identifies consensus with curbing the hedonistic impulse and instinct, and with Durkheim's notion of solidarity and social cohesion generally.[11] Our last author sees consensus in its pure form as a sharing of perspective, as "nothing more or less than the existence on the part of two or more persons, of similar orientations toward something."[12] The concept of consensus has aroused such intense interest because it seems to satisfy

[6] J. O. Hertzler, *American Social Institutions: A Sociological Analysis.* Boston: Allyn and Bacon, 1961, p. 63.
[7] Neal Gross, "The Sociology of Education," in *Sociology Today: Problems and Prospects*, edited by R. K. Merton, L. Broom, L. S. Cottrell, Jr. New York: Basic Books, 1959, p. 140.
[8] Leonard Broom and Philip Selznick, *Sociology: A Text with Adapted Readings*, second edition. Evanston, Ill.: Row, Peterson & Co., 1958, p. 278.
[9] Arnold W. Green, *Sociology: An Analysis of Life in Modern Society*, third edition. New York: McGraw-Hill, 1960, p. 65.
[10] Ibid., p. 67.
[11] Ely Chinoy, *Society: An Introduction to Sociology.* New York: Random House, 1961, pp. 344-6.
[12] Theodore Newcomb, "The Study of Consensus," in *Sociology Today, op. cit.*, p. 279.

the requirements of both social equilibrium and social development. Most frequently consensus is identified with functional efficiency and with the social requisites of political democracy in advanced nations.[13] In its simplest form, this means that an increase in the amount of social consensus yields an increase in functional efficacy and democratic polity; while, inversely, a decrease in the amount of social consensus creates social disorganization and dissensus. On a broader front, advocates of censensus avoid the knotty issue of how conflicts arise by concentrating on how men achieve agreements "in principle." By defining the core of social action in terms of establishing a pattern of orientation and locating one or more situational objects—consensus comes to be equated with the maintenance of social equilibrium.[14]

Conflict theory suffers less from the problem of ambiguity, since the nature of conflict, being a more "positive" act, makes possible a clearer theoretical position. The early development of sociology from Marx to Simmel took as its point of departure the idea that society is best understood as a selective and collective response to the needs of social interaction in a "nonequilibrated" world. This involved a rejection, conscious or otherwise, of the idea that society rests upon a contractual or informal agreement made between equals to secure common goals.[15] Simmel sees the Roman Empire not as a union of the general will with particularized wills, but rather as an illustration of the efficiency, the functionality of political dissensus; what he terms "Caesaristic types of rule." Thus consensus consists only in the "tendency of domination by means of leveling." This apparent consensual apparatus is but disguised superordination. In discussing Philip the Good of Burgundy, he notes that "legal differences were created exclusively by the arbitrary pleasure of the ruler. They thus marked all the more distinctly the common, unalterable subordination of his subjects."[16]

13 Seymour M. Lipset, "Political Sociology," in Sociology Today, op. cit., p. 114.
14 Talcott Parsons, The Social System. Glencoe: The Free Press, 1951, p. 507. This same view is even more forcefully developed in his "The Point of View of the Author," The Social Theories of Talcott Parsons, edited by Max Black. Englewood Cliffs, N.J.: Prentice-Hall, 1961, p. 327.
15 For an excellent general statement of conflict theory, see Don Martindale, The Nature and Types of Sociological Theory. Boston: Houghton Mifflin Co., 1960, pp. 127-49.
16 Georg Simmel, "Subordination Under an Individual," The Sociology of Georg Simmel, edited and translated by K. H. Wolff. Glencoe: The Free Press, 1950, pp. 201-7.

Similarly for Marx, the economic system called capitalism does not come into existence because of the clamor of public opinion, or to express the general will, but simply to satisfy the historical process which brings a social class to power. The welding of such power to a new social class is the purpose of the state, which in turn enters the historical picture as the central agency of coercion while posing as the agency of social consensus.

The practical struggle of these particular interests, which constantly run counter to communal interests, both real and illusory, makes it necessary for the state to intervene and seize control. The social power, i.e. the multiplied productive force, which arises through the co-operation of different individuals as it is determined within the division of labor, appears to these individuals, since their co-operation is not voluntary but natural, not as their own united power, but as an alien force existing outside them, of the origin and end of which they are ignorant, which they thus cannot control.[17]

Seen from this viewpoint consensus appears as an idealized form of coercion. Modern expressions of conflict theory rest upon the fact that the social world exists in equilibrium as a consequence of conflict situations. The world is imperiled by threats, gambles, strategic moves, interdependent decisions, limited wars, etc. As Thomas Schelling notes:

> Though "strategy of conflict" sounds cold-blooded, the theory is not concerned with the efficient application of violence or anything of the sort; it is not essentially a theory of aggression or of resistance or of war . . . Such a theory is nondiscriminatory as between the conflict and the common interest, as between its applicability to potential enemies and its applicability to potential friends.[18]

In a broader sense, conflict theory strongly emphasizes dissensus and deviance because it has been focused on the problem of social change instead of on the nature of social structure. Conflict thus appears as the "motor force" or the "drive shaft" of the developmental process. As a result, the emphasis was then placed upon human agencies which would

[17] Karl Marx and Friedrich Engels, "The German Ideology," in *Basic Writings on Politics and Philosophy: Marx and Engels*, edited by L. S. Feuer. Garden City: Doubleday and Co., 1959, pp. 255-6, also p. 253.
[18] Thomas C. Schelling, *op. cit.*, p. 15.

perform such a role. For Marx, it was the urban proletariat; for Gumplo-
wicz, the ethnic minority transformed into a majority; and for Sorel, the
creative elite culled from the ranks of the exploited.[19] Obviously, the
very language of conflict involves a negation of integration, or at least a
postponement of the consideration of such matters. And this is the significant difference between various analysts of the development process
—for whether one accepts a consensus or a dissensus model in large measure determines how one fills the content of development with "social
forces" or "social engineering."

But conflict theory shares with consensus theory a faith in "two
player" situations. As such, their utility in meeting the challenge of the
Third World or of multi-national situations remains dubious. Formulations which start with *either* capitalism *or* socialism, *either* democracy
or autocracy, *either* West *or* East are a reflection of the "bilateralism"
in conflict theory. They have dubious relevance to those newly emerging
societies for which economic and political experimentation is a felt
necessity.

Critics have reacted to conflict theory by resurrecting "unilateral"
faiths. They have particularly relied upon the brilliant social historian
Alexis de Tocqueville.[20] The rallying point in de Tocqueville is the comment that "a society can exist only when a great number of men consider a great number of things from the same point of view; when they
hold the same opinion upon many subjects; when the same occurrences
suggest the same thought and impressions to their minds."[21] This would
seem to be the historical progenitor for the new theory of consensus, and
it would seem to be the rejoinder to those political sociologies which seek
to define social structure in terms of holders and seekers of power.

Perhaps the most widespread claim made by advocates of this theory
is that consensus is a necessary condition for social structure. Social

[19] Cf. Irving Louis Horowitz, *Radicalism and the Revolt Against Reason*. London: Routledge & Kegan Paul Ltd., 1961.
[20] Seymour M. Lipset, *Political Man: The Social Basis of Politics*. Garden City:
Doubleday and Co., 1960, pp. 26-8, 65-6. Lipset's continual juxtaposition of de
Tocqueville and Marx is a strong indication that the differences between consensus and conflict theories involve something more than scientific requirements.
Indeed, he has made them ideological poles: consensus representing democracy
and conflict representing authoritarianism.
[21] Alexis de Tocqueville, *Democracy in America*, trans. by H. Reeve. New York:
Century and Co., 1899, Vol. 1, p. 398.

structure has been seen to exclude those patterns of human action which are spontaneous.[22] Social structure is said to consist in a "set of statuses" defined by relatively stable relationships between people. Consensus and conflict thus appear as structured and unstructured modes of behavior respectively. Consensus involves a general acceptance of the authority of the group, common traditions and rules for inducting and indoctrinating new members; while conflict is seen as external to social structure, as spontaneity, impulsive action, lack of organization, and intuitive response to immediate situations.[23] In short, consensus differs from conflict as organization differs from deviance. Thus to discuss social structure is by definition not to examine conflict situations and, of course, to examine conflict situations is to discuss something extraneous to social structure.[24]

To place conflict outside the framework of social structure, or to go further and see dissensus as necessarily destructive of the social organism is to place a definite premium on social disequilibrium. It strongly implies that a society can be changed only by apocalyptic or spontaneous methods. The identification of consensus with social structure reinforces the stereotyped view that social development is inferentially synonymous with social chaos. Consensus theory thus tends to become a metaphysical representation of the fully developed societies, i.e. the "consensual society."[25] It rests on a principle of "general interests" which every member of every society is supposed to imbibe if he wishes to avoid the onus of being deviant with respect to his society. Such a view implies that social conflict necessarily produces a world of deviants quite incapable

[22] Cf. Paul F. Lazarsfeld, "Political Behavior and Public Opinion," in *The Behavioral Sciences Today*, edited by Bernard Berelson. New York: Basic Books, 1963, pp. 176-87.
[23] Cf. Robert E. Park, "Reflections on Communication and Culture," *The American Journal of Sociology*, XLIV, 1939, pp. 191-205.
[24] Kurt Lang and Gladys E. Lang, *Collective Dynamics*. New York: Thomas Y. Crowell Co., 1961, pp. 13-14. This is one of the few serious efforts at fusing a theory of social structure with the facts of social psychology and political movements. The pioneer effort in this direction was made by Herbert Blumer, "Collective Behavior, " in *New Outline of the Principles of Sociology*, edited by A. M. Lee. New York: Barnes & Noble, 1946.
[25] For example, the position taken by Edward A. Shils, in "The Calling of Sociology," *Theories of Society: Foundations of Modern Sociological Theory*, edited by T. Parsons, E. Shils, K. D. Naegele, J. R. Pitts. New York: The Free Press of Glencoe, 1961, pp. 1405-48.

of attending to problems of functional survival.[26] The possibility that different goals can be registered within a single functional agency, such as a unified national party, is too rarely entertained.[27]

A social structure might be considered as a dynamic balance of disharmonious parts. If we start from the real position of societies, it is evident that conflict situations are intrinsic and organic to social structure. Considered in this manner, the group, the community, or the nation are the particularized areas of social activity in which conflicts arise and are resolved. Recent students of social problems have shown that dissensus is intrinsic to social structure. Indeed, the form of society is itself defined by the quality and types of conflict situations tolerated if not openly sanctioned.[28]

Types of conflict cannot be considered apart from types of social structure. Internal social conflicts, which concern goals, values, or interests that do not contradict the basic assumptions upon which conflicts are founded, tend to be positively functional for the social structure. Such conflicts tend to make it possible to readjust the norms and power relations within groups in accordance with the felt needs of its individual members or subgroups.[29]

III

Consensus theory has been advanced as better suited to dealing with the difficulties of a social examination of unstable relations than is dissensus theory. Three factors in particular are emphasized; first, conflict situations are transitory in nature. That is, the actual behavior of a mass in an extreme situation, such as civil war or revolution, is so short-lived and capricious that it is impossible to predict conclusions or consequences in

[26] Theodore Newcomb, "The Study of Consensus," *Sociology Today, op. cit.,* p. 284.
[27] Gideon Sjoberg, "Contradictory Functional Requirements and Social Systems," *Journal of Conflict Resolution,* Vol. IV, 1960, pp. 198-208; also see Eugene Litwak, "Modes of Bureaucracy Which Permit Conflict," *The American Journal of Sociology,* LXVII, 1961, pp. 177-84.
[28] See, for example, the recent text by R. R. Dynes, Alfred C. Clarke, Simon Dinitz, Iwao Ishino, *Social Problems: Dissensus and Deviation in an Industrial Society.* New York: Oxford University Press, 1964.
[29] Lewis A. Coser, *The Functions of Social Conflict.* Glencoe: The Free Press, 1956, pp. 151-2.

such situations. Second, since conflict situations must be dealt with in their natural social environment it is impossible to conduct controlled experiments as one finds in strictly delineated microscopic types of research. Third, evaluations must be made in terms of second- and third-hand materials such as newspaper reports, autobiographical sketches, and historical studies of unique events—all of which clearly involve the sociological researcher in commitments to many styles of research.[30]

These objections actually reveal a transparency and shallowness that poses a serious threat to social research as such. Analysis in sociology has never been reducible to the simplicity of a scientific investigation. While it is correct that conflict situations, even of major proportions, are generally of "short" duration (but not in regard to their consequences), this does not represent a serious objection either to the empirical study of conflict situations, or, more to the point, to an investigation of the causes of such situations. The brief time all but the most protracted physical conflicts take indicates that certain sampling devices used in stable contexts are ineffectual in dealing with certain kinds of happenings. To reason that to go beyond the borders of current methodological safeguards is to go beyond social science itself is sheer casuistry.

It is equally transparent to object to studying conflict situations because they have no well-defined contours or boundaries. The anthropologist almost always faces this problem in relation to a given culture. Would anyone seriously contend that anthropological research is any less a social science because it has a natural setting? The surest guarantee against provincialism and ethnocentricism would be to develop techniques of study suitable to this "natural" social setting. The sociologist has too often failed in this endeavor. For instance, he has tried to apply questionnaries devised for particular situations to other cultural and social settings where they have little relevance or validity. The natural setting within which dissensus arises is far from being an obstacle; it provides an incentive for moving beyond the highly structured world of the small group into the world at large. That this opportunity has not been seized is a sad reflection on the current limits of sociological practices rather than a true estimate of the legitimate boundaries of sociology.

[30] A fuller catalogue of objections to the study of conflict situations is contained in Kurt Lang and Gladys Lang, *op. cit.*, pp. 545-53.

To equate the worth of a theory (such as consensus or conflict theory) with degrees of control is an arbitrary device which means that the only things that can be studied are those for which data already exist—which may help to account for sameness and duplication of research efforts present in small-group sociology today, and the relative absence of studies on the social structure of developing areas. The most important task for sociology today is to fashion methods adequate for studying problems of social order in a world of conflicting interests, standards, and values. Social order must itself be defined, and in turn must define the larger universe of social change. And both structure and process must be analyzed in terms of the more generic concept of development. The sociologist can hardly run the risk of being surprised by current events because he has been bewitched by order and befuddled by change.

The faith in consensus is often reflected in a deep respect for the amazing complexity of social organization in industrial economies: the automation of production, the mechanization of human responsibilities, the precision of "chain of command" and "line" matrices, and the opportunities of regulating and manipulating man in mass society on the part of highly articulate elites leads to a vision of the social system as inviolable. The Parsonian model of development in particular seems impressed with the regularities which obtain between organization and society as such. This is the consequence of equating organization with consensus. The stress and strain of organizational life gives rise to a definition of social action as that auto-regulative mechanism which adjusts for such "alienative" factors as may arise in the maintenance of the whole system.[31]

Such a view faces the same dilemma as traditional laisser-faire economics, namely, the assumption that automatic marketing "laws" somehow operate over and above the actual desires and ends of men. To meet the laisser-faire implications in the theory of social consensus, certain functionalists have developed a theory of the "safety-value," where organizations "provide substitute objects upon which to displace hostile sentiments as well as means of a reaction to aggressive tendencies."[32] But

[31] Cf. Marion J. Levy, Jr., *The Structure of Society*. Princeton: Princeton University Press, 1952, esp. pp. 288-9.
[32] Lewis A. Coser, *op. cit.*, pp. 155-6.

this safety-valve notion only reinforces the equilibrium model surrounding the theory of social organization, since the assumption of institutional omnipotence and omniscience is strengthened.

Consensus theory, particularly as a replacement for conflict theory, bears a close historical and analytical connection to the attempt to replace the language of social class with that of social status. It is a shift from viewing industrialism as an aspect of many and varied forms of society to a vision of the industrial complex as growing omnipotent and dominating the society. Essentially the Weberian theory of bureaucracy is a pessimistic vision, a view of organization once and for all superseding production as the master lever of industrial life. Under bureaucracy, the question of which class or group of classes holds the reins of power is secondary, since the "basic" bureaucratic factor continues to grow, whichever form of industrial organization might obtain. Bureaucracy comes to be viewed as omnipotent and universal, subject to temporary setbacks but never to any real or sizeable defeat. If such is the case, then consensus theory applies equally to the study of an African state, an aboriginal community, and an industrial city.

Consensus theory has led to such a stress on continuities and similarities in the life of an industrial complex, that all real differences between democracy and autocracy, ruling and being ruled, exploiting and being exploited, are eliminated. The "natural history of society" technique, which sees everything in terms of functional identities, has made a universe in which only grey cats and clever hounds exist. Political systems are reduced to "quantifiable" terms which evaluate how decisions are arrived at in system A or system B. The fusion of Michels' "iron law of oligarchy" and Weber's bureaucracy is not a resolution of the crisis in consensus theory, but a symptom of that crisis.[33] Consensus becomes the ideological celebration of the corporate personality, possessing a reality which transcends human society as such.

Consensus theory seems reinforced by the complex organization. Its basic feature is total specialization: the narcotizing effect of role-sets and the insistence on constraint and persuasion as an exclusive way of bringing about change. The paradox is that consensus theory does not really act as a bulwark for democratic social theory; quite the reverse. It is not a

[33] Seymour M. Lipset, "Political Sociology," op. cit., pp. 89-91.

theory for reaching agreements. It advocates harmony intrinsic to the organization of the bureaucratic life, one which exists over and above the actual accords reached by men. And so it must remain, since any serious theory of agreements and decisions must at the same time be a theory of disagreements and the conditions under which decisions cannot be reached. Yet consensus theorists, starting from the metaphysical "need" for universal consensus, can only talk about absolute and relative consensus, complete or partial integration, but never about conflict as a means of expressing genuine social needs and aspirations.[34]

On this point, Gouldner has stated that "instead of telling men how bureaucracy might be mitigated, they insist that it is inevitable. Instead of explaining how democratic patterns may, to some extent, be fortified and extended, they warn us that democracy cannot be perfect. Instead of controlling the disease, they suggest that we are deluded, or more politely, incurably romantic, for hoping to control it. Instead of assuming responsibilities as realistic clinicians, striving to further democratic potentialities wherever they can, many social scientists have become morticians, all too eager to bury men's hopes."[35]

If we equate "rebellion" with "alienation" and "conformity" with "equilibrium," we are *a priori* ruling out the possibility that a condition of rebellion is consonant with equilibrium at any level.[36] Correspondingly, this equation ignores the possibility that extreme states of consensus might create rather than alleviate social or personal stress.

The concept of deviant behavior itself rests on a faith that normative behavior is in every situation observable and functionally relevant. From the point of view of established consensus on the matter of the sanctity of private property, an act of juvenile vandalism might be measured in the same way as an act of political rebellion, such as the physical damage involved in the Freedom Riders' actions. But from the point of view of the goals sought, what is meant by consensus demands a study

[34] See in particular Chester I. Barnard, *The Functions of the Executive.* Cambridge: Harvard University Press, 1938; James D. Mooney and Alan C. Reiley, *The Principles of Organization.* New York: Harper & Co., 1939; Talcott Parsons, "Suggestions for a Sociological Approach to the Theory of Organization," *Administrative Science Quarterly,* Vol. 1, 1956, pp. 63-85; Philip Selznick, "Foundations of the Theory of Organization," *American Sociological Review,* Vol. XIII, 1948, pp. 25-35.
[35] Alvin W. Gouldner, "Metaphysical Pathos and the Theory of Bureaucracy," *American Political Science Review,* Vol. 49, 1955, pp. 506-7.
[36] Talcott Parsons, *The Social System.* Glencoe: The Free Press, 1951, pp. 257-259.

of group objectives no less than group norms; and no less, the difference between means and ends must itself be considered as a factor existing over and beyond the supposed functional damage the social order sustains from the deviant behavior. Too often, deviance is ambiguously formulated so as to cover extremely different situations, i.e. a departure from the rules on the part of an isolated member of a group, and no less, defiance of group rules.

Consensus does not carry an implication of social equilibrium, nor for that matter does dissensus entail disequilibrium. Different kinds of conflict exist. For instance, there is a great distinction between conflicts on the basis of consensus and conflicts arising within the consensual apparatus. To draw an analogy from game theory, there are conflicts programmed for continuation of the game (such as parliamentary debates), and those programmed to end the game through a change of the rules (such as take place in *coups d'état*). In neither case is dissensus tied to social disorganization or to deviance from norms. This is not to say that conflict situations do not contain possibilities of social disorganization. Of course they do. For example, the absence of a formal constitution over an extended period of time can create political chaos and turmoil. But, likewise, a perfect constitution, preparing the ground for every sort of contingency, can have a boomerang effect; it can increase stress by failing to bring about common standards of belief and action. In short, consensus and dissensus are phenomena which can equally promote or retard social co-operation or political cohesion.

Simmel caught the authentic spirit of the relation of conflict to co-operation when he noted:

> If a fight simply aims at annihilation, it does approach the marginal case of assassination in which the admixture of unifying elements is almost zero. If, however, there is any consideration, any limit to violence, there already exists a socializing factor, even though only as the qualification of violence. One unites in order to fight, and one fights under the mutually recognized control of norms and rules.[37]

Thus, dissensus, no less than consensus, operates within the social structure, within the system of mutually established laws, norms, and values; and hence there is no scientific need to choose between the two.

[37] Georg Simmel, *Conflict*, pp. 25-6. Quoted in Lewis A. Coser, *op. cit.*, p. 121.

Socialization defined exclusively in terms of consensus becomes a euphemism for gamed responses. Being a member of the social system becomes a game played in a way that formal obedience to the rule system is never challenged. Those who do not accept such a view, those who consider social development from the viewpoint of mass movements and spontaneous happenings are described as pariahs, deviants, abnormals, marginals, and even clerics.[38] The multiple definitions of consensus, connected as they are to games-playing and organizational performance, are the perfect completion of the legitimated bifurcation of values and actions, beliefs and behavior. In this form, consensus is reduced to the exclusive mechanism for resolving problems. And social development is seen as taking place only within the social system. Consensus theory has reduced itself to "thinking together."[39] Whether this proves an adequate replacement for the old-fashioned idea of thinking for oneself remains to be demonstrated.

IV

The difficulties in describing any but the most permissive and tolerant communities in terms of consensus matrices leads to a re-examination of conflict theory, with its openness to problems of coercion, pressure groups, social classes, political myths, cultural clashes, and racial strife, factors which more nearly approximate the actual state of affairs in developing areas. From a descriptive point of view, conflict theory covers a wider and more profound range of questions than consensus theory. To be sure, it is better for men to settle their differences on the basis of free agreement rather than external pressures. Neither consensus nor conflict theory has any exclusive claims as a problem-solving technique.

The particular significance of this controversy (concerning conflict and consensus) for developmental research has to do with the position of social change vis à vis social structure. If social conflict is seen as necessarily destructive of social order, the tendency will be for a society to rely heavily on spontaneity and on the operations of the free market.

[38] S. M. Lipset and Neil Smelser, "Change and Controversy in Recent American Sociology," *The British Journal of Sociology*, Vol. XII, 1961, pp. 41-51.
[39] Edward Gross, "Symbiosis and Consensus as Integrative Factors in Small Groups," *American Sociological Review*, Vol. XXI, 1956, pp. 174-9.

Laisser-faire, laisser-passer links up well with a view of life in which the consensual apparatus is held to be supreme. On the other hand, if conflict is seen to be equal to consensus in terms of its abilities to provide social cohesion, then an increase in the machinery of regulation rather than the much more complicated change in social organization is in order. There are two essential types of conflict: one form which arises out of the root differences between social forces, and which generally goes unchecked; and another form which a political regime can build into the social system and hence plan for. There is nothing especially deceptive about planning for conflict, any more than the rules of a game are sinful because they lay down rules of combat or competition. To plan for social change very often means to anticipate social conflict and devise programs for meeting the problems which arise out of such conflict.

To reject conflict as a generative, causal agency in social change is to deprive a society of an essential mechanism for reaching order. The rejection of conflict is an invitation to violence and coercion. That is to say, dissensus is as "natural" to a social system as consensus—and frequently more fruitful in nations and areas where parliamentary democracy is an unknown quantity. Co-operation can be a consequence of conflict, *if* the rules for governing conflict are as clearly worked out as those which regulate consensus. The instinct to break the rules is no greater in conflict situations than in consensual situations. The history of parliamentary "cheating" can be considered strong evidence that the simple existence of legal organizations is no mandate for a consensual approach. In brief, the planning of social change in underdeveloped regions carries with it the understanding that conflict is as subject to rules as consensus. Indeed, conflict may often turn out to be a "safety valve" for minimizing violence and terrorism in the new regions.

The definition of a social system in terms of small collectivities and interacting groups assumes the presence of self-sufficiency in each unit, and this upon investigation very rarely obtains. A social system can more readily be understood as component parts of a larger multi-national complex which embraces a number of interacting and coexisting societies, e.g. an area cluster, sharing a common culture, a specific geography, on a common ethnic basis. The kind of regional analysis necessary to understand social change is simply not possible if we start from the assumption that all problems can be resolved within a systematic model.

The difficulty with consensus schemes is that they too readily spill over into equilibrium models. Any conceptual scheme which dissolves the region and civilization within the same amorphous concept that is used to distinguish specific social systems is submerging a series of vital distinctions which need independent articulation. The failure to work out this articulation in the contemporary social sciences helps to explain why the "structural imperatives" governing large-scale development have been largely ignored. The failure to consider societies as functioning within a more inclusive civilization helped to create an artificial image of a social system as functioning in an isolated society without external factors impinging upon or impeding the operations of that society. Little recognition was taken of the pressures and mechanisms which have evolved out of the participation of individual social systems in larger complex civilizations. The boundaries of a society are not rigidly drawn, but are marked by zones of interaction of relative degrees of intensity. The analysis of a social system from a consensual framework can yield fruitful results precisely to the extent that it is seen as auto-functioning and self-regulating. But this focus on inner balancing agencies has as its upper limit the force of surrounding areas, and the interactive process of a world scale.

An acute danger in consensual analysis is the relative ease of constructing models which ignore patterns of conflict at a large-scale level. Colonialism, imperialism, spheres of influence, military sites, etc., are also "inter-actional" in character. But since it is an interaction which is involuntary, and hence not derived through mutual consent or common institutionalization, it is easily excluded from the analytic account of the social system as such. The scientific limits of this sort of functional-structural accounting are characterized ideologically by an avoidance of the divisive elements between nations and peoples which are *no less binding* upon both parties, as the things which a community mutually agrees upon. Interaction does not signify knowing or willing consent. When an equivalence between interaction and consent is set up, the wide possibilities of developing mechanisms of co-operation that leave conflicting national economies and politics intact are severely curbed.

Consensus theory has a narrowing effect on the study of interest elements and sectoral phenomena in the Third World. Consensual units are too frequently seen in terms of small group and small community relations. In this sense, consensus theory has a self-fulfilling prophetic dimension, in that what is examined presupposes a high degree of social cohesion and interaction.[40] Such unifying agencies and symbols are absent precisely in larger forms of social and national development. Immigration waves; differences in cultural, racial, and ethnic backgrounds; sectional, caste, and class antagonisms; these types of situations stand in continual need of a sociological theory of conflict resolution, one which makes no assumptions as to the auto-regulative or equilibriated conditions of a specific social system. To declare that the only viable avenue of scientific study open to the sociologist is the small group, since only in group relations can all the variables be controlled for, is not to prove the worth of consensus but only to demonstrate the extent to which larger units of social research have been surrendered because of the difficulties in explaining dissensual elements in the macroscopic world.[41]

The original intent of consensus theory—to establish a measurement of what public opinion maintains as true or desirable at any given point —has been subverted. This has been forcefully made clear by the elitist corruption of consensus to signify what "prestige" judges think consensus to be.[42] The assumption that consensus is intrinsically more democratic than dissensus is about as sound as the "theory" that clean-shaven men are kindlier than bearded men. As Leonard Reissman has well pointed out, consensus theorists "create an uncomfortable suspicion

[40] This is not to imply that conflict situations, and thus conflict theory, are inoperative at small-group levels. Quite the contrary; the most significant literature of this genre has shown a marked concern with conflict and conflict resolution as the essence of group interaction. See, for example, Arthur J. Vidich and Joseph Bensman, *Small Town in Mass Society: Class, Power and Religion in a Rural Community*. Garden City: Doubleday-Anchor Books, 1960; Judith R. Kramer and Seymour Leventman, *Children of the Gilded Ghetto: Conflict Resolutions of Three Generations of American Jews*. New Haven: Yale University Press, 1961; and Kenneth Wilson Underwood, *Protestant and Catholic: Religious and Social Interaction in an Industrial Community*. Boston: The Beacon Press, 1957. These kinds of studies are conspicuously absent for other societies.

[41] A monumental effort to develop a quantitative statement of international affairs is that of Bruce M. Russett, Hayward R. Alker, Karl W. Deutsch, Harold D. Lasswell, *World Handbook of Political and Social Indicators*. New Haven: Yale University Press, 1964.

[42] Harold Kaufman, *Prestige Classes in a New York Rural Community*. Ithaca: Cornell University Agricultural Experiment Station, March 1944, Memoir 260, p. 46.

about what consensus means and how valid is the use of prestige judges as a research technique. There is something unexplained that badly needs elucidation when a measure can turn up eleven or more distinguishable classes in a community with a total population of some 1200." Reissman goes on to explain the central weakness of consensual definitions of social class:

> There is the tendency, although not an inevitable one, to consider behavior as the result of the value system of class rather than as the effect of, say, economic factors, social power, education, or political forces. The crux of class distinction, thereby, becomes one of values, which in turn become the presumed causes of class difference in behavior.[43]

It must not be concluded that status factors are inoperative as independent variables, but rather that such a conclusion is not necessarily arrived at by a theory of consensus. Shifts in modes of behavior from class to prestige lines can be more readily and accurately gauged on historical grounds than on psychological grounds of the instinctual need for togetherness and social acceptance.

Why then has the great shift from dissensus to consensus taken place in the United States at precisely the same time as the reverse is the case at the international level? Several hypotheses suggest themselves. First, that as American society becomes more democratic, more easy-going, the search for the consensual basis becomes more pronounced. However, this view of the end of ideology seems not so much a consequence of an expanding democratic temper as it is simply a reflection of domestic affluence and more United States inhabitants' benefiting from the affluent society.[44] A more powerful line of reasoning is that technical bureaucracies and team-member proficiency have tended to usurp the older power of formal authority as distinct from science.[45] The older situation of science as isolated from policy-making has disintegrated.

[43] Leonard Reissman, *Class in American Society*. Glencoe: The Free Press, 1959, pp. 127 and 75.
[44] Seymour M. Lipset, *Political Man*, *op. cit.*, pp. 403-17; see also in this connection, Daniel Bell, *The End of Ideology*. Glencoe: The Free Press, 1960.
[45] Morris Janowitz, *Sociology and the Military Establishment*. New York: Russell Sage Foundation, 1959, pp. 27-39. Janowitz's remarks are confined to the military. Responsibility for enlarging the scope and context of his argument is mine.

With this, authority shifts from outright reliance on domination to a wider utilization of manipulation, demonstrated managerial skills, operational proficiencies, and the capacity to develop positive organizational loyalties. In such a context, consensus comes to be the decisive pivot upon which the success or failure of the managerially oriented society hangs.

Perhaps the most cogent explanation for the shift to consensus theory is the "enlightened" recognition that mass terror is not as powerful an instrument for extracting economic and political loyalties as mass persuasion. The entire edifice of small-group theory comes to rest on the idea that the formal sanctioning of force is less potent a factor in individual or group motivation than informal reinforcement of the immediately involved reference-set. The belief in consensus as a strategem is well articulated by Frank:

> The idea has spread that employers were wasting human energy by the traditional authoritarian ways of imposing their decisions on their employees. Psychologists—collaborating with engineers and economists and, more recently, anthropologists—have made many studies concerned with the impact of physical aspects of the workplace, such as lighting, color of walls and machines, temperature and humidity; with working conditions, such as hours, shifts, rest periods, piece rates, and especially relations of foremen and supervisors to their groups. Such studies helped to articulate a new view of corporate life.[46]

What is the content of this new view of corporate life? Is it a theory of the corporation or simply a technique of mass persuasion and manipulation? Is it a sociological statement of the nature of the corporate structure, or the uses by the corporate structure of sociological statements? The promotion of consensus as a theory has had as its asking price the conversion of sociology from a science to a tool of policy. A policy, moreover, which fails to reach the goal of harmony. As White recently indicated: "There is nothing new in manipulated opinion and engineered consent . . . Even the sheer bulk of distortion is not alto-

---

[46] Lawrence K. Frank, "Psychology and the Social Order," in *The Human Meaning of the Social Sciences*, edited by Daniel Lerner. New York: Meridian Books, Inc., 1959, p. 230.

gether new, merely more refined. What is new is the acceptability, the mere taken-for-grantedness of these things."[47]

V

The terrain of human co-operation, while related to consensus and conflict, has a unique dimension and operational range. A decision in favor of consensus theory is not automatically a decision on behalf of co-operation. It is simply a decision to examine social structure to the partial or total exclusion of social dynamics; a decision to act as if breaks with traditional shifts in the culture complex, disruption of moral patterns, can be described as marginal in character. There is a kind of safety in the traditional, the prolonged, the enduring. But this safety, gratuitously cloaking itself in the mantle of social order, represents in fact the abdication of the field of social change, and hence an abandonment of the ongoing problems confronting those most directly concerned with achieving human co-operation at group, regional, national, or international levels.

What then is the difference between consensus and dissensus on one side, and co-operation on the other? There seem to be three distinguishable factors to be identified.

First: dissensus and consensus each stands for agreement internally, i.e. in terms of shared perspectives, agreements on the rules of association and action, a common set of norms and values. Co-operation for its part makes no demands on role uniformity but only upon procedural rules. Co-operation concerns the settlement of problems in terms which make possible the continuation of differences and even fundamental disagreements. One can legitimately speak of co-operation between labor and management, while one speaks of the degree of consensus each side brings to bear at the bargaining table. This is of particular significance for the newer developing nations, since co-operation would legitimize rather than outlaw differences, and hence reduce the fear that negotiation means capitulation.

Second: consensus is agreement on the content of behavior, while co-operation necessitates agreement only on the form of behavior. We speak of consensus if all members of the Women's Christian Temper-

[47] Howard B. White, "The Processed Voter and the New Political Science," *Social Research*, Vol. XXVIII, 1961, p. 150.

ance Union agree to abstain from drinking alcoholic beverages. But we speak of co-operation when agreement is reached on the forms allowed for drinking and the forms allowed for curbing the intake of liquor. As the Prohibition Era dramatically showed, the substitution of co-operation for consensus did not lead to a new morality but simply to chaos. There is similarly the danger that too heavy an emphasis on consensus in the African states would result in a resurrection of racial warfare as a mode of settling conflicts, since the demand for racial hegemony would undoubtedly precede all else. The very multiplicity of nations in Africa offers some comfort that co-operative forms of polity will prevail. Interestingly, African leaders generally call for racial equality and not for racial supremacy, although the continued policy of *apartheid* in South Africa could change this situation.

Third: co-operation concerns toleration of differences, while consensus demands reconciliation of these same differences. If a games theory analogy be preferred, the distinction between co-operation and consensus might be stated in the following terms: both conflict and consensus program the *termination* of the game by insisting on the principle of unity and unilateral victory, whereas co-operation is pluralistic because it programs the *continuation* of the game by maintaining and insisting upon the legitimacy of differences.

What is required at this juncture is a stipulation of the conditions of the minimum set of beliefs about man and his social universe that is consonant with continued survival and growth. Such a theory of co-operation would insist on the need for maintaining life, although leaving open the question of what to do with it; the need to secure the material and cultural needs of man, although differing on the sort of social system best able to meet such needs. Beyond this, there is a need for a theory of conflict, a programming of conflict that would allow people to shift and choose their conceptions of what constitutes progress, pleasure, and the institutionalization of avenues for action to implement these conceptions. Consensus theory might contribute its share to melt the present freezing of attitudes by indicating ways in which co-operation can be converted into consensus through a re-examination of present interests.

The unity required to evolve such a sociological theory of co-operation is methodological rather than systematic. The concept of co-operation is essentially the programming of common standards in a world of conflicting interests and even different notions as to what constitutes interests. Precisely because a general theory of co-operation would offer no transcendental commitments to the eternal righteousness of any existing social order, it can place itself in the service of social development.

The existence of a Third World does not in itself reduce the areas of conflict, nor enhance the growth of a new consensus. What it does is introduce a new dimension for the political consideration of old power blocs, and hence make possible channels of co-operation which, in the long run, can minimize the friction created by the present bi-polarization in the economic, political, and military realms. The new economic and political mixes introduced by Third World countries create new social forms which make "hard postures" embarrassing and obsolescent. It is not necessary to maintain that the Third World will lead the way to a recasting of present political dilemmas. What is more likely to occur is a loosening of ideological postures by the major power blocs in a manifest effort to "capture" Third World sympathies. But a latent byproduct of this shifting and casting may come about in the vitalization of present agencies for international settlement such as the United Nations; and the creation of yet new institutions for settlement. In brief, bilateral co-operation will be made possible, if not inevitable, precisely because of the rise of new nations of power. This co-operation may not be altruistic in character. It may be stimulated by a common fear that the failure to institutionalize norms of co-operation now, when the power "players" are few in number, would make it only that much harder later, when the number of players in the world power struggle multiply.

The fact that co-operation offers some viable paths to survival and conflict resolution does not mean that development may not be adversely affected. Indeed, co-operation is itself an ambiguous notion; it can refer to a "balance of powers" or to a "balance of numbers." The developing regions already have come to outnumber (and in the United Nations, to outvote) the traditional centers of power. However, it is clear that ultimate decisions affecting the fate of the world still reside in the holders of nuclear power. Under such conditions, the best that developing nations can hope to achieve is the arrangement of "nuclear free" zones in the hope that a wider basis of co-operation between the power blocs can be effected. Even if a maximum degree of co-operation is maintained regarding procedural matters—i.e. an adequate definition of the conflict situation, maximization of factual information regarding potential conflicts, and testing of proposals for breaking tensions in terms of past experience—the overriding conflict of interests may forestall any basic settlement. It must be noted that only where basic big-power interests coincide, as in matters of the unlimited use of nuclear weapons, has a general theory of co-operation been successfully employed. Beyond that point, special interests come to the foreground. And the developing regions are very much considered part of these "interests" of major powers. Hence, a basic stumbling block to co-operation is the limited feasibility of maintaining the "rules of the game" under conditions where each "side" does indeed have something to "lose" and something to "gain" by any fundamental shift in social structure. Every nation becomes a "vital" sphere of influence instead of a sovereign autonomous area.

This raises the more generic problem that co-operation is a negatively induced condition. The likelihood of co-operation under conditions of one side winning and the other losing is a most treacherous plausibility—quite subject to violation. Therefore, the growth of a Third World has a dangerous side to it: the abandonment of co-operation even as to the rules for programming future conflicts. But along with the risks are the advantages. If one or more area clusters in the Third World manage to gain great power, this would forestall a two-player game between the United States and the Soviet Union. For such an event to occur, the developing areas would themselves have to develop independent nuclear deterrents—and hence expand the size and scale of arms races. This in turn would compel the old power centers to reconsider their own postures.

There is a circularity to the problem of co-operation because there is a circularity to the facts involved. To expand the bargaining power of the Third World entails an expansion of the risks of war. Yet, to curtail or limit this bargaining power is to jeopardize the Third World entirely, to make it subject to precisely the forms of big power settlement which is found so abhorrent by the emergent nations.

The assumption of the major powers is that co-operation is possible because social structure presupposes social development. The assumption of the Third World is that co-operation is possible because social development presupposes social structure. The Third World may be willing to sacrifice life to preserve the principle of development. Formulas cannot break this dichotomy—only the general recognition that anything pushed to its ultimate, either structure or process, may prove to be self-defeating. Hence, that much abused term "moderation" may still prove to be the handmaiden of human reason.

Co-operation may prove a slender reed upon which to hang our hopes for both conflict resolution and social development. However, any return to consensus theory would mark a step backward in the toleration of social differences; while any return to conflict theory would mark a return to nineteenth-century geo-politics that would eliminate even that amount of "internationalization" of life thus far registered. Human reason has posed the problems in this ultimate way by virtue of the scientific and technological achievements it has painfully gained. It is not too much to hope that this same sort of reason will prove to be the basic variable needed in social and political life. Peace is not likely to be gained without establishing a functional common ground upon which men can stand. Any common ground can easily be turned into a divisive barrier if parochial interests are allowed to displace man's universal need of men for survival.

That something is drastically wrong with the contemporary world scene, and that this something is directly connected to our failure to establish machinery for the preservation of life and limb will come as a shock to no one. What is shocking, however, is the fact that the historical effort to secure international peace through the arts of compromise has been thoroughly discredited.

> Nowhere is the failure of compromise so obvious in our Western societies as in the wars by which they have been ravaged. A review of the processes whereby the West has sought to avoid the increasingly deadly wars which have followed upon one another in an infernal round would bring to mind the various plans for "perpetual peace," all of which have had one thing in common—their pathetic inadequacy. The international institutions set up to maintain world peace proved no more effectual as long as they did not reflect an actual situation making war particularly terrible . . . it can now be said that, in the past, the West has

failed in its efforts to reach a peaceful settlement of its international conflicts.[48]

If we are to avoid a surrender to the pure utilitarianism of *Realpolitik* or to the equally pure cynicism of the advocates of Doomsday, an alternative to the classical arts of big-power diplomacy must be located. These remarks on conflict resolution are intended as a step in that direction. They are an appeal for world peace which would make extensive use of Third World nations irrespective of their social systems. They take for granted the fact that social problems are a consequence of social development. We have demanded either/or solutions for too long: either dissensus or consensus; either anarchy or behemoth. But when we examine the social infra-structure, what becomes most apparent is that conflict can be programmed no less than consensus. We are in a position not only to tolerate conflict, with a low yield of violence, but induce dissensus—for the purpose of avoiding all-out conflict which is unstructured. Political parties, voluntary social organization, and athletic events are examples of the safety-valve factor in such forms of conflict.[49] By taking conflict as a social constant it may yet be possible to avoid the consequences of *maximum* conflict. There is abundant evidence that low-yield violence is at least as plausible within a world of programmed conflict as it is in the diplomatic world of compromise.

[48] Cf. Charles Moraze, "The Settlement of Conflicts in Western Cultures," *International Social Science Quarterly*, Vol. XV, No. 2, 1963, pp. 248-9. A first attempt to deal with the problem is contained in *Economic and Social Consequences of Disarmament*. New York: United Nations, May 1963 (E-3736).
[49] The significance of strategic concepts such as the safety-valve factor, programmed conflict, and low-yield violence, is undeniable. What is mistaken is the elevation of such strategies into principles for the maintenance of the social system. Strategies are not miracles, nor are they theoretical resolutions of the dilemmas of development.

Chapter 13

Which Way The Third World? Developmentalists and Development

I

Three problems loom large in the decision to accelerate development: First, should the rate of national development be determined by the needs of the sovereign citizens, by other nations' rates of growth, or by general principles of planning? Second, are entrepreneurial or proletariat classes best suited to carry forth the developmental process, or, to state the issue another way, should elites or masses determine the tempo and themes of development? Third, what is the proper proportion of coercion and consensus in the developmental process?

At a more generic level, the solution would seem to hinge upon whether there is an economic basis to politics, as in the First World and Second World, or a political basis to economics, as in most of the Third World. In some measure this is an analytic problem of how the world is "carved up," and not exclusively a pragmatic one of how men shape their world. This combination of analytical, empirical, and practical may be untidy, but it is precisely the intellectual blend which we must ultimately come to terms with.

Putting the master issue in paradigm form, there is an economic continuum between capitalism and socialism and a political continuum extending from elite totalitarianism to mass democracy. The Third World mix is essentially unstable. What is at issue for the immediate future is the proportion of the "mix," that is, the particular combinations involving capitalism, socialism, democracy, and authoritarianism. The unstable mix is often taken to indicate the "transitional" character of the Third

World. The problem is no longer traditionalism versus modernism, but rather the different political and economic arrangements covered by the word "modern."

Revolution is now being made in terms of socialism *plus* maximum social control. The alternative is not capitalism plus democracy, but rather capitalism and maximum social control. Third World revolutions have overthrown absolute tyrants, shiekdoms, petty militarists in the service of foreign rulers, and even some of the feudal "remnants." That these revolutions are not at the same time democratic is due to a multitude of factors—from the backwardness of the peoples involved to the political elitism bred by traditionalism. Modernization may be rapid, but development is still a slow and laborious process. The former is defined by industrialism while the latter must locate industrialism in an overall developmental scheme. One has to choose not simply between freedom and slavery, as free enterprise apologists maintain. The choice is really between socialism, with a minimum of conventional democratic safeguards, and colonialism, with little more conventional democracy than now obtains. To expect any more is simply asking for utopia. The Cuban Revolution of 1959 did not "crush" democracy, as there was precious little of it to crush. The Algerian Revolution did not abolish personal freedoms; under the French colonialists there were none to guarantee. The Egyptian Revolution did not deprive the bourgeoisie of the free trade it did not possess.

Second World socialism differs in its political profile from Third World adaptations of it. Socialism in the Afro-Asian nations replaces traditionalism or a semi-colonialism which contain little in the way of political democracy, except in so far as democracy was part of the colonialist rhetoric. In such East European countries as Czechoslovakia and Poland, however, an externally induced socialist economy replaces neo-capitalist systems which had already achieved some measure of formal democracy. It is futile to consider rapid development exclusively in terms of democracy or autocracy, without also examining the specific social systems at the point of "liberation." Astute observers of the developmental processes have indeed avoided such banalities. The difference between socialism in the Second and Third Worlds illustrates the shift from an economy imposed by an outside power as the "spoils of war" to an economy imposed by the internal logic of post-World War Two colonialism.

Not every nation needs to go through every phase of the developmental process. Historic backwardness makes possible a "law of combined development," an amalgam of archaic and contemporary forms.[1] This "law" does not mean that such combined development is automatically advantageous to the newly emergent nations. In the process of grafting on new forms of industrial production to a traditional culture, privileged sectors in emerging societies often seek to preserve old social relations. "Backward" classes no less than "established classes"—peasants no less than landlords—may show this instinct. The Third World, lacking as it does a well-defined and well-developed mass, runs the risk of uneven development rather than accelerated development.

Latin America reveals just how far deformities can be carried. In the absence of a mobilized class of urban proletarians, development is continually fragmented. The Argentine middle classes merge with the big oligarchical landholders to forestall national control of basic utilities and mineral wealth. The Peruvian cities preserve their commercial, administrative, and military features and remain centers of consumption instead of bases of production. The Central American "banana republics" become "industrialized" only insofar and to the degree that the processing of crops for export is involved. The simple emergence of industrialism, however decisive a part of the developmental process it may be, can never be equated with development as such. It must always be judged in terms of the character of class relations within a nation and of political relations between nations.

The most successful societies to have achieved full development, such as the United States in the First World and the Soviet Union in the Second World, were extremely backward in regard to the industrial gains already registered by Western and Central Europe, but they were never "underdeveloped." The United States was not freighted with a society to be removed from obstructing a new establishment, and hence political compromise did not act to thwart or retard industrial growth. This in turn made possible a consensual value system functionally attuned to the modes of economic production. The same is not the case for present-day satellite cultures—whether they be in South America or East-

[1] See on this Leon Trotsky, *The History of the Russian Revolution*, Vol. 1. New York: Simon & Schuster, Inc., 1932, pp. 4-9.

ern Europe.[2] The continued organizational and structural backwardness which exists in present-day satellite societies indicates quite clearly that a modernizing society is not necessarily a developing one. This is not an argument based upon the "little" against the "big," otherwise we should have to defend little Belgium against the big Congo. What is required is a recognition that imperialism—old military style or new monetary style—is not simply morally reprehensible. It is socially and economically deforming in regard to the general needs of a people. The negative effects of imperialism enable nationalism to serve as a drive-shaft of the developmental process.

To equate development with rapid and high industrialism is to avoid a number of critical issues. First, industrialism does not settle the question of the social relations best suited to a given social system. Second, industrialism often adds to, rather than minimizes, the deformities of national development by putting a profound strain on the various "popular classes." Third, industrialism may stimulate rather than discourage a confrontation between social classes, since it may provide the organizational network needed for successful revolutionary agitation. Fourth, industrialization may provide the foundations either for a viable capitalism or a viable socialism. The actual growth of an economic system may be "apolitical." This is the basic impulse behind the technocratic approach taken by de Gaulle in France.[3]

There are nations in which a highly developed bourgeoisie exists in an environment of small-scale industry. Argentina is a case in point. It has a fully developed, ideologically sophisticated middle class, whose manufactured output is confined to consumer production for an internal market by the pressures of imperialism. In such a condition, the infusion of foreign investment capital to stimulate rapid industrialization would serve to stabilize the bourgeoisie so that they would be the unques-

[2] For a very useful accounting of satellitic and dominant patterns in the industrialization process, see Bert F. Hoselitz, "Patterns of Economic Growth," *Sociological Aspects of Economic Growth*. New York: The Free Press of Glencoe, 1960, pp. 85-109.

[3] See on this T. B. Bottomore, "The Administrative Elite," in *The New Sociology*, edited by Irving L. Horowitz. New York: Oxford University Press, 1964, pp. 357-69; also see his recent work, *Elites and Society*. London: C. A. Watts & Co. Ltd., 1964.

tioned dominant force in the nation for the first time. Japan has already pointed the way in this direction. But while this may extend the number of people who achieve affluence, it leaves intact the traditional class divisions.

In new nation-states, it is difficult to expect industrialization to take a capitalist path, which would mean that the state would bring into existence a situation where the private sector would dominate the economy, which would raise the bourgeoisie to political pre-eminence. Furthermore, if development along private enterprise paths were intensified, it is entirely possible that popular sentiments for socialist action would be intensified, too. For the most part, motivational stimulants to industrialization based on the "profit motive" are already being made in the confines of socialist-oriented states.

The study of development has thus far tended to underscore and underline differences in sociological theory rather than to resolve them. The dual tradition in theories of social change handed down to the twentieth century by such thinkers as Marx and Durkheim serves to highlight the sharp gap between entrepreneurial and mass doctrines of development. In effect, the entrepreneurial group believes: (a) Change derives from those who take high risks and are willing to try new patterns. (b) The entrepreneurial group alone can at one and the same time be innovative with respect to the social structure and remain sufficiently within it to effect real change. (c) Social change is a consequence of anticipatory responses to new situations, and only a scientific or technological elite is now prepared to meet such challenges. (d) In effect, the conservative elements in a situation are those which have the least to gain by innovation—such as the factory or office workers in modern capitalism. Thus, it is maintained that responsibility for genuine social development is directly in the hands of those who combine managerial, organizational, and scientific skills.

In contrast to this business theory of development, the structural group puts forth a contrary view: (a) While change may entail certain high risks, it is debatable that such risks are uniquely taken by an entrepreneurial group. It is even more questionable that individual entrepreneurial decisions really determine actual social development. (b) The innovative aspects of the modern entrepreneur are no less subject to serious question since this group can hardly go beyond an equation between industrial society and managerial control—however "unprofitable" such an arrangement may be. Whether in fact this group, through its use of monopoly, cartels, and directed research, does more to promote than to curb innovation, is questionable. More important, the business theory of development rests on the idea that innovation and social development are the same. This is merely a restatement in different form of the classical economic argument which views development as equivalent to industrialization. (c) Whether social change is a response to the breakdown in present human interactions, or an anticipation of future human needs is certainly arguable. Clearly, both elements are required as stimuli to further social change. The entrepreneurial view separates social *change* from social *class*, and puts the burden on a trained elite.

It may be that in Western Europe, as Alain Touraine has suggested, technical elites rather than traditional classes have been instrumental in bringing about social development, even changes in human relations.[4] But this technological order would still be a long-run consequence of very high industrialization. The technological perspective cannot be applied to the basic demands and tensions of the Third World since it reverses the empirical order of things. It makes the technological perspective a cause rather than a consequence of industrialization. The argument that elites are radical and masses are conservative, or that elites are at least "modern" and masses are at least "traditionalist," rests on serious prejudices transmitted from the most advanced nations and superimposed on the most backward nations. This argument shifts the burden of research from an analysis of class relations to an analysis of personal behavior. It may well be that this shift from political sociology to social psychology has itself helped produce the new wave of consensual doctrines of social change based on models of norms and deviances.[5]

There is no question that the various types of developmental theories greatly influence the kinds of strategies which are likely to be adopted, and the kinds of policies which are likely to be carried forth. If consensual models are correct, then the problems of the Third World are simply those of historical backwardness, capable of resolution

[4] Alain Touraine, "Sociologie du développement," *Sociologie du Travail*, Vol. 5, No. 2, April-June 1963, pp. 156-74.
[5] Irving L. Horowitz, "Consensus, Conflict and Cooperation," *Social Forces*, Vol. 41, No. 2, December 1962, pp. 177-88.

through a crash program in the communications and transportation fields.[6] But if conflict models are more appropriate, then problems of the Third World are far graver than those faced by the United States or the Soviet Union when they were in a condition of backwardness. Third World nations contain structural defects which can only be overcome by forceful economic and political action.

There is real doubt whether the consensual sociologists really understand the Third World. This becomes clear if we examine the history of the least understood part of the Third World—Latin America. This vast continental area reveals a higher degree of economic development than any other area outside of Europe and North America. Latin Americans achieved their political independence almost at the same time as the United States. They continued to grow at rates comparable to North Americans until the post-Civil War period. Thus, throughout the eighteenth century, and despite the retarded view of colonialism held by the Spanish Empire, the "leisure" ethnic of the Catholic religion, the ethos of traditionalism, and the social psychology of the "Pot of Gold," economic facts support the view that the comparative decline of Latin America with respect to North America is directly and proportionately related to the heavy-scale North European and North American capital investments in the region.

On an international scale, foreign colonialism has been a root factor in the process of holding back economic progress—or, more piquantly, in the devolution of falling expectations. Within the domestic context, a home-grown class of exploiters has managed to develop an economic system based on internal colonialism.[7] The connections between national bourgeoisie and foreign colonial sectors, the economic fusion of the two, have served to define the present situation in Latin America. Latin America offers abundant evidence that the Third World is not underdeveloped because it is historically backward, but that its development was aborted by foreign and native interests which derive great ad-

[6] Phillips Cutright, "National Political Development," *American Sociological Review*, Vol. 28, No. 2, April 1963, pp. 253-64.
[7] Pablo Casanova, "Société plurale, colonialisme interne et développement," *Tiers-Monde*, Vol. 5, No. 18, April-June 1964, pp. 291-312; in this same connection, see also Torcuato S. Di Tella, "Los Procesos Políticos y Sociales de la Industrialización," *Desarrollo Económico*, Vol. 2, No. 3, Oct.-Dec. 1962, pp. 19-48.

vantages from keeping the nation as a whole politically and economically subordinate.

II

A number of works have attempted to define development as a problem of delinquent economics. The consequence of viewing development as an escape from stagnation has been fully developed by Walt W. Rostow. He has sought to understand the grievances and the dilemmas of people in Jakarta, Rangoon, New Delhi, and Karachi, but he brings his analysis of stages of economic growth "to an end" with the emergence of a Third World. There is a clear implication in his work that the only real model of development is the United States since it is highest on the measurements of economic growth he deems crucial.[8]

Rostow's doctrine of "take-off" and his "non-communist manifesto" are a "natural" combination, if the problem of development is seen as the same as that of stagnation. But whatever the deficiencies in Rostow's polemic, he at least appreciates the fact that, to seriously confront the master problems of development, one must come to grips with Marxist theories of growth and change.[9]

Marxists view economic development as the unfolding of five stages of economic growth: primitive communism (an equality of scarcity), slavery, feudalism, capitalism, socialism, and communism (an equality of abundance).[10] Rostow charts economic stages differently: Traditional Society (with a high proportion of production in the agriculture sector); The Preconditions for Take-off (marked by the translation of scientific discovery into technological channels, and by external dominion of advanced societies over less advanced societies); The Take-off (where the rate of effective investment sharply increases, new industries expand rapidly, and agriculture is commercialized); The Drive to Maturity (in

[8] Walt W. Rostow, *The Stages of Economic Growth: A Non-Communist Manifesto.* Cambridge: Cambridge University Press, 1960.
[9] See George I. Blanksten, "Transference of Social and Political Loyalties," *Industrialization and Society*, edited by B. F. Hoselitz and W. E. Moore. Paris: UNESCO-Mouton, 1963, pp. 175-92.
[10] For a sophisticated examination of economic doctrines of "stages of growth" in Marxian and conventional economies see Maurice Dobb, *Economic Growth and Underdeveloped Countries.* New York: International Publishers, 1963, pp. 45-59.

which the national income is invested, permitting output regularly to outstrip population); and The Age of High Mass Consumption (in which the leading sectors shift toward durable consumer goods and services and away from production as such). Despite the employment of a jargonized language more suitable to the language of *Machtpolitik* than economic analysis, his plotted course of growth has elicited wide attention.

Both Marx and Rostow have sought to evolve an ideal typology for the study of economic stages. It is doubtful that Rostow, even less than Marx, could really accept his theoretical system as anything less than a perfect description of the empirical world. Rostow's analysis leads him into the familiar nationalistic trap of viewing American society as the top of the ladder. In the United States there is a degree of mass consumption unparalleled anywhere else in the world. And for Rostow, the display of these wares is universally necessary and worthwhile in itself. Marx's typification was made in relation to social classes—slaves, serfs, noblemen, capitalists, proletarians, peasants, etc.—whereas Rostow rarely mentions economic *relations*. Instead, everything is said to hinge on the *level* of social production and not on the character of social relations. In this way, the essential pattern of developmental economics is falsified, since it is precisely the relationship of ownership to production that largely determines the allocation of wealth and the investment procedures of the Third World.

Even if we ignore the tremendous imbalances in the American economy—the disproportionate ownership and control of industry, the continued gap between rich and poor, the huge ecological and economic separation of Negroes, the disparity of wealth between areas of the country, the growing chasm between high payments for intellectual activities and low payments for manual skills[11]—and we take Rostow's last stage of High Mass Consumption, or to shorten the matter Galbraith's "affluence"—it is difficult to see how he can escape utopian conclusions. Ultimately Rostow is saying that the road to the communist ideal, to absolute equality, is through American capitalism. There is always for the non-utopian the question, what next? And Rostow's incredible answer speaks to us as caricature: "Americans have behaved as if, having been born

[11] See Gabriel Kolko, *Wealth and Power in America: An Analysis of Social Class and Income Distribution*. New York: Frederick Praeger, 1962.

into a system that provided economic security and high mass-consumption, they placed a lower valuation on acquiring additional increments of real income in the conventional form as opposed to the advantages and values of an enlarged family." While it is a "shade too soon to create a new-stage-of-growth based on babies," it is clear a Baby-Boom Stage is Rostow's rosy-pink (or baby-blue) picture of the economic future.[12] And as long as changes in social relations are *a priori* considered superfluous, if not worse, the construction of economic fantasies can scarcely be opposed. We are left with middle-class utopianism, without middle-class justification or courage for dominion.

A less cozy picture would take into account the following facts of our Mass Consumption Society. There has been a virtual stagnation in the field of new consumer products since the 'forties. With the saturation of the television, washing machine, and dishwasher market, the Gadget Society has arrived. Affluence has come to be represented by useless trimmings for necessary products and by duplication of items instead of new product research—for instance, the new family standard of two cars and three television sets. The Mass Consumption Society has produced an enormous cultural and psychic strain on Americans. The phenomenon of privatization, of withdrawal from social involvements, and a collapse of common goals has been accentuated by the emphasis on private property and private wealth. The general anomic qualities of American life, filled with instrumentalities and emptied of meaningful goals, have created apathy along with the heralded affluent society.[13]

While it would be foolhardy to insist that other peoples, or the Third World in general, eschew the road to high consumption, it is no less foolish to imagine that every deformity that accompanied product innovation or labor-management relations in the United States will be repeated elsewhere. There is an advantage to coming last not only in the technological sphere but also in consumer attitudes. To cite a simple current example, television is enjoyed just as much in other nations as it is in the United States, but often without the banalities of programming and advertising Americans have accustomed themselves to. Public trans-

[12] Walt Rostow, *op. cit.* pp. 12-13.

[13] See Harold Ephraim Mizruchi, *Success and Opportunity: A Study of Anomie.* New York: The Free Press of Glencoe, 1964; and for a general study of this theme, see Seymour Melman, *Our Depleted Society.* New York: Holt, Rinehart and Winston, 1965.

portation systems can be improved in order to avoid the crush of private transport that is customary in the United States and Western Europe. The list of contrasts could be extended indefinitely, but the point to be made is the same: the Mass Consumption Stage is simply not a stage so much as it is a byproduct of extreme asymmetry in the economic growth of the United States. To label something which is a function of inequality and status disequilibrium a "stage of economic growth" and a "reply to Marxism" is bizarre. Rostow does not deny the place of commodity production in modern societies. But his model does not have any realistic application to the Third World. It assumes an immense transfer of bourgeois values which, even if possible, would tend to exacerbate rather than alleviate the pressures for social change.

The United States has maintained its mass consumption stage partly by selling off its excess production to foreign markets. The spectacle of a city like Buenos Aires with six heavily imported television channels is a case in point. But consumer orientation in Buenos Aires only increases, in marked fashion, the separation of masses from classes. Furthermore, when national income is expended to indulge such luxuries as automobiles and washing machines, it only accelerates the demands for highways and electric power, which in themselves are essentially waste of energy sources in an economy where supplying such sources will only extend the economy's imbalance. In contrast to Rostow's views, such misapplication of energy sources postpones the actual take-off period by using economic wealth to supply the amenities and comforts of the moment and postponing indefinitely the basic needs of a solid future.

If the Rostow model were to be introduced by political and administrative fiat in the underdeveloped areas, it could well result in intensified class and social hostilities. The asymmetrical character of a society becomes most transparent when there is a drive for consumer affluence. In the United States, poverty is easily disguised and buried from sight—through the ecological concentration of the lower class population in ghetto communities—often with official connivance. Given the high proportion of people involved in mass consumption, inequalities become temporal annoyances rather than structural aggravations; they serve as opportunities to extend the benefits of the welfare state even more widely. The possibility that "wider" might mean "thinner" for most Third World countries, where the gap between wealth and poverty is already great, and that status disequilibrium might become increasingly pronounced as the Consumer Society dumps its wares on the Backward World is not entertained by Rostow. The irony is that to take the "non-communist manifesto" literally might actually serve to stimulate those abrasives between "haves" and "have-nots" which would put the *Communist* Manifesto back on the agenda of history.

III

The basis of the mass consumption society outlined by Rostow is strongly akin to the notion of the affluent society produced by John Kenneth Galbraith several years prior to the famed "non-communist manifesto."[14] But since the mid-'fifties, Galbraith has attempted to apply the argument of the affluent society to the underdeveloped world. This is the aspect of Galbraith's work we shall focus upon. His reputation as a liberal and as a friend of the developing peoples was summed up practically by his appointment as Ambassador to India, and theoretically by a series of lectures entitled "Economic Development in Perspective."[15] His reputation is not in contention here. What is in contention is the utility of the theory of affluence to the emergent nations.

From the point of view of economic theory, Galbraith never left Adam Smith. If *The Affluent Society* obscured this classical orientation because it was directed toward the novelty of mass wealth, his discussion of the developmental process is not covered by the same shroud. For this reason, his lectures on economic development retrospectively shed new light on the character and message of *The Affluent Society*.

Galbraith sets out to prove a set of connecting propositions: that the world is *not* divided into developed and underdeveloped countries; and that modern technological knowledge and a sound plan for using capital are *not* the main missing elements in an underdeveloped society. As it turns out, Galbraith considers the most serious deficiency in the developmental process to be the absence of popular education and proper education. The eighteenth-century doctrine of salvation through knowl-

[14] See John Kenneth Galbraith, *The Affluent Society*. Boston: Houghton-Mifflin Co., 1958.
[15] See John Kenneth Galbraith, *Economic Development in Perspective*. Cambridge, Mass.: Harvard University Press, 1962.

edge and reason is again employed. The hunt for a rational *homo economicus* is resurrected.

Generally, but not uniformly,[16] it has been asserted that Galbraith represents the firmest adherent to Keynesian economics. At the same time it has often been said that the conclusions in *The Affluent Society* represent a consistent critique of the mindlessness and amorality of private-sector approaches to an advanced capitalist society such as the United States. While it is true that Galbraith is discontented with the operations of government by the corporate elites, the ambiguities and blindspots he reveals in his alternatives to corporate direction should caution us against considering him a firm advocate of public-sector economics. It is one thing to criticize the operations of the corporate elite in the United States, and another to argue for socialist alternatives in Asia and Africa. As a matter of record, Galbraith's recommendations never extend beyond a call for the government to sponsor economic reforms based on increased planning. But he never surrenders the equilibrium model whereby the government (any government) becomes strangely equated with public sector, and business (any business) with the private sector, and both with an abstract theory of the harmonious society. Thus, Galbraith's lectures on development shed considerable light on his general economic views.

Galbraith's argument resembles the attitude of nineteenth-century Victorian commentators, who spoke of the drastic need for the indolent working classes to pull themselves up by their bootstraps. Of course, the middle class was blamed for failing to conduct "operation bootstrap." There is a strange set of omissions in his discussion on the nature of exploitation. These omissions permit Galbraith to speak of development without ever once mentioning colonialism, foreign or internal. This, in a series of lectures before an Indian public.

Galbraith has a perspective on development, which like that of Rostow, comes stratified in five stages. These stages are spaced analytically and horizontally rather than historically, as in Rostow: (1) The construction of organs for public administration and provision for an educated mentality, which would furnish a nucleus of people able to build

[16] See Stephen W. Rousseas, "Peaceful Coexistence in a World of Nuclear Power," in *Conference on Conflict, Consensus and Cooperation*, edited by Irving L. Horowitz. Geneva, N.Y.: Hobart & William Smith, 1962.

a system of public administration and, for that matter, other instruments of organization. (2) A period of popular enlightenment, during which the masses are able to participate in economic activity and in the administrative apparatus—although Galbraith does not indicate the specific forms of such participation. (3) The construction of a system of popular rewards. Underlying Galbraith's position is the utilitarianism of Smith. Galbraith believes that no person will bend his best energies to the enrichment of something or someone else. Social justice, hence, is either economically efficient on ego grounds, or not worth dealing with. (4) Here capital becomes the touchstone of development. Economic wealth is a factor in countries which are well along the developmental line. Indeed, Galbraith maintains that there is a strong possibility that capital provided for countries in their earliest stages of development will be wasted. This comes close to the neo-classical argument against "excessive" foreign aid. (5) Finally, capital ceases to be a limiting factor to development. Instead, development becomes dependent upon scientific and technological skills, the quality of the work force, and the ability to make full use of available resources.

Since Galbraith's five stages are considered here only in terms of their rationality, they represent at best a rule of thumb for describing types of national development. But beyond this rule of thumb Galbraith exhibits an extraordinary degree of eclecticism and evasiveness. It is not that he shares the pragmatic disrespect for economic prescriptions, but rather that he thinks of development atomistically, in terms of autonomous nations undergoing autonomous stages. The pragmatism in Galbraith's economic approach admits of few possibilities of generalization. When Galbraith does deal with such relevant economic issues as planning or mechanisms of organization, he comes very close to a simplified pragmatism in which economic decisions are rational and independent of the social circumstances or purposes involved. Since he does not admit that there are many commonalities among underdeveloped countries, he cannot grant the premise that planning is a requirement of development. The only "law" of economics thus turns out to be the law of exceptionalism—that is, lawlessness.

While Galbraith sees that no group of nations is uniquely qualified to extend assistance to other nations, and no other group of nations is condemned to the role of recipient, he fails to provide guidelines for the transformation of the present economic gap between producing nations and supplying nations. There *are* donor nations and recipient nations. The degree to which donor nations can be manifestly distinguished from recipient nations is itself a powerful index of the gap between developed and underdeveloped areas.[17] Galbraith declares that backward nations would be wise to copy from advanced nations what they need in the way of technological innovations. Selective borrowing in any event is done wherever necessary. The advantage of coming historically last has been virtually exhausted. The copying of advanced technological modes does not seem to lessen the dependence of the poor nations upon the rich nations, nor concomitantly does it seem to unduly disturb the wealthy classes of the rich nations.

In effect, Galbraith's admonition for poor nations to copy from rich nations represents a form of patriotic piety rather than an actual solution to the problem of world development. Galbraith's overemphasis on education as a panacea for developmental problems would seem more nearly to represent the attitude of an enlightened philosopher than the remarks of an economist interested in structural growth. When Galbraith says that a dollar invested in the intellectual improvement of human beings will often bring a greater increase in national income than a dollar devoted to railways, dams, machine tools, or other tangible capital goods, he simply forgets what schools are made of—namely, bricks and mortar and all the products of machine tools and other tangible goods. He also tends to see in education something other than learning. It becomes a "consumer good." He speaks of university education in particular as being a consumer service.

The business civilization which underwrites this philosophy of education needs little elaboration. It is extremely significant to note, however, that Galbraith has not considered seriously enough the *social consequences* of education. It may function not as a capital investment in the good life, but as a capital investment in the agonized life. The man of education who is, at the same time, immobilized by social stagnation, who is educated beyond the abilities of his society to absorb his knowledge, is a frustrated man. And a society of educated men in a condition

17 See, for example, Raúl Prebisch, *Nueva Política Comercial para el Desarrollo*. Mexico-Buenos Aires: Fondo de Cultura Económica, 1964.

of semi-development is a frustrated society. The consequences of such frustrations are not the good life, but the revolutionary life. As one writer recently pointed out:

> The dilemma is clear. Developing countries desperately need a large pool of intellectual capital in reserve, but it is not always possible to find employment for all of them until a rather advanced state of development has been reached. Unfortunately, this is one resource that cannot be stored away until it is ready to be put to use. If professionals cannot find employment they go away (if they can) or they begin to use their talents to change things so that they *can* practice their profession. In trying to do so, they sometimes learn a new one—that of revolutionary! The rewards derived from being a successful political militant are often such that students prefer to keep on in this new role than to go outside the university and seek unsuccessfully for a position in an already overcrowded profession such as law or a profession where personal connections rather than scientific ability are often the criteria for gaining access to scarce research instruments, as in medicine.[18]

As a matter of fact, we find that the command posts of revolutionary parties in the developing areas are drawn precisely from the best educated. It is therefore clear that only in a special sense can education provide a consumer service. Galbraith ignores the fact that it is a consumer service which is customarily gratified *after*, rather than before, the construction of the material conditions of a mature economy.

In Galbraith, as in Rostow, defense of corporate practices takes precedence over an analysis of development as such. Hence, both are equally committed to monetarist, pump-priming solutions that would leave intact the structural bases of society. Galbraith provides an interesting case of those who conceive of development in terms of laisser faire, laisser passer. He speaks of a public sector not as a massive build-up of capital accumulation but in terms of monetary intervention and price supports. In Galbraith's world the private sector and the public sector

[18] David Nasatir, "University and Politics in Latin America" (unpublished monograph). An abbreviated version of this study appeared as "Student Action in Latin America," *Trans-Action*, Vol. 2, No. 3, March-April 1965, pp. 8-11.

both resolve themselves into a theory of the autonomous economy. What is at stake is the belief that economic solutions are possible, independent of political systems. Above all, Galbraith does not want to upset the image of industrial life with which he is acquainting his audience, namely, the United States model of development. Even though the functional autonomy of the economy is found only in advanced nations, Galbraith persists in raising the autonomous economy as a *general* principle of development.

To deal with the corporate personality as sovereign, and to speak exclusively of the negative aspects of any influence which impairs the autonomy of the private-economic sector is already to prejudice the outcome of the analysis. Galbraith performs this kind of juxtaposition by assuming that the industrial firm is the necessary basis for *all* economic development. He says that the industrial plant has a highly demanding personality. But if the industrial firm, which is at the same time an autonomous firm, is necessary for social development, then we are presented with a truism. It is a tautology to define the problem of industrial development in terms of an industrial firm. What is really at issue is whether industry is going to be run by private management or by public authority.

The familiar clichés about the risks of a public-sector economy are repeated by Galbraith. He refers especially to abuse in the hiring and firing of personnel and the intrusion of politics and patronage into the corporation. Galbraith holds that both of these practices subvert the subtle relationships on which an effective development of the corporate personality depends.[19] Interestingly, Galbraith discusses only the autonomy of the industrial firm rather than the autonomy of the nation (the prime reason why a nation often enters the developmental race). Galbraith maintains that the corporate "personality" must be protected from intrusion by outside authorities.[20] But that very personality of the cor-

---

[19] This seems to have become the theoretical justification in India for the failure to complete, or even extend, the socialized sector of the nation.

[20] It appears that recent ambassadors to India must meet two qualifications: first, they must be politically liberal, and, second, believers in private enterprise. Chester Bowles likewise sees the "greatest need" of the developing nations to be "private investment to aid the free sectors of their economies." See "The Developing Nations' Greatest Need," *The New York Times Magazine*, April 12, 1964, pp. 15, and 87-92.

poration is exactly the element within a developing nation that is least concerned with overall national aims and the overall social planning.

Galbraith's conclusion comes in the form of an admission: the autonomy of the corporation may not protect the public commonweal adequately. But this statement comes too late, in the form of a pious wish. Galbraith offers no guidance, mechanism, or human agency which could in fact control the private corporate personality. The accumulation of private wealth is not made accountable to any public body because the corporate personality underlying wealth is basically irresponsible. In a social setting in which the very corporate personality is a contributing element to the political and economic difficulties of an emergent nation, Galbraith's remarks seem singularly out of place. If this kind of thinking came in the form of straight polemicizing for a Carnegie-like solution to economic ills, "self-help," then one could not feel any real chagrin or discomfort. It would be understood that this was a natural position to be taken by a business man. What is disturbing about Galbraith is that he stands as a popular spokesman for what in the United States is conceived to be an excessive dose of economic liberalism. This is the case despite the fact that the substance of Galbraith's developmental orientation involves a repetition of the entrepreneurial virtues. The tragedy of Galbraith is that he has steadfastly remained a man of the New Deal, and has not seriously considered the problems of the Third World from a perspective removed in time and in place from American society.

In a brilliant, well-reasoned paper on "Economics and the Quality of Life," Galbraith has now taken up problems of social development as they manifest themselves at an advanced stage. One finds that Galbraith actually has a double standard: one for newly emerging nations and another for fully mature nations. For the newly emerging nations he argues in favor of extending the private-economic sector; for the mature nations he argues that the "growing proportion of the requirements of an increasingly civilized community—schools, colleges, libraries, museums, hospitals, recreational facilities—are by their nature in the public domain."[21] He further points out that modern technology, such as the automotive industry, requires a vast network of public highways and traffic regulations which clearly fall into the public sector. In general, his

[21] John Kenneth Galbraith, "Economics and the Quality of Life," *Science*, Vol. 145, No. 3628, July 10, 1964, pp. 117-23.

message is that *developing* economies have economic growth as an upper-most concern, while *mature* economies have as their uppermost concern *social* and *political growth*—that is, mass participation.

The courageous aspects of Galbraith's argument cannot be denied or ignored. He has shown categorically and clearly that as the world marches forward, economic concerns recede in importance—if not for the professional economist with a vested interest in the rhetoric of his discipline, then at least for the mass of humanity. What Galbraith cannot seem to accept is that the gap between underdeveloped and developed is not made along the lines of *homo economicus* and *homo sociologicus*. Problems of development at every step of the way involve sociological and political decisions. It is no less a political act to determine the allocation of scarce resources in eighteenth-century England than it is to determine the allocation of abundant resources in twentieth-century America. It is easier for an economist to make general rules than for nearly any other scientist. To argue the need for a broadened private sector in India, and a broadened public sector in the United States is a respectable position, but it is quixotic against a background of world affairs which seeks to promote the private sector as a bulwark against the public sector—rather than a joint strategy.

In connection with Galbraith's emphasis on the private sector, it should be emphasized that this sector in India has been a dismal failure. The landholders have not adopted Gandhian measures of agrarian reform; manufacturers have not engaged in the sort of large-scale production which would be less profitable but more socially useful. It is also a fact that the public sector in the United States has become so identified with the bureaucratic sector that it is hard to say whether an enlargement of this public sector really suits the needs of the nation today. Perhaps Galbraith's use of the terms private and public sector are in need of some more adequate frame of reference—one which would enable us to move beyond the quandary of multiple policy recommendations based on geographic locale and economic strategies, and into the area of long-range goals. Galbraith is unquestionably correct in saying that "we do not have development in order to make our surroundings more hideous, our culture more meretricious, or our lives less complete," but it should be duly noted that hideous environment, cultural bankruptcy, and fragmented lives—the very warp and woof of life in the Third World—are precisely a consequence of incomplete, partial development—a process of imitative modernism that ultimately makes structural reform more, rather than less, difficult.

IV

Gunnar Myrdal points up the problems faced by an economist who starts with a theory of equilibrium and a faith in socialism. His view of development is a case of misplaced concreteness. Myrdal, whose work on an international economy is the nearest thing we have to a meaningful global theory of a post-class "one-world,"[22] and whose slim volume on rich lands and poor lands is one of the very few treatises on the subject by an orthodox Western economist which recognizes the culpabilities no less than the capabilities of the First World,[23] has simply reversed the Galbraith paradox. He has gone from a general theory of international development, which is broadly liberal, to a re-evaluation of United States development which is in general more restrained and conservative than the views expressed earlier in *An American Dilemma:* an emphasis on trade and commerce, coupled with a consensual attitude phrased in terms of monetary and fiscal supports for the less developed areas. This position rests on adopting a static viewpoint from which crucial variables in growth, such as limits in natural resources and trade blockages, are excluded. His view converges on the same point: the need to retain the present ratio and balance of the two economic sectors. Neither Myrdal nor Galbraith resolves the dilemmas of dual sectors in a single nation, or between nations. Both offer the hope that such equilibrium will ultimately be resolved by evolution, education, and enlightenment—by the conventional forces which are generally grouped under "moral suasion." But why such persuasion should fare better in the present era, and with the present pressures of power and interests, remains magnificently cloudy, mainly because Myrdal concentrates almost exclusively on Western institutions and Western democratic norms of behavior.

[22] See in particular Gunnar Myrdal, *An International Economy: Problems and Prospects.* New York: Harper, 1956; and *Beyond the Welfare State: Economic Planning and Its International Implications.* New Haven: Yale University Press, 1960.
[23] Gunnar Myrdal, *Rich Lands and Poor: The Road to World Prosperity.* New York: Harper, 1957.

Challenge to Affluence is structured in terms of formal economic paradoxes that can find resolution only in an equilibrium theory.[24] The underlying theme is that the American economy exhibits relative stagnation, that the record of economic development in the United States is highly unsatisfactory, given the fact that there is a continued high and rising level of unemployment, and a prolonged consumer orientation in which there is too little left both for saving and for investment to keep the economy growing quickly. While Myrdal holds that the American economic crisis is structural in character, he does not indicate anything in the economy which would need alteration in order to change present tendencies, nor is there any theory of overdevelopment. The very reverse seems to emerge. A series of political implications are made which would indicate that Myrdal thinks that the American economy is free to act as it wishes. There is, for example, a statement that business should be encouraged to expand rapidly by means of a revised tax structure, which in fact contradicts Myrdal's earlier rejection of the classical theory of the perfect market and the perfect economic integration.[25] Myrdal's exhortations that Americans need to have a new educational orientation, a new training and retraining for the age of automation and specialization, and that they ought not run the risk of "clamping a class structure upon the nation" are a set of rhetorical statements which seriously weaken his claim as an authentic student of American society.

Likewise, the concept of an "underclass" represents a powder-puff substitution for "hungry masses" or "poverty-stricken." It is a term which in fact removes the issue of social mobility in America beyond structural analysis. There is a strong element of paternalism in Myrdal's suggestions. He uses the concept "underclass" in the same way the social welfare establishment uses the word "poor." The United States has a particularly heavy responsibility for these underprivileged since traditionally they are the least able to articulate their interests. This lack of political articulation is not confined to any underclass, though, but is a general property of the United States social order in an age which has emphasized elitist *policies* in place of spontaneous mass *politics*.

Everyone will have something to enjoy and quote. Businessmen will

---

[24] Gunnar Myrdal, *Challenge to Affluence*. New York: Pantheon Books, 1963.
[25] Gunnar Myrdal, "Methodological Note on the Concepts and the Value Premises," *An International Economy*. New York: Harper & Row, 1956, pp. 336-40.

be pleased by Myrdal's statements that working-class organization is strong in America and business organizations should emulate this by building up their own organizational efficiency. Economists will be made happy by the view that, since the United States has had a heavy dose of short-range planning, it needs much more emphasis on long-range planning. Free trade and low tariff men will find joy in Myrdal's advocacy of the widest possible free trade and of tariff aids rather than tariff barriers as a means of integrating an international economy. American liberals will be happy to know that American democracy is strong, but saddened to learn that the Negro question remains unsolved. Hence they can look forward to making American democracy stronger by an open-ended social mobility system. The politicians in Washington will be pleased to know that, even though they form a tight little policy-making elite with a low level of mass participation, they are motivated by altruistic responses (as everyone knows); the country has nothing to worry about.

In effect, Myrdal supports every sober economic principle ever held by every sober economic man. He can do this because he is always dealing with the benefits and the consequences of affluence and never with the social costs or psychological penalties inflicted by economic development. No one can really take issue with Myrdal, since he is not stating a problem but only a fact: affluence is the essential drive of modern man, and therefore roadblocks to affluence, such as mass poverty, have to be removed. But the roadblock theory comes upon hard times when it is realized that not everything in life, not even in American life, can be packaged into an equilibrium model and resolved by the good sense and good will of good people.

These criticisms notwithstanding, there are sound elements in Myrdal's analysis of the developmental process in advanced countries. He calls attention to the lack of participation in public life, which he claims derives from the heterogeneous composition of the population in the United States. His further point—that the lower down the economic scale one goes, the less membership and participation exist in voluntary organizations—is a fundamental social problem no less than an economic fact.

Myrdal's economic liberalism was then foreshadowed in his earlier book, *Rich Lands and Poor*. This work dealt more specifically with development in the Third World. He states the basic position which has been adopted by pamphleteers and popularizers the world over: (a) There is a world divided between many poor nations and a few rich ones. (b) The basic weapon of the poor nations is to make such nuisances out of themselves so as to attract widespread attention. (c) The rich nations, in their own self-interest, must eschew any Anglo-American bias and push for a more equitable distribution and sharing of the natural and the national wealth. At the same time, the new nations must also eschew traditional Marxism, with its emphasis on social relations at the expense of social production and internal trade. The assumption underlying each of Myrdal's premises is that the Third World is now at the same stage as the developed world formerly was. The problem is therefore temporal rather than structural.[26]

Myrdal wants to steer a course between a "stable equilibrium" of Western economics and a "perpetual disequilibrium" of the Soviet bloc. While it is clear that Myrdal is close in *sentiment* to the aspirations of Third World nations, it is clearer still that he finds it difficult to see the Third World as something different from the "Third Way" of his native Sweden. His "theory of international trade" falls prey to the kind of narrow and confined thinking of which he accuses most economists. For a concept of balanced trade involves a deeper concept of internationalism as such, which contradicts Myrdal's own grudging acknowledgment that the nationalism of the Afro-Asian bloc is positive and useful even necessary. In fact the Third World is moving further away from an international economy and closer to an economy integrated along national or regional bloc lines. At some point in the future these continental blocs may contribute to an integrated world economy, but not at present.

Myrdal is fully aware of the technical dilemmas involved in integrating a world economy, and of the "ideological connotations" involved in aid programs from the International Monetary Fund. But he fails to indicate that this ideological connotation is a natural corollary of economic institutional facts. The absence of an international organization, of a World State, becomes central to Myrdal's thinking, since for him it is only through such international banking agencies that development can proceed through a tranquil and meaningful trade policy. Thus

---

[26] Gunnar Myrdal, *Rich Lands and Poor, op. cit.*; an updated and more popular version of this middle way solution is contained in Chester Bowles, "The Developing Nations' Greatest Need," *op. cit.*

Myrdal's "economic liberalism" is confounded by a "scientific conservatism"—since it permits him to speak of development, the excesses of
colonialism, the need for planning agencies, etc., without ever specifically
mentioning what kinds of development are needed, for whom, at whose
expense. There is no examination of which colonialists have perpetrated
what kinds of excesses, or of which continue to perform a colonial role
through economic control, who will direct the agencies of planning, and
what mechanisms of control are and are not permissible.

Without such information Myrdal becomes an economic ideologist.
He cannot move beyond pointing out to his colleagues the standpoints
of their researches. But moral suasion still does not confront the political
dimensions of development—the struggle to control the state in order to
promote development, and the struggle against the colonial powers for
the control of development per se. Myrdal reflects the gradualist philosophy that entails mutual understanding, men of good will, co-operation,
etc., which in effect ignores the reasons for international economic and
political schisms in the first place. Increasingly, theorists are divided
between those who feel development must come about through international co-operation, and those who feel development can only succeed
at the national or regional level regardless of whether international co-
operation exists. Myrdal stands with the first group. But by so doing he
has isolated himself from the empirical facts of development.

V

Wilbert Moore is a sociologist who is not only aware but is also self-
critical. Not many sociologists will admit that they have "been challenged particularly (and correctly) on a fundamental point of social
stratification." Fewer still recognize the handicap of studying social
change after having "been long subject to the discipline of thought in
sociology that discouraged the study of change." Unfortunately, to recognize the shortcomings in sociology does not resolve these problems. And
if Moore has shown insight into the sociological aspects of development,
he also provides a case study of the disintegration of scientific firmness
when the values of the fully developed nations come in conflict with
those of the emerging nations.

Wilbert Moore represents a special dimension in developmental analysis partly because he places a heavy premium upon non-economic factors. The study of social polarities, such as status incongruity and status coalescence, the achievement-ascription axis, particularism and universalism, normative and deviant patterns of behavior, all of these are tributes to the social systems approach, to Talcott Parsons and his variety of functionalism. There can be little doubt that men like Moore have creatively carried this language over into the study of development. But it is more than a special language. It is also an ideological style and a form of advocacy. There is, first, the felt need for studying social stratification as an expression of the forms of inequality rather than as the relationships between power and powerlessness, wealth and poverty. There is, second, the displacement of the concept of economic development by the more vague term "social change," and, finally, there is the tautological identification of the developmental process with the industrialization process.[27] In short, at this point where sociology could produce a unique point of view it fails to supply a meaningful vocabulary of motives.

The world of Wilbert Moore is one in which "mobilization" takes place without the active participation of masses, and "integration" takes place through administrative fiat—open-ended to be sure. The exaggerated costs of such perfect mobilization and integration are seen in elitist terms, rather than as an activity of the popular classes, hence the cost factor in "social evolution" is unaccounted for. The problem of industrial development is isolated from the problem of social transformation. Development becomes non-historical, a process which takes place through the Archimedean lever of social engineering. Since social inequality is "universal," the problem is said to be an "operational" one: how to transfer loyalties from old rulers and elites to new rulers and elites.[28] Since low-wage policies engender animosity, the solution is to expand consumer purchasing power. Since an industrial system is more vulnerable to "civil disorders" than earlier systems, the task is to consol-

[27] See on this Wilbert E. Moore, "Industrialization and Social Change," in *Industrialization and Society*, edited by Bert F. Hoselitz and Wilbert E. Moore. Paris: UNESCO-Mouton, 1963.
[28] See Wilbert E. Moore and Arnold S. Feldman (eds.), *Labor Commitments and Social Change in Developing Areas*. New York: Social Science Research Council, 1960.

idate effective control by the state (without, of course, making such control total).

The magical words in Moore's position are consensus, equilibrium, and maintenance.[29] The segmentary nature of social forces is covered by an umbrella which at one and the same time prevents any person or class from seeking shelter outside it and also offers the shelter of sociological togetherness. One could dismiss such an approach perfunctorily. Yet, it is clear that the sociological dimension does add something to the economic viewpoint. At the same time, the process whereby the "hard" science of economics is "softened" by sociological inquiry is itself worthy of further examination.[30] Wilbert Moore is faced with the Herculean task of explaining the existence of social change from the vantage point of a theoretical system which ignores change.

Moore first emphasizes the "normality of change." But this normality implies only a modification, not a discarding of functional equilibrium models, with their assumptions of near perfect integration, the presence of strains but the absence of conflicts, and their foreclosure on questions of the *sources* of change. But whether a view of elite social agencies functioning as instruments of "tension management" does more than treat change as a secondary factor in social structure remains unresolved. To believe that a "golden mean" exists for the solution of conflicts is a form of faith that has little factual basis underlying it.

Moore is aware of the historical theories implicit in any doctrine of evolution. He raises critically "qualities of change," especially the "myth" of a singular theory of change or direction. Moore launches a powerful critique against monistic doctrines, such as those developed by Spengler, Sorokin, and the evolutionists. But whether Moore's "eclectic and tolerant" acceptance of *all* theories of change as potentially valuable in the study of different aspects of social systems can really escape the weaknesses of extreme historical relativism remains uncertain.

Moore better appreciates the weaknesses in dialectical doctrines of change than the equally serious shortcomings in strict cyclical theories.

[29] See Wilbert E. Moore and Arnold S. Feldman, "Society as a Tension-Management System," *Behavioral Science and Civil Defense Disaster Research*. Washington: National Academy of Sciences, National Research Council, 1962, pp. 93-105.
[30] Wilbert E. Moore, *Social Change*. Englewood Cliffs, N.J.: Prentice-Hall, Inc., 1963.

He has a tendency to dismiss the possibility that the past was in fact ever better than the present in any sense whatsoever. Even if the "noble savage" approach represents a distortion based on nostalgia, still it is quite possible to speak of stagnation as well as progression.

It might be possible to deal with change in terms of primary pivots: the eighteenth century in terms of national struggles, the nineteenth century in terms of class struggles, and the twentieth century in terms of race struggles. It may well be that a uni-deterministic theory of change can be so structured and limited in space and time that the reductionistic features, most objectionable in any deterministic system, can be removed. A general theory of conflict examining the relationship between individualism and socialism, logos and mythos, reason and unreason, may offer an understanding of change no less objectionable and more practicable than a theory of action which makes wide assumptions as to the functionality of consensus. Although Moore is willing to grant that it is the beginning of wisdom to identify dichotomies, he sees such polarities as reflecting only the weaknesses of sociological thought, instead of the paradoxes in the social world.

Moore's analysis of the specific factors involved in generational cycles, changes in formal organization, and inter-group conflict in preclusive groups is a model of good sense. Particularly noteworthy is his appreciation of the fact that the ascription-achievement axes are not mutually exclusive alternatives, but conflicting principles present in every social system. These conflicting principles are particularly important in the study of the developmental process, given the tendency to view achievement as a higher stage in the social system, and one which cancels out the importance of ascription in the developed societies. It should be pointed out, however, that the struggle is not simply between partisans of tradition and upholders of rational innovation. This dichotomy assumes too neat a world, one in which "irrational" processes are simply ruled out on the grounds that they entail unstructured or spontaneous behavior.[31] Development occurs at specific levels which may or may not

[31] The recent sociological studies of mass behavior should be consulted on this problem; in particular, Herbert Blumer, "Collective Behavior," *Review of Sociology*, edited by J. B. Gittler. New York: John Wiley & Sons, 1957, pp. 127-158; Kurt Lang and Gladys E. Lang, *Collective Dynamics*. New York: Thomas Y. Crowell, 1961; and Neil J. Smelser, *Theory of Collective Behavior*. New York: The Free Press of Glencoe, 1963.

affect other levels of society, or may indeed have an adverse effect, as did the suppression of musical and artistic creativity under Hitler and Stalin. This raises anew the question of how social liberation is related to economic expansion. But these problems are not dealt with in Moore's work since he is overwhelmed by an extreme rationalism in his denial of the role of ideals and utopias in the actual conduct of social change. Were Moore not so taken with evolutionary development, he would consider that revolutionary changes and demands can be based on a vision of a more perfect future as well as on a simple response to material exigencies. Moore sometimes sounds as if he actually believes that men live by bread alone.

That his approach to the developmental process is called "modernization" is itself highly revealing. The choice in the newly emerging nations is precisely one between modernism and structural innovation. The process of modernization is *not* synonymous with economic development. Modernization is related to a special form of economic change which emphasizes bureaucratic innovation and a host of mending processes such as education and legal reform. In contrast to modernization, the structuralist school of development holds that the process of development requires smashing even more than mending; that is, requires an overhaul in social relations as well as in industrial productivity as such. Moore's failure to grapple with this problem leads him to describe, as "radically inappropriate," structuralist options to modernization. On the other hand, since he recognizes that continuous growth involves the direct intervention of the state at those points where voluntary choice breaks down, he is hard put to explain how developing regions can respond to the necessity of continuous growth without calling upon mechanisms of persuasion and coercion which are lodged in the state. Moore tends to speak of modernization as an autonomous social process. Hence, in the name of pluralism he avoids the political problems of development occasioned by the role of planned processes.

At the root of Moore's equilibrium theory of social change is his attitude toward business civilization.[32] What particularly disturbs him is "collectivism" and its economic equivalent "socialism." Juxtaposed to

[32] Wilbert E. Moore, *The Conduct of the Corporation*. New York: Random House, 1962. This book forms the basis of my discussion of Moore's concept of the fully modernized society.

this is "individualism" and its imagined economic equivalent "capitalism." Indeed, when Moore is critical of the conduct of the corporation, it is precisely on the grounds of the sentiments of corporate collectivism and company patriotism—which smack too much of the socialist evil. "Private socialism"—the gigantic industrial empires which exist for autos, chemicals, and utilities, and combine the worst features of bureaucratic socialism and capitalist inefficiency—is condemned, and it is urged that severe, genuine competition can remove such evils. Lacking this restoration of competitive capitalism, Moore feels that the "professionalization of business management" would be best. Indeed, the concept of professionalization is held to be the only real protection workers have against company tyranny.

Moore fully appreciates the fact that the concentration of economic power is a critical necessity for modern productive technology, forms of mass organization, and for social development as such. What he rejects as reactionary is the argument that public-sector control can solve any of the problems raised by private-sector ownership. In his view such public ownership would only exaggerate the problem. Again it is the "inhibition" of a super-organized bureaucracy with which he is concerned. And since the idea of abolishing big business is held to be reactionary, "a silly attempt to recreate a simpler life," we are left with no alternative to the present but to accept it. This super-imposition of the American growth model on all foreign economies conditions Moore to modernism and moves him away from structural alteration. Since modern business civilization has satisfied creature comforts and greatly expanded consumer goods, it seems only natural that socialist alternatives would be viewed as everything from nostalgic to reactionary. Moore has broadened the equation of development with industrialism to one which asserts that development equals modernization. But this only introduces sociological variables; it does not help solve problems.

The problem is that the "super-bureaucracy" is no less a feature of the United States than of the Soviet Union, and hence it cannot be used as an argument in support of a private-sector economy over a public-sector economy. Further, the existence of this super-bureaucracy is nowhere larger than in underdeveloped nations of Latin America. Here again the threat of a burgeoning bureaucracy is no argument in defense of the present against the future. Moore does not seem to appreciate the distinction between abolishing big business, an effort which might indeed be reactionary, and abolishing big businessmen—which might be the only way left to many nations to establish genuinely profitable big business.

The assumption that social development is best under a system of checks and balances—when an alert business community can prevent "politically disembodied trustees" from acting irresponsibly—substitutes a constitutional utopian longing for the present realities in which business functions as part of a developmental trusteeship. In the United States such a system of dynamic equilibrium may be an effective barrier to tyrannies of management, government, or labor. But Moore also falls into an ethnocentric trap by assuming that the rest of the world has nurtured the kind of middle class which has emerged in the United States, or has the kind of resilient state apparatus that has grown up in the United States since the New Deal. The United States is an economic society. The state is the regulatory mechanism for this society. Third World nations are distinguished by precisely the reverse processes. They are political societies. And the economy becomes the dependent variable in the operations of the state.

Even if modernization and industrialization are equivalent processes, which is extremely difficult to accept on empirical grounds, neither defines the intensely *political* attack on economic issues in Third World nations. Neither modernization nor industrialization are full-scale developments. The three-hundred-year record of Latin America's subservience to Europe and North America proves this beyond a shadow of a doubt. For here, in this huge area, one finds modernization and industrialization as ongoing processes—yet both take place in a developmental vacuum. They occur without a corresponding transformation in social relations, and hence Latin America remains part of the "developing" world, irrespective of how many business establishments are set up, or how many goods for consumer satisfaction are produced. The paradox is that individual initiative is the last thing to be found in these individualistic economies. For individualism is an ideology of independence that can only become effective through a high degree of political organization.

VI

With the passage of time, and the apparent success of the Third World in developing an ideology based on "popular classes" and "working masses," the idea of sectoral in contrast to national approaches to the development process have become prominent. Indeed, a kind of Marxism-in-reverse has come to the fore. In its most exaggerated form, the unilinear theory of history is based upon the notion that development is best achieved by placing chief responsibility in the hands of a primary social force or economic sector. According to this view, there is good reason to believe that a single class must take command of the developmental process, but there is no good reason to believe that this class must be drawn from the popular classes. In its conservative form the unilinear theory of history is based on the elitist possibilities of the traditional and/or middle classes.[33] This desperation theory of development —desperate because it attempts to preserve the social *status quo* by employing revolutionary theories of the vanguard for its purpose—is best seen in the work of the American historian John J. Johnson. Given his role in planning American strategy for Latin America, his view can scarcely be considered peripheral or insignificant.

In constructing his theory, Johnson calls upon military history and modern Communist regimes to vindicate his claims. There is a nostalgic yearning for a return to Colbert's use of the French army to build an economy of primary accumulation. And there is the inevitable side glance at Mao Tse Tung's transformation of the Chinese army into a vanguard labor force. It is seen as the key to building an industrial network, just as under the old Confucian emperors the military were used to build the imperial tombs and stone walls. In the doctrine of counterinsurgency, the assumption is made that anti-guerrilla activities are merely the logical opposite of guerrilla activities. And in this extension of RAND Corporation thinking to the problem of development, it is assumed that one army under socialist supervision is the same as another army under capitalist or feudal supervision. If human history moved ac-

---

[33] John J. Johnson, *Political Change in Latin America: The Emergence of the Middle Sectors.* Stanford: Stanford University Press, 1958.

cording to pure logic, this approach might be valid. But this assumption is precisely what is most questionable in the Johnson thesis.

If this thesis is applied to the Third World, Latin America has some special incongruities. It is an area which turns to its military as the court of ultimate national redemption, while at the same time it is aware that the military has crushed democratic and constitutional processes more often and more painfully than any other social force in the hemisphere. The traditional military has been the bulwark of anti-Communist crusades without whom, as Johnson himself makes plain, nearly every republic in Latin America would be much more radical politically than it now is.[34] At the same time, and in the midst of a declining trend in left-wing mass civilian politics, with the exceptions of Chile, Bolivia, and perhaps Venezuela, a modernizing *military* has been in the ascendancy in such diversified political climates as Mexico, Guatemala, Brazil, and Cuba. Indeed, "socialism from above" is just as much a rallying cry among some military elites as the "anti-Communist crusade" was in the last decade. In their public behavior the military establishments of Latin America exemplify lawlessness; in their political action, undemocratic processes. At the same time, they always make their *golpes* and *manifestaciones* in the name of law, legitimacy, order, and security. And they have no peer as a self-seeking and self-promoting segment; yet they insist equally strongly (sometimes with considerable justice) that they alone are entitled to act as guardians of the national morality and the national treasury.

Johnson etches these ambiguities in a way which elicits respect and admiration for his firm ethnographic capacity and, no less, for his documentary use of writers on the subject of Latin American militarism who preceded him. Particularly outstanding is his ability to weave the historical background to current possibilities for vitalizing the military in terms of developmental needs. Johnson's fusion of history and theory is best exemplified by his discussion of the soldier as citizen and bureaucrat and of the function and role of military ideology. By seeing the Latin

[34] John J. Johnson, *The Military and Society in Latin America.* Stanford: Stanford University Press, 1964; in this same connection see his earlier paper on the same theme, "The Latin-American Military as a Politically Competing Group in Transitional Society," in *The Role of the Military in Underdeveloped Countries.* Princeton: Princeton University Press, 1962, pp. 91-129.

military first and foremost as an example of bureaucratic behavior, Johnson spares himself the needless dilemma of distinguishing the military from all other bureaucratic agencies. However limited his typology of "civil-militarism" may turn out to be, it deserves serious attention from students of economic development no less than from specialists in social organization.[35]

Johnson's discussion of the social origins and early backgrounds of professional military men in Latin America provides a significant clue to his support of the military, rather than the middle class, as an agent for change. He points to seven fundamental variables: racial origin, educational levels, small-town background of the officer corps, Roman Catholicism, non-propertied origins, and the immigration patterns. These are woven into an interesting mosaic which adds up to the perspective that in Latin America, unlike North America, social origins and sectional backgrounds count for a great deal in defining military stratification. His elaborate discussion of the concept "civil-militarism" and his belief that it has a long life ahead are likewise well reasoned.

There can be no doubt that the conclusion drawn by Johnson, if correct, can be vital to the future. The economically developing nations of Latin America show a weakening tendency on the part of the military to perform or even desire political roles. It may become intrinsic to development that military specialization increases to a great extent. This specialization is not to be confused with the continued rise in military operations throughout the Third World. Sometimes it is not quite clear whether Johnson realizes a distinction between the *size* of the armed forces and its *character*. Development has meant a distinct rise in military expenditures from Argentina to Zanzibar. "Independence" is sometimes measured by such military power. While the size of the Latin American military has continued to increase, the character of this establishment in most cases has not undergone significant change.

The Brazilian military offers important evidence on the develop-

[35] Two good examples of the interpenetration of civilian and military functions are Edward A. Shils, "The Military in the Political Development of the New States," in John J. Johnson (ed.), *The Role of the Military in Underdeveloped Countries*, pp. 7-68; and Moshe Lissak, "Social Change, Mobilization, and Exchange of Services Between the Military Establishment and the Civil Society," in *Economic Development and Cultural Change*, Vol. XIII, No. 1, Part 1, October 1964, pp. 1-19.

mental stimulus it can create under exceptionally powerful civilian leadership. But it also illustrates how quickly such a military can return to its classical *coup d'état* role in the absence of such civilian leadership. We should resist the tendency to lump militarisms together in an undifferentiated way, without taking into account some of the special features of the Brazilian historical development which led to a peculiarly non-violent military ideology. Nonetheless, it must be pointed out somewhat somberly in the light of political developments between 1954 and 1964 that the Brazilian military, while historically distinctive, has increasingly acted less responsibly in recent years and resembles more and more the military of other Latin American countries. The interference of the Brazilian military in the Vargas regime of 1954, in the Quadros regime of 1961, and in the Goulart regime of 1964 makes perfectly plain that its behavior is unfortunately more militaristic than it is developmental. The whole concept of guardianship which the Brazilian military elite relies on has become part of *Falangist* rhetoric throughout the hemisphere.

Although the distinction between Hispanic and Brazilian military patterns is made sharply, other distinctions between military establishments are not drawn as clearly. For example, the highly professionalized military elite of Mexico and Uruguay contrasts sharply with the highly politicized military elites of Argentina and most Central American republics. But this distinction is not related to the problems of Latin American social development as such. Likewise, Johnson does not distinguish between "revolution from above" and "revolution from below" or describe the role each plays in the developmental process.

Despite Johnson's disclaimer of having any special knowledge or special qualifications to deal with Castro's Cuba, most of his large-scale generalizations stand or fall on the Cuban experience. And this reticence to examine the Cuban experience sheds some doubt on his modest disclaimer. For example, his statement that nowhere in Spanish America is there a situation comparable to what is found in some of the Third World nations of Africa and Asia, where officers can claim the right to direct government activities on the basis of both acquired skills and moral leadership, is challenged by the Cuban experience. Castroism is precisely the same manifestation which is seen elsewhere in the policies of Tito, Nasser, Touré, Sukarno, and other Third World leaders.

The dilemmas in this approach have perhaps best been understood by Johnson himself. His recent work can be read as a refutation of his own past faith in the middle classes. His earlier book on *Political Change in Latin America* was basically a paean of praise to the middle classes. But in *The Military and Society in Latin America* he points out that: (a) The middle sectors have forsaken radicalism in favor of conservatism. (b) The higher the stake middle classes have in society, the lower the risks they are willing to take to promote social change. (c) Middle-class support for militarism and the growing reciprocity of that support—that is, militaristic support of the middle sectors—invalidates any claims for middle-class democracy. (d) Statism is defined as a bureaucratic control of economic resources, and this bureaucracy is the source of middle-class strength. (e) On the very last pages—irony of ironies—Johnson promulgates the strange idea that the military will save Latin American civilization for, if not from, the middle classes. The assumption is clear: for the middles classes, life in the villages and in the underdeveloped portions of their own nations is held to be an impossible status demotion, a "virtual banishment from civilization." At this point the military are to be conscripted into a gigantic domestic "Military Peace Corps," or what is more likely, into an enormous Works Progress Administration, all because the middle classes have no stomach for the kind of national sacrifice that identification with nationalism entails. Presumably, if the military fail to behave as a proper surrogate for the bourgeoisie, the Church will stand next in rotation.

Nonetheless, the same sort of criticisms can be leveled against his present attraction toward a military approach to rapid development. The ultimate assumption which Johnson makes about the role of the military in the developmental process is that it is the most readily mobilized sector of society; it is subject to military discipline and can therefore be employed efficiently and inexpensively in public works. There are three flaws in this theory: First, the actual costs of maintaining a military establishment are far higher than the actual yield in the developmental process. They serve to drain off potential sources of new investment, rather than add to them. Second, the nature of the military establishments in the Third World is such as to discourage rather than to encourage the developmental process. These military regimes are top-heavy, with a low rate of enlistment and even lower morale in the non-officer corps, and with an officer corps more concerned with politics than military organization and discipline. Third, Johnson assumes that the military will act in a restrained manner, but in fact, wherever these military establishments have replaced colonial or semi-colonial armies, they have to be more rather than less militant than other social forces.

Despite the disclaimer by Johnson, the absence of any discussion of the role of the United States Government Military Assistance Programs to Latin America weakens his notion of the local "internal" military as an independent force for development. Between 1933 and 1953 the basic United States position was based upon Roosevelt's Good Neighbor Policy, in which economic assistance was emphasized at the expense of military assistance. Even during World War Two, United States military assistance to Latin America was not especially significant, with only token military combat on the part of Latin American troops. Such military assistance programs got under way only *after* 1953. They have had tremendous effect in professionalizing the military and in increasing its political role within every nation.

Johnson notes the fact that the military budgets of each Latin American nation range from between 0.1 per cent to 3.3 per cent. But what is left out of his reckoning is that these percentages are based on the Gross National Product. The defense expenditures do not include foreign aid receipts. Once this adjustment in the defense budget is made, we find that the total military expenditures zoom to approximately three to five times the figures based exclusively on the GNP. For example, in Argentina, military allocation is 13.2 per cent of the Total National Budget (TNB), while it is only 2.6 per cent of the Gross National Product (GNP). Chile has 18.0 per cent of its total budget earmarked for military purposes, but if the GNP is used as the base line, only 2.8 per cent is. Peru also has 18.0 per cent of its budget allocated for military purposes, of which only 3.2 per cent is derived from the GNP. Since less than a quarter of the military allocation is generated internally, the "balance" is made up of foreign military loans. Similar differentials occur across the Latin American board. The statistical gap is made up almost entirely by United States foreign aid programs. Not to deal with this factor, not even to mention it, is not a symbol of modesty but an illustration of default.

Johnson is making the same error with respect to the military in the 'sixties that he made with respect to the middle classes in the 'fifties. He is endowing a private "sector" with a national dimension and a capacity for self-sacrifice which only rarely exists in reality.

VII

In the major statements on development discussed above, a series of paradoxical statements are presented. They do not account for history in social relations. They all assert a belief in the "revolution of rising expectations," but none can accept the implication that this carries with it a concurrent "revolution of falling profits." They refuse to believe that the situation of the Third World is derived from the omnipotent position of the First and Second Worlds. They are insensitive to the fact that the underdeveloped condition of the Third World results from structural deformities and not simply from a historical lag or backwardness. They are blind to the fact that "system maintenance" is futile to "social development." They refuse to believe that the clever manipulation of power by an elite, or collection of elites, defines the absence of real democracy and hence the deformities of political development.

The source of their evasion from the real situation in the Third World is the same for all; each scholar believes in the benefits of private enterprise (a domesticated variety, to be sure), and disdains the idea that a public-sector economy can be organizationally or historically more advanced. They all treat the quarrel which the Third World leadership has with Stalinist and Maoist forms of socialism as a way to reintroduce private-enterprise solutions. They cannot absorb the fact that the economic philosophies of entrepreneurial leadership and economic pump-priming are viewed as anachronistic by the elites of the emerging nations. The Third World's position is that the anachronisms of capitalism offer no real option to the aberrations of socialism. If they have not yet arrived at any unified formula, it is not because these nations do not know where they are going so much as they are worried about how long it will take to get "there," and at what price. The essential pragmatism of Third World spokesmen lies in their capacity to define goals heuristically rather than hysterically.

Chapter 14

Social Structure and Political Change

The sociology of development has received great impetus from four separate sources: professional economists, political scientists, socialist theorists from within and without the Soviet bloc, and sociologists residing in, or concerned with, Third World regions.

Economics, long ridiculed as the "dismal science," is nonetheless the discipline most directly concerned with the political economy of development. The work of Kuznets[1] on the economic growth of nations, Gerschenkron[2] and Heilbroner[3] on the forms of social backwardness, P. J. D. Wiles on the ideology and theology of "full communism,"[4] Rostow on the relationship between economic "thrust" and self-sustained growth,[5] and Viner on the connection of social savings and economic change[6] have all made significant contributions to the study of economic development.

[1] Simon Kuznets, *Quantitative Aspects of the Economic Growth of Nations*. Chicago: Research Center in Economic Development and Cultural Change, 1962, esp. Vol. X, No. 2, Part II.
[2] Alexander Gerschenkron (ed.), *Economic Backwardness in Historical Perspective*. Cambridge: Harvard University Press, 1962.
[3] Robert L. Heilbroner, "The Revolution of Economic Development," *The American Scholar*, Vol. 31, No. 4, Autumn 1962, pp. 541-9. See also his book, *The Great Ascent*. New York: Harper & Row, 1963.
[4] P. J. D. Wiles, *The Political Economy of Communism*. Cambridge: Harvard University Press, 1962.
[5] Walt W. Rostow, *The Stages of Economic Growth*. Cambridge, England: Cambridge University Press, 1960.
[6] Jacob Viner, *International Trade and Economic Development*. London: Oxford University Press, 1956.

427

Socialism, long held to be stagnant and unable to deal effectively with new conditions, has nonetheless witnessed a "great debate" recently which represents both an off-shoot of the economic sciences and an independent force in the evolution of a social science of development. The orthodox Marxists Dutt[7] and Baran[8] have conducted an effective dialogue with the reform Marxists Strachey,[9] Myrdal,[10] and Bronfenbrenner.[11] This debate is concerned with the problem of economic expansion in relation to political coercion and consensus. Political directives affect the allocation of national wealth and human energies, and these in turn generate distinctive and explicit world views. Both classical and socialist economists have been quite willing in recent discussions to acknowledge the sociological roots of the problem of development.

The developing nations of Asia, Africa, and Latin America, long held to be very backward in matters of education and scientific know-how, represent nonetheless that part of the world where sociologists are tackling head-on the master issues of social development. The work of Celso Furtado[12] and Costa Pinto[13] in Brazil; of Germani in Argentina,[14] and of Alfredo Navarette[15] and Jesus Herzog in Mexico[16] indicates that an expression of the meaning of the degree of development is not a simple matter of linguistic nuance but a complex matter of the life and death of man in society. Real strides have been taken to evolve a general theory of social development. Sociological conferences held throughout

[7] R. Palme Dutt, The Crisis of Britain and the British Empire. London: Lawrence and Wishart, 1953.
[8] Paul A. Baran, The Political Economy of Growth. New York: Monthly Review Press, 1957.
[9] John Strachey, The End of Empire. London: Victor Gollancz Ltd., 1959.
[10] Gunnar Myrdal, Rich Lands and Poor: The Road to World Prosperity. New York: Harper, 1957.
[11] M. Bronfenbrenner, "The Appeal of Confiscation in Economic Development," in The Economics of Underdevelopment, edited by A. N. Agarwala and S. P. Singh. New York: Oxford University Press, 1963.
[12] Celso Furtado, Desenvolvimento e Subdesenvolvimento. Rio de Janeiro: Editora Fundo de Cultura, 1961.
[13] L. A. Costa Pinto, "O Desenvolvimento: Seus Processos e Seus Obstáculos," Journal of Inter-American Studies, Vol. IV, No. 3, July 1962.
[14] Gino Germani, Política y Sociedad en una Época de Transición. Buenos Aires: Editorial Paidós, 1962.
[15] Alfredo Navarette Jr. and Ifigenia M. de Navarette, "La Subocupación en las Economías Poco Desarrolladas," El Trimestre Económico, Vol. 18, No. 4, Oct.-Dec. 1951.
[16] Jesus Silva Herzog, Mexico y su Petróleo: Una Lección para América. Buenos Aires: Universidad de Buenos Aires, 1959.

the world for the past decade have been deeply concerned with developmental issues. The emergence of such periodicals as *Revue Tiers Monde, The International Development Review, Desarrollo Económico, Comparative International Development,* and *Economic Development and Cultural Change* reflects the attempt to evolve a working body of systematic knowledge in this area.

Clearly, with such an extensive literature available, social scientists must either summarize the work already done or select problem areas which remain unsolved. I shall attempt to summarize these findings by means of a series of verifiable propositions on development. Perhaps in this way, the real problem areas can be more readily ascertained.

Why is it that sociology in the United States has been delinquent in forging a general theory of social development? Historically, sociologists were pioneers in precisely this field. Ferdinand Toennies' remarkable typology of *Gemeinschaft* and *Gesellschaft* socio-cultural structures is at its source an historical account of the machinery through which community-agrarian patterns dissolved and gave way to a societal-industrial pattern. Toennies' description of European capitalism still forms the basis for much discussion of what a developed society necessarily includes and excludes. Max Weber's work on the sociology of religion has as its fundamental motive to account for the transition from feudalism to capitalism in European and Asian societies. Indeed, the impulse behind Weber's interests in religion is economic—i.e. an effort to understand the social function of ideas as a catalytic agent in social development. Werner Sombart's studies of religious forces in the evolution of European capitalism likewise had as a basis the need to find out the sociological variables in the full flowering of the bourgeois system of production. Studies by such other major sociological figures as Simmel, Thomas, Znaniecki, and Mannheim could similarly be introduced in support of my contention that the problem of development was uppermost in the minds of the "classical" sociologists.

But why have we become negligent, and even indifferent, to such problems of "big-range" sociology? The answers are manifold. And since this is not intended as an exercise in the sociology of sociology, it is only possible to list briefly some of the more outstanding reasons.[17] One of the root problems seems to be that the rise of socialism has confounded

[17] For a further examination of these problems, see Irving L. Horowitz (ed.), *The New Sociology.* New York and London: Oxford University Press, 1964.

sociology. On the American scene, sociology and socialism have for so long seen each other as "enemies" that each side does everything possible to avoid slipping into the language of the "generalized other." Furthermore, sociology, even in its generous moments and in the hands of its more radical practitioners, viewed socialism as a historical "moment" in the evolution of the social sciences. On the other hand, socialist spokesmen have always considered sociology as a middle-class effort to improve a decadent social order—a bourgeois "moment" in the development of socialist theory.

Sociologists have so taken for granted the language of structure and function, stability, and pattern maintenance that socialism has come to be viewed as a form of deviance, a conflict-laden ideology devoid of the hard facts of social structure. Socialists, on their side, have for so long held out the need for radical social change that problems of order and structure have indeed come to be viewed as a sort of betrayal of radical principles. The sociologist is as "deviant" from the socialist standpoint as the other way around. Any suggestion that the development of *both* socialism and sociology has been one-sided, to the detriment of both, has only produced howls of protest from ideologues in both camps.

It is not my purpose, however, to allocate blame. From the standpoint of advancing sociological theory, neither side is living up to its obligations very well. Both sociological and socialist *ideologies* tend to act as a brake on the development of a theory of social change.

By outlining in proposition form the main features of a theory of development, features about which there is a broad consensus, we can help the critical issues in the sociological theory of economic development to emerge more clearly. Then we shall be in a better position to see just how much of a contribution sociology can make to the resolution of such a big-range problem. But to present these propositions satisfactorily requires honesty; a recognition that the traditional animus between sociology and socialism is outmoded and outdated. The traditional animus is made obsolete by the operational character of sociology and by the pragmatic character of contemporary socialism. Sociology as a heuristic device has replaced sociology as the *bête noire* of socialism. The question is not what kind of sociology but whither sociology. If the Soviets have come so far as to set up an Institute for Social Research in Leningrad modeled after the Bureau of Applied Research in New York, we can do no less than try to understand ways in which socialism and sociology can pool their information to bring about a better understanding of the social, political, and economic bases of human development.

We know that concrete problems cannot be separated into neat social science disciplines. Such divisions have no basis in social reality. Concrete problems are never exclusively economic, sociological, or political. A theory of development and underdevelopment based on any one set of variables is destined to failure. Gunnar Myrdal, in concluding his argument for a science of development, speaks of a need for a "model of models" which would be based on a close reading of social history as well as social science.

I submit the following "model of models" as my own attempt to come to terms with the problem of development by considering the interplay of social order and social change. Its obvious imperfections are partly the result of the difficulties involved in projecting forms of development which do not fully account for psychological and ethical factors.

The logical structure of propositions concerning social development is introduced. Then we move successively to the economic, political, political-economic, and, finally, the sociological dimensions proper. The scheme of exposition employed obviously owes a considerable debt to the work of Vilfredo Pareto in sociology and, no less, to Ludwig Wittgenstein in linguistic philosophy. But it is not my purpose to imitate their styles of work. There are many departures from their efforts, as many as were necessary to make the following scheme meaningful.

1   The social world is the totality of human forces.

1:1   The social world is the totality of processes and structures, not of objects and ideas.

1:1:1   The totality of processes and structures defines what is socially the case, and also what is not the case.

1:2   Processes and structures are social categories for discussing change and becoming.

1:2:1   All processes take place within structures, and all structures are subject to processes.

Note: The extensiveness or speed of process, like the durability and solidity of being or structure, is an empirical consideration and not determined a priori.

1:2:1:1   That portion of social facts concerned with processes refers to changes in class, power, occupation, and prestige. Such changes may occur at the individual, group, or societal level. Such changes may be measured by both objective and subjective indices—i.e. by an "absolute" growth in power or by a "relative" shift in how a person, group, or society is viewed by other persons, groups, and societies.

1:2:1:2   That portion of social facts concerned with structures refers to how the processes of the social world appear to the observer at any specific moment in time and space. Such structures may be measured by both objective and subjective indices—i.e. the actual durability of a social structure is a consequence both of its "real" power and of the social members' view of such power.

1:2:2   Social structure is then the sum total of social processes, and social processes define the social structure.

2   All the processes and structures in a society define the stage of development of that society.

2:1   Development refers to the level of complexity achieved by a social structure and to the degrees of alteration achieved by a social process.

2:2   Full development refers to the ideal standards entertained in our perceptions of structures and processes.

2:2:1   Underdevelopment refers to a social condition in which anticipated processes and structures are being aborted.

2:2:1:1   Underdeveloped differs from undeveloped as the sociological differs from the natural: or the biological from the ecological.

2:2:2   Overdevelopment refers to a social condition in which processes and structures are realized out of proportion to, and in excess of, available resources, manpower, etc.
Example: One speaks of the overdeveloped society when the cost factors outweigh the benefits derived from high productivity—i.e. when human "suffering" (anomie, alienation, anxiety) caused by high industrial output levels outweighs advantages of material acquisitions and short working days.

2:2:2:1   Overdevelopment differs from overexhaustion of natural wealth as the sociological differs from the natural, biological, or the geographical.

Note: Overdevelopment is observable through its "Franken-stein effect"—anomie, alienation, and anxiety on a mass scale.

3 Development, underdevelopment, and overdevelopment are social concepts. The underdeveloped and the overdeveloped are representative norms of a social system.

3:1 The developing society is one in which there is a "proper mix" between the maintenance of social structures and the acceleration of social processes.

Note: This proposition clearly has a subjective quality. Yet, unless one assumes that the nature of development is exclusively economic, this "subjectivity" is not so much a short-coming as an additional factor in analysis.

3:1:1 An "improper mix" is indicated by a breakdown in processes, or a disruption in the structures.

3:2 Underdeveloped societies have difficulty in initiating and accelerating new social processes while overdeveloped societies are characterized by the disintegration of structures.

3:2:1 Processes which are in excess of what the structures deem sufficient lead either to the sacrifices of the processes or of the structures.

3:2:1:1 Structures which are made rigid beyond the point where they can absorb new processes lead either to the sacrifice of the structure or of the processes.

3:3 Process is the totality of social changes in a specific situation. Structure is the totality of social institutions in a specific situation.

3:3:1 Revolution is that condition in which structures are drastically changed without necessarily being replaced, and in which processes cannot be modified without being abandoned or thwarted.

3:3:2 Reaction is that condition in which an attempt is made to preserve structures and processes which can no longer be meshed or fused.

Note: The difference between revolution and reaction is that the former overthrows the structure, while the latter thwarts the process.

3:4 Change and stability are the logical totality of all social facts.

3:5 Full development refers to the ideal-typification of a social system. All actual social systems reveal an imperfect relationship between change and stability.

3:5:1 The social problem of development concerns the point at which change should be emphasized at the expense of stability, or stability emphasized at the expense of change.

3:6 The difference between political postures and policies is defined by the degree of change or stability advocated.

3:6:1 Those who emphasize stability under conditions of a private-sector economy—one in which the allocation of resources and profits is in the hands of individual owners and enterpreneurs of corporate wealth—are called capitalists.

3:6:2 Those who emphasize stability under conditions of a public-sector economy—one in which the allocation of resources and profits is regulated by a collectivity of owners, managers, and workers of corporate wealth—are called socialists.

3:7 The above represents the polarities of economic change and stability. Those who adopt a position between these polarities are defined by the nature of the economic mix advocated —state capitalism, state socialism, welfare economy, etc.

3:8 The point at which some person or party ceases being capitalist and becomes socialist is determined by the cross-over between public-sector and private-sector investment.

4 Social development requires both a consensus apparatus (voluntary association) and a coercive apparatus (involuntary association—the state).

4:1 The forced maintenance of the social process at the expense of the social structure is called social coercion.

4:1:1 The forced maintenance of the social structure at the expense of social process is called social coercion.
Note: Any enforced asymmetry can only be maintained by a coercive apparatus.

4:2 The unobstructed transformation of an old structure into a new structure is called social consensus.

4:2:1 The unobstructed transformation of old processes into new processes is called social consensus.

4:3 The acceleration of social development by means of maximum control of the mechanical and human sources of production is characteristic of coercion.

Note: Coercion does not necessarily entail the use of violence. More often than not, coercion is applied by means of formal and informal sanctions; that is, through pressures of an indirect variety such as extra financial bonuses for working in "virgin lands" projects or through the deprivation of financial assistance to areas declared "unessential."

4:3:1　The acceleration of social development by means of minimum regulation of the mechanical and human sources of production is characteristic of consensus.

Note: As a rule, a "consensual society" will exhibit a higher regard for human sacrifice than it will for high productivity. It generally holds "the humanization of labor" as a social constant, and thus adjusts production rates to the constant.

4:4　The ratio between coercion and consensus at any given time determines the character of the political structure, just as the mix between public investment and private investment of capital determines the economic structure.

5　The intersections between coercion and consensus in the polity and between public and private investment in the economy define the area called political economy.

5:1　The political-economic "mix" is at any point a consequence of internal (national) pressures and external (international) pressures.

5:1:1　When the political-economic processes are primarily determined by internal pressures, such processes are designated as the "role of the state."

5:1:2　When the political-economic processes are primarily determined by external pressures, such processes are designated as the "role of the imperium."

5:2　State and imperium are two legalized modes of expressing coercion.

5:2:1　The voluntary minimization of state and imperium, their replacement with decisions arrived at through voluntary agencies, is an expression of consensus.

Note: The state and the imperium do not necessarily have equal weight in determining the political economy, since the state in itself may come under the domination of a more pervasive imperium.

5:3   The purposes and direction of the state and the imperium (when they are not one and the same) may be inharmonious.

5:3:1   The state may emphasize stability at any moment, while the imperium may emphasize change.

5:3:1:1   The state may emphasize change at any moment, while the imperium may emphasize stability.

5:4   The underdeveloped state and the fully developed imperium come into a condition of competition, or even conflict, when each puts emphasis on one factor of social development at the expense of the other—that is, either structure or process.

5:4:1   The underdeveloped state and the fully developed imperium come into a condition of consensus when each emphasizes the same factors at the same time. This is expressed by the difference between the vocabulary of "foreign aid" and that of "foreign exploitation."

6   Expropriation is the re-allocation of social wealth through agencies of political coercion.

6:1   The forms of expropriation determine the type of social structure.

6:1:1   The forms of expropriation determine the rate of social processes.

6:2   There can be no social change, or new social modes, without some form of expropriation—i.e. without the political re-allocation of economic wealth.

6:3   Capitalism is an economic system in which political power resides in the hands of the national bourgeoisie.

6:3:1   Socialism is an economic system in which political power resides in the hands of the national planning board.

6:3:2   Latifundism is an economic system in which political power resides in the hands of the national land-owning classes.

6:3:3   Peasant socialism is an economic system in which political power resides in the hands of the national peasantry.

6:4   Imperialism is a limiting factor for a symmetrical economic system.

6:4:1   Imperialism is an economic system of supra-national proportions in which political power resides (either fully or partially) in the hands of the imperium as such.

6:5 The conflict between the developing nations and the advanced nations often appears as a struggle between the nationalism of the former and the imperialism of the latter. This is so because capitalism, socialism, latifundism, and peasant socialism, whatever their differences, represent forms of national control and allocation of wealth, while imperialism, whether of an "enlightened" or "despotic" variety, represents the foreign control and allocation of wealth.

6:6 For the developing nations, the forms of political economy are subordinate to the right to have a national economy.

6:6:1 For the highly developed nations, the forms of political economy are central and foremost since the "nationalization" of the economy as such has been achieved.

7 Consciousness of underdevelopment produces emphasis on social change; whereas consciousness of being highly developed produces emphasis on stability.

7:1 Awareness of different rewards for similar kinds of work can perform a revolutionary function in so far as it creates tensions between underdeveloped and highly developed economic units.

7:1:1 Awareness of different rewards for similar kinds of work in so far as it can perform a conservatizing function creates tensions between highly developed and underdeveloped economic units.

Note: Revolutionary and conservative frameworks are thus defined by the response to the problem of development as such. Emphasis on rapid unfettered development, combined with a negative attitude toward underdevelopment as such, creates the political base for revolutionary ideologies. Emphasis on controlling development and fear of loss of wealth and prestige through independence and development creates the base for a conservative ideology.

7:2 Ideological aspects of consciousness are defined in terms of interests.

7:2:1 If interests are to achieve a higher stage of social development, the ideological consciousness is called revolutionary. If interests are to preserve an existing developmental stage, the ideological consciousness is called conservative.

7:3   Consciousness of poverty and wealth are comparative in nature. Both terms are significant in relation to each other.
Note: This proposition rules out theories of "absolute" poverty or "absolute" wealth as superfluous on economic grounds and undemonstrable on sociological grounds.

7:3:1   Consciousness of poverty in relation to wealth is the determining element in the ideology of social progress.

7:3:2   Consciousness of wealth in relation to poverty is the determining element in the ideology of social stability.

7:4   The poor of the poor nations tend to adopt a revolutionary ideology.

7:4:1   The poor of the rich nations, in so far as they identify with country rather than class, tend to adopt a conservative ideology, e.g. the phenomenon of "working-class authoritarianism."

7:4:2   The wealthy of the poor nations, in so far as they identify with their country rather than social class, tend to adopt a revolutionary ideology, e.g. the phenomenon of "middle-sector radicalism."

7:4:3   The wealthy of the rich nations tend to adopt a conservative ideology.
Note: For each of these conditions, there are contravening factors. The wealthy of the poor nations may derive their funds from interests in the rich nations, and hence, their "interests" would be split: to protect their "national" position or to preserve their "imperial" position. Similar intervening or contravening elements exist in each case. But as a phase rule, the propositions in 7:4 are empirically confirmable.

7:5   Revolutionary ideology can be modified when the costs of development are seen to outweigh its benefits.
Example: Lower levels of consumer accommodation and agriculture often accompany the "transitional" period from agriculture to industry. Rationalization of the costs of development in terms of delayed gratification and future advantages for the children often demand greater personal sacrifice than people are willing to accept.

7:5:1 Conservative ideology can be modified when the costs of structure maintenance are seen to outweigh the benefits.

Example: Mass pressures from non-elite sectors may be so unremitting and unrelenting that the mere ability to maintain control of an economic or political structure no longer suffices to maintain an ideological posture of conservatism intact. In this way, "reform" doctrines and "liberalism" emerge to minimize the costs of structure maintenance without resort to revolution.

7:6 The type of economic ideology propounded depends heavily on the evaluation of the potential costs of development in relation to the actual costs of development.

7:7 The consciousness of development accounts for the forms of ideology, as such forms interact with the social system as such.

Note: There is, of course, the phenomenon of unconsciousness. But this is usually associated with tribal areas so isolated as not to have information about other civilizations. At the other end of the historical scale, there are societies so affluent and economically self-reliant that they become equally aware of how they are perceived by others.

8 Underdeveloped, developed, and overdeveloped societies are definable by all factors involved in social structure and social processes.

8:1 The various sociological "mixes" signify imperfect or unfinished forms of development, such as "transitional" and developing societies.

8:2 The sociological properties of the underdeveloped society are characterized by a series of social forces which, by convention, can be considered under the polar terms of structure and process, or stratification and mobility.

8:2:1 In the sphere of social structure, the underdeveloped society bases its actions on authority systems.

8:2:2 In the sphere of social relations, there is a high degree of personal interaction and personal sanction. Personal factors rather than professional factors are decisive in human associations.

8:2:3   In the sphere of technology, the underdeveloped society exhibits high reliance on manual instruments and on human and animal energy.

8:2:4   In the sphere of economy, one finds "subsistence" patterns—production to satisfy concrete necessities of individuals or groups functioning within a traditional cultural framework.

8:2:4:1   An undeveloped economy is undifferentiated and indifferent to the social system as such.

8:2:4:2   On a national scale, the assignment of labor tasks is based upon sex, age, race, and caste.

8:2:4:3   On an international scale, the assignment of labor tasks is based upon color, language, and geography.

8:2:4:4   When the laborer owns the instruments of production, craft rather than machinery is the essential production ingredient.

8:3   When the psychology of undevelopment reveals an absence of specific motivations, production is connected to subsistence rather than to savings.

8:3:1   Psychological attitudes toward the work process emphasize fulfillment of living necessities rather than competition to produce a surplus or an abundance for "the next generation."

8:4   The inheritance of status and economic power has as a corollary a high degree of stratification. Work norms are guaranteed through tradition and not through competition.

8:4:1   Types of property relations in underdeveloped areas are personal; with a clear distinction between owners and owned, rulers and ruled, masters and slaves, lords and serfs, etc.

Note: The role of intermediary classes increases as a society crosses over from an underdeveloped to a developing situation. This is due to an increase in occupational differentiation, and to the rise in consumer demands in contradistinction to production demands. Class polarization begins to give way to work specialization. It is for these reasons that a gap sets in between ideologies on the one hand and interest attitudes determined by parochial and local considerations on the other.

8:5   In the sphere of social processes, one finds a parent-oriented society, with movement determined by age and sex, no less than class and caste. Veneration based on age is a characteristic of underdeveloped or traditional societies such as "feudal" China.

8:6 In the sphere of demography, the underdeveloped society exhibits a high birth rate and a high mortality rate; or, at times, a low birth rate and a high mortality rate.

8:6:1 Immigration tends to be limited to the extent that industrialization is absent, or the chances for rapid industrialization minimal.

8:6:2 Ecological mobility, the movement of internal population to new areas, is either very low or non-existent.

Note: Again, a hallmark of the developing or transitional society is the imperfect breakdown of traditional patterns. Thus, there is high ecological mobility in Brazil and Argentina, but due to inherited conditions—the absence of urban planning, the poor development of transportation, etc.—such mobility or high population explosions tend to set in motion a game of hare and hound, a struggle to avoid having "social savings" or "primitive accumulation" eaten away by population expansion or rapid urbanization. Nonetheless, it would be dangerous to confuse the problems of a developing nation (often accompanied by inflationary spirals, for example) with the problems of underdevelopment per se. The absence of pressure on a social structure may indicate the extreme state of backwardness and not the intrinsic stability of a society.

8:7 The types of authority and control exercised are traditional and take a form in which law is subservient to custom.

8:7:1 Authority is reinforced through a religious machinery, through considering society as "sacred" and "divine" in origin and in rule. There is a proliferation of "Divine Right" and "Natural Law" theories.

8:7:1:1 Psychological antagonism for the "outsider" or the "innovator" is reinforced by the authority of custom and tradition. An equation is made between the outsider and the enemy.

8:7:1:2 Further reinforcement of authority occurs through "group decision-making" and through exclusive reliance upon primary associations.

Note: This "group decision-making" also characterizes rapidly developing societies such as modern China, and it may be a feature integral to a coercive society as such, rather than to a particular stage of development.

8:8　The value system of the underdeveloped society moves along parallel axes of "tradition" . . . "blood lines" . . . "the land" . . . "divinity," etc. Values are absolute and insular.

8:9　Underdevelopment tends to accentuate ethnic heterogeneity and to emphasize structure at the expense of process.

Note: Ethnic heterogeneity in contrast to structural differentiation leads either to total stagnation or total revolution. The underdeveloped society is in an unstable condition: first, because it has insufficient agencies available—if any at all—to cope with the novel and the changing; and, second, because changes in one part of the underdeveloped society have wide repercussions on all other parts.

9　The sociological properties of the developed or rapidly developing society take the form of a series of social forces which can be considered under the polar terms of structure and process, or stratification and mobility.

9:1　In sociological terms developed or developing societies are those which have achieved a mass distribution of national wealth (either in the form of ownership or consumption) within the context of a relatively stable social system. It is a "mass society" in contrast to a "traditional society."

9:1:1　A shorthand rule is that the developed society emphasizes social mobility at the expense of social stratification.

9:2　In the sphere of social structure, the developed society exhibits a nominalist character—the individual wills his world rather than being determined by a willful world.

Note: Above all, change is itself built into the structure. This may be done via direct planning, federal allocation of resources, or indirect monetary manipulations.

9:2:1　In the sphere of social relations, the feeling of community responsibility is replaced by a concept of individual self-determination, social distance, functional associations in terms of occupation rather than in terms of community, and universalism, that is, a "worldly perspective" or a "national perspective."

9:2:2   In the sphere of technology, the developed society makes wide use of mechanical, electrical, and nuclear energy in place of human energy; and mass-production techniques and automation in place of craft techniques.

Note: The "alienation effect" is a consequence of this process. Alienation, the separation of personal satisfaction from public production, is thus a characteristic of development. Like social "deviance" in general, alienation is a cost factor in advanced forms of industrial living.

9:2:3   In the sphere of economy, production is geared to the satisfaction of high demands made by an anonymous public. Developed societies are oriented toward creature comforts; monetary relations replace bartering relations; the emphasis moves from the quality of production to quantity in production.

Note: The drive toward high production creates a set of special problems concerned with distribution, transportation, communication, monopolization, and the manipulation of wealth as such.

9:3   The functional differentiation of roles and positions leads to a high degree of legal prescriptions. It further leads to measuring social worth in terms of consumer satisfaction on a mass scale. The rise of status as an independent variable apart from class is directly linked to the crossover from productivity as a value to consumption as a value.

Note: A measure of the overdeveloped society is its inability to make full use of its energy potential because of social drives in the direction of mass leisure. The break-up of work patterns and work incentives and their replacement by leisure or non-productivity as a fundamental value distinguish the overdeveloped from the developed. The psychology of underdevelopment once more appears: the distinctions between master and servant (those who have everything but don't work, and those who have nothing but do work) reappear in their overdeveloped form in terms of the relations between nations. In place of have and have-not classes, there are have and have-not nations. This is what makes for "class cohesion" rather than "class conflict" on a national scale. The character of social conflict changes as the units shift from social classes to political nations. This shift also helps to explain the "racial" dimension in underdevelopment—racialism as a consequence of nationalism.

9:4 On a national scale, the pace of development may be measured by the size of the bureaucracy in relation to other classes. The division of labor is made on the basis of efficiency rather than birth. The growth of professionalism increases the significance of the intermediary classes and decreases the importance of the classes engaged in production. Managerial functions usurp new areas, formerly held by ownership classes and laboring classes. *Note:* Nonetheless, it is important to realize that the managerial expansion is not a managerial revolution. Ownership still remains distinct from management and still has the power to direct the managerial estate, and not the other way around. This is as true of the United States as it is of the Soviet Union—despite the different ownership classes in each country.

9:4:1 On an international scale, the developed society controls world markets by means of protective tariffs, import and export regulations, and a struggle for the control of underdeveloped regions—by direct military means in the older developed nations and by indirect economic means in the more recently developed nations. Development does not necessarily imply imperialism (so underdeveloped a nation as Portugal can yet be an imperial power, while so highly developed a country as Sweden has no colonial pretensions or imperial domains). It does mean that one way that the rate of growth has been maintained after a certain level of development is through imperial colonization.

9:5 The psychology of the developed society reveals specific motivations. Production is connected to credit, and credit tends to become an instrument of ensuring future gratifications. *Note:* In this connection, the shift from the extended family to the nuclear family in the developed society has served to focus positive attitudes toward savings. Here, too, we see a peculiar dovetailing of underdevelopment and overdevelopment: the re-emergence of a strong "we" and "they," outsider-insider relationship. The high degree of "socialization" required by the developing society gives way to a high degree of alienation in the overdeveloped society. Even the phrase "the sick society" betrays just such an impression of over-development.

9:6 The attitude toward work in the developed society produces impersonal human relations. There is a shift from one job to another, one elite position to another. Impersonalism is reinforced by the notion of working for the highest bidder. Personal loyalties tend thus to be minimized in industrial life; they are reserved for the life of the family or associates outside the place of work.

9:6:1 In work attitudes the shift from traditional communities to modern societies becomes apparent. It is not so much that feelings as such, or even values as such, undergo drastic revision, as it is the object of such feelings and values which is revised.

9:6:2 The specialization of work tends to undermine wider identifications with class or the nation as a whole.
Example: The higher degree of industrial development, the more difficult it is to distinguish between different social classes. Clothing styles, living quarters, and transportation means become standardized. Mass culture replaces class culture. A unified "culture of the people" replaces the different cultures of traditional society, such as the "art tradition" of the rich and the "folk tradition" of the poor. The "tradition-bearing" role of the intelligentsia seeks to support the older cultural inheritance, but there can be small doubt that the "art" of the developed countries is fully embodied in the design of utilitarian objects. It is as a special product and consequence of scientific and technological innovation that design tends to become functional. The overdeveloped society is thus not synonymous with the existence of mass culture. In the overdeveloped society, there is an attempt to recreate and reconstruct traditional distinctions between cultural and functional entities; as Eric Larrabee suggests, overdevelopment is defined in part by the over-designing of artifacts.

9:6:3 Types of property relations tend to become impersonal. The distinction between the property-owner and the propertyless is determined by law rather than fixed by class inheritance. Ownership of property is no longer closed to members of the laboring classes—whether, as under capitalism, because wealth is limited by taxation and poverty by insurance programs, or whether, as under socialism, because private property as such is abolished. The impersonality of class distinctions is achieved by defining every person functionally—in terms of occupational activities instead of property ownership.

9:6:3:1   When development spills over into overdevelopment, there is a breakdown in the functional definition of roles. Status performs a role equivalent to class in the underdeveloped society: it builds up distinctions which lead to an intensification of stratification at the expense of mobility.

9:7   In the sphere of social processes in a developed society, one finds a child-oriented society, the movement of which is determined by skills acquired, educational "rites of passage," and professionalism as such. Conflict occurs between generations; the older generation is no longer venerated.

Example: "Cutting the umbilical cord" assumes the same dimensions in the modern developed society as "cutting the class bonds" did in the past century. This tends to confirm Mannheim's comment that the conflict between generations is now as intense as the class struggle was in older societies.

9:7:1   In part, the "child-centered" family is a consequence of having the larger society define an individual's social roles rather than the family.

9:7:1:1   Social processes are ensured by individual achievement rather than by inheritance. Educational opportunity and leadership in decisive social and political organizations assist in making individual autonomy a factor in its own right.

9:8   Social processes are set in motion by secular forms of belief, by ideological systems rather than religious systems. Values become autonomous and public rather than connected to supernatural beliefs about rewards and punishments for virtue and vice. Utilitarian impulses are released from their previous religious enclosures. There is, in brief, a general rise in concern with this world rather than with any supernatural one.

9:8:1 The same process is exhibited by religious agencies themselves. Ministers become psychiatric counselors. Churches become social meeting halls (and sometimes even gambling casinos). Theology becomes general and "ecumenical" rather than specific and "separatist."

9:8:2 Social processes are occupationally defined. Prestige becomes based on money independent of class background. Occupational loyalties increase as class affiliations grow weaker. This is the basic content of professionalism as such.

9:9 In the sphere of demography, the developed society exhibits a combination of either high birth rates and low mortality rates, or a low birth rate and a low mortality rate.

9:9:1 At the point of industrial "take-off" there is usually a higher birth rate than the population size of the traditional society would warrant. Rapid capital formation usually (although not invariably) shows a parallel rise in the birth rate.

9:9:1:1 When an economic plateau is reached—that is, when the rate of capital formation becomes stabilized—population usually becomes stabilized too.

Example: In the United States, middle-class Catholics tend to have "average" (slightly under three children) families as do their Protestant equivalents. Lower-class Catholics tend to have many offspring, as do their counterparts in other sectors of the lower classes. These differential birth rates indicate that the main factors governing birth rates are economic and not religious. It is only when Catholics are "outside" the developed society that procreation patterns follow an "underdeveloped" course. We may thus say, with some assurance that population inclines and decreases are rarely autonomous. They move in accord with the overall trajectory of development.

9:9:2 Immigration tends to be high in developed countries when industrialization is present. The increase in artificial barriers to immigration serves, as does the maintenance of small families, to widen the share in the products of industrial life.

Immigration restrictions are thus more characteristic of fully developed societies than of those at the initial "take-off" stages, where labor power (particularly of a skilled and cheap variety) is both needed and scarce.

Note: Intervening factors may affect this pattern. "Excessive" immigration from a "highly developed" culture to a "developing" culture—from Europe to South America, for example—may so upset the national ethnic pattern that, despite the dire need of skilled labor power, restrictions are imposed on immigration in order to maintain the social structure as such.

9:9:3 Shifts of population within a country tend to vary directly with the level of social development. For a nation to be "on wheels" assumes the wide distribution of transport facilities.

Note: The essential problem in discussing the relationship of development to population is precisely a matter of relationship. It is as silly to talk of a "population explosion" as it is to talk of "industrial affluence." Each is measurable in terms of the other. If the growth rate of an economy, however high, cannot allocate more per person per annum because its population increase is "eating up" the growth rate margins, then such a society does indeed have a "population problem." But the simple numerical increase in population is not itself cause of a crisis in the economy. Throughout history, the reverse has more nearly been the case. Thus, India has a "population crisis" while Brazil has a "population boom" (even though the rate of population increases is proportionate). For the economic rate of growth in India cannot absorb a population increase, while the rate of growth in Brazil can. As a matter of fact, it is likely that the high population rise in Brazil will give it a marked advantage in the future industrialization process over its Latin American "under-populated" and "under-industrialized" neighbors.

9:10 Types of authority and control exercised in the developed society are rationalistic and bureaucratic rather than personalistic and charismatic. The authority network serves to institutionalize change in the developed society.

9:10:1 Reinforcement of authority comes about through conformity to the legal code and to the informal censorship—with remote authority becoming increasingly important as a check on change as society becomes increasingly complex.

9:10:2 Authority itself is established through the manipulation of public opinion by mass communications media, and by the conscious formation of "political slogans" and "social myths."

9:10:2:1 Secondary associations become increasingly important in the formation of consensual patterns, replacing the "group consensus" of traditionalist societies.

9:10:2:2 There is an increased reliance upon indirect controls rather than direct prohibitions. The institutionalization of a system of rewards and punishments replaces the direct terrorism of state authority, or the capricious nature of personal authority that is characteristic of traditional societies.

9:11 The developing society is directed toward "pre-eminence." Such pre-eminence might be measured in terms of political power over other nations, technological-scientific weaponry, and mass affluence which cuts across traditional class lines.

9:11:1 The characteristic feature of a developed society is diversity— not as a moral virtue, but as a consequence of role differentiation and occupational specialization.

9:11:2 The value structure of a developed society supports the society by putting an emphasis on "openness," on "experimentalism," and on "experience."
Note: In this sense, the revival of the "quest for certainty," the "return to faith," etc., is indicative of overdevelopment, of an inability to cope with the very forces which make development possible.

10 Full development is equivalent to absolute pre-eminence. And absolute pre-eminence in the modern world is measured in terms of material levels of production, distribution, and consumption.

10:1 The concept of development as pre-eminence may come into competition and conflict with the concept of the fully developed personality.

Note: This is another way of stating the philosophic paradox between authority and individualism, and material growth and mental freedom.

10:1:1 The individual is most likely to be pre-eminent when a society is dedicated to the central achievement of high rates of production.

Note: The "schism" in contemporary socialism is precisely between those who hold that rapid industrialization is a value exceeding any personal hardship or deprivation, and those who hold that at a certain point in human suffering the ends of industrialism are no longer to be pursued. There is no longer any question that "terrorism" is an effective instrument for achieving rapid economic development. The only question is whether the "costs" of such development are worth the sacrifices entailed. This is a question for each society to examine as it enters the "take-off" stage of development.

10:1:2 Social development as pre-eminence is least likely to be achieved when a society is dedicated to the ends of personal freedom as an immediate goal—one which must precede general social development as such.

Note: It is easy to assume that democracy and production increases are necessary corollaries. Yet, historically, this correlation has rarely been the case. Class conflict was most intense, and personal freedom most violated, at those points of industrial expansion in Western Europe and the United States which showed the highest increases in productivity. Affluence may well produce a consensual society democratically organized. But the advanced nations ought not to forget their own histories when they warn the developing nations on the need for maintaining and extending personal liberties. *Example:* The end of colonial rule was registered in India in 1948, while the victory of "socialism" was registered in Bolivia in 1952. Yet, in neither nation can one say that a firm pattern of economic development has emerged. The rate of growth in India, measured in terms of industrial reinvestment and expansion, is low. In large part, it is precisely the retention of libertarian values which frustrated rapid industrialization. It might appear shocking to point out that the achievement of one "good"—rapid industrial development—and the achievement of another "good"—mass liberation—are customarily in conflict with each other. At best, they can be achieved sequentially and hardly ever (if ever) simultaneously. Without some social sector in charge of "forced savings" or guaranteeing "delayed gratifications" (whether through coercive or voluntary means), stagnation and a dependent economy will only continue. The manifest function of revolutions is to make things "better" for more people. But a "Revolution" which sees the very act of transferring state or civic authority as a goal in itself ignores the difference between the transfer of authority and the achievement of material abundance. A revolutionary *event* which is not at the same time a revolutionary process is a fraud—a fact which Bolivians and Indians must recognize by now with painful awareness—the "armed workers' militia" of the former and the "people's army" of the latter notwithstanding.

10:2   The function of planning is to achieve rapid social development at a minimum social cost.

10:2:1   Planning is the basic public-sector mechanism for achieving high production as an instrument of policy—the policy of international pre-eminence.

10:2:2   The function of the free market is to achieve rapid social development through "natural" means—by the laisser-faire system.

10:2:3   The free market is the basic private-sector mechanism for achieving high production as an instrument of policy—the policy of international pre-eminence.

10:3   The "choice" is not between development and underdevelopment, since the search for international pre-eminence might be considered as something of a "psychological constant," but between public-sector and private-sector economies.

10:3:1   Whether the drive toward the developed society is carried out under the auspices of the public sector or the private sector, through planning or laisser-faire, depends on the selection of instrumentalities used and the priority of goals sought.

Note: Behind the talk about planning as a central agency for rationalizing economic production is the basic fact that politics has increasingly come to define economic possibilities, rather than the other way around. This development is just as much an agonizing reality for socialists as for capitalists (perhaps much more so in the light of the binding nature of socialist ideology and the flabby nature of capitalist ideology). Is development to be viewed as a new humanism or as a new way to world power? In India, where development has been identified with a bureaucratic system of authority, humanism has correspondingly been indefinitely postponed. Many social developmentalists ignore the basic paradox of development itself: rapid and bold forms of development cannot be achieved without human sacrifice. The need for sacrifice is even more evident in the "newly developing nations," since time itself has become a major factor. Those new nations must develop very rapidly, or face the fact that they are falling even further behind the advanced nations. The alternative—low levels of industrial development and relative security through remaining a supplier nation—is quite feasible on sociological grounds, but hardly feasible on either political or competitive grounds. No one social science exhausts the issues raised, because no single social dimension as such exhausts the problem.

10:3:2   The "answer" to the question of the appropriate type and tempo of development is therefore both empirical and ethical. It cannot be resolved by a logical model of models. The real value of a model is to telescope the problems in a meaningful way. Beyond this, logic turns into intellectual tyranny. *Note:* Social scientists might make an inventory of the actual benefits and costs of development. The worth of the sacrifices, however, will be viewed differently by people with different social interests. The Catholic bishop may consider the destruction of traditional mores as inherently wicked, while the Communist organizer might consider any attempt to impede the highest possible industrial development in the shortest possible time as a form of obstructionism punishable by death and imprisonment. Between such extremes, there are a whole range of postures based on different social, political, economic, ideological, and ethical moorings. In confronting the issues of development, sociology must first identify these various positions in terms of their bases in coercion and consensus, elite and mass, traditionalism, modernism, and structuralism. Nostalgia, the ideology of backwardness, has no more place in social science than utopianism, the ideology of future perfection. But of the two, utopianism is infinitely preferable—if for no other reason than it points sociology in the right direction.

Name Index

455

Subject Index

achievement, 291; and development, 343-8

affluence, 411; military, 35; sociology of, 70; in U.S., 20, 105, 398-9

affluent society, 401-9

Africa, 28-9, 31-2, 34, 37, 116, 118-21, 123-4, 147, 164, 174, 199, 205, 215, 228, 230-32, 234-6, 241-2, 244-5, 254-5, 308, 321, 335, 340, 344, 361, 385, 428; North, 37, 263; sub-Sahara, 229, 258; and the Third World, 18, 44-6, 159, 249, 256, 261-3, 265, 270, 309, 327, 349, 359, 423; and U.S., 115, 122; West, 322

Afro-Asian bloc, 94, 119, 391, 412; and party charisma in single-party states, 250-53

agriculture, 6, 146-7, 205; in the Soviet Union, 145; in the Third World, 198-9, 202, 206

Algeria, 5, 28, 217, 255, 258, 263, 268, 271, 278, 280, 304; party charisma in, 250-53; and production, 22; and the Third World, 18, 31, 44-6, 219

alienation, 3, 315

alienation effect, 445

Alliance for Progress, 353

anarchy, of market, 17

Angola, 241

anomie, 315; collective, 66-7

anthropology, philosophical, 53

apartheid, 119, 385

Apristas (Peru), 232

Argentina, 68, 187, 217, 231, 232, 233, 277, 280, 289, 290, 293, 353, 355, 423, 425, 441; and development, 357, 392; middle class of, 393-4; party charisma in, 250-53; and U.S. G.N.P., 19

arms race, 272

ascription, 291; and development, 343-8

Asia, 31, 32, 34, 123, 124, 164, 174, 199, 205, 211, 215, 219, 230, 235-6, 242, 245-5, 335, 340, 344, 428; East, 300; and the Second World, 41-4, 124; Southeast, 123, 187, 263; and the Third World, 18, 44-6, 159, 249, 256, 262-3, 270, 309, 327, 349, 359, 423; and U.S., 115, 116, 122

Asunción, 69

Athens, 91

Atlantic community, 93, 173

Austria, 18

authoritarianism, 17, 222-3; and development, 339-40; in the Soviet Union, 155-63; working class, 233, 438

authority, 441; in developed societies, 448-9; legitimation of, 228

automation, 3

backwardness, 4; economic, 12, 13; Soviet Union and, 11, 13, 16; tribes, 69

balanced growth, 24

Bandung Conference (1955), 17, 164

463